The American Journalist in the 1990s
U.S. News People at the End of an Era

LEA's COMMUNICATION SERIES
Jennings Bryant/Dolf Zillmann, General Editors

For a complete list of other titles in LEA's Communication Series, please contact
Lawrence Erlbaum Associates, Publishers.

The American Journalist in the 1990s
U.S. News People at the End of an Era

David H. Weaver
G. Cleveland Wilhoit
Indiana University

LEA LAWRENCE ERLBAUM ASSOCIATES, PUBLISHERS
1996   Mahwah, New Jersey

Lawrence Erlbaum Associates, Inc., Publishers
10 Industrial Avenue
Mahwah, New Jersey 07430

Library of Congress Cataloging-in-Publication Data

Weaver, David H. (David Hugh), 1946–
    The American journalist in the 1990s : U.S. news people at the end
of an era / David H. Weaver, G. Cleveland Wilhoit.
        p.   cm.
    Includes bibliographical references and index.
    ISBN 0-8058-2135-X. — ISBN 0-8058-2136-8
    1. Journalists—United States. 2. Journalism—United States—
History—20th century. I. Wilhoit, G. Cleveland. II. Title.
PN4871.W42 1996
070'.922'73—dc20   96-17622
                                                                CIP

Books published by Lawrence Erlbaum Associates are printed on acid-free paper,
and their bindings are chosen for strength and durability.

Printed in the United States of America
10 9 8 7 6 5 4 3 2

To Jerry Sass,
without whom many good things
in journalism education and
in our careers would not have
been possible, including
this book.

Contents

Foreword:
Background Check—Why the Public Needs to Know More About News People

Everette E. Dennis
The Freedom Forum Media Studies Center

Once again we are indebted to Professors David H. Weaver and G. Cleveland Wilhoit for their anthropological exploration of America's newsrooms to identify and catalog the species found therein, that of *homo journalisticas*. Conducted with sociological care, their decennial inquiry could also be used to trace what might be the ultimate demise of journalism as we know it. We are in an era of sea changes in the media industries, when news people with different characteristics and values from those of the past are emerging to create the new journalistic jungle.

It is appropriate to ask, however irreverently, why we care about such an exercise. The fact that Leo Rosten provided a vivid portrait of Washington correspondents in the 1930s, replicated by William L. Rivers in the 1960s, or that John Johnstone and his colleagues at the University of Illinois provided earlier evidence, built on by Weaver and Wilhoit in 1982 and again in 1992, is not reason enough. The reason we care at all about the nature, characteristics, and "mating habits" of American journalists, more than we seem to care about similar data on doctors, lawyers, accountants, or undertakers, is that we think it matters and that it has been the cause of much controversy.

It is worth noting that the findings of this study run counter to and break through several realities of and about journalism and journalists, such as:

1. *The isolated nature of the craft and profession.* Journalists lack sufficient knowledge about others like them beyond their own workplace, and often have little knowledge of the history of their field.

2. *The belief that there is danger in definition.* Courts and constitutional scholars have been wary about defining *who* journalists are and *what* journalism is. When one asks who they are, there is a debate over whether the designation *journalist*

applies only to those employed by media organizations or also to "lonely pam-
phleteers," freelance writers, and others. This was underscored in an exchange
between Carol Simpson of ABC News and talk show host Larry King at a
Harvard conference when he said, "I may not be a journalist, but what I do
makes journalism."

There is also a fear of saying what journalistic standards should be, both in terms
of education and theory, as well as what they actually produce. There is no
requirement for responsibility or fairness, the courts say. Still, this means that the
First Amendment can serve as a great bulwark for free expression, or a convenient
rationale for ignorance or an arrogant refusal to discuss journalistic definitions.

3. *The belief that studies like this one will be misused.* Some people believe that
research will be fodder for forces trying to influence, coddle, and manipulate the
media. Forbes' *Media Guide*, marketed to public relations (PR) firms and other
organizations, for example, is largely used by those who want to prepare for
interviews. Additionally, when one mentions detailed information about journalists, some critics immediately will misuse or distort it. For example, there is
a lust for information about ideology, which ideologues use to prove their case
that the press is too liberal or too conservative, anti-business or pro-business,
and hostile or not to minorities and women. In light of the 1992 presidential
campaign, when claims of media bias were made, studies of this kind would be
helpful in providing factual information based on evidence, not just opinion.
Thus, research about journalists can be useful in: (a) satisfying the sheer curiosity
of media watchers and news junkies; (b) considering the relationship between
news people's backgrounds and what news consumers actually get; (c) taking
the temperature of the newsroom and making an inventory of the workforce to
learn whether there is any link between public attitudes about journalists and
who journalists actually are and what they believe; and (d) moving beyond
generic generalizations about "the media" and understanding people who work
for the media.

In the Weaver–Wilhoit data, there is much to celebrate about the vitality
and vibrancy of American journalism. The size, scope and composition of the
workforce are impressive by any worldwide standard. There are some suspicions
and expectations confirmed, a few surprises, and some reasons to be worried
about the future and robustness of this singularly important occupation and
profession. In fact, I am concerned enough about what these findings tell us
about healthy American journalism to wonder whether this study is merely an
inquiry, or whether it can be characterized also as a preliminary inquest.

Beyond the natural curiosity of the media navel gazers and news junkies, the
only reason the public should care about research on journalists is that there is
good cause to wonder whether there is any relationship between *who* these
journalists are and *what* we ultimately get from them in our news products. This
also leads quite naturally to the subject of professionalism, and whether that

intervening factor somehow transforms the human frailties of journalists, who are rather unlike most of the American population. We do not worry much about a doctor's politics or religion influencing the kind of care we get, and we assume that even lawyers with whom we disagree on most things are capable of defending our interests in court. At the same time, we care greatly about the health and sanitary habits of those who work in restaurants or sausage factories. For such reasons, we should care about journalists and their news-processing practices.

If *who* American journalists are influences, shapes, and biases the news, we should care very much about the current inventory of this species. Of course, there has been controversy about bias in the press for a long time. In recent years, various media-watcher lobbies and special interests have told us that the press is too liberal or too conservative, insensitive to critical issues in American life, or out of touch on such matters as race and gender. Still, in 1986, when Professors Weaver and Wilhoit reported their findings at a news conference in midtown Manhattan, Edwin Diamond of *New York Magazine* (certainly not a heavy-breathing ideologue eager to inject opinion into the news) characterized the journalists in their study as "the best and the blandest."

Interest in studies like this one is weighed because of a penchant in this country for certainty, and there is a comforting certainty in numbers. The numbers in this sample, which represents about 1% of the 122,000 practicing journalists in America, give a better sense of who they are by age, gender, race, and income; the venues in which they ply their craft; their attitudes about their profession; and the way they do their work. This study has value, and will either reassure or dismay consumers of the news product, depending on their point of view.

But whatever consumers' reaction, no one can deny that the Weaver–Wilhoit study is good social science, rigorously conducted and open to replication by others. This has not been true for many other studies of the press, especially those conducted by ideologically oriented study groups and advocates. In contrast, the Weaver–Wilhoit study was prepared by master chefs in a clean, carefully inspected, and uncontaminated kitchen.

Some will find solace in these data, which portray a news corps dedicated to public service—idealistic, practical, relatively well educated, and connected to the rest of society by religious and political affiliations. It is an elite group to be sure, but few would want a press corps that was utterly mediocre because it is the front line force that gathers the information on which the rest of society depends. Vested interests here and elsewhere will seize on one or more statistics in the study to reinforce their views, often distorting the data and their context in the process. Women, critics of the right or the left, minorities, and journalism school deans will all view some numbers with alarm. Editors of news magazines will use this study to tell their employees that they are financially better off than they think they are.

Much of what is reported here, however, is a function of an economic recession that has hit the news industries especially hard. Although incomes are up slightly, the workforce is not growing very fast, women are not increasing in sheer numbers, fewer people are leaving the business, and there are relatively fewer new hires. Even the increase in journalists who identify with the Democratic party may be, as much as anything, a function of the economy and dissatisfaction with the years of Republican rule between this study and its predecessor.

Despite the economy, however, it appears that many media executives have made good on their promises to hire and promote more minorities. Clear gains in raw numbers, job responsibilities, and incomes are reported. At the same time, it is worth noting that minority group members, especially African Americans, are more likely than all journalists to be Democrats than Republicans, which will prove worrisome to those seeking a professionally oriented, impartial journalistic corps.

One of the difficulties in any national study is that data "brown out" the sharper edges of the field. We get little insight here into the elite media that really rule the roost in American journalism and that have a much greater impact on the nation than does the "Median Journalist in Middle America."

For example, a study like this one suggests that the best-paid journalists in America work on news magazines, but anyone who looks closely at relative compensation in the national media sees that this is just plain wrong. Television people get the highest salaries, followed by some leading newspaper people, followed by news magazine people. This is from an informal, but widely accepted survey in such places as New York, Washington, and Los Angeles—the centers of the media industries. Still, when averaged out over the whole field, Weaver and Wilhoit are not wrong, although their data can be distorted.

People will always debate the alleged political bias of the press. The day after the 1992 presidential election, Robert Teeter of the Bush/Quayle campaign charged the media with a pro-Clinton slant—a claim that has been heard before. The question of political bias has been around for a long time, and there is never a satisfying answer for anyone. In the 1992 election, all three candidates were unhappy with the media most of the time, and yet evidence indicates that we have just seen the best performance by the press in any modern election. This raises questions about the nature of informing the public and with what approach versus the relative popularity of the press and other news media.

Still, anyone who looks back very far finds shifting ground. Franklin D. Roosevelt thought the press "about 200%" against him, and did an end run much like this year's candidates by airing his "fireside chats" directly to the American public. A few years later, Adlai Stevenson denounced the "one-party press," and he was most assuredly not talking about Democrats and liberals. In 1964, an aged Dwight Eisenhower received the greatest applause at the Republican National Convention by denouncing "sensation-seeking columnists and commentators." By the end of the decade, Spiro Agnew, in speeches written by Patrick Buchanan and William Safire, took on the media with gusto and warned against "nattering nabobs of negativism." A beleaguered Jimmy Carter complained about "an unrelentingly negative press." When Ronald Reagan left office, the news media themselves admitted to "an 8-year honeymoon" for "The Great Communicator."

Most recently, George Bush saw both sides of the equation with great intensity, being portrayed both with fawning adulation after the Persian Gulf War and, by contrast, as a wounded leader in the 1992 campaign. If the press tried to be biased and partisan, it could not send more mixed signals, and would have to be declared incompetent on its face. No, the story of positive and negative portrayals is far deeper than political preferences.

As we celebrate the kind of responsible public scholarship demonstrated in the Weaver–Wilhoit study, we might also ask what studies like this do not tell us. There is not much here about the individual psychology of the journalist that from Freud forward has been terribly important in understanding who people are and what they do. We learn little here of their personal lives—whether these journalists are married, single, or cohabiting; what their sexual preferences are; and whether any of these factors are evident in their professional behavior. Although we have the numbers that describe politics and religion, we do not know much about the intensity of those personal choices and how they play out in people's daily lives.

It is hard to know whether we are asking the right questions that will yield cues in the future about the most important influences on how people actually live their lives, do their work, and shape their thinking and professional practice. Sexuality, health, lifestyle, housing, transportation, use of technology, and other issues may, in fact, tell us a great deal more about a journalist and his or her work than do political and religious preferences, especially in an era when political parties and organized religion may be less relevant than before. The point is that our outlook and attitudes are shaped by many forces and change over time.

Any study of journalists today is beset with problems, beginning with the question, Who is a journalist? This is not a new question, but, for First Amendment reasons, Americans are reluctant to come to a concrete definition. There was a time when a *journalist*, a rather pretentious term by the way, simply meant "an unemployed newspaperman." Now, the term applies to all kinds of news people, but apparently not to those on the business side of publications who often become publishers and really influence the organization.

By the same token, the philosophies of professionalism and journalistic fairness—fair play being a fundamental American value—are also not defined. This study gives some clues as to why there is a declining support for an adversarial role for the press, whether in relationship to government or business. At the same time, it appears that journalists have considerable respect for the operations and values of the organization for which they work. Fairness is never defined here or elsewhere, although it is at the heart of virtually every dispute about the media, whether generated in the business community, politics, or a racial group. Again, the courts have given comfort to vagueness, saying that the Constitution does not require that the press be either fair or responsible.

This study, like others these days, accepts the assumption that employees in the media should mirror the racial and gender composition of the rest of the U.S. population. I can think of no other profession or field of endeavor where this is the case, or where such goals are being pursued voluntarily. Of course, equity is championed everywhere, and people increasingly believe that the workforce of the government and apparently the media should look like the rest of America. But that is different from saying it ought to be numerically correct in exact or nearly exact proportion. The hot buttons these days are race and, to a much lesser degree, gender.

The proportional representation argument ironically was not forced on the media by minority journalists' associations (although they supported it), but accepted almost uncritically by the influential American Society of Newspaper Editors (ASNE), which urged that minorities be represented in the workforce in line with national demographics by the year 2000. No one I know currently thinks this can happen, but the goal remains and sets a standard that influences studies like this one and various groups' expectations. Despite special programs, job fairs, scholarships, preferential hiring policies, and other efforts, the goal has proved elusive, and results will surely be disappointing.

Again, the issue of equity and equal opportunity is one thing, but ASNE's goal raises disturbing questions. There are fewer accepted quotas or even expressed concerns for Asian Americans, Native Americans, or other ethnic groups less vocal at the moment. Similarly, we do not seem to worry much about age, class, or even gender as much these days. Whether any profession or field should precisely reflect the larger population may seem a desirable social goal, but what about some future time when those doing the hiring will use the same rationale to deny entry to an individual because "we already have a quota for your group"?

If we are going to worry about race, then we should also care about age. For example, since when do we happily entrust our information to people in their mid-30s? If we are going to insist on racial quotas, what about quotas for social classes, educational levels, single and married people, gays, and other legitimate social groupings and demographics? The idea that the media industries should be open to all and that there should be incentives for minorities is noble and highly desirable. However, rigid racial and ethnic quotas developed selectively and leaving out most of America hardly achieve the goal of making the media look more like America.

Without putting words into the mouths of respondents in this study, I am intrigued by the finding that broadcast journalists apparently do not agree with the widespread view that the line between news and entertainment is blurring, or that there is much concern about business values superseding editorial values. I believe that these nearly clichéd assumptions are ahistorical. Some leaders of the news media—who push the image of a once eleemosynary and beneficent media dedicated to the public interest versus the money-grubbing and venal media of today—seem to forget the principal concerns of figures such as Joseph Pulitzer, William Randolph Hearst, or even William S. Paley.

Similarly, there is incontrovertible evidence developed elsewhere that the entertainment culture is playing an increasing role in both print and electronic media. One intriguing example is author Patricia O'Brien's recent observation that many of her classmates in a New York screenwriting course were young television news producers. When she asked them why they were there, they explained that "we have to learn more about dramatic presentation in order to survive in this business today"—a far cry from the sanctimonious responses of the broadcast news people in the Weaver–Wilhoit study.

In the end, we ask what it is we really know about news people. The answer, despite some blind spots and flaws, is quite a bit. What we do not know is just how the demographics of journalists really connect, or fail to connect, with what they do and write. However, the precepts of professionalism covered in this study suggest that, ultimately, when basic news decisions are made, professionalism, and not personal bias, prevails. Part of that reason may be something not covered in detail in the study—and that, of course, is ownership. Whatever the politics of individual journalists, media owners continue to be business people, and every intelligent source I know says that they are likely to be fiscally conservative and typically Republican in their politics. At the same time, like their employees, owners are not ideologues who are driven by political passion and personal political agendas—that simply is not the American way of doing media business.

A study of this kind always demands context, and the operative question is, Compared to what? News people today, compared with those a generation or two ago, are more professional, better educated, and more self-aware. On so-called ethical matters, however, they seem to veer far from what was once the norm for personal privacy and professional conduct. Yet contrasted with news people in other countries and cultures, the American genus is almost saintly.

Elsewhere in the world, where special interests and governments still own and dominate the media, journalists regularly promote pointed or partisan political views, disdain ordinary people, and accept bribes. They often work both sides of the fence by identifying with their media bosses while accepting the largess of their sources. When journalists and their critics complain about these practices, reform using "the American example of media ethics" is suggested. The American journalist, in a global context, is a progressive creature, and we should, I believe, be grateful. By the same token, the Weaver–Wilhoit data suggest many areas where higher standards and a more representative workforce are imperative for the media to maintain credibility and to authoritatively play their continuing role in American life.

It is also clear that the American journalist, like the media industries, is changing. Journalists today see themselves as less clinically detached than they were once expected to be, more likely to be self-conscious about themselves and their work, less dedicated to journalism as a career for life, and more likely to find job satisfaction in journalism. Yet journalists are also apparently deeply disturbed and even confused about the future. Indeed, the next time this study is done, researchers may have to look at new venues to find journalists in such places as cable, business information, telephone-information services, newsletters, corporate video/telecommunication, institutional news bureaus, the Internet, and elsewhere.

The value of a study like this is in its clarity and pointed presentation as expressed in numbers. However, that does not excuse journalists and their critics from making historical connections, relying not on the instant photograph, but on the long-term view, remembering that the end product of American journalism is a mixture of several creatures and cultures.

Journalists are truly the worker bees, but they rarely own the hive and they never exist outside the prevailing society and culture. We have heard what journalists think of themselves. The other side of the ledger not covered is what the public thinks of the news it receives, of the media in general, and of journalists in particular. Unfortunately, most of the criticism of the media is overly broad and general. While disdaining "the media," ordinary Americans like their local newspapers and often admire journalists, despite their relatively low prestige ratings compared with other professionals and occupations.

Although some figures in journalism, mostly TV anchors or prominent owners like CNN's Ted Turner, are public figures and even celebrities, they are not well known to ordinary Americans. While Tom Brokaw, Peter Jennings, Dan Rather, and Bernard Shaw enter our living rooms nightly, few know much about them personally or could recite their biographies from memory. Their faces are known and people may have opinions and suspicions about their personal views, but even these most famous journalists are only vaguely known. On the local scene, only sports and TV columnists are household names, but neither they nor their colleagues are really known to average citizens.

A journalism that began in America with people, often colorful people, is increasingly hidden from public view. People rail about "the media," but say they like and trust America's most visible journalists. In the 150 years since people relied on Horace Greeley's *New York Tribune* or Pulitzer's *New York World*, tying what we now call *media institutions* to individuals and personal accountability, much has changed. The corporatization of journalism is clearly with us, yet the enterprise is still made up of people trying to do their work with honesty and professional standards.

Studies like this give us hope that we can once again learn more about the people who take part in the increasingly impersonal manufacturing process we call *journalism*. This will happen to the extent that the Weaver–Wilhoit study and others that follow in its path are available to the American people. That is what this exercise in public scholarship is all about. I submit that the media in America or elsewhere will never be understood or appreciated until America's journalists step out of their newsrooms, where they are shielded from the public, and become better known to the rest of us. That is the challenge for people in the media who have a vested interest in that process because it will help them, their enterprises, and, ultimately, society.

Preface

It used to be said that a lot more was known about American farmers than about journalists. No occupational group is more important than the providers of much of the world's grain, but the suppliers of some of the mental foodstuff of democracy and governance are important, too.

Two decades ago, sociologist John Johnstone and his colleagues, working in America's heartland at the University of Illinois at Chicago, changed what we know about journalists. Their landmark national study of journalists in the mainstream news media gave, for the first time, a baseline of important data. The book by John W. C. Johnstone, Edward J. Slawski, and William W. Bowman, *The News People*, published in 1976, will remain a durable analytical portrait of news crafters for future historians studying the uncertain democracy of late 20th-century America. Our goal—in our first study in 1982–1983 and in our book, *The American Journalist*, published in 1986—was to build on the important groundwork laid by the Johnstone team. This was also our aim with this 1992 study and this book, published 20 years after the original Johnstone volume.

Our chief concerns here are with: (a) the role perceptions of journalists working in America's news media over the last quarter of the century; (b) the changes in the backgrounds and education of those choosing journalistic life; (c) professional attitudes, beliefs, and values of journalists; and (d) the problem of retaining the best and brightest people in journalism. In addition to providing a "third wave" of information to studies from two previous decades, this book has two new dimensions. First, the attitudes of minority journalists are assessed more deeply than previously possible. Second, the book contains more open-ended comments, giving a richer perspective from the journalists themselves on critical issues of quality and autonomy.

ACKNOWLEDGMENTS

We are indebted to many people for the opportunity to conduct this study. Most important is the generosity of The Freedom Forum, an international, nonpartisan foundation dedicated to enhancing the prospects of a free press and the professional development of journalists. Charles Overby, president; Gerald Sass, executive vice president; Félix Gutiérrez, vice president; Everette Dennis, senior vice president; and the trustees of The Freedom Forum made the present book possible. Their support for the national study came with no strings attached: There was never a request nor the slightest hint by the foundation that anything be included or excluded. It was, in short, the ideal situation for independent researchers, and we are deeply grateful for their support of this research.

At our request, Everette Dennis, executive director of The Freedom Forum Media Studies Center in New York City, reacted to the wording of some new questions in the latest study and generously wrote the foreword to this book. Jane Coleman and John Pavlik, then at The Freedom Forum Media Studies Center, also made helpful suggestions on the questionnaire.

Félix Gutiérrez, vice president, and Brian Buchanan, director of journalism professional development of The Freedom Forum, assisted us in preparing for the conference, "The American Journalist in the 1990s," where a preliminary report of the present findings was presented at The Freedom Forum World Center in Arlington, Virginia, on November 17, 1992. A videotape of that conference is available from the C-SPAN archive at Purdue University in West Lafayette, Indiana.

We are indebted to many persons at Indiana University for assistance on this project. With the late Richard Gray, then dean of the School of Journalism, we proposed the idea for the first study. Colleagues at that time—Trevor Brown, Dan Drew, Eric Fredin, and Edmund Lambeth—made helpful suggestions on the 1982 study. Lori Bergen, Sue Lafky, Jo Ellen Fair, Mary Alice Sentman, and Hemant Shah (then graduate students who are now faculty members at other institutions) assisted us in coding and data processing on *The American Journalist* in 1986. Drew, Bergen, and Lafky performed additional analyses and contributed new material for the second edition of *The American Journalist*, published in 1991.

Trevor Brown, dean of the School of Journalism, encouraged us and gave us critical support on the present project. Brown also generously wrote the afterword for the book. Douglas Walker and Lars Willnat, then graduate students who are now faculty members at other institutions, gave important assistance in drawing the sample, corresponding with respondents, processing the data, and preparing charts. Walker provided special help in processing the extensive open-ended comments for analysis. Scott Lewis, a graduate student at the time, provided extensive data processing and preparation of tables and charts for several pre-liminary reports based on the 1992 survey.

Wei Wu and Divya C. McMillin, presently doctoral students at Indiana, helped us greatly in the final stages of the book's preparation. McMillin executed the content and data analysis, and is the first author of chapter 7, "Journalists' Best Work," based on an earlier analysis by Bergen and Lafky. Wu did data runs, prepared tables, and compiled the bibliography and indexes. Cathi Norton assisted in many important ways with manuscript preparation.

Significant support for research assistance in the preparation of the book was also provided from the Roy W. Howard Research Professorship established by Jack Howard, Jane Howard, and the Scripps Howard Foundation, with generous bequests to the Indiana University School of Journalism.

John Kennedy, director of the Center for Survey Research at Indiana University, assisted us in editing the final questionnaire, and provided a highly motivated staff of technicians and well-trained interviewers equipped with computer-assisted facilities for high-quality interviews. We also thank the 1,410 U.S. journalists who provided what we believe to be reliable and valid information about themselves and the field, giving us a response rate of 81% of our original sample.

Frances Goins Wilhoit, head of the Weil Journalism Library, did reference work and kept us informed about books and studies related to both projects. Connie Carter, head of the Science and Technology Division of the Library of Congress, introduced us to electronic library searching in the early 1980s, and provided important bibliographic support for the first project. Also helpful were Keith Buckley, Douglas Freeman, Ralph Gaebler, and Michael Parrish—all librarians at Indiana University.

Although we lay no claim to the slightest hint of the kind of fame achieved by U.S. journalism's best-known reporting team—who came to be called "Woodstein"—we can say that our partnership lasted longer than that of Bob Woodward and Carl Bernstein. This marks our 27th year of working together, beginning with a research paper on news coverage of U.S. senators presented at the 1969 annual convention of the Association for Education in Journalism in Berkeley, California. Although our last names have not been fused, we have been called "the odd couple" because of our vastly different work styles. No matter. Our research partnership and friendship have survived the trials and tribulations of two national surveys, each containing more than 150,000 pieces of information and producing results that were called "silly" by broadcast "talker" Rush Limbaugh. Of that we are proud.

David Weaver
G. Cleveland Wilhoit

Chapter 1

Basic Characteristics of U.S. Journalists

It is risky to write in general terms about the traits of U.S. journalists in the early 1990s, as was true in the early 1980s, because they comprise such a large and diverse group. The statistical "profile" of the typical U.S. journalist in 1992 was much like that of 1982–1983: a married White Protestant male with a bachelor's degree in his 30s. However, some changes occurred between 1982 and 1992. The typical U.S. journalist in 1992 was 4 years older, more likely to be of a race other than Caucasian, somewhat more likely to identify with the Democratic party, less likely to claim to be a political Independent, and more likely to hold a college degree. Of course, this picture, based on the central tendencies of demographic measures, masks many of the important differences and changes in U.S. journalists.

This chapter looks at the size of the journalistic workforce in the United States in 1992 compared with earlier years, the geographic dispersion of U.S. journalists, their age and gender, their ethnic and religious origins, their political views, and their media use patterns. (See Appendix I, this volume, for details of the survey methods.)

SIZE OF THE JOURNALISTIC WORKFORCE

In 1971, Johnstone and his colleagues estimated the total full-time editorial (journalistic) workforce in U.S. English-language mainstream news media to be 69,500, with more than half employed by daily newspapers.[1] In late 1982, we estimated this workforce to be 112,072, an increase of 61%, with slightly less than half employed by daily newspapers.[2] In 1992, we estimated the total number of

TABLE 1.1
Estimated Full-Time Editorial Workforce in U.S. News Media

News Medium	April 1971[a]		November 1982[b]		June 1992	
	Number	%	Number	%	Number	%
Daily newspapers	38,800	55.8	51,650	46.1	67,207	55.1
Weekly newspapers	11,500	16.5	22,942	20.5	16,226	13.3
News magazines	1,900	2.7	1,284	1.1	1,664	1.4
Total print media	52,200	75.1	75,876	67.1	85,097	69.8
Television (and combined radio and TV stations)	7,000	10.1	15,212	13.6	17,784	14.6
Radio	7,000	10.1	19,583	17.5	17,755	14.5
Total broadcast media	14,000	20.2	34,795	31.1	35,539	29.1
News services	3,300	4.7	1,401	1.2	1,379	1.1
Total workforce	69,500	100.0	112,072	100.0	122,015	100.0

[a]From John Johnstone, Edward Slawski, and William Bowman, The News People (Urbana: University of Illinois Press, 1976), p. 195.

[b]From David H. Weaver and G. Cleveland Wilhoit, The American Journalist (Bloomington: Indiana University Press, 1986 and 1991), p. 13.

journalists working for mainstream news media to be 122,015, an increase of just under 9%, with more than half employed by daily newspapers (see Table 1.1).

Compared with the 1970s, the growth in number of full-time mainstream news media journalism jobs in the United States in the 1980s was very small—almost stagnant. As New York Times columnist Russell Baker put it, the newspaper business is often referred to as "a mature industry." Baker wrote that when people use that term, "they are breaking the bad news gently. What they mean is that your industry is not long for this world, pal."[3]

Although we don't agree that U.S. newspapers are not long for this world, we do suspect that, during the 1980s, there was more growth in news and information jobs in specialized magazines, newsletters, computerized information services, and various cable television programs than in daily newspapers and the other more traditional news media included in this study (news magazines, wire services, weekly newspapers, radio and television news departments).

Although it is difficult to obtain estimates of employment for all branches of the mass communication field, the U.S. Bureau of Labor Statistics estimated that, from 1981 to 1989, the field of "communication" (which includes telephones, radio-TV broadcasting, and cable and pay TV) actually shrank by 9%—from 1.384 million to 1.265 million jobs.[4] The U.S. Department of Labor's prediction is that "employment in communications is projected to decline by 13 percent" between 1990 and 2005, reflecting labor-saving technology and industry competition.[5]

However, the field of "printing and publishing" (which includes newspapers, periodicals, books, and miscellaneous publishing) grew 19%—from 1.292 million jobs in 1982 to 1.538 million in 1990.[6] The U.S. Department of Labor's prediction is that professional, technical and managerial positions in manufacturing firms will increase, although manufacturing jobs in general will decline by 3% during the 1990–2005 period.[7]

The figures for total number of jobs in communication and publishing include many technical and clerical jobs, of course, so they are rough estimates of growth (or lack of it) in news-related jobs in these broader fields. But they do raise questions about whether there has been (or will be) much growth in jobs in the broader field of communication outside of the traditional news media. There has also been a blurring of the lines between news and entertainment in various publications and "tabloid" TV shows, such as "Inside Edition" or "A Current Affair." This blurring may call for a broader definition of *journalist* the next time a study such as this is conducted.

Our estimates of U.S. journalistic employment do not include part-time correspondents, freelancers, or stringers working on an occasional basis, although their numbers seem to have increased during the 1980s, especially in radio.[8] Our estimates are subject to varying amounts of sampling error because they were based on different sized random samples of news organizations in relation to their actual numbers. The most reliable estimates are those for news magazines and wire services, whereas the least reliable estimates are those for daily newspapers and radio. (For more details on how these estimates were calculated and how our sample of journalists was drawn, see Appendix I, this volume.)

In 1983, we concluded that the dramatic increase in the size of the editorial (or news) workforce during the 1970s appeared to have exceeded the overall growth in the number of news organization employees, at least for daily newspapers, including those working in advertising, circulation, production, and the business side. In the 1980s, the small growth in the editorial workforce was matched by little growth in all news organization employees, again taking daily newspapers as an example. The growth in the total workforce of daily newspapers—including those employed in advertising, circulation, editorial, production, and the business side—was barely 8% from 1980 to 1992,[9] compared with an estimated increase of just under 9% for all full-time journalists in our study from 1982 to 1992.[10]

Compared with the growth in total U.S. employment from 1980 to 1992, which the U.S. Bureau of Labor Statistics put at about 18%,[11] the figures for daily newspapers and for journalists in general suggest that U.S. mainstream journalism grew at about half the rate of the overall U.S. workforce during the 1980s—and this is an optimistic estimate. If the American Society of Newspaper Editors' (ASNE) estimates for total number of daily newspaper journalists (54,530) and the Radio-Television News Directors Association's (RTNDA) estimates for the total number of radio and television journalists (39,400) in 1992 are substituted for ours, then the estimate of U.S. journalists in 1992 drops to 113,199—and this includes considerable numbers of part-time journalists in radio and television.[12] Compared with our estimate of 112,072 in 1982, this more conservative (and possibly more accurate) estimate of 113,199 in 1992 suggests virtually no growth during the 1980s in full-time U.S. journalists working for mainstream news media.

Whichever estimates are used, in 1992, about two thirds of all U.S. journalists worked for the print media (daily and weekly newspapers, and news magazines). This is even more true if the wire services are classified as *print media*. But there are some signs that the percentage of broadcast journalists inched up a bit (from 31% in 1982 to nearly 35% in 1992, if the ASNE and RTNDA estimates are used). If only television journalists are considered, it is clear that they increased between 1982 and 1992—by at least 2,500 according to our estimates, and possibly by as many as 6,000 according to the RTNDA estimates.[13] The number of radio journalists declined 2,000 to 4,000, depending on which estimates are used.

When we speak of *journalists* in this study, we are using virtually the same definition employed in the 1971 Johnstone study: those who have editorial responsibility for the preparation or transmission of news stories or other information, including full-time reporters, writers, correspondents, columnists, news people, and editors. In broadcast organizations, only news and public affairs staff are included. Our definition of *journalists*, like Johnstone's, includes editorial cartoonists, but not comic-strip cartoonists.

In this 1992 study, we included photographers as journalists; in the earlier two studies, only photographers who were also reporters were included. We think that in 1992, as compared with 1982 and 1971, photojournalists had more discretion than in the past about which pictures to shoot and were more likely to write copy to accompany these pictures.

As in the previous studies, we excluded librarians and visual and audio technicians because most of them usually are directed by reporters and editors (or assist them), and therefore do not have direct editorial control over the information they communicate.

GEOGRAPHIC DISTRIBUTION OF JOURNALISTS

Johnstone and his colleagues argued that, from its beginnings, the American news industry has been concentrated in the Northeast, largely because that region has been the center of population, trade, and commerce.[14] In 1971, the Johnstone study found journalists overrepresented by 12% in the Northeast, as compared with the total population, and underrepresented in all other major regions of the country (see Table 1.2). During 1982–1983, there was a dramatic decline in the percentage of journalists working in the Northeast, significant increases in the proportions employed in the North Central (Midwest) and South regions, and almost no change in those located in the West. In 1992, the proportion in the Northeast remained constant, with a small decline in the North Central (Midwest) and small

TABLE 1.2
Regional Distribution of Journalists Compared with
Total U.S. Population (Percentage in Each Region)

Region	Journalists			Total Population		
	1971[a] (N = 1,328)	1982–1983[b] (N = 1,001)	1992 (N = 1,156)	1970[c]	1981[d]	1990[e]
New England	7.5	9.7	5.0	5.8	5.4	5.3
Middle Atlantic	28.8	11.2	14.8	18.3	16.1	15.1
East North Central	15.3	19.2	12.0	19.8	18.2	16.9
West North Central	7.4	11.5	12.8	8.0	7.5	7.1
South Atlantic	11.0	12.8	20.6	15.1	16.5	17.5
East South Central	4.6	6.8	11.6	6.3	6.4	6.1
West South Central	9.1	13.3	6.0	9.5	10.7	10.7
Mountain	6.4	4.5	6.7	4.1	5.1	5.5
Pacific	9.9	11.1	10.5	13.1	14.1	15.7
Total	100.0	100.1[f]	100.0	100.0	100.0	99.9[f]
Total Northeast	36.3	20.9	19.8	24.1	21.5	20.4
Total Midwest	22.7	30.7	24.8	27.8	25.7	24.0
Total South	24.7	32.9	38.1	30.9	33.5	34.4
Total West	16.3	15.6	17.2	17.2	19.3	21.2

[a]From Johnstone, Slawski, and Bowman, *The News People*, p. 195.

[b]From Weaver and Wilhoit, *The American Journalist*, p. 16.

[c]U.S. Bureau of the Census, 1971, Table 11, p. 12.

[d]U.S. Bureau of the Census, *Statistical Abstract of the United States, 1982–1983*, 103rd ed. (Washington, DC: U.S. Government Printing Office, 1982), p. 30.

[e]U.S. Bureau of the Census, *Statistical Abstract of the United States, 1991*, 111th ed. (Washington, DC: U.S. Government Printing Office, 1991), p. 20.

[f]Does not total 100% because of rounding.

increases in the South and West (see Table 1.2). In general, the changes in the 1980s were minor compared with those in the 1970s, as one might expect from the negligible growth in U.S. journalism in the 1980s.

The proportion of journalists living and working in different regions of the country in 1992 matched the distribution of the overall population quite closely—slightly more than in 1982–1983 and certainly more than in 1971. But in terms of national prominence and influence in 1992, the major broadcast networks, news magazines, news services, and some of the most influential newspapers tended to be heavily concentrated in the Northeast, so the regional imbalances in prestige and influence were much greater than Table 1.2 suggests, as was true in the two earlier studies. This point is reinforced by data on journalists' media exposure patterns presented later in this chapter.

In 1982–1983, we concluded that with the rapid growth of broadcast journalism jobs, the U.S. news industry seemed less concentrated in the Northeast,
at least in terms of numbers of jobs.[15] Even without much growth in full-time
U.S. journalism jobs in the 1980s, except in television, there was not much
concentration in the Northeast in numbers of journalists working for different
media, except for news magazines and, to a lesser extent, news services (see
Table 1.3). For the other media, the greatest concentrations tended to be in the
Midwest (North Central) or the South, as one would expect from looking at
the overall U.S. population distribution and the growth of population in the
South during the 1980s.

AGE AND GENDER

On average, U.S. journalists in 1992 were older than in 1982–1983, but no more
likely to be female, despite dramatic increases in women journalism students and
the emphasis on hiring more women in journalism in the 1980s (see Tables 1.4
and 1.5). Although the median age of journalists (36 years) was virtually identical
to that of the total U.S. labor force, in 1992 U.S. journalists were disproportionately clustered in the 25–34 and 35–44 age brackets, and substantially underrepresented in the 24 and younger age categories.

The drop of nearly eight percentage points in the two youngest age categories
for journalists can be explained by the negligible growth in journalism during
the 1980s, and by the fact that the U.S. civilian labor force under 24 years of
age also declined as a relative percentage by five percentage points, although
the total U.S. workforce grew nearly 18%.[16] The sharp increase in the proportion
of journalists in the 35–44 age category can be explained by the dramatic growth
in the 1970s of U.S. journalism (from an estimated 69,500 full-time to just over
112,000—a 61% increase).

Many of those hired in the 1970s were in their late 30s or early 40s in 1992,
thus still a long way from retirement. With no real growth in number of full-time
journalism jobs, this left little room for those seeking to enter the field in the
early 1990s. It also means that, in 1992, U.S. journalism was less a younger
person's occupation than it was in the early 1980s or even the early 1970s.

Among most racial minorities, however, results show that journalism was
more a younger person's world in 1992. The median age of Asian-American,
African-American, and Hispanic journalists was 32, compared with 37 for Cau-
casians. Native-American journalists were the oldest on average, with a median
age of 40. Among the different news media, television journalists tended to be
youngest (33 on average), followed by those in radio (35), wire services (38),
daily and weekly newspapers (39), and news magazines (40). There was not
much difference in the median age between men (37) and women (35) in U.S.
mainstream journalism in 1992.

TABLE 1.3
Distribution of Journalists by Region and News Medium (Percentage in Each Region in 1992)

				News Medium			
Region	Daily Newspaper (n = 636)	Weekly Newspaper (n = 162)	News Magazine (n = 61)	News Service (n = 58)	Radio Station (n = 101)	Television Station (n = 138)	Total (n = 1,156)
Northeast	13.2	29.0	83.6	34.5	13.9	9.4	19.8
North Central	22.0	40.7	0.0	27.6	31.7	23.9	24.8
South	42.8	24.1	16.4	32.8	41.6	42.8	38.1
West	22.0	6.2	0.0	5.2	12.9	23.9	17.2
Total	100.0	100.0	100.0	100.1[a]	100.1[a]	100.0	99.9[a]

[a]Does not total to 100% because of rounding.

TABLE 1.4
Age Distribution of U.S. Journalistic Workforce
(Percentage in Each Age Group)

Age Group	Journalists			U.S. Civilian Labor Force		
	1971[a]	1982–1983[b]	1992	1971[c]	1981[d]	1989[e]
Under 20	0.7	0.1	0.0	5.1	8.3	6.4
20–24	11.3	11.7	4.1	13.9	14.8	11.4
25–34	33.3	44.9	37.2	22.2	28.0	29.0
35–44	22.2	21.0	36.7	20.0	19.5	24.7
45–54	18.8	10.9	13.9	21.0	15.6	16.1
55–64	11.3	8.9	6.6	14.1	11.0	9.6
65 and older	2.3	1.6	1.5	3.9	2.8	2.8
Total	99.9[f]	99.1[f]	100.0	100.2[f]	100.0	100.0
Median age	36.5	32.4	36.0	39.2	33.6	36.1

[a]From Johnstone, Slawski, and Bowman, *The News People*, p. 197.
[b]From Weaver and Wilhoit, *The American Journalist*, p. 19.
[c]U.S. Department of Labor, 1971, Table A-3, p. 29.
[d]U.S. Bureau of the Census, *Statistical Abstract of the United States, 1982–1983*, 103rd ed., p. 379.
[e]U.S. Bureau of the Census, *Statistical Abstract of the United States, 1991*, 111th ed., p. 392.
[f]Does not total to 100% because of rounding.

Although 45% of all full-time journalists hired between 1988–1992 were women, the virtually negligible growth in full-time journalism jobs between 1982–1992 meant that not enough women in absolute numbers were hired to make a difference in the overall workforce percentage. As Table 1.5 shows, in 1992 it remained at 34%. Figure 1.1 also shows that the proportion of women steadily declined with number of years in journalism, suggesting that fewer women were hired in earlier times, or that women did not stay in journalism as long as men, or both.

The 1992 results show that the average number of years of journalism experience was 15 for men and 12 for women. Men were considerably more likely

TABLE 1.5
Gender of U.S. Journalists (Percentage)

Gender	Journalists			U.S. Civilian Labor Force		
	1971[a]	1982–1983[b]	1992	1971[c]	1981[d]	1989[e]
Male	79.7	66.2	66.0	66.4	57.5	54.8
Female	20.3	33.8	34.0	33.6	42.5	45.2
Total	100.0	100.0	100.0	100.0	100.0	100.0

[a]From Johnstone, Slawski, and Bowman, *The News People*, p. 197.
[b]From Weaver and Wilhoit, *The American Journalist*, p. 19.
[c]U.S. Department of Labor, 1971, Table A-2, p. 28.
[d]U.S. Bureau of the Census, *Statistical Abstract of the United States, 1982–1983*, 103rd ed., p. 379.
[e]U.S. Bureau of the Census, *Statistical Abstract of the United States, 1991*, 111th ed., p. 392.

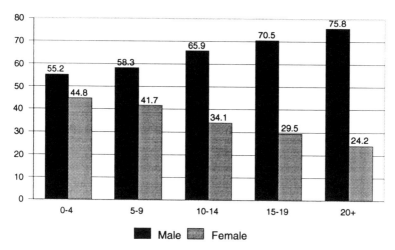

FIG. 1.1. Gender of journalists by years in journalism (%).

than women (46% vs. 32%) to have 15 or more years of experience in journalism, lending some support to the idea that women, in general, have not stayed in journalism as long as men have, regardless of their numbers.

Table 1.5 shows that, compared with the total U.S. labor force, the percentage of women in journalism in 1992 lagged behind by more than 11 points, and was at about the same level as the percentage of women in the total U.S. labor force in 1971 (34%). But when compared with other professional occupations, women in 1992 were better represented in journalism: Only about 27% of U.S. college faculty were women, 22% of attorneys were women, 9% of dentists were women, and 18% of physicians were women.[17]

It also appears from the data that women journalists gained responsibility in journalism. Forty-one percent said they supervised news or editorial employees, compared with 43% of men journalists. In addition, 18% of women journalists were owners, publishers, or upper level managers (city editor, news director, and higher), compared with 22% of male journalists. Finally, 32% of women journalists were lower level managers (desk editors, assignment editors, or assistant editors), compared with 30% of men.

U.S. journalists' gender was related to their marital status and family situation in 1992, just as it was in 1982–1983. Women were still less likely to be married (48%) than men (65%), and were much less likely to have children living with them (28%) than men (44%). But men and women journalists did not differ much with respect to education, religious background, membership in journalism organizations, or employment in group-owned versus independently owned media.

The proportion of women journalists varied by news medium, as Table 1.6 indicates—from about one fourth in the wire services and television to nearly one half in weekly newspapers and news magazines. But overall, there was not as much variation in 1992 as there was in 1971, when only 5% of radio journalists

TABLE 1.6
Representation of Women Journalists in Different Kinds of U.S. News Media

	Percentage Women			Case Base		
News Medium	1971[a]	1982–1983[b]	1992	1971[a]	1982–1983[b]	1992
Radio	4.8	26.3	29.0	89	118	100
Television	10.7	33.1	24.8	162	121	137
Wire services	13.0	19.1	25.9	46	47	58
Daily newspapers	22.4	34.4	33.9	920	462	635
Weekly newspapers	27.1	42.1	44.1	78	183	161
News magazines	30.4	31.7	45.9	33	63	61
Total	—	—	—	1,328	994	1,152

[a]From Johnstone, Slawski, and Bowman, *The News People*, p. 198.
[b]From Weaver and Wilhoit, *The American Journalist*, p. 21.

were women, compared with nearly a third of those working for news magazines. The biggest increases of women during the 1980s were in news magazines and, to a lesser extent, news services. Women actually lost ground in television newsrooms and held steady in daily and weekly newspapers.

The largest increase in women journalists during the 1980s was in the youngest age category (under 25), as might be expected from Fig. 1.1, and the only decline was in the 45–54 age bracket (see Table 1.7). The proportion of women in the youngest category slightly exceeded that for the total U.S. civilian labor force in 1989. This was the first time that happened in the three major studies of journalists done from 1971 to 1992, confirming the success of mainstream news media in hiring young women for entry-level positions during the 1980s.

TABLE 1.7
Representation of Women Journalists in U.S. Media and in
U.S. Labor Force by Age (Percentage of Women)

	Journalists			Total Labor Force		
Age Group	1971[a]	1982–1983[b]	1992	1970[c]	1981[d]	1989[e]
Under 25	25.5	42.0	48.9	40.9	46.5	47.6
25–34	17.9	35.1	37.9	32.3	42.5	44.5
35–44	15.5	28.6	30.6	35.6	42.6	45.7
45–54	22.5	33.0	30.6	38.4	41.8	45.2
55–64	25.5	24.7	27.6	36.8	40.1	42.9
65 and older	9.1	31.2	35.3	32.8	38.7	41.5

[a]From Johnstone, Slawski, and Bowman, *The News People*, p. 198.
[b]From Weaver and Wilhoit, *The American Journalist*, p. 22.
[c]U.S. Bureau of the Census, 1971, Table 328, p. 211.
[d]U.S. Bureau of the Census, *Statistical Abstract of the United States, 1982–1983*, 103rd ed., p. 379.
[e]U.S. Bureau of the Census, *Statistical Abstract of the United States, 1991*, 111th ed., p. 392.

But when we move to the next age group (25–34), we can see that the percentage of women journalists began to lag behind the percentage of women in the overall labor force. However, considering all the age groups, the differences between the percentages of women journalists and women in the labor force from 1982 to 1992 have declined in all but two categories—those 35–44 and 45–54 years old. Despite this progress, the overall percentage of women in U.S. mainstream journalism did not increase significantly from what it was a decade previous, as Table 1.5 indicates. Among racial minorities in U.S. journalism, however, the percentage of women was considerably higher: 52.5% of Asian Americans, 53.2% of African Americans, 48.1% of Hispanics, and 42.9% of Native Americans.

ETHNIC AND RACIAL ORIGINS

In their 1971 study of U.S. journalists, Johnstone and his colleagues concluded that, in general, journalists come from the established and dominant cultural groups in society.[18] Table 1.8 suggests that in 1992 that still was the case, even when the percentages of racial and ethnic minorities were compared with their percentages in the U.S. population. There was some improvement in the representation of minorities in U.S. journalism between 1982–1992, except for those of Jewish background. But Jewish journalists have been, and still are, overrepresented in U.S. journalism, as compared with their relative proportions in the overall population.

TABLE 1.8
Ethnic Origins of U.S. Journalists Compared with
Total U.S. Population (Percentage in Each Group)

	Journalists			Total U.S. Population		
Ethnicity	1971[a]	1982–1983[b]	1992	1970[c]	1980[d]	1990[e]
African American	3.9	2.9	3.7	11.1	11.8	12.1
Hispanic	1.1	0.6	2.2	4.4	6.5	9.0
Asian American	—[f]	0.4	1.0	0.5	0.7	2.9
Native American	—[f]	—[g]	0.6	—	—	0.8
Jewish	6.4	5.8	5.4	2.6	2.6	2.4
Other (includes Caucasian)	89.7	90.3	87.1	81.4	78.4	72.8
Total	100.0	100.0	100.0	100.0	100.0	100.0

[a]From Johnstone, Slawski, and Bowman, The News People, pp. 26, 198.
[b]From Weaver and Wilhoit, The American Journalist, p. 23.
[c]From U.S. Bureau of the Census, Statistical Abstract of the United States, 1972, 93rd ed., pp. 29, 33, 45.
[d]From Statistical Abstract of the United States, 1982–1983, 103rd ed., pp. 32, 33, 54, 55.
[e]From Statistical Abstract of the United States, 1991, 111th ed., pp. 22, 56.
[f]Not reported by Johnstone, Slawski, and Bowman, The News People.
[g]Not reported by Weaver and Wilhoit, The American Journalist.

Excluding Jewish journalists, the overall percentage of racial minorities in full-time U.S. mainstream journalism jobs increased from 3.9% in 1982–1983 to 8.2% in 1992, if the .7% who identified themselves as "Other" minorities is included. This 8.2% lagged far behind the 25% estimated by the U.S. Census for the total U.S. population. But when compared with the percentage of minorities who had bachelor's degrees (9.1), which was the minimum requirement for most full-time journalism jobs in 1992, it is clear that U.S. journalism did not lag very far behind the qualified population percentage, as Stephen Hess of The Brookings Institution pointed out.[19]

If only those full-time journalists hired during 1982–1992 are considered, the overall percentage of minorities was considerably higher than 8.2% (11.9% for those with 0–4 years of experience, and 12.4% for those with 5–9 years of experience)—both percentages well above the 9.1% estimated by the Census to hold bachelor's degrees (see Fig. 1.2). These figures suggest that there were increased efforts, and some success, in minority hiring in U.S. journalism during 1982–1992.

But Fig. 1.2 also shows that, after 10 years of experience, the percentage of minority journalists dropped sharply, probably because of a combination of less emphasis on hiring minorities before the 1980s and a tendency for minorities to leave journalism. Our data show that, in 1992, minority journalists had an average of 9–11 years of work experience in journalism, compared with an average of 14 years for nonminority journalists.

As with women, some news media have done better than others in recruiting full-time journalists of races other than Caucasian. Figure 1.3 shows that the broadcast news media of radio and television had the highest percentages, whereas weekly newspapers had the lowest. It is likely that the low percentages for weeklies reflect that most racial minorities in the United States lived in larger urban areas,

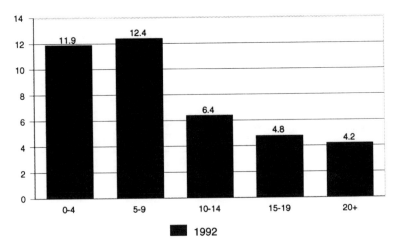

FIG. 1.2. Minority journalists by years in journalism (%).

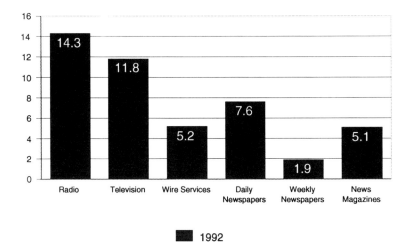

FIG. 1.3. Representation of minority journalists in different kinds of U.S. news media (%).

rather than in the small towns where weeklies tend to be published. However, the same cannot be said for news magazines and wire services, which tend to be located in larger urban areas.

The higher percentages of minorities in broadcast news media in 1992 were consistent with more interest in these media by minority journalism students in 1980[20] and 1987.[21] In our 1982–1983 study of U.S. journalists, we speculated that "minorities are more likely to be attracted to the faster-growing broadcast media than to the more traditional print media of newspapers, news magazines, and news services."[22] This appears to have happened during 1982–1992 perhaps because of additional efforts by broadcast news managers to recruit minorities, or because of more interest in broadcast media by minority journalism students, or both.

Although there were real increases in the proportions of racial minorities working in U.S. mainstream news media during the 1980s and early 1990s, it will likely be difficult to retain many of the brightest and most ambitious, given the limited opportunities for advancement in a field that did not grow much, if at all, during 1982–1992.

RELIGIOUS BACKGROUNDS

Table 1.9 shows that U.S. journalists did not change much during 1982–1992 in terms of religious backgrounds, and they reflected the overall U.S. population fairly closely. There was a drop in the percentage of journalists from Protestant backgrounds, but that was also true in the larger society. There was also an increase in the percentage of journalists claiming to be brought up in no religion

TABLE 1.9
Religious Backgrounds of U.S. Journalists Compared with
U.S. Adult Population (Percentage in Each Group)

Religion	Journalists			U.S. Adult Population		
	1971[a]	1982–1983[b]	1992	1974[c]	1981[d]	1992[e]
Protestant	61.5	60.5	54.4	60	59	55
Catholic	24.5	26.9	29.9	27	28	26
Jewish	6.4	5.8	5.4	2	2	1
Other or none	7.7	6.8	10.2	11	11	18
Total	100.1[f]	100.0	99.9[f]	100.0	100.0	100.0

[a]From Johnstone, Slawski, and Bowman, The News People, pp. 90, 225. Figures calculated from Table 5.9.

[b]From Weaver and Wilhoit, The American Journalist, p. 24.

[c]From George H. Gallup, The Gallup Poll: Public Opinion, 1972–1977, Vol. 1 (Wilmington, DE: Scholarly Resources, 1973), p. 393.

[d]From The Gallup Poll: Public Opinion, 1982, p. 37.

[e]Gallup Organization national telephone survey of 1,001 U.S. adults, July 31–August 2, 1992. Question: What is your religious preference? Data provided by The Roper Center, University of Connecticut.

[f]Does not total to 100% because of rounding.

or one other than Protestant, Catholic, or Jewish—also true in the larger society. Catholics and Jews were slightly overrepresented in journalism as compared with the U.S. population, but, in general, U.S. journalists closely reflected the religious preferences of the entire society.

There was variation by news medium, however, with news magazine and wire service journalists being much more likely to be of the Jewish faith than the population at large (23% in news magazines and 17% in the news services). There were also some differences by race, with African Americans more likely to be Protestant (67%), Hispanics much more likely to be Catholic (82%), Asian Americans more likely to be of no religion (29%), and Native Americans more likely to be of another religion (37%).

When it comes to the importance of religion or religious beliefs, however, U.S. journalists in 1992 were not in step with the larger society. Our survey results show that the percentage of journalists rating religion or religious beliefs as very important was significantly lower (38%) than in the overall U.S. population (61%). But 34% of journalists said religion was somewhat important, compared with 30% of the population.[23] The results also indicate differences by news medium, with journalists working for news magazines and wire services less likely to consider religion very important, and those in radio more likely. African-American and Native-American journalists were also more likely to say that religion or religious beliefs were very important (57% and 63%, respectively), and Asian Americans were least likely to say so (19%).

These findings raise the issue of whether U.S. journalists in 1992 were "elites" or whether they were representative of the larger society. In our previous study,[24] we argued that U.S. journalists were more reflective of the general society than removed from it. But, as these findings on religion suggest, there were some areas where there were notable differences, depending on what was measured. We return to this issue later.

POLITICAL VIEWS

Journalists have often been portrayed as social reformers who are likely to be more liberal than conservative politically.[25] Lichter and Rothman's 1981 study of elite journalists found 54% placed themselves to the left of center, compared with only 19% who chose the right side of the spectrum.[26] These elite journalists' voting records strongly supported the Democratic party in presidential elections from 1964 to 1976. In our 1982–1983 national survey of U.S. journalists, we found a slight left-leaning tendency among journalists, but it was much less pronounced than that found in Lichter and Rothman's sample of Northeastern elite journalists.

Political Leanings

Table 1.10 shows that journalists' trend of gravitating to the middle of the political spectrum from the early 1970s to the early 1980s was reversed from 1982 to 1992. In the early 1990s, journalists were much more likely to consider

TABLE 1.10
Political Leanings of U.S. Journalists Compared with
U.S. Adult Population (Percentage in Each Group)

Political Leanings	Journalists			U.S. Adult Population	
	1971[a]	1982–1983[b]	1992	1982[c]	1992[d]
Pretty far to left	7.5	3.8	11.6	—	—
A little to left	30.5	18.3	35.7	21	18
Middle of the road	38.5	57.5	30.0	37	41
A little to right	15.6	16.3	17.0	32	34
Pretty far to right	3.4	1.6	4.7	—	—
Don't know/refused	4.5	2.5	1.0	10	7
Total	100.0	100.0	100.0	100	100

[a]From Johnstone, Slawski, and Bowman, *The News People*, p. 93.

[b]From Weaver and Wilhoit, *The American Journalist*, p. 26.

[c]From George H. Gallup, *The Gallup Poll: Public Opinion, 1983* (Wilmington, DE: Scholarly Resources, 1984), p. 82.

[d]From Gallup Organization national telephone surveys of 1,307 U.S. adults, July 6–8, 1992, and 955 U.S. adults, July 17, 1992.

themselves left of center politically, and much less likely to claim to be middle of the road. There was also a slight increase in the percentage of U.S. journalists considering themselves pretty far to the right politically. However, in general, in 1992 journalists were less likely to think of themselves as on the right side of the political spectrum than was the public in general (22% of journalists vs. 34% of the public). Journalists were much more likely to consider themselves on the left (47%) than was the public (18%). In contrast to the striking changes in the political views of U.S. journalists, the U.S. public did not change much during 1982–1992.

Stephen Hess found similar political leanings in 1991 for White House reporters, but fewer said they were liberal (42%) and considerably more said they were conservative (33%).[27] Whereas Hess found White House reporters becoming more conservative from 1978 (19%) to 1991 (33%), we found U.S. journalists in general becoming more liberal from 1982 (22%) to 1992 (47%).

When we analyzed the political leanings of U.S. journalists separately for executives (those who supervise editorial employees) and staffers of prominent and nonprominent news organizations,[28] we found more journalists (both executives and staffers) from prominent news organizations claiming to be left of center than from nonprominent news media, as was true in the previous two studies (see Table 1.11). As in 1982–1983, the differences between prominent and nonprominent news organizations in 1992 were less than in 1971, but there were striking differences between the 1982–1983 and 1992 figures for both kinds of organizations and for both executives and staffers.

In all groups, there were significant increases from 1982–1983 to 1992 in the proportions of journalists saying that they were far or a little to the left. There were significant declines in the percentages claiming to be middle of the road politically, reflecting the general trends for all U.S. journalists. The proportions leaning to the right did not change much during 1982–1992 for staffers of prominent organizations or for executives of nonprominent news media, but there was a drop in self-proclaimed conservatives among the executives of prominent news organizations and an increase among staffers of nonprominent news media.

In the 1971 and 1982–1983 studies, managers in nonprominent news media were the most likely to claim political conservatism, but in 1992 there was no significant difference in percent leaning right between managers and staffers in these nonprominent organizations. Journalists in the nonprominent news organizations were more likely to say they leaned to the right (and a bit less likely to lean left) than those in the prominent media, regardless of position, as was true in the earlier studies.

In the 1982–1983 study, with its dramatic shift from the left to the center of the political spectrum, we concluded that there was "almost no evidence to support Rothman and Lichter's prediction that the next generation of journalists is likely to be more to the left than is the current generation."[29] In 1992, we had evidence that Rothman and Lichter[30] were better forecasters than we were,

TABLE 1.11

Political Leanings of U.S. Journalists in Prominent and Nonprominent Organizations (Percentage in Each Group)

	Prominent Organizations						Nonprominent Organizations					
	Executives			Staffers			Executives			Staffers		
Leaning	1971[a]	1982–1983[b] (n = 58)	1992 (n = 35)	1971[a]	1982–1983[b] (n = 78)	1992 (n = 32)	1971[a]	1982–1983[b] (n = 413)	1992 (n = 452)	1971[a]	1982–1983[b] (n = 450)	1992 (n = 622)
Left	6.8	6.9	14.3	12.4	9.0	15.6	4.1	5.6	11.3	9.5	6.4	11.7
Leaning left	56.1	24.1	42.9	40.4	24.4	43.8	24.4	16.2	36.5	31.0	18.4	35.0
Middle of the road	27.1	56.9	37.1	29.9	55.1	28.1	46.7	56.9	30.5	41.0	58.7	29.9
Leaning right	8.7	12.1	5.7	15.1	11.5	12.5	19.7	19.1	17.7	15.3	14.9	17.7
Right	1.4	0.0	0.0	2.2	0.0	0.0	5.1	2.2	4.0	3.2	1.6	5.6
Total	100.1[c]	100.0	100.0	100.0	100.0	100.0	100.0	100.0	100.0	100.0	100.0	99.9[c]

[a]From Johnstone, Slawski, and Bowman, *The News People*, p. 226. Ns are not reported for 1971 because they are weighted and therefore not directly comparable to those in 1982–1983 and 1992. See Johnstone et al., p. 225.

[b]From Weaver and Wilhoit, *The American Journalist*, p. 28.

[c]Does not total to 100% because of rounding.

17

although all journalists, not just the next generation, swung to the left during the 1980s, possibly in reaction to the conservative climate of the 1980s.

Political Party Identification

Another indicator of U.S. journalists' political views is political party identification. In 1971, Johnstone and his colleagues found that U.S. journalists were predominantly Democrats or Independents. We found the same to be true in 1982–1983, but to a greater degree because of a shift of about 7% from Republican to Independent. In 1992, as Table 1.12 shows, there was an increase of more than five percentage points in those considering themselves Democrats, a slight decrease in those claiming to be Republicans, and a decline in those claiming to be Independents. These trends ran counter to those for the general public, where there was an increase in Republicans and a decrease in Democrats from 1982 to 1992.

Thus, when compared with the U.S. population in 1992, journalists were about 10 percentage points more likely to say they were Democrats and about 16 points less likely to say they were Republicans. Journalists were slightly more likely than the public to claim to be Independents. Part of the increase in journalists identifying with the Democratic party came from the increase in minorities and in recently hired women in journalism. In general, minorities were much more likely to consider themselves Democrats than were the majority Caucasian journalists, especially African Americans (70%), Asian Americans

TABLE 1.12
Political Party Identification of U.S. Journalists Compared
with U.S. Adult Population (Percentage in Each Group)

Party	Journalists			U.S. Adult Population		
	1971[a]	1982–1983[b]	1992	1972[c]	1982–1983[d]	1992[e]
Democrat	35.5	38.5	44.1	43	45	34
Republican	25.7	18.8	16.4	28	25	33
Independent	32.5	39.1	34.4	29	30	31
Other	5.8	1.6	3.5	—[f]	—	1
Don't know/refused	0.5	2.1	1.6	—	—	2
Total	100.0	100.1[g]	100.0	100	100	101[g]

[a]From Johnstone, Slawski, and Bowman, The News People, p. 92.

[b]From Weaver and Wilhoit, The American Journalist, p. 29.

[c]From George H. Gallup, The Gallup Poll: Public Opinion, 1983 (Wilmington, DE: Scholarly Resources, 1984), p. 43.

[d]From The Gallup Poll: Public Opinion, 1983, p. 42.

[e]Gallup Organization national telephone survey of 1,307 U.S. adults, July 6–8, 1992. Data provided by The Roper Center, University of Connecticut.

[f]Not reported by Gallup.

[g]Does not total to 100% because of rounding.

(63%), and Hispanics (59%). There was also a wide gender gap, with women much more likely to say they were Democrats (58%) than men (38%). Men were the most likely (40%) of all these groups to say they were Independents.

When we look at political party identification by position in prominent and nonprominent news organizations, it is clear that the biggest gains in Democrats came in the prominent news organizations, among both managers and staffers, with the staffers the most likely (63%) to be Democrats (see Table 1.13). The biggest losses for the Republicans came among the executives of both prominent and nonprominent organizations, contrary to the common wisdom that managers are likely to be more conservative than younger staffers. The managers of prominent news media were much more likely to say they were political Independents, however, than were other groups.

Attitudes About Abortion

Still another indicator of journalists' political attitudes in 1992 was their response to a question about a specific issue (abortion) asked by the Gallup polling organization in a national survey. Although this question—Do you think abortions should be legal under any circumstances, legal under only certain circumstances, or illegal in all circumstances?—by no means covers the issue fully, it does allow a comparison of journalists' opinions with those of the public.

Not surprisingly, given the previous findings, journalists were inclined to respond in a more liberal manner, with 51% saying that abortion should be legal under any circumstance, as compared with 33% of the public.[31] Whereas 14% of the public agreed that abortions should be illegal in all circumstances, only 4% of journalists agreed.

In our 1982–1983 study of U.S. journalists, we concluded that there was a trend among U.S. journalists toward the center of the political spectrum and away from the right and the Republican party, but no visible swing to the left. In 1992, there was a noticeable swing to the liberal side of the spectrum and the Democratic party, almost entirely at the expense of the middle-of-the-road Independents. This trend was just the opposite of that for the general public, which may help to explain why journalists were recently criticized for the perceived unfairness of their news coverage, especially during the final months of the 1992 U.S. presidential election campaign. The swing to the political left was especially apparent among women and minority journalists, as well as among staffers of the more prominent Northeastern news media.

MEDIA USE

As was true a decade previous to this study, U.S. journalists in 1992 were heavy consumers of not only their own media, but also the news produced by journalists in other media, especially newspapers. Journalists in 1992 reported reading an

TABLE 1.13
Political Party Identification of U.S. Journalists in Prominent and Nonprominent Organizations (Percentage in Each Group)

	Prominent Organizations						Nonprominent Organizations					
	Executives			Staffers			Executives			Staffers		
Party	1971[a]	1982–1983[b] (n = 58)	1992 (n = 35)	1971[a]	1982–1983[b] (n = 78)	1992 (n = 30)	1971[a]	1982–1983[b] (n = 413)	1992 (n = 449)	1971[a]	1982–1983[b] (n = 450)	1992 (n = 619)
Democrat	44.0	33.3	48.6	43.2	50.7	63.3	31.1	37.7	44.5	35.3	39.8	44.1
Republican	8.5	8.8	0.0	15.6	4.0	6.7	31.8	22.4	15.4	27.8	19.8	18.9
Independent	44.7	57.9	51.4	33.7	44.0	30.0	30.6	37.7	36.3	31.8	39.1	33.3
Other	2.7	0.0	0.0	7.4	1.3	0.0	6.5	2.2	3.8	5.2	1.4	3.7
Total	99.9[c]	100.0	100.0	99.9[c]	100.0	100.0	100.0	100.0	100.0	100.1[c]	100.1[c]	100.0

[a]From Johnstone, Slawski, and Bowman, *The News People*, p. 226. Ns are not reported for 1971 because they are weighted and therefore not directly comparable to those in 1982–1983 and 1992. See Johnstone et al., p. 225.
[b]From Weaver and Wilhoit, *The American Journalist*, p. 31.
[c]Does not total to 100% because of rounding.

TABLE 1.14
Frequency of General Media Use by U.S. Journalists
(Percentage in Each Category)

Frequency	Number of Different Newspapers Read per Week	Number of TV Network News Shows per Week	Number of Local TV News Shows per Week	Number of Magazines Read Regularly
0	0.9	34.0	10.8	9.1
1	11.1	15.5	7.8	13.3
2	24.0	12.1	9.1	19.9
3	20.5	11.6	8.6	17.6
4	19.8	7.3	10.2	15.3
5	8.9	10.3	18.6	9.3
6	7.4	3.3	7.7	6.5
7	3.1	5.8	27.3	4.0
More than 7	4.5	—	—	5.0
Total	100.2[a]	99.9[a]	100.1[a]	100.0
Average	3.5	2.2	4.2	3.2

[a]Does not total to 100% because of rounding.

average of 3.5 different newspapers each week and watching 4.2 local TV news shows—the same as in 1982. But journalists in 1992 reported viewing an average of only 2.2 TV network news shows each week—down from an average of 3.3 in 1982. This decline may have been due to more frequent viewing of Cable News Network (CNN) television newscasts (3.2 times a week on the average in 1992, and even more for broadcast, male, and African-American and Hispanic journalists). The average number of magazines read regularly in 1992 was 3.2—a slight drop from the 3.7 figure from 1982 (see Table 1.14).

Newspaper Reading

These figures suggest that, in 1992, U.S. journalists were much heavier readers of newspapers than were nonjournalists. In 1987, only 15% of the total population read two or more newspapers on a given day,[32] as compared with 88% of journalists who reported reading two or more different newspapers each week in 1992. Although these measures are different, they suggest that journalists were considerably more likely to read more than one newspaper than were nonjournalists. These findings support an earlier study's conclusions that "information suppliers are information addicts,"[33] at least for newspaper information.

In contrast, U.S. journalists apparently were not heavy consumers of the less traditional media. The results show that they watched the *MacNeil/Lehrer Newshour* on public television only .7 days a week on average (higher for news magazine and Asian-American journalists, and those who did reporting frequently). They viewed TV "tabloid" programs, such as *Hard Copy*, and TV talk shows, such as *Oprah Winfrey*, only .5 days a week (less for those of higher income and those who did reporting frequently).

Table 1.15 shows that the most frequently read newspapers by U.S. journalists in 1992 were *The New York Times*, the *Wall Street Journal*, and *USA Today*. In 1982–1983, the *Washington Post* was in third place behind the same top two, but it slipped into a distinct fourth place in 1992. In 1971, the *Washington Post* was in second place. Readership of *The New York Times* dropped from one third to about one fourth, and readership of *USA Today* more than doubled, probably because of the losses in readers of *The New York Times* and the *Washington Post*.

Broadcast journalists in 1992 were much more likely to read *USA Today* regularly than the other top newspapers, and news magazine journalists were especially likely to read *The New York Times*. Regardless of these differences, those newspapers with nationwide visibility among substantial proportions of

TABLE 1.15
Newspapers Most Often Read by U.S. Journalists
(Percentage Reading Once a Week or More)

Newspaper	Percentage of Journalists Mentioning $(N = 1,156)$[a]
The New York Times	26.1
Wall Street Journal	23.4
USA Today	21.9
Washington Post	11.1
Los Angeles Times	5.4
Chicago Tribune	4.6
San Francisco Chronicle	4.4
Charlotte Observer	4.0
Philadelphia Inquirer	4.0
St. Paul (Minn.) Pioneer Press	3.9
(Norfolk) Virginia Pilot	3.8
Memphis Commercial Appeal	3.5
Boston Globe	3.5
Sacramento Bee	3.1
Denver Post	3.0
Minneapolis Star Tribune	2.9
Rocky Mountain News (Denver)	2.9
Atlanta Journal and Constitution	2.7
Milwaukee Journal	2.7
New York Post	2.7
Detroit Free Press	2.4
Miami Herald	2.2
Dallas Morning News	2.2
New York Daily News	2.0

[a]Percentages total to more than 100% because each journalist could name up to 12 different newspapers. Only those newspapers mentioned by 2% or more of all responding journalists are listed here.

U.S. journalists were small in number and tended to be located in the Northeast or Washington, D.C. area, just as was true in the 1971 Johnstone study.

Magazine Reading

The same was true for the magazines that U.S. journalists read regularly, as Table 1.16 indicates. But the percentages of journalists reading almost every issue of these magazines declined noticeably from 1982 to 1992—from about 50% for *Time* and *Newsweek* to about 30%, and from 16% for *U.S. News and World Report* to about 9%. The percentage reading *Sports Illustrated* regularly stayed about the same from 1982 to 1992. Other changes included *Newsweek* replacing *Time* as the most often read magazine, and the addition of the *Utne Reader* and *Entertainment Weekly* to the list mentioned by 2% or more of all responding journalists. In general, the list in 1992 focused on the leading information and

TABLE 1.16
Magazines Most Often Read by U.S. Journalists
(Percentage Reading Almost Every Issue)

Magazine	Percentage of Journalists Mentioning (N = 1,156)[a]
Newsweek	32.2
Time	28.5
Sports Illustrated	16.5
U.S. News and World Report	9.2
National Geographic	8.9
The New Yorker	8.7
Rolling Stone	6.9
Esquire	5.8
Atlantic Monthly	5.2
People	4.9
Reader's Digest	4.7
Smithsonian	4.4
Harper's	4.2
The New Republic	3.8
Utne Reader	3.8
Life	3.2
Business Week	3.0
Consumer Reports	2.9
Entertainment Weekly	2.9
Fortune	2.7
Sporting News	2.3
Money	2.2
Better Homes and Gardens	2.0
Forbes	2.0

[a]Percentages total to more than 100% because each journalist could mention any number of magazines. Only those magazines mentioned by 2% or more of all responding journalists are listed here.

opinion publications, rather than on the more mass-circulation entertainment ones, with a few exceptions.

A slightly higher percentage of journalists in 1992 said they did not read any magazines regularly (8.3%), as compared with 6.1% in 1982–1983. In general, however, journalists in 1992 were more likely to read at least one news magazine regularly than was the U.S. public. Table 1.16 shows that nearly one third of all journalists in 1992 read either *Newsweek* or *Time*, whereas in 1988 the unduplicated audience for three weekly news magazines was about 23%.[34] Among magazine journalists, not surprisingly, the percentage reading *Newsweek* (56%) or *Time* (52%) regularly was more than twice that of the general population.

In short, as in 1982, journalists in 1992 paid more attention to newspapers than did average Americans, although no single paper commanded a majority of readers. Journalists were also more likely to read one of the three weekly news magazines (especially *Newsweek* or *Time*) than was the public. When it came to electronic media use, however, journalists did not seem to be unusually heavy users.

In all, only four newspapers and three magazines were read regularly by more than 10% of U.S. journalists in 1992. All these publications are based on the east coast, which reinforces the conclusions of the 1971 Johnstone study regarding the pyramidal shape of the prestige hierarchy within the news industry and the dominance of the eastern seaboard.[35] (For a discussion of journalists' exposure to specialized professional publications, see chap. 4, this volume, on professionalism.)

CONCLUSIONS

This analysis of the basic characteristics of U.S. journalists in the early 1990s finds more similarities than differences to those characteristics in the 1982–1983 study. The most prominent similarities include:

1. The size of the full-time mainstream news media journalistic workforce in the United States in 1992 did not change much, and perhaps not at all, from 1982.

2. The bulk of full-time U.S. journalists in 1992 were still concentrated in the print media, especially in daily newspapers.

3. Changes in the geographic distribution of U.S. journalists in the 1980s were minor compared with those in the 1970s, as one might expect from the negligible growth in U.S. journalism in the 1980s. The proportion of journalists living and working in different regions of the country matched the distribution of the overall population quite closely—as was true in 1982–1983, but not in 1971.

4. U.S. journalists in 1992 were not more likely to be female, despite the increases in women journalism students and the emphasis on hiring more women

in journalism in the 1980s. There was an increase in women among journalists hired during 1982–1992, but a notable decrease in women among journalists with more than 10 years of experience.

5. Women journalists in 1992 were still less likely to be married than male journalists, and women were much less likely to have children living with them than were men.

6. U.S. journalists did not change much during 1982–1992 in terms of religious backgrounds, and they still reflected the overall population fairly closely.

7. Journalists in 1992 read the same number of newspapers regularly and watched the same number of local TV news shows each week as in 1982, but there was a slight drop in network TV news viewing and magazine reading.

8. *The New York Times* and the *Wall Street Journal* were still the most regularly read newspapers among U.S. journalists in 1992, as were *Newsweek* and *Time* news magazines. Overall, as in 1982–1983, only a handful of newspapers and magazines were read regularly by more than 10% of all U.S. journalists—and they were all based on the East Coast, reinforcing the dominance of the eastern seaboard in U.S. journalism.

This analysis also finds some notable differences from 1982–1983, including the following:

1. U.S. journalists in 1992 were older, on average, than in 1982. The median age for all journalists increased from 32 to 36 years. Print journalists in 1992 were older on average (39 years) than were broadcast journalists (33 years). Journalists under 24 years of age shrunk dramatically as a percentage of all journalists in 1992, compared with 1982–1983.

2. There was some growth in the percentage of racial minorities in U.S. journalism, from 4% in the early 1980s to just over 8% in 1992. Among journalists hired between 1987–1992, the percentage of minorities was 12%. Radio and TV had the highest proportions of minorities, and weekly newspapers the lowest, supporting our 1982 prediction that minorities would be more likely to be attracted to the faster growing broadcast media than to the more traditional print media.

3. Journalists in 1992 were somewhat more likely to identify with the Democratic party than in 1982, and much more likely to consider themselves to be left of center politically rather than middle of the road. The swing to the left was especially apparent among women and minorities, and among news magazine and daily newspaper journalists. This trend ran counter to that for the general public, where there was an increase in self-proclaimed Republicans and a decrease in Democrats from 1982 to 1992.

4. There was a decline among U.S. journalists in the average number of network TV news shows watched each week during the 1980s, and a slight drop

in the average number of magazines read regularly. But there was an increase in the viewing of CNN television news.

5. The *Washington Post* was replaced by *USA Today* as the third most widely read newspaper by U.S. journalists during 1982–1992, and *Newsweek* overtook *Time* to become the most widely read news magazine.

These are the main similarities and differences in the basic characteristics of U.S. journalists working for both print and broadcast mainstream English-language news media from the early 1980s to the early 1990s. They suggest some progress in the recruitment of minorities, but some formidable problems for young people who want to advance in mainstream U.S. news organizations. Because of stalled growth during the 1980s, which followed on the heels of dramatic growth in the 1970s, many of the most desirable jobs in U.S. journalism are held by people in their late 30s or early 40s, who are still a long way from retirement. Without new growth in the field, there will be few opportunities for advancement for the next 20 years or so. This will make it very difficult to retain the brightest and most ambitious young journalists, especially women and minorities who have perceived their chances for advancement to be reduced in the past by their gender or race.

NOTES

1. John W. C. Johnstone, Edward J. Slawski, and William W. Bowman, *The News People: A Sociological Portrait of American Journalists and Their Work* (Urbana: University of Illinois Press, 1976), pp. 18, 195.
2. David H. Weaver and G. Cleveland Wilhoit, *The American Journalist: A Portrait of U.S. News People and Their Work* (Bloomington: Indiana University Press, 1986; 2nd ed. 1991), p. 13.
3. Russell Baker, "Terror in the Sunlight," *The New York Times*, June 12, 1993, Op-Ed, p. 15.
4. U.S. Bureau of the Census, *Statistical Abstract of the United States 1991*, 111th ed. (Washington, DC: U.S. Government Printing Office, 1991), p. 411.
5. U.S. Department of Labor, *Occupational Outlook Handbook*, 1992–1993 ed., Bulletin 2400 (Washington, DC: U.S. Government Printing Office), p. 11.
6. U.S. Bureau of the Census, *Statistical Abstract of the United States 1992*, 112th ed. (Washington, DC: U.S. Government Printing Office, 1992), p. 734.
7. U.S. Department of Labor, *Occupational Outlook Handbook*, 1992–1993 ed., p. 11.
8. Vernon A. Stone, "TV News Work Force Grows, Declines Continue in Radio," *Communicator*, May 1993, p. 26.
9. Newspaper Association of America, *Facts About Newspapers*, 1993.
10. Our estimate of 1992 total daily newspaper full-time journalists (67,207) is considerably higher than the estimate from the American Society of Newspaper Editors' 1992 newsroom employment survey (54,530), probably because we received numbers of full-time newsroom employees from somewhat fewer small and mid-sized newspapers (under 50,000 circulation) than called for by our stratified random sample of daily newspapers, and from more larger papers (50,000–100,000 circulation). Thus, our estimate is likely to be higher than the actual numbers in the population. Another estimate, based on the newspapers in our sample in each circulation category separately, is much smaller (47,991), suggesting that the true figure is somewhere in between this and the

aggregate estimate of 67,207. The ASNE figure of 54,530 is likely to be the most accurate of the three estimates because it is based on responses from far more daily newspapers (more than 900) than the 114 in our sample.

11. Newspaper Association of America, *Facts About Newspapers*, 1993, p. 14.

12. American Society of Newspaper Editors, "News Release," March 30, 1993 and ASNE Census Projections for 1992; and Stone, "TV News Work Force Grows, Declines Continue in Radio," p. 26.

13. Stone, "TV News Work Force Grows, Declines Continue in Radio," p. 26.

14. Johnstone, Slawski, and Bowman, *The News People*, p. 20.

15. Weaver and Wilhoit, *The American Journalist*, pp. 15–17.

16. Newspaper Association of America, *Facts About Newspapers*, 1993, p. 14.

17. Susan H. Russell et al., *Profiles of Faculty in Higher Education Institutions, 1988* (Washington, DC: National Center for Education Statistics, U.S. Department of Education, 1991), p. 133; and Sylvia Nasar, "Women's Progress Stalled? Just Not So," *The New York Times*, October 18, 1992, p. 10.

18. Johnstone, Slawski, and Bowman, *The News People*, pp. 25, 26, 198.

19. U.S. Bureau of the Census, *Statistical Abstract of the United States*, 1991, p. 386; and Stephen Hess, Remarks at "The American Journalist in the 1990s," The Freedom Forum World Center, Arlington, Virginia, November 17, 1992.

20. Paul V. Peterson, *Today's Journalism Students: Who They Are and What They Want to Do* (Columbus, OH: School of Journalism, Ohio State University, 1981), p. 15.

21. Lee B. Becker and Thomas E. Engleman, "Class of 1987 Describes Salaries, Satisfaction Found in First Jobs," *Journalism Educator*, 43 (Autumn 1988), p. 6.

22. Weaver and Wilhoit, *The American Journalist*, p. 22.

23. Gallup Organization, National telephone survey of 1,002 U.S. adults, April 9–12, 1992. Data provided by the Political Science Data Lab, Indiana University, Bloomington, IN.

24. Weaver and Wilhoit, *The American Journalist*.

25. Leo Rosten, *The Washington Correspondents* (New York: Harcourt, Brace, 1937; reprint ed. Arno Press, 1974), p. 191; William L. Rivers, "The Correspondents After Twenty-five Years," *Columbia Journalism Review*, 1 (Spring 1962), p. 5; and Stephen Hess, *The Washington Reporters* (Washington, DC: The Brookings Institution, 1981), pp. 87–90.

26. S. Robert Lichter and Stanley Rothman, "Media and Business Elites," *Public Opinion* (October/November 1981), pp. 4, 5.

27. Stephen Hess, "All the President's Reporters: A New Survey of the White House Press Corps," *Presidential Studies Quarterly*, 22 (Spring 1992), pp. 311–321.

28. Our definition of a *prominent* news organization is similar to that used originally in the 1971 Johnstone study, where a prominent news organization was any one mentioned by more than 10 journalists in the national sample as either one of the fairest or most reliable news organizations in the country, or as one of the three they relied on most often in their own work. See pages 89, 90, and 224 of Johnstone, Slawski, and Bowman, *The News People*. We did not ask journalists to rate the fairness or reliability of news organizations, but we did ask which media they used. Based on their responses, the prominent news organizations that were represented in our study were the three weekly news magazines (*Newsweek*, *Time*, and *U.S. News and World Report*) and the Associated Press. We did not have journalists from any of the top five most read newspapers in our sample.

29. Weaver and Wilhoit, *The American Journalist*, p. 29.

30. Stanley Rothman and S. Robert Lichter, "Are Journalists a New Class?" *Business Forum*, Spring 1983, p. 15.

31. Gallup Organization, National telephone survey of U.S. adults, September 5–8, 1991. Data provided by the Political Science Data Lab, Indiana University, Bloomington, IN.

32. Leo Bogart, *Press and Public: Who Reads What, When, Where, and Why in American Newspapers*, 2nd ed. (Hillsdale, NJ: Lawrence Erlbaum Associates, 1989), pp. 82–83.

33. Judee K. Burgoon, Michael Burgoon, and Charles K. Atkin, *The World of the Working Journalist* (New York: Newspaper Advertising Bureau, Inc., 1982), p. 5.
34. Bogart, *Press and Public*, p. 206.
35. Johnstone, Slawski, and Bowman, *The News People*, p. 89.

Education and Training

In 1971, nearly 60% of all U.S. journalists were college graduates, and 34% majored in journalism. In 1982–1983, nearly 75% of all U.S. journalists completed a college degree, and 40% majored in journalism. In 1992, 82% of all U.S. journalists earned a college degree, and 40% majored in journalism. Thus, in 21 years, the proportion of U.S. journalists with at least a college bachelor's degree jumped from 58% to 82%, and the proportion of those college graduates with a journalism degree increased from 34% to 40%. But if radio and TV, telecommunications, and communications are added to journalism, the percentage of college graduate journalists who majored in any of these communications subjects increased from 41% to 56% during the 1971–1992 period.

This chapter discusses the educational backgrounds and preferences of U.S. journalists in light of a decade of significantly increased numbers of journalism school graduates entering the media job market. Comparisons are made with the earlier 1971 and 1982–1983 studies of journalists, and also with U.S. Census figures for the population in general.

PAST DEVELOPMENTS IN JOURNALISM EDUCATION

In our earlier book on American journalists, based on the 1982–1983 survey, we divided the history of journalism education in the United States into four rough periods: 1700s–1860s, 1860s–1920s, 1920s–1940s, and 1940s–early 1980s.[1] We do not repeat all the details of that brief historical sketch here, but pick up from the final part of it, where we traced the growth of schools and departments of journalism–mass communication since the turn of this century.

U.S. schools and departments of journalism have grown greatly in number, and in numbers of students, since the turn of the century. Lindley argued that journalism's emergence in the academic world was part of a great surge in education for the professions.[2] A tabulation of the number of schools with 4-year journalism programs by the *Journalism Bulletin* showed an increase from 4 in 1910 to 28 in 1920 to 54 in 1927. These programs produced fewer than 25 graduates a year in 1910, but this figure ballooned to 931 in 1927.

Forty-four years later, in 1971, when the Johnstone survey of U.S. journalists was conducted, Peterson reported 36,697 students who claimed journalism as a major, 7,968 degrees granted, and "slightly more than 200 colleges and universities offering majors in journalism."[3] By the fall of 1982, just before our earlier national survey of U.S. journalists was carried out, 304 schools reported programs in journalism.[4] Of these, 216 participated in Peterson's annual enrollment survey and reported 91,016 journalism–mass communication majors and 20,355 degrees granted. In the fall of 1992, just after our summer 1992 survey of journalists was conducted, Becker reported 413 U.S. degree-granting programs in journalism–mass communication, with a projected total enrollment of 143,370 students and 36,171 degrees granted for all 413 programs (see Table 2.1).[5]

RECENT DEVELOPMENTS IN JOURNALISM EDUCATION

It is obvious from these numbers that there has been tremendous growth in the number of college-level journalism–mass communication programs in the United States since early in the century. Even during the 1980s, when there was little or no growth in mainstream news media full-time editorial positions, there was substantial growth in the number of college programs (from 304 to 413) and in total enrollment of students (from 91,016 to 143,370). As Table 2.1 shows, the growth rates for programs, numbers of students, and degrees granted far outstripped the negligible growth in U.S. mainstream journalism during 1982–1992, and even that of the broader communication field (estimated at a negative 9% by U.S. Bureau of Labor Statistics, 1991) and the printing and publishing industries (estimated at 24% by the U.S. Bureau of Labor Statistics, 1991).

The nature of journalism–mass communication education has also changed over time. The early programs were concerned mostly with reporting, copy reading (editing), feature writing, editorial writing, criticism, history, comparative journalism, and ethics, according to a survey of about 40 institutions in 1924.[6] Modern journalism–mass communication education programs offer most of these same "news-editorial" subjects, but in addition often include courses in photojournalism or visual communication, public relations, advertising, broadcast news, and telecommunication.

In a 1982 survey of 216 journalism schools, Peterson found that, of 17,316 journalism bachelor's degrees identified by sequence, 26% were in news-editorial,

TABLE 2.1
Number of U.S. College Programs, Majors, and Degrees
in Journalism–Mass Communication Compared with
Number of U.S. Jobs in Journalism–Mass Communication

Variable	1971[a]	1982[b]	1992[c]	Growth, 1982–1992 (%)
Number of degree-granting programs	200+	304	413	36
Number of students enrolled	36,697	91,016	143,370	57
Number of degrees granted	7,968	20,355	36,171	78
Number of undergraduate degrees granted	6,802	18,574	33,752	82
Estimated full-time journalism jobs in mainstream U.S. news media[d]	69,500	112,072	122,015	9
Estimated number of jobs in communication[e]	1.129 million	1.384 million	1.265 million	–9
Estimated number of jobs in publishing[f]	1.104 million	1.292 million	1.538 million	19

[a]Paul V. Peterson, "Journalism Growth Continues at Hefty 10.8 Per Cent Rate," *Journalism Educator*, 26, 4 (January 1972), pp. 4, 5, 60.

[b]Paul V. Peterson, "J-school Enrollments Hit Record 91,016," *Journalism Educator*, 37, 4 (Winter 1983), pp. 3, 4, 7, 8.

[c]Lee B. Becker, personal communication from 1992 annual enrollment census and 1991–92 annual graduate survey, July 22 and 28, 1993.

[d]The 1971 figure is from Johnstone et al., *The News People*, 1976, p. 195. The 1982 figure is from Weaver and Wilhoit, *The American Journalist*, 1986, p. 13. The 1992 figure is from Weaver and Wilhoit, "The American Journalist in the 1990s," November 1992, p. 3.

[e]From *Statistical Abstract of the U.S. 1991*, p. 410. Figures are for 1970, 1981, and 1989, and are for *all* jobs, including technical, clerical, and production.

[f]From *Statistical Abstract of the U.S. 1992*, p. 734. Figures are for 1970, 1982, and 1990, and are for *all* jobs, including technical, clerical, and production.

21% in radio-TV, 13% in public relations, 19% in advertising, and 21% in other areas.[7] A decade later, in their survey of 2,648 spring 1991 graduates of 79 journalism–mass communication programs, Becker and Kosicki found that bachelor's degrees in news-editorial had dropped to 17%, broadcasting (radio-TV) had stayed steady at 21%, public relations had increased to 18%, advertising had declined to 14%, and other areas had increased to 29%.[8]

Employment Patterns

Of about 18,600 journalism–mass communication graduates who received bachelor's degrees in 1982, slightly more than one half (53%) found media jobs, with 12% going to daily newspapers, 10% to public relations, 8% to advertising agencies, and 6% to TV stations. The remaining graduates who found media jobs went to weekly newspapers, radio stations, magazines, and news services. Those who did not find media jobs went to graduate and law schools (about

9%) or nonmedia jobs (nearly 23%). Nearly 12% were unemployed after gradu-ation, and 3% said they were not looking for work.[9]

In 1991, of 34,000 bachelor's degree graduates in journalism–mass commu-nication, only 22% found jobs in the more traditional media, with 5% going to daily newspapers, 2% to public relations agencies, 4% to advertising agencies, and 3% to TV stations. The remaining graduates who found media jobs went to weekly newspapers (about 3%), radio stations (3%), magazines (1.5%), and news or wire services (.2%). Some of those who did not find media jobs went to other jobs in communication—about 26% in corporate public relations and advertising; educational, military, or government communications; or produc-tion/other companies. Some went into noncommunication work (27%), or con-tinued in school (7.5%). About 16% were unemployed.[10]

Thus, from 1982 to 1991, the proportion of journalism–mass communication graduates who went into the more traditional media jobs declined sharply—from just over one half (53%) to less than one fourth (22%). The percentage going into other communication work (e.g., corporate, educational, military, or gov-ernment) increased, and the unemployed proportion also rose from 12% to 16%. As in our earlier study, but even more dramatically, the career patterns and interests of journalism–mass communication students have both reflected and spurred the expansion of journalism education into a more general mass or public communication field.

But what about the educational backgrounds of those journalists still working for the more traditional news media in this country? Did they change much during 1982–1992? How many graduated from college? From a graduate program? What fields of study did they pursue? Where did they attend university classes? Where did they end up working? How many journalists thought they needed additional training or education? In what subjects? To answer these and other questions about the education of U.S. journalists, we turn to our survey findings from interviews with them during the summer of 1992.

EDUCATIONAL BACKGROUNDS
OF U.S. JOURNALISTS

For most professionals, it would be redundant to ask about educational background because their professional standing is based on certain programs of studies.[11] Although that is certainly true for medical doctors, lawyers, licensed nurses, and certified public accountants, it is not true for U.S. journalists. There is no single set of requirements for becoming a journalist, although it is more and more necessary for one to have at least a bachelor's degree from a college or university. As of 1992, there was still no specific credential necessary to enter the field of journalism, but it was clearer than 20 years previous that a bachelor's degree in journalism–mass communication was becoming the most common qualification among those recently hired. In fact, Becker estimated that 75% of entry-level daily newspaper journalists in the early 1990s were graduates of journalism–mass communication programs. Our data show that 77% of journalists in all news media with 1 year or less of work experience took courses in journalism or media studies.[12]

Years of Schooling

Most journalists in 1992 graduated from college. Of those who did, about 40% majored in journalism, as noted earlier. The figures in Table 2.2 indicate significant increases in college graduates during 1982–1992 among all age groups of U.S. journalists, except those 55 years and older. Overall, the proportion of college graduate journalists rose from 74% to about 82% during 1982–1992, but the proportion holding a graduate degree remained constant at 11%. There was a modest increase in the proportion holding a graduate degree among journalists 45 years and older. The percentage of journalists with only a high school diploma decreased in every age category. Thus, a bachelor's degree was the minimum requirement for a full-time job as a U.S. journalist in the early 1990s.

When journalists in the early 1990s were compared with the overall U.S. population, it became evident that a bachelor's degree was the necessary qualification for being a journalist. Whereas the percentage of U.S. journalists with 4-year college degrees increased by about 10 points to 82% during 1982–1992, the percentage of the overall population with college degrees increased by only about 5 points—from 16% to 21%.[13]

In 1971, Johnstone and his colleagues argued that there was substantial heterogeneity in educational backgrounds of journalists. Then, there were sizable minorities of journalists who had never been to college, especially among those 55 years and older (nearly one third). But 21 years later, we found very few who had not attended college, even among the oldest journalists. The proportion of journalists without a college degree declined sharply from 42% to only 18%. Thus, the basic undergraduate college degree in 1992 was much more the standard educational credential of U.S. journalists than 21 years previous, especially for those just entering journalism.

Variation Among Media

In 1971, Johnstone found that different kinds of news organizations varied greatly in the percentage of college graduates they employed. There was still some variation by news medium in 1992, but Table 2.3 indicates that it was less than in 1971, when the extremes were 37% for radio and 88% for news magazines. In 1992, the range was still from radio to news magazines, but it shrunk from 51 to 36 percentage points. This difference was less than in 1982–1983. The differences between the top four news media (news magazines, wire services, daily newspapers, and television) were much less pronounced than in 1971 and 1982–1983. Radio

TABLE 2.2
Amount of Formal Schooling by Age (Percentage of U.S. Journalists with Different Amounts of Schooling)

Highest Educational Attainment	Under 25			25–34			35–44		
	1971	1982–1983	1992	1971	1982–1983	1992	1971	1982–1983	1992
Some high school	1.7[a]	0.9[b]	0.0	0.8	0.0	0.0	1.8	0.0	0.2
Graduated from high school	3.8	8.6	2.1	8.6	3.3	2.6	11.4	5.2	2.6
Some college	44.4	16.4	19.2	26.6	14.0	7.9	22.7	21.4	12.8
Graduated from college	41.4	69.8	76.6	41.4	63.3	78.5	42.7	45.7	61.5
Some graduate training	6.0	1.7	0.0	13.9	10.2	3.3	9.9	9.5	8.3
Graduate degree(s)	2.6	2.7	2.1	8.7	9.1	7.7	11.4	18.1	14.5
Total	100.0	100.0	100.0	100.0	99.9	100.0	99.9	99.8	99.9
N	130	116	47	409	449	427	310	210	421

Highest Educational Attainment	45–54			55+			Total		
	1971	1982–1983	1992	1971	1982–1983	1992	1971	1982–1983	1992
Some high school	1.8	0.9	0.0	3.9	1.9	0.0	1.8	0.6	0.1
Graduated from high school	12.3	16.5	8.8	28.8	20.2	11.8	12.2	9.4	4.2
Some college	29.9	26.6	20.7	21.8	20.2	29.0	27.9	19.7	13.6
Graduated from college	37.8	34.9	45.0	31.5	43.3	40.9	39.6	50.3	64.5
Some graduate training	10.6	8.3	10.0	7.4	6.7	6.5	10.5	8.7	6.2
Graduate degree(s)	7.6	12.8	15.6	6.6	7.7	11.8	8.1	11.1	11.4
Total	100.0	100.0	100.1	100.0	99.1	100.0	100.1	99.8	100.0
N	274	109	160	180	104	93	1,303	988	1,148

[a] 1971 figures from John Johnstone, Edward Slawski, and William Bowman, *The News People* (Urbana: University of Illinois Press, 1976), p. 200.

[b] 1982–1983 figures from David Weaver and G. Cleveland Wilhoit, *The American Journalist* (Bloomington: Indiana University Press, 1986), p. 47.

TABLE 2.3
Number of U.S. Journalists Who Are College Graduates
by Media Type (Percentage Who Graduated from College)

Media Type	1971 (%)[a]	1982–1983 (%)[b]	N	1992 (%)	N
News magazines	88.2	93.7	63	95.1	61
Wire services	80.4	95.7	47	94.7	58
Daily newspapers	62.6	74.4	462	84.3	634
TV	58.7	80.2	121	83.2	137
Weekly newspapers	43.6	69.8	182	77.0	161
Radio	36.6	52.5	118	59.0	100
Total print sector	59.4	76.4	754	84.4	914
Total broadcast sector	47.7	66.5	239	73.0	237
Total sample	58.2	73.7	998	82.1	1,151

[a]Johnstone's cases are not reported here because they were weighted and not directly comparable to ours. From Johnstone, Slawski, and Bowman, *The News People*, p. 200.
[b]From Weaver and Wilhoit, *The American Journalist*, p. 48.

and weekly newspaper journalists in 1992 were least likely to hold a college degree, as in 1971, but even these journalists were much more likely to have a bachelor's degree. The largest increase from 1982 to 1992 was among daily newspaper journalists, who jumped 10 points from 74% to 84% college graduates.

Johnstone and his colleagues attributed much of the difference in percentage of college graduates among the different news media to differences in sizes of media organizations and the communities in which they operated. Table 2.4 shows that differences by size of news organization were almost gone in 1992. Only among the smallest news organizations (those with 10 or fewer full-time journalists) was the proportion of college graduates less. There was virtually no difference in the percentage of college-graduate journalists in the other size categories, including the largest news organizations, which still had more college graduates in 1982–1983.

TABLE 2.4
Number of Journalists Who Are College Graduates by News Organization Size

Size of Editorial Staff	1971 (%)[a]	1982–1983 (%)[b]	N	1992 (%)	N
1–10	44.0	68.7	415	73.6	292
11–25	48.1	76.7	176	85.3	116
26–50	58.1	75.9	133	84.4	212
51–100	59.4	77.8	117	84.3	166
More than 100	76.2	81.0	142	85.4	343
Total			983		1,129

[a]Johnstone's cases are not reported because they were weighted and not directly comparable to ours. From Johnstone, Slawski, and Bowman, *The News People*, p. 201.
[b]From Weaver and Wilhoit, *The American Journalist*, p. 50.

Thus, size of news organization and, by inference, size of community were not significant predictors of holding a college degree in journalism in the 1990s, as they were 21 years previous. Given the tremendous increase in the numbers of journalism school bachelor's degrees from 1971 (6,802) to 1982 (18,574) to 1992 (33,752), it is not surprising that more college graduates had to seek journalism jobs in smaller news organizations.

Regional Differences

In 1971, Johnstone and colleagues found "a surprising consistency" in the percentages of college-graduate journalists working in the nine census divisions of the country.[14] We found less such consistency in 1982–1983, with almost a 17-point difference between the divisions with the lowest and highest proportions of college-graduate journalists.[15] Ten years later, in 1992, we found even less consistency, with just over a 19-point difference between the lowest (East North Central) and highest (New England) divisions (see Table 2.5). But aside from these two extremes, there was not much difference among the other seven divisions (from 79% to 85% college graduates).

The proportion of college-graduate journalists increased from 1982 to 1992 in every division of the country except the East North Central and West South Central, with the largest increases in New England, the South Atlantic, and the East South Central areas. In 1971 and 1982–1983, the Middle Atlantic and Pacific boasted the largest percentages of college graduates; in 1992, New England, the Middle Atlantic, and the South Atlantic areas were the leaders.

Journalism–mass communication majors in 1992 varied more widely by area of the country than did college graduates, as Table 2.6 indicates. The highest proportion of these majors came from undergraduate colleges in the South Central states (i.e., Alabama, Arkansas, Kentucky, Louisiana, Mississippi, Oklahoma, Tennessee, and Texas) and Mountain states (i.e., Montana, Idaho, Wyoming, Colorado, New Mexico, Arizona, Utah, and Nevada). This was a notable change from 1982, when the largest percentage of journalism–mass communication majors came from colleges in the Midwest—an area that historically has been strong in journalism programs. But journalism–mass communication education in 1992 still had the least influence in New England and the Middle Atlantic states, as was true in 1982–1983, where the majority of the most prominent news media are headquartered.

This conclusion regarding the impact of journalism education assumes that graduates of journalism schools in various regions of the country tend to work in the same areas they attended college. As Table 2.7 shows, this assumption held up better in some regions than in others, especially in the South Atlantic states (i.e., the Virginias, Delaware, Maryland, the Carolinas, Georgia, and Florida) and the Pacific and Middle Atlantic areas. It did not fare as well in the New England or East North Central regions, where only two fifths of journalists

TABLE 2.5
College-Graduate Journalists by Region of Employment
(Percentage Graduating from College)

Region of Country[f]	Journalists			U.S. Population		
	1971[a]	1982–1983[b]	1992	1970[c]	1980[d]	1990[e]
New England	52.2	76.3	91.4	12.1	19.3	27.4
Middle Atlantic	61.0	81.3	84.7	10.9	17.1	22.6
East North Central	58.5	71.9	71.9	9.5	14.5	18.8
West North Central	52.4	71.9	82.3	9.8	15.1	19.3
South Atlantic	58.1	67.2	85.3	10.5	15.8	21.0
East South Central	59.1	64.7	82.0	7.7	12.0	14.7
West South Central	52.9	79.5	79.4	10.0	14.9	20.5
Mountain	58.2	68.2	79.2	14.6	18.3	22.7
Pacific	61.8	79.3	82.6	15.8	19.5	24.3
Total U.S.	58.2	73.9	82.1	10.7	16.3	21.3

[a]From Johnstone, Slawski, and Bowman, *The News People*, p. 202.

[b]From Weaver and Wilhoit, *The American Journalist*, p. 51.

[c]From U.S. Bureau of the Census, *Statistical Abstract of the U.S., 1973*, 94th ed., p. 117. Percentages are those residing in each region.

[d]From U.S. Bureau of the Census, *Statistical Abstract of the U.S., 1982–83*, 103rd ed., p. 144.

[e]From U.S. National Center for Education Statistics, *Digest of Education Statistics, 1992*, Table 12, p. 21.

[f]*New England* includes Maine, New Hampshire, Vermont, Massachusetts, Rhode Island, and Connecticut. The *Middle Atlantic* region includes New York, New Jersey, and Pennsylvania. The *East North Central* region includes Ohio, Indiana, Michigan, Illinois, and Wisconsin. The *West North Central* area includes Minnesota, Iowa, Missouri, North and South Dakota, Nebraska, and Kansas. The *South Atlantic* region includes Delaware, Maryland, Washington DC, Virginia, West Virginia, North and South Carolina, Georgia, and Florida. The *East South Central* area includes Kentucky, Tennessee, Alabama, and Mississippi. The *West South Central* region includes Arkansas, Louisiana, Oklahoma, and Texas. The *Mountain* region includes Montana, Idaho, Wyoming, Colorado, New Mexico, Arizona, Utah, and Nevada. The *Pacific* area includes Washington, Oregon, California, Alaska, and Hawaii. Source is U.S. Bureau of the Census, *Current Population Reports*, Series P-25, no. 913.

who attended college ended up working in the same region. There was greater discrepancy in 1992 between areas of the country than in 1982, possibly because of the tighter job market in journalism, which encouraged people to move to wherever they could to find a job.

In the early 1980s, there was a tendency for journalists to work in regions adjacent to where they attended college, if not in the same region. This was no longer generally true in 1992, except in the Northeast, where those who attended college in New England were next most likely (27.4%) to work in the Middle Atlantic states (New York, New Jersey, or Pennsylvania) or the South Atlantic area (16.1%), reinforcing an attachment to the East Coast. For the other areas of the country, this pattern of working in adjacent regions was not present, again probably because of the tighter job market.

TABLE 2.6
College Major of U.S. Journalists by Region of College
(Percentage of College-Graduate Journalists in 1982–1983 and 1992)

Region of College[a]	Journalists Majoring in Journalism–Mass Communication[b]	
	1982–1983	1992
New England	31.7	30.8
Middle Atlantic	33.3	34.0
East North Central	62.4	56.1
West North Central	68.9	60.7
South Atlantic	45.5	49.3
East South Central	44.1	65.7
West South Central	55.6	67.9
Mountain	56.7	65.6
Pacific	59.8	61.6
Total	53.2	53.5

[a]See Table 2.5 for a listing of states included in each region of the country.
[b]Includes journalism, radio and TV, telecommunications, and other communications.

Fields of Study in College and Graduate School

Although journalism was the most popular major field of study for both under-graduates and graduates in 1971, formal training in journalism was not typical among all practicing journalists (not just college graduates) because only 23% held journalism undergraduate degrees and just 7% had completed graduate degrees in journalism.[16] In 1982–1983, we found the same pattern, although the proportion of working journalists with an undergraduate journalism degree in-

TABLE 2.7
Region of College by Region of Employment of U.S. Journalists

Region of College[a]	Percentage of Journalists Employed in the Same Region in Which They Attended College	
	1982–1983[b]	1992
New England	63.5	41.9
Middle Atlantic	54.1	65.8
East North Central	63.6	39.6
West North Central	55.6	56.4
South Atlantic	61.4	81.8
East South Central	70.6	69.1
West South Central	72.8	57.1
Mountain	61.3	57.4
Pacific	79.3	66.3

[a]See Table 2.5 for a listing of states included in each region of the country.
[b]From Weaver and Wilhoit, The American Journalist, p. 53.

TABLE 2.8
Fields of Study of U.S. Journalists in College (Percentage of U.S. Journalists)

Subjects	Major Field in College (1971)[d]		Major Field in College (1982–1983)		Major Field in College (1992)	
	Sample	Subjects who finished college	Sample	Subjects who finished college	Sample	Subjects who finished college
Journalism	22.6	34.2	29.5	39.8	34.9	40.6
Radio and TV	1.8	2.8	4.4	5.9	4.3	5.0
Other communication specialties	3.1	4.7	6.7	9.0	9.2	10.7
Total communication field	27.5	41.7	40.6	54.7	48.4	56.3
English, creative writing	15.1	22.9	10.9	14.7	13.9	16.2
History	6.4	9.7	4.7	6.3	3.8	4.4
Other humanities	2.9	4.4	4.9	6.6	4.8	5.6
Political science, government	5.0	7.5	3.6	4.9	5.3	6.1
Other social sciences	3.6	5.5	3.3	4.4	3.8	4.4
Liberal Arts, unspecified	1.1	1.6	1.0	1.4	1.0	1.1
Mathematics	0.4	0.6	0.2	0.3	0.4	0.5
Physical or biological sciences	0.8	1.2	1.2	1.6	1.8	2.1
Total Liberal Arts & Sciences	35.3	53.4	29.8	40.2	34.8	40.4
Agriculture	0.2	0.3	0.4	0.5	0.1	0.1
Business	1.0	1.5	1.7	2.3	1.7	2.0
Education	0.5	0.8	1.3	1.8	0.8	0.9
Law	[a]	0.1	0.1	0.1		
All other fields	1.5	2.3	0.3	0.4	0.2	0.2
Total other fields	3.2	5.0	3.8	5.1	2.8	3.2
Total	66.0[b]	100.1[c]	74.2[b]	100.0	86.0[b]	99.9[c]

[a]Less than one tenth of 1%.

[b]Does not total to 100% because some journalists were not college graduates, and does not total to percentage of those college graduates because some majored in more than one subject.

[c]Rounding error.

[d]From Johnstone, Slawski, and Bowman, *The News People,* p. 203.

creased to nearly 30%, and those holding a graduate journalism degree inched up to 7.5%.[17] In 1992, 35% of all U.S. journalists held undergraduate journalism degrees, and just over 7% held graduate journalism degrees (see Table 2.8).

Thus, between 1971–1992 there was considerable growth in the proportion of all U.S. journalists (not just college graduates) holding undergraduate journalism degrees (from 23% to 35%), but no growth in the percentage with journalism graduate degrees (about 7%).

Table 2.8 shows that, when radio and television (telecommunications) and other communication subjects (e.g., advertising, public relations, and speech communication) were combined with journalism, nearly one half of all working journalists in 1992 majored in communication in college—a significant increase from 1982, and a huge increase from the one fourth who did so in 1971.

In the 1971 study, Johnstone et al. cited data compiled by the Newspaper Fund showing that just 25% of journalism graduates in 1971 found employment in the news media.[18] In 1982, the annual Newspaper Fund survey of journalism–mass communication graduates showed 53% going into media jobs.[19] In 1991, the annual survey of 2,648 journalism–mass communication graduates by Becker and Kosicki showed 49% going into communication work (but only about 16% into traditional news media).[20]

Other research by Becker showed that 75% of entry-level daily newspaper hires were journalism–mass communication program graduates. Our survey of U.S. journalists indicates that nearly half majored in communication, with 77% of those hired in 1991 having taken undergraduate courses in journalism or media studies.[21] These figures suggest that formal college-level education in journalism–mass communication in 1992 was a necessary condition for an entry-level journalism job in U.S. mainstream news media.

In 1982–1983, we noted that the increase in journalism–mass communication majors came largely at the expense of English and creative writing—from 23% of college graduates in 1971 to 15% in 1982–1983.[22] But in 1992 (Table 2.8), there was little change in the percentages majoring in subjects other than communication, as compared with 1982. English rose slightly, history dropped a bit, and political science was up slightly, but overall there were no significant changes in the majors of those journalists who completed college. There was a five-point jump in the percentage of all journalists with a liberal arts and sciences major, and an eight-point increase in communication majors, mainly because of the increase in the percentage of journalists who completed a college degree.

Among those few journalists who completed graduate degrees, there was a significant increase in the percentage majoring in journalism–mass communication in comparison with 1982 (nearly 10 points), largely at the expense of majors in other humanities and education. But there was also a six-point increase in the percentage of English majors, in contrast to the drop in English during the 1970s. This was perhaps due to increased interest in the media, particularly film, in English departments during the 1980s, or an increase in graduate student interest in more creative kinds of writing, which are usually not taught in journalism programs.

As in 1982–1983, in 1992 those earning graduate degrees in journalism–mass communication were most likely to major in these subjects at the undergraduate level. Thirty-seven percent of journalists who earned graduate degrees in journalism–mass communication also earned undergraduate degrees in these same subjects, compared with 40% in 1982. But the next most common undergraduate major was English (up to 34% from 21% in 1982–1983), followed by history (18.7%) and political science (16%).

Thus, the "high degree of educational diversity" of journalists found in the 1971 study eroded somewhat in the 1980s, except for the increases in English majors among those earning graduate degrees. More journalists graduated from college, and more majored in journalism–mass communications at both under-graduate and graduate levels. Still, in most undergraduate journalism programs, the major classes totalled only about one fourth of all classes taken; in many of these programs, a second major or concentration was required.

Are Journalism Majors Different?

Given the increases in proportions of journalists majoring in journalism, it is even more tempting than before to ask what difference that makes. In 1982, we found no indication that majoring in journalism was correlated with job stability (number of previous jobs in journalism), job satisfaction, gender, race, or type of ownership of news organization.[23] In 1992, this was also true, except that journalism majors were more likely to be women (38%) than were other majors (32%).

In 1982, the most notable differences between journalism majors and others were in type of medium, size of media organization, region of employment, and age. A decade later, in 1992, there were still significant differences by type of medium, size of news organization, region of employment, and age. Table 2.9 shows that the college-graduate journalists working in news magazines and radio and TV were much less likely to have majored in journalism than those working for other kinds of journalism organizations. Daily newspaper journalists were most likely to be journalism majors. When the percentages of those majoring in communication or telecommunications (radio and TV) were added, the figures for radio and TV increased substantially, but not so for news magazines, which were the least likely of any of the mainstream news media to employ journalism majors.

Table 2.10 indicates that journalism majors in 1992 were more likely to work for larger news organizations than smaller, although this was not a linear trend

TABLE 2.9
College Major of U.S. Journalists by Media Type
(Percentage of College-Graduate Journalists in 1982–1983 and 1992)

Media Type	Journalists Majoring in Journalism–Mass Communication[a]			
	1982–1983	N	1992	N
News magazines	25.9	58	24.1	58
Wire services	53.3	45	47.2	53
Daily newspapers	56.3	348	53.7	533
Television	62.9	97	78.6	112
Weekly newspapers	50.4	127	40.8	120
Radio	53.1	64	64.4	59
		739		935

[a]Includes journalism, radio and TV, telecommunications, and other communications.

TABLE 2.10
College Major of U.S. Journalists by News Organization Size
(Percentage of College-Graduate Journalists in 1982–1983 and 1992)

Editorial Staff	Journalists Majoring in Journalism–Mass Communication[a]			
	1982–1983	N	1992	N
1–10	53.3	287	54.9	215
11–25	62.5	136	67.7	99
26–50	54.5	101	52.6	171
51–100	58.7	92	55.7	140
More than 100	35.3	116	48.6	292
Total		732		917

[a]Includes journalism, radio and TV, telecommunications, and other communications.

because a substantial proportion worked for news media with 11–25 full-time news staff. Still, the average staff size for journalism majors was 85, compared with 68 for other majors, no doubt reflecting the high percentages of journalism majors working for larger daily newspapers. One noticeable change in 1992 was that about the same percentage of journalism majors worked for the largest news organizations as for the next largest, whereas 10 years previous the figure for the largest was considerably lower. This suggests that journalism majors were infiltrating the ranks of even the largest newspapers in the early 1990s, some of which were resistant to hiring journalism graduates in the past.

Taken together, these findings, plus those illustrated in Tables 2.3, 2.5, and 2.6, suggest that in 1992 the influence of journalism education was least where the percentages of college graduates were the highest for journalists and the general population—in the Northeast and in news magazines. This was also true in 1982, probably because of the relative scarcity of major journalism schools in the Northeast, as compared with other regions of the country, as well as the tendency for news magazines to hire journalists who were more specialized in a subject (and more likely to have a graduate degree) than the other news media.

In their 1971 study, Johnstone and colleagues found that the number of journalists with undergraduate degrees in fields other than journalism–mass communication was fewer among more recent graduates, leading them to wonder whether this suggested a trend toward declining media recruitment of persons from other occupations.[24] We found in 1982–1983 that, among more recent college graduates, there were fewer majoring in fields other than journalism–mass communication. This suggests that the news media (except for news magazines) were indeed recruiting from journalism schools more heavily than in the past.

Table 2.11 shows that, among 1992 graduates, fewer than in earlier years majored in other fields, although there was no real increase in the proportion of journalism majors among the youngest (under 25 years of age), as compared with those journalists in the next decade of their lives. This finding is also supported by

TABLE 2.11
College Major of U.S. Journalists by Age
(Percentage of College-Graduate Journalists in 1982–1983 and 1992)

| Age | Journalists Majoring in Journalism–Mass Communication[a] | | | |
	1982–1983	N	1992	N
Under 25	65.9	88	67.6	37
25–34	59.8	373	63.8	376
35–44	39.6	154	49.3	353
45–54	40.3	62	33.0	112
55 and over	45.8	59	44.4	54
Total		736		932

[a]Includes journalism, radio and TV, telecommunications, and other communications.

analyzing the percentage of journalism majors by years of experience in journalism. There was no significant difference in this percentage for those journalists with one or fewer years of experience (41%), as compared with those with 10 or fewer years of experience (39%).

When the percentages of journalism majors were added with those who took some journalism or media studies classes as undergraduates, the figure for all journalists jumped from 39% to 56%. For those journalists with 3 or fewer years of experience, it was 71%, suggesting more influence of journalism education than previously thought. A recent study by Lee Becker of Ohio State University indicated that 75% of all new hires by daily newspapers in the U.S. in the early 1990s were journalism school graduates, again suggesting that some news media recruiters relied quite heavily on journalism graduates at the expense of majors in other fields.[25]

Continuing Education of Journalists

In the 1971 study, Johnstone and colleagues found that just over a third (35.7%) of the journalists in their national sample said they had participated in some kind of education program since becoming journalists. Twenty years later, that figure jumped to 58.4%, with daily newspaper journalists most likely to have done so (68.9%), and radio (39%) and television (40.1%) journalists least likely.

Counter to this trend of increased participation in short courses, sabbaticals, workshops, or fellowships by U.S. journalists, we also found a decrease in the percentage who said they wanted additional training—from nearly 77% in 1982–1983 to about 62% in 1992 (see Table 2.12). Part of this decrease may have been due to a slight change in question wording; in 1992, we asked if journalists felt they needed additional training, whereas in previous studies, the question was whether they would like additional training.

Nevertheless, Table 2.12 shows that the subject preferences for additional training did not change much from 1982 to 1992, with a few exceptions. Slightly

TABLE 2.12
Preferences of U.S. Journalists for Continuing Education
(Percentage of Total Sample Mentioning)

Variable	1971[a]	1982–1983[b]	1992
Total who said they would like some			
kind of additional training	57.7	76.8	61.6
Journalism	10.1	15.4	11.4
Political science, government	8.9	4.3	4.9
English, literature, writing	7.2	8.9	4.7
History	3.9	3.1	3.8
Economics	3.6	3.6	2.9
Law	2.7	3.3	2.2
Business	2.6	9.2	7.2
Photography	2.2	2.1	1.6
News analysis, clinics, seminars	1.7	12.9	9.8
Shorthand	1.5	0.0	0.3
Modern languages	1.5	2.2	2.6
Total who said they would not like			
additional training	42.3	23.2	38.4
	100.0	100.0	100.0
	($n \cong 1,000$)	($n = 987$)	($n = 1,148$)

[a]From Johnstone, Slawski, and Bowman, *The News People*, pp. 45, 207. Subjects mentioned by fewer than 1.5% of journalists are not included in this table. Therefore, the percentages for the individual subjects do not total to the percentages wanting additional training.

[b]From Weaver and Wilhoit, *The American Journalist*, p. 61.

fewer journalists in 1992 were interested in training in journalism broadly defined (communications, advertising, broadcasting), in English literature and writing, and in news analysis. Compared with 1971, however, in 1992 there was more interest in business training (marketing, accounting, management, and computer science), news analysis, and clinics and seminars dealing with subjects such as use of computers, applied ethics, interviewing, investigative reporting, and layout and design, especially among minority journalists. In 1971, Johnstone found that academic subjects were cited more frequently than those he called *vocational*, whereas in 1992, we found (as we did in 1982–1983) an increased tendency to mention more vocational subjects, especially if business is considered more vocational than academic.

A similar pattern emerged from 652 daily and weekly newspaper journalists working at 123 newspapers in a 1992 study carried out by The Freedom Forum and the Roper Center for Public Opinion Research. The most often cited interests for additional training were in ethics, writing, privacy, libel law, management, editing, and reporting.[26] This study also found a fairly high ranking of computer-assisted or database reporting, and a strong showing for special expertise in subjects such as environment, race, and gender.

The Freedom Forum study found that those journalists who were under the age of 40, women, college graduates, and journalism majors had generally more interest in continuing education than those who were older than 40, men, and nongraduates or nonjournalism majors. In our study, journalists most likely to want additional training were those who had worked in journalism 5 years or less, were minorities, were very dissatisfied with their jobs, and had made less than $15,000 in 1991.

As in 1982–1983, it was not surprising that in 1992 younger, less experienced journalists were more likely to want some form of continuing education, especially education that they thought would help them advance their careers. What was different from a decade previous, however, was that plans to stay in journalism and college education were no longer associated with wanting additional training. Thus, commitment to journalism no longer seemed correlated with interest in more instruction. Instead, it was experience, job conditions, and race that predicted the desire for continuing education.

CONCLUSIONS

In 1992, it was more the case than ever before in American journalism that a bachelor's degree in journalism–mass communication was becoming the necessary qualification for being hired as a journalist by the mainstream news media, especially radio and TV and daily newspapers. At the same time, the lack of growth in mainstream news media jobs during the 1980s, coupled with dramatic growth in journalism–mass communication degrees granted, resulted in a sharp decline in the proportion of journalism–mass communication graduates taking traditional news media jobs—from just over one half to less than one fourth. More of these graduates in 1992 were going into other communication-related work (e.g., corporate, educational, military, or government), and somewhat more were unemployed several months after graduation than was true in 1982.

In 1971, Johnstone and colleagues concluded that there was substantial heterogeneity in educational backgrounds of U.S. journalists, but predicted that differences in these backgrounds would become less pronounced as those in the oldest age groups were replaced by younger journalists. This prediction was supported by our 1982–1983 study, and was even more strongly confirmed in 1992. As of 1992, there were few U.S. journalists without a college degree (18%), as compared with 1971 (42%), and the percentage of all journalists who majored in journalism or communication was nearly twice what it was in 1971 (from 27% to 48%).

Differences in proportions of college graduates by media type and size of organization were notably less in 1992 than in 1971 or 1982–1983, but differences in college major by region of the country persisted, with journalists who studied in the Northeast much less likely to have majored in journalism–mass communication than those who attended college in another region of the country. As in 1982, in 1992 news magazines (nearly all located in the Northeast) were by far the least likely of all the news media to employ graduates of journalism–mass communication programs, although they were the most likely to hire college graduates and those with graduate degrees. This tendency not to employ journalism–mass communication majors may have reflected: (a) the relative lack of these programs in colleges in the Northeast, (b) a desire by news magazines to hire journalists who specialized in subject areas such as economics and science, (c) a less favorable view of journalism–mass communication education, or (d) some combination of these reasons.

In 1982, we concluded that the increase in journalism–mass communication majors from 1971 to 1982 came largely at the expense of English and creative writing, but in 1992, there was little change in the percentages of journalists majoring in subjects other than communication since 1982–1983. At the graduate level, however, there was a significant increase in the proportion majoring in journalism–mass communication since 1982 (nearly 10 points), largely at the expense of majors in other humanities and education, and a 6-point increase in English majors.

Thus, the "high degree of educational diversity" of journalists found in the 1971 study eroded somewhat in the 1980s, except for the increases in English majors among those earning graduate degrees. More journalists graduated from college, and more majored in journalism–mass communications at both undergraduate and graduate levels. Still, in most undergraduate journalism programs, the major classes totalled only about one fourth of all classes taken, and, in many of these programs, a second major or concentration was required.

In addition to the increases in college graduates and journalists majoring in journalism–mass communications, we also found an increase in those who had participated in a continuing education program (short course, sabbatical, workshop of fellowship) since beginning work as a journalist, especially among daily newspaper journalists. The subjects of interest in 1992 tended to be more applied or vocational than in 1971, and were more closely tied to a desire to advance one's own career, again suggesting somewhat less educational diversity than two decades previous.

Because the educational backgrounds of U.S. journalists in 1992 were not as diverse as they were 10 or 20 years ago, we might expect their views on the importance of different aspects of work and on professional values and ethics to be more homogeneous than in the earlier studies. But the following chapters on working conditions, professionalism, women, and minorities demonstrate that, as of 1992, there was still much diversity (more attitudinal than demographic) and disagreement among U.S. journalists, perhaps more than ever before. In fact, we think the amount of professional fragmentation and lack of consensus, coupled with declines in resources for reporting, were troubling signs in U.S. journalism in the early 1990s.

NOTES

1. David H. Weaver and G. Cleveland Wilhoit, *The American Journalist: A Portrait of U.S. News People and Their Work* (Bloomington: Indiana University Press, 1986, 2nd ed., 1991), pp. 41–44.
2. William R. Lindley, *Journalism and Higher Education: The Search for Academic Purpose* (Stillwater, OK: Journalistic Services, 1975), p. 3.
3. Paul V. Peterson, "Journalism Growth Continues at Hefty 10.8 Per Cent Rate," *Journalism Educator*, 26, 4 (January 1972), pp. 4, 5, 60.
4. Paul V. Peterson, "J-school Enrollments Hit Record 91,016," *Journalism Educator*, 37, 4 (Winter 1983), pp. 3–8.
5. Lee B. Becker, personal communication from 1992 annual enrollment census and 1991–92 annual journalism–mass communication graduate survey, July 22 and 28, 1993. See also Lee B. Becker and Gerald M. Kosicki, "Annual Census of Enrollment Records Fewer Undergrads," *Journalism Educator*, 48, 3 (Autumn 1993), pp. 56–57, where the figure for total degrees granted was adjusted from 36,171 to 36,336.
6. Lindley, *Journalism and Higher Education*, p. 4.
7. Peterson, "J-school enrollments hit record 91,016," p. 9.
8. Lee B. Becker and Gerald M. Kosicki, "Summary Results from the 1992 Annual Enrollment & Graduate Surveys," presented at the 1993 convention of the Association for Education in Journalism, Table 2.
9. The Dow Jones Newspaper Fund, Inc., *1984 Journalism Career and Scholarship Guide* (Princeton, NJ: Dow Jones Newspaper Fund, 1984), p. 14.
10. Becker and Kosicki, "Summary Results," Table 9.
11. John W. C. Johnstone, Edward J. Slawski, and William W. Bowman, *The News People: A Sociological Portrait of American Journalists and Their Work* (Urbana: University of Illinois Press, 1976), p. 31.
12. Lee B. Becker, personal communication, July 28, 1993, based on unpublished research by him for The Dow Jones Newspaper Fund.
13. U.S. Bureau of the Census, *Statistical Abstract of the United States 1991*, 111th ed. (Washington, DC: U.S. Government Printing Office, 1991), p. 139.
14. Johnstone, Slawski, and Bowman, *The News People*, p. 34.
15. Weaver and Wilhoit, *The American Journalist*, p. 50.
16. Johnstone, Slawski, and Bowman, *The News People*, pp. 36, 203.
17. Weaver and Wilhoit, *The American Journalist*, pp. 54, 56, 57.
18. Johnstone, Slawski, and Bowman, *The News People*, p. 36.
19. Dow Jones Newspaper Fund, *1984 Journalism Career Guide*, p. 14.
20. Becker and Kosicki, "Summary Results," Table 9.
21. Becker, personal communication, July 28, 1993.
22. Weaver and Wilhoit, *The American Journalist*, p. 54.
23. Weaver and Wilhoit, *The American Journalist*, pp. 55–60.
24. Johnstone, Slawski, and Bowman, *The News People*, p. 39.
25. Becker, personal communication, July 28, 1993.
26. Brian J. Buchanan, Eric Newton, and Richard Thien, *No Train, No Gain: Continuing Training for Newspaper Journalists in the 1990s* (Arlington, VA: The Freedom Forum, 1993), pp. 10–12.

Job Conditions
and Satisfactions

Novels, movies, and television have often portrayed journalists at work, but never has the actual production of the news behind the front pages and the daily broadcasts been so visible to the public as now. Audiences of the C-SPAN public affairs TV cable channel see journalists asking questions at press conferences and conducting interviews with news sources that formerly were seen only rarely. Viewers occasionally are taken inside news organizations by C-SPAN cameras to watch editorial decisions in the making. It appears that the old homily about the adverse impact on the appetite of seeing the "sausage being made" has relevance for the public's perception of newsmaking as well.

Public disparagement of journalists, although certainly not new, seems more biting, particularly among the nation's elites. For example, Alice Rivlin, the economist who became director of the White House Budget Office in the Clinton administration, told an academic audience during the 1992 presidential campaign that it was not "until the journalists got out of the way" that serious issues could be debated.[1] Jon Katz, a media critic, later said news reporting on the federal government has become "the Capital gang bang" that results from the press corps' susceptibility to social bribery, transparent flattery, and its own vengeance.[2] Richard Neustadt, a long-time scholar of the presidency, called the press corps in the Clinton White House "obnoxious, arrogant, pampered and self-important baby-boomers."[3]

Others have couched their disdain in futuristic barbs about the eclipse of journalism by evolving communication technology. Michael Crichton, writer of *Jurassic Park*, told a National Press Club luncheon—broadcast live by C-SPAN in April 1993—that journalists will not be needed much longer. Soon, he said, audiences who want "high-quality information" will mediate it for themselves.

Using computerized databases and personalized systems of artificial intelligence to sift through them, audiences will bypass journalists altogether, he predicted. Although Crichton stopped short of calling journalists dinosaurs, the implication was clear.

Journalists themselves and scholars of the press sometimes join in the chorus of criticism. Many of their concerns focus on what some call the "final phase" of corporate concentration of ownership. Since the 1960s, large media corporations that already owned many media have acquired smaller "chains" in increasing numbers.[4] Many of these companies are publicly traded through the major stock exchanges. Of the 30 companies that control the preponderance of media revenues in the United States, few are privately held or controlled by individuals or families. Most are now media conglomerates that own large numbers of different media.[5] The New York Times Company's 1993 purchase of The Boston Globe, one of the last large dailies that was under family control, signaled that the end may be in sight for news traditions nurtured by powerful families living in their cities of publication.[6]

James D. Squires, former editor of the Chicago Tribune, said a "plundering" of newsrooms is taking place as media conglomerates struggle to deal with declining profits and splintering audiences.[7] Doug Underwood, a journalism scholar at the University of Washington, argued that the "professional managers" who increasingly run America's newsrooms for absentee corporate owners are responsible for a declining quality of news and an erosion of journalists' job satisfaction and professional pride.[8] He said more than 50 interviews with journalists around the country found many who said "they feel increasingly unwelcome in a business that once was a haven for the independent, irreverent, creative spirits who have traditionally given newspapers their personalities."[9]

An intensive study of 12 West Coast newspapers by Keith Stamm and Doug Underwood found in 1991 that those newspapers, particularly ones owned by large corporations, were becoming market-driven and reader-oriented. However, their analysis also suggested that increased devotion to profitable business practices did not always compromise journalistic principles.[10] In those news organizations where business-oriented policy changes allowed news personnel to be "about the business of journalism—rather than the business of business," the journalists were happier with their jobs.[11]

Clearly the journalistic process and the people who craft the news are now largely in the hands of corporations.[12] More than 70% of American journalists work in newsrooms of group-owned media, and half of those work for companies whose shares are publicly traded on major stock exchanges. What changes in news work, in the eyes of journalists, occurred during the recent decade of corporate ascendancy? This chapter summarizes journalists' perspectives on their jobs and working conditions, and compares them, where possible, over two decades of change since the early 1970s. To begin, we look at the reasons our respondents gave for going into journalism as an occupation.

WHY JOURNALISM?

Russell Baker, a shrewd observer of the journalistic mind, began his newspaper career after serving in World War II. This *New York Times* columnist said that all the newsrooms he has known have "... attracted people whose minds were open and interesting, people who were curious instead of preachy, people who distrusted people who had all the answers, people with a taste for the raffish, people who wanted life to be interesting rather than safe."[13] Other images of the personality types drawn to journalism are not so favorable. In a 1991 speech at the 75th anniversary celebration of the awarding of the Pulitzer Prizes at Columbia University's School of Journalism, Baker noted that, "most of the creative and scholarly people" he knew agreed with the "fellow" who defined a *journalist* as "a man with nothing on his mind, and the power to express it."[14]

What were the attractions of journalistic life for those in the field in 1992? We asked our respondents: In looking back, why did you become a journalist? Their open-ended replies offer interesting "freeze-frames" of memories about career choice. The sketches of journalism's attractiveness cover a wide range of categories, and more than one was cited in many of the answers. The most common themes, however, were an early "love" of writing, an aptitude for the "digging" of reporting, a desire to "make a difference," the field's being intrinsically "interesting," a penchant for "current events" or immediacy, and college experiences.

An Early "Love" for Writing

It was no surprise that 37% of our respondents cited an aptitude for writing as their main reason for being in journalism. Elite journalists often talk about this aspect in biographies, as Russell Baker did in remembering what attracted him to the campus newspaper at Johns Hopkins University in the 1940s: "I went there looking for the company of people who liked to write."[15]

But among our respondents, the creative bent frequently was tied to other important reasons, sometimes with an altruistic twist. For example, a daily newspaper journalist said, "I always liked to write, [and] I thought it was a real noble profession." Another answered: "Writing seemed to be the thing I was better at than anything else, [and] I felt I could make a difference in society by reporting the good, the bad, and the ugly."

Print journalists were more likely than broadcast personnel to remember a talent for writing as a draw for journalism. Almost half of them cited an early interest in writing. A little less than 20% of broadcast journalists remembered writing as an attraction to the field.

Among journalists mentioning writing, there was often a connection to other interests, such as current events. For example, a wire service journalist said, "I like to write, to tell stories [and] I like covering big events." A magazine journalist struck a similar tone, saying, "I enjoyed writing [and] learning about the world.

I wanted to inform people about what was happening, [and] it was chance to meet interesting people."

Many of the comments about writing reflected a fascination with language and "the word," but there was often a connection to action as well. For example, a daily newspaper staffer said: "I was a good writer and I have a pretty decent command of the English language. I employed the skills I know the best [and] it was a way to reach other people and make a positive impact." A weekly newspaper journalist said, "I just liked writing, and later I discovered what I wrote about had an impact on people."

Particularly among newspaper journalists, the sense of being a good writer was linked to student newspaper experience or a high school teacher. One daily newspaper journalist commented: "I got hooked in junior high school. I worked on the school newspaper, loved writing and telling stories and I've been hooked ever since. I think it's an addictive business. It's so unique it spoils you for anything else."

For television journalists, the interest in writing was sometimes remembered a little differently: "I enjoyed talking and telling people information, telling stories [and had a] keen interest in writing. I had done performing and speech in school, [so television news] seemed like a natural progression." A radio journalist said, "I like to write, [and] for me it's a creative outlet, being able to disseminate information that informs people [and] also to entertain people."

Aptitude for Newsgathering

About 13% of the journalists mentioned some aspect of reporting as drawing them to the field. This theme was somewhat harder to pin down than a talent for writing because it was expressed in a variety of ways, ranging from a "nose" for news to an unusual curiosity, particularly about politics. As we saw earlier, aspects of reporting were often mentioned with other factors, particularly an interest in writing. For example, a wire service journalist said, "Because I love to write and I love reporting, especially reporting stories that would expose truth or injustices to help a fellow person."

Television and news magazine journalists (about 20%) were a little more likely to mention reporting and newsgathering than were others in our sample. Wire personnel (15%) were followed by weekly and daily newspaper journalists (about 12%), with radio (5%) being least likely to remember an aspect of reporting as attracting them.

One television journalist responded, "I like to listen and I like to ask questions. I like the excitement of changing assignments on a daily basis." Another commented, "I wanted to do something different, and I liked getting the news and gathering it . . . [and] it's fun, enjoyable work." The television personnel used the word *excitement* fairly often, as this journalist, who said, "I like the excitement of newsgathering and helping to inform people."

Writing, as noted previously, often was tied to reporting, as in the answer from this magazine journalist: "Because I enjoy writing and I enjoy research as well. I like putting everything I learn into one package." The perception of unusual curiosity was often mentioned in connection with reporting, but so was the idea of "nosiness." A newspaper journalist responded, "Because I'm naturally nosey and like to ask questions, and I like to write." Another said, "Because it gave me a license to be nosey."

To "Make a Difference"

As some of the previous quotations suggest, a sense of altruism was sometimes commingled with other reasons for choosing journalism. For about 11% of our respondents, however, the idea of "making an impact" seemed to be a strong theme. Newspaper journalists (14%) were a bit more likely to couch their career path in these terms than were personnel in other media. Minority journalists—one in four—were considerably more likely to see their career decision as having been driven by idealism than were others.

Newspaper journalists tended to describe the notion of "making a difference" in somewhat more idealistic terms than those in other media. For example, one newspaper journalist said, "I wanted to go out and tilt at windmills, right the wrongs, shine a light in the dirty corners so someone would come along and clean up the messes." A minority newspaper journalist said: "I saw the newspaper as a forum or recourse for bringing injustices to the public's attention in a way that would spur government to action to remedy those injustices. And, . . . as a forum for ideas and dialogue, for an exchange of ideas and dialogue between the common people and government."

A television journalist—fairly typical of the succinctness of those expressing idealism—answered, "I really believed that news stories could make a real difference in people's lives." Another added, "[There is] something appealing about the lasting effect of journalism. What we do makes a difference to most people, [and there is something] appealing about being in the center of information."

Field Is Intrinsically "Interesting"

One in 10 journalists in our study said their career was influenced by the engaging nature of the work or a general "fascination" with it. Television journalists (25%) were especially likely to cite this. Weekly and daily newspaper personnel were least likely (about 6%) to frame their reasoning in a way that suggested the field itself was inherently interesting. As we noted earlier, print personnel—particularly in newspapers—often found the writing process interesting, but that was different.

For example, a television journalist commented, "I was fascinated with television news when I was about 12 or 13 years old . . . [so] I placed myself in position to pursue it." Another remembered, as a child, being "inspired by watching [TV anchors] Huntley and Brinkley and Walter Cronkite" in a home with "lots of newspapers." Few mentioned deadlines fondly, but one said, "[It] looked like an interesting job. The deadlines looked like they were fun!" Another responded, ". . . I love news, and television is one of the best media for getting news to the public quickly."

An Attraction to "Current Events"

The journalists in our sample sometimes tied their career choices to an early sense of unusual interest in the latest happenings, often political events. About 10% mentioned this, with radio journalists being slightly more likely to cite it (16%) than those in other media. In a typically terse reply, one radio journalist said, "Just wanting to know what was going on all the time." Another added, "[I] like being involved in doings of state and local government . . . [and being] the first person knowing about what is going on." Another linked current events to a slightly different aspect, saying, "[I was a] story teller and interested in what was going on, and I put the two together."

The idea of the newspaper as a "first draft of history" appeared occasionally among those mentioning current events. For example, a weekly journalist responded, ". . . I've always been an amateur historian, and journalism is history in the making in most cases." Others mentioned an innate curiosity. A television journalist said: "I'm naturally a curious person. I love news. I love world events." The notion of journalism's "detachment"—sometimes seen by critics as an attraction of the field—was hardly ever mentioned, but one newspaper journalist linked it to current events, saying, "I liked the idea of being able to observe the processes of life up close but not actually having to be a part of it."

College Experiences

Campus newspapers have long been remembered as nurturers of journalism talent, as Russell Baker suggested in The Good Times.[16] Among our respondents, campus media, journalism schools or courses, and other campus experiences were mentioned by almost 8% as being important to their discovery of journalism as a career. A television journalist said: "When I went to school, I didn't know what I wanted to do. I stumbled upon the journalism school. I knew in the back of my mind that [television] is what I wanted to do because I did a lot of public speaking and getting across ideas. . . ." A daily newspaper journalist commented, "I liked the classes. In college I had majored in a lot of things, and I just somehow ended up in the journalism department."

Luck was mentioned by some as playing a role in their career choices, as this newspaper journalist described: "I was majoring in something else, and the computer mistakenly assigned me to a journalism class and I stayed with it. It was a real challenge [and] something I enjoyed doing."

Other Influences

A variety of other reasons for career choice were mentioned. The importance of a high school teacher or the high school newspaper was remembered by about 5% of our respondents. A life-long interest in sports was a factor for about 5% of our sample. A weekly newspaper journalist said, "I read newspapers growing up. I loved the sports page and have an avid interest in sports." A daily newspaper journalist observed, "I was interested in sports and writing. Put them together and you have a sportswriter."

An early love of photography was mentioned by about 4% of our sample. For example, a daily newspaper journalist commented, "I'm a second-generation news photographer [who likes] the excitement and the chance to meet interesting people." A television journalist remembered looking at photographs in news magazines while in high school, saying, "[I] always wanted to take photos like that and win a Pulitzer Prize."

Family influences were remembered by about 3% of our sample. One daily newspaper journalist, whose family was involved in weekly journalism for 70 years, answered, "In all honesty, in a family as the only child, I felt some obligation to follow the family trade." A magazine journalist commented: "My father was a newspaper man . . . [and] I liked what he did. I liked his friends; it seemed like a fairly natural thing to do. I like the diversity of the field."

No survey, of course, can ever capture more than a glimpse of the complicated forces that attract people to journalistic life. However, The Paperboy, Pete Dexter's haunting story of two young Florida reporters, dramatized the heart of our survey findings. Dexter, a former journalist, created his Miami Times characters as "exact opposites."[17] For reporter Ward James, the smell of a "story" was as strong as the proverbial odor of the unsavory, back-swamp character awaiting execution for a murder he may not have committed, the setting of Dexter's book.

The author wrote, "A story had authority of its own to [James], and under that authority he was able to approach subjects of intimacy that he would never approach on his own." Fold into the novel's plot Ward James' opposite, a stubborn "pretty boy," Yardley Acheman, who was possessed of a "literary grace" that enabled him to take the enormity of details amassed by Ward James, the reclusive reporter, and become "flush with the telling" of them.

In the novel, the two characters are a team, playing on each others' strengths.[18] In the "real life" of our survey findings, the powerful images of the novel pick up the threads of many of the things that seem to drive journalists into a craft that journalist Lewis Lapham once called "sculpting in the snow." Cropping up most frequently in the open-ended responses to our question about career choice were two themes in Dexter's novel: The feeling at an early age of a kind of "literary grace," and the gift of not being able to "quit" as long as there was some digging to do on a "story."[19]

But it was Russell Baker who most succinctly captured another strong theme in our narratives about career choice. Joseph Pulitzer's legacy of the Pulitzer

Prizes, Baker said, ". . . simply confirms what journalists have always known: When the world needs improving, a journalist will beat a politician every time."[20]

PROFILES OF NEWSWORK

Most journalists in 1992 had worked for more than one news organization. Employed at their present organization for about 7 years, the typical journalist entered the field during the first year of the Reagan presidency and had been in news for about 12 years. A major demographic change between 1982–1992 was a rise in the median age of journalists, reversing a dramatic shift to a younger work force in the 1980s (see chap. 1, this volume). The age profiles of news personnel in 1992 were roughly similar to those of the 1970s, as the younger workforce of the early 1980s aged in the midst of a sharp decline in new hires.

Still, journalism in 1992 was a field that had fewer "elders" and "mid-life adults"—the traditional "leadership" age cohorts—than other fields, such as law, medicine, or the professoriate. It was a field dominated by "rising adults," the age grouping of 22–43 years, which was seen by some social historians as typically "testing" the values of an earlier generation.[21]

The Reporter

The "typical" news reporter in 1992 was born in 1958, during the second Eisenhower administration and near the end of what is called the idealistic "Baby Boom Generation." Few elders of the adaptive "Silent Generation" who were born prior to 1942 are left in the newsroom as reporters, although 1 in 10 is.[22] Robert Woodward and Carl Bernstein, the most famous journalists of their day, had already helped topple the Nixon presidency by the time typical 1992 reporters were juniors in high school. For many, the movie *All the President's Men*, as former *Times* columnist Anna Quindlen remembers, gave, ". . . the distinct impression that if you worked hard and were a tenacious reporter, you could bring down the President of the United States."[23]

Still likely to be male, in a newsroom where 3 in 10 were women and about 1 in 10 was a minority, the reporter's median age in 1992 was 34. Slightly likely to be unmarried, the typical reporter was also unlikely to have children even if he were married. A graduate of a public university, the typical reporter in 1992 had about 10 years of journalism experience, having entered the field the second year of President Ronald Reagan's first term in office. The typical reporter in 1992 also had been in the present newsroom job for about 7 years and had only 3 years less professional experience than his immediate supervisor. Most reporters had been in the newsroom long enough to have the "rude awakening," as *Times* writer Quindlen noted, to find ". . . themselves covering proposals for solid waste treatment plants at zoning board meetings," far from the romantics of Woodward and Bernstein.[24]

In 1992, reporters' fundamental news values were fairly close to those of the editors, although reporters were more likely to see interpretative analysis, investigating government claims, and an adversarial stance with government as higher priorities than did news management, particularly top management. In political views, reporters were likely to lean toward the liberal side, but saw the editorial stance of their news organizations as middle of the road.

The dominant job titles among reporters were general-assignment reporting and specific beat reporting. A little more than half of those in our sample who said they did reporting on a regular basis were general-assignment reporters covering a variety of areas. Reporters in 1992 were more likely to be assigned to specific beats, such as government or police, than in 1982, with 45% saying they had beats, compared with 38% a decade previous. Among daily newspapers and news magazines, a majority of reporters (57%) had beats. Wire service and broadcast journalists were still much more likely to be general-assignment reporters than were their colleagues in other media. The most common beats in 1992 were government and sports. Business, crime, education, and entertainment were other typical specialties. More than half of all journalists who reported also edited others' work. That was especially true for journalists who worked for the smaller sized media, such as weekly newspapers.

The Photojournalist

The typical photographer and graphics staff member in 1992 was about 2 years older and more experienced than was the median reporter, and was likely to be married. This journalist was also more likely to be middle of the road politically, and tended to be closer to top management on news values than other staffers.

News Management

Supervisory personnel in print media were somewhat younger than their counterparts in the early 1970s, but the typical supervisor in 1992 was older than in the early 1980s. Managers of broadcast news departments had a median age comparable to that of the early 1970s, and were notably older than were the journalists in their positions in the early 1980s (see Table 3.1).

A slightly lower percentage of the workforce (42.6%) had supervisory duties in 1992 than a decade previous. Although the typical supervisor in 1992 was still male, the gender gap narrowed between 1982–1992. Women were about one third of those with supervisory roles, compared with 28% in 1982. Proportionally, 43% of male journalists had supervisory duties, compared with 41% of their women colleagues.

TABLE 3.1
Comparison of Median Ages of Print and Broadcast Journalists
Who Perform Various Journalists' Functions

Type of Function	Median Age (years)		
	1971	1982–1983	1992
Print journalists			
Cover a specific news beat	35.2	31.8	36.2
Do reporting regularly	35.6	31.8	36.0
Manage a news desk[a]	41.5	35.0	39.5
Do a great deal of editing	41.7	33.5	37.5
Have an influence on hiring and firing	45.2	37.0	40.2
Manage a daily newspaper	48.5	38.7	41.5
All print journalists	38.1	33.5	37.9
Broadcast journalists			
Cover a specific news beat	30.6	27.8	31.9
Do reporting regularly	31.0	28.6	32.4
Do a great deal of editing	29.7	28.3	31.7
Have an influence on hiring and firing[b]	32.8	30.8	34.1
Manage a news department[a]	36.2	31.0	36.6
All broadcast journalists	30.8	28.3	32.5

[a]Includes all those in upper level news management.

[b]Includes respondents who said they had little, some, or a great deal of influence on decisions on hiring and firing news or editorial employees.

Most supervisors (70%) in 1992 did at least some reporting, down by 10 percentage points from the 1980s. The likely explanation is that recessionary layoffs and "buy outs" in 1992, particularly at the very large media, resulted in a leaner management structure, with fewer of them doing part-time reporting than in the previous decade. Also, some supervisory personnel in 1992 were engaged in graphics and design work with no reporting (see Table 3.2).

Lower Level Managers

Desk editors, assignment editors, and news producers, like the staff who reported to them, tended to be older in 1992 than were their counterparts during the early 1980s. At a median age of 37, the typical lower level manager was born in 1955 and, like the slightly younger reporting staff, was a member of the "Boom Generation." With 13 years professional experience, the typical lower level manager became a journalist during the Carter presidency.

Upper Level Managers

Managing editors, editors, and news directors typically were only a year older and more experienced than lower level supervisors. The typical manager was likely to be married and more likely to have children than were other journalists.

TABLE 3.2
Types and Percentages of Job Functions Journalists Perform, by Media Sector

Functions	Weeklies (N = 162)	Dailies (N = 635)	Magazines (N = 61)	Wire (N = 58)	Radio (N = 101)	TV (N = 137)	1992 Total (N = 1,154)	1982 Total (N = 1,001)	1971 Total (N = 1,328)
Reporting, newsgathering, and news-writing functions									
Total who do reporting[a]	88.9	60.3	73.8	87.9	90.1	67.2	69.9	79.8	78.8
Covered a specialized newsbeat	41.2	57.5	57.1	35.4	13.6	26.1	44.7	38.4	34.7
Editing and news-processing functions									
Total who edit or process other people's work[b]	83.4	71.6	65.5	91.4	74.3	84.0	75.7	71.4	64.8
Managerial and supervisory duties									
Total with managerial or supervisory functions[c]	54.9	37.5	44.3	51.8	45.5	45.3	42.6	47.1	41.9
Influence hiring and firing[d]	69.3	29.8	33.3	17.2	43.5	29.0	37.6	34.2	28.1
Supervise one or more reporters[e]	30.7	36.5	25.9	55.1	50.0	71.0	41.6	42.9	27.9

[a]Percentage of the entire sample who said they did reporting regularly or some of the time.
[b]Percentage of the entire sample who said they edited others work a great deal or some of the time.
[c]Percentage of the entire sample who said they supervised news or editorial employees.
[d]Percentage of those with managerial or supervisory functions who said they had a great deal of influence on hiring and firing.
[e]Percentage of those with managerial or supervisory functions who said they met at least daily with reporters to discuss stories.

The top-level manager was significantly different from lower management and rank-and-file reporters on some news values. Interpretative analysis, investigating government claims, and an adversary stance toward public officials were not likely to be deemed quite as important by top management as for lower level personnel on their news staffs. The top-level manager leaned slightly to the left politically, but tended to see the news operation as middle to right in editorial stance.

Size of Organizations

Staff size, of course, varied widely in 1992, with print organizations typically employing larger staffs than broadcast news operations. With the exception of news magazines, which increased their staff sizes substantially during 1982–1992, print media staffs shrunk. Both daily and weekly newspapers had smaller news staffs in 1992 than a decade previous. Between 1990–1992, more than a dozen of the largest daily newspapers, ranging from the Los Angeles Times to the Philadelphia Inquirer, engaged in editorial employee "buy-out" programs, usually targeting personnel with 10–15 years experience.[25] Radio stations, too, reduced their news operations to typically one person (see Table 3.3).

An aggregate profile of jobs held by persons with various lengths of professional experience suggested another broad change in the field. In 1982, a journalist with 21–25 years of experience was more likely to be a supervisor than just a reporter. In 1992, it was somewhat more likely that such a veteran was a reporter with no supervisory responsibilities. This was likely a result of the slow growth in the workforce during the recessionary decade of the 1980s, which meant there were fewer management positions into which the experienced journalists could move (see Fig. 3.1).

PERCEIVED AUTONOMY OF JOURNALISTS

The early 1980s was a time of considerable concern that rank-and-file journalists had gotten too heady in their post-Watergate exercise of aggressive reporting and, in the eyes of some, advocacy. Some of the nation's leading editors questioned whether young journalists had been given too free a hand.

Janet Cooke's fabrication of the principal elements of a Pulitzer Prize-winning story for the Washington Post in 1981 touched off a serious debate. Did her actions symbolize the costs of giving too much autonomy to ambitious young reporters who were eager to be noticed by their editors?[26] In a convocation speech to journalism students at Indiana University in 1983, Eugene Patterson, then publisher of the St. Petersburg Times, said, "We've had a time in the last decade or so when on some newspapers, the sailors were running the ship." That has changed, he said: "Editors are beginning to edit again."[27]

In that context, reporters in our 1982 study were asked how much freedom they had in selecting the news stories they worked on and in deciding which

TABLE 3.3
Median News Staff Size, by Various Media

	Median Staff Size	
Medium	1982–1983	1992
News magazines	100.9	146.6
Daily newspapers	41.5	32.5
Television	21.8	25.7
Wire service bureau	6.2	7.0
Weekly newspapers	4.6	2.9
Radio	3.0	1.0

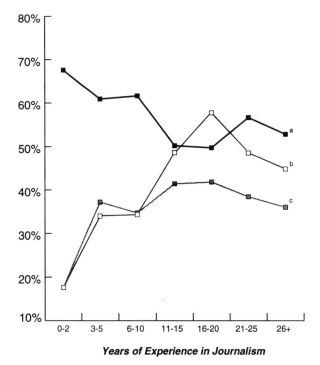

Years of Experience in Journalism

a Percent of those who do reporting "regularly"

b Percent of those who have supervisory responsibilities

c Percent of those who do "a great deal" of editing

FIG. 3.1. Types of journalistic functions performed by years of experience in news media.

aspects of a story should be emphasized, and whether they could get a subject covered if they thought it important. They were also asked about the extent of editing their copy received (see Table 3.4). Compared with the early 1970s, journalists in the 1982 sample reported a significant decline in their freedom to decide news story emphasis and editing. This was especially true for journalists working in large organizations (i.e., 100 or more news workers).

Declining Efficacy in the Newsroom

The 1992 interviews suggested that newsroom autonomy diminished further and at a startling pace. For the first time in three decades, barely half of reporters saw themselves as having the kind of clout in the newsroom that their predecessors did. The lessening autonomy occurred at a time when many in the workforce—who entered the profession during a tide of heavy hiring of young staff in the late 1970s and early 1980s—had been in the newsroom long enough to have established their authority.

Those who said they almost always could get a story covered, if they thought it should be, numbered only 55% in 1992, down from 59% a decade previous. Just 44% thought they had almost complete freedom in selecting the stories they worked on, compared with 60% in 1982 (see Figs. 3.2, 3.3, and 3.4).

Reporters in 1992 were also less likely to say they could decide independently which aspects of a story should be emphasized. Fifty-one percent said they had almost complete freedom to decide the emphasis with which a story was written, compared with 66% a decade previous.

The exception to the disturbing decline in perceived autonomy was at weekly newspapers, where reporters were more likely to think they could get a story covered in 1992 (63%). Their efficacy to select and determine the emphasis of stories appeared to be roughly similar to the journalists on weeklies in our earlier study.

In general, print journalists in 1992 were much more likely than broadcast journalists to say their work was edited by others (see Table 3.4). The explanation appears to be that broadcast journalists tended to work on smaller staffs, with radio journalists often on single-person operations. More important, the question about editing was less clearly a question of professional autonomy than the others. As suggested in the earlier remarks about editors "editing again" after a hiatus of the "sailors running the ship," many viewed the finding about editing positively. That suggests a need for a deeper look at a critical open-ended question that asks journalists to elaborate on the nature of constraints on them.

REASONS FOR AUTONOMY'S DECLINE

Some saw the diminution in autonomy as a result of the ascendance of a corporate culture that thrived on a top-down management style. Even *The New York Times*, regarded by many as "America's family-owned newspaper of record,"

TABLE 3.4

Indicators of Professional Autonomy Among Those Who Do Reporting, by Type of Medium

Indicators of Autonomy Percentage Who Say	Medium Type						
	Dailies (%)	Wires (%)	News Magazines (%)	Weeklies (%)	TV News (%)	Radio News (%)	All Reporters (%)
They are almost always able to get a story covered that they think should be covered							
1982–1983	64	63	45	50	61	60	59
1992	56	51	34	63	52	50	55
They have almost complete freedom in selecting the stories they work on							
1982–1983	56	46	39	67	47	73	60
1992	38	31	34	63	35	59	44
They have almost complete freedom in deciding which aspects of a news story should be emphasized							
1982–1983	67	63	32	64	67	73	66
1992	49	38	27	63	39	69	51
Their stories are not edited by other people							
1982–1983	14	8	23	29	39	59	29
1992	12	0	7	34	32	59	23

Note. 1992 Sample Sizes = Dailies, 383; Wires, 51; News Magazines, 45; Weeklies, 144; TV News, 92; Radio News, 91; All Reporters, 806.

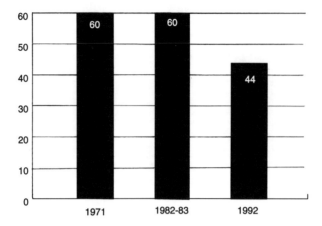

FIG. 3.2. Freedom to select stories (% of reporters saying "almost complete freedom").

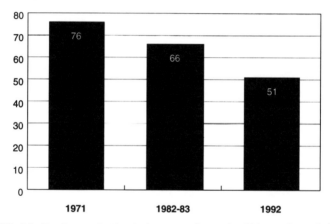

FIG. 3.3. Freedom to decide which aspects of story should be emphasized (% of reporters saying "almost complete freedom").

was struggling with perceptions in both the news *and* business departments of the paper that an authoritarian decision-making process was hampering initiative. Arthur Sulzberger, Jr., publisher, said, "For *The New York Times* to become all it can and for it to flourish in the years ahead, we must reduce our dependency on hierarchy in decision-making of every sort."[28] Anna Quindlen, columnist for the paper, said, "I don't think it makes sense for an editor to tell reporters how to cover a story, how long it has to be, or how it should be played."[29]

Yet the problem was much more complex than just a prevailing corporate culture. The audience was changing, both in informational preferences and in their modes of accessing information. The mass media, at first laggards on technology, were overtaken by it. To probe more deeply the growing perceptions of diminished

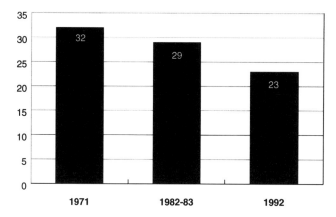

FIG. 3.4. Amount of editing stories got from others (% of reporters saying "none at all").

authority in a greatly changed media world of the 1990s, journalists in our sample were asked to comment on possible limits to their professional autonomy and freedom. The open-ended item asked was this: On the whole, what do you consider to be the most significant limits on your freedom as a journalist?

The query was done in the context of the other specific questions about autonomy, but the journalists had great latitude in describing constraints. They were free to elaborate on factors that were salient to them, regardless of whether the comments were about internal organizational constraints or roadblocks outside the newsroom. Most were eager to describe bothersome limits to their independence.

About one half of the journalists described *internal* organizational constraints of editorial control, time-space limits, or inadequate staffing. *External* pressures from government, advertisers, or a hostile public were cited by one third of our interviewees as the major impediments to their autonomy. A small minority, only 8%, said they were sometimes hindered by *professional* standards of ethics, good taste, and objectivity (see Fig. 3.5).

Internal Organizational Constraints

When news organizational constraints were mentioned by journalists, about two thirds of the comments focused on the impact of *inadequate staffing or time and space* on news coverage. These impediments to autonomy were largely budgetary and impersonal, and were somewhat more likely to be mentioned by journalists on daily newspapers and news magazines than by their colleagues on other media. Newspapers reduced their staffs, thus the concerns were not surprising. In contrast, news magazines increased their editorial staffs during 1982–1992.

Many journalists described the corrosive effects of a concern for *profit over quality*—a complaint that has been widely discussed in the trade journals. A

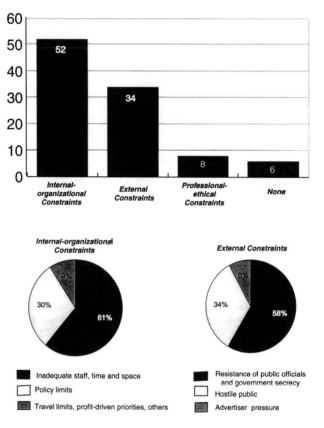

FIG. 3.5. Types of constraints on autonomy considered most significant by journalists (%).

young newspaper reporter on a large metropolitan daily in the South had a typical comment: "There is increasing pressure from large corporations, including my own, for bottom-line profit and gains at the expense of long-term quality." Another reporter, a 29-year-old woman at a mid-size daily newspaper in the Northeast, said:

> We have a large work load and that inhibits our ability for investigative reporting. There's just not time . . . [and we] end up being forced to rely on press releases . . . or on the testimony of public relations representatives. It takes time to uncover things that people may be trying to hide, and we just don't always have the time.

A midwestern news director of a large radio operation complained of time constraints "imposed on everyone in the department by the programming and sales department." He added, "Since I've been here the number of newscasts and length of newscasts have steadily declined."

A desk editor for a large metropolitan daily said, "We don't have enough time to devote to getting the best stories, [and] too much time is spent on insignificant stuff." Another newspaper journalist, a young woman reporting on a mid-size northeastern daily, said, ". . . If I want to do a more in-depth story, I have to neglect or not do the story because of breaking news." A 28-year-old, female wire service reporter in the Northeast said, "I have very little time to work on [in-depth] projects because we are constantly on deadlines and must get out stories as fast as possible." Some daily newspaper journalists complained about inadequate newshole, as did a desk editor at a mid-size newsroom in the Midwest: "You have to fight for every [column] inch."

Also mentioned were *limits on travel.* A veteran newspaper reporter at a daily in the South said that when she wanted to travel to important political events, "the other side of the office, the business side, usually says that with air fares being what they are, we can't afford it." She added that a lot of reporters "grumble that the front office is too cheap and you can't cover everything you want."

About one third of the complaints about internal organizational constraints on journalistic autonomy related to informal or formal *policy restrictions on what is newsworthy.* A 35-year-old desk editor on a large daily newspaper in the West said, "There are many men [in management] who are very or somewhat conservative, and who often take a rather dim view of some of the more trendy or more important issues that are not mainstream or middle of the road." She added: "We just did a story on gay teens which was frowned upon. I think management can be a little too conservative or out of touch with the needs of society and what they need to know in their world."

At a large daily newspaper, the managing editor, a woman, complained of "top management—and very occasionally, the publisher—personally intervening in the news gathering process and writing."

Management's emphasis on *reader-driven news values* was cited by some as a hindrance. At a large newspaper in the South, a reporter said she had to follow a formula:

> We have to fill out a checklist with every story, making sure we talk to minorities and have a "common man" in every story. If we don't, we have to justify it. We frequently spend more time finding people to fit the checklist than we do putting news in the story.

Another angle on the impact of the audience was shown in the complaint of a desk editor for a large daily in the Northeast, who said, "Too much emphasis in recent years on graphics . . . and page design are driving the paper rather than news, information and substance." A photographer at a large southern newspaper complained about the "narrow-minded attitudes" of management:

Sometimes they go overboard in making one group of people happy. The newspaper is very cognizant of getting minorities into the paper, so the best picture may not be used because it doesn't have a minority in it. . . . There's a definite need to have minorities represented in the paper, but sometimes they [editors] go overboard.

Others complained about the "biases" of editors. At one news magazine, a young female writer said, "There are a lot of stories near and dear to my heart that never make it into print . . . because the editors have to approve the story ideas."

External Constraints

Some journalists (34% of our sample) saw forces outside their organization—such as government, a hostile public, or powerful advertisers—as great hindrances to their autonomy. Of those citing external pressures, a majority of the comments (58%) pointed to *resistance by public officials, violations of open-records laws,* or *government secrecy* in general. Journalists in all media voiced the problem, but those in radio news and at weekly newspapers were somewhat more likely to cite external constraints.

A young radio reporter in the Midwest expressed the necessity of informally yielding to official constraints:

Being in a small town and having to see public officials [socially] everyday, there are sometimes restraints that . . . in a bigger town might not be a factor. But, in a smaller town, I may hold off on a . . . story at the personal request of a public official or else that particular source may dry up. . . .

Reporters in larger cities, particularly on daily newspapers, were more likely to see official constraints as less personal. A young reporter in the Midwest said: "[Even] with the Freedom of Information Act and [the state] open-meetings act, a lot still takes place behind closed doors. A big limit is access to information, getting people to play . . . [by] the rules as to what can be discussed in the open. . . ." At a large newspaper in the South, another reporter, 36, added: "Some of the privacy laws are unnecessarily restrictive. Their intent is good but they impede what I believe [is] the public's legitimate right to learn about events in the community."

Located in the Northeast, a young woman reporter at a mid-size daily newspaper cited official secrecy as a major hindrance:

The reporters and editors are dogged in their pursuit of news . . . [but] we don't have access to all the records. . . . [The state's open records law] is very limited and the political climate is very closed. For example, the major police department denied us access to arrest bookings, and we have no recourse. Under state law they don't have to show them to us. So, we have no way of fighting to get them back.

A news director at a large television station in the South said, "Government agencies frequently dodge the issue and are slow to provide requested information." At a large radio station in the Midwest, a news director said the biggest constraints were "federal government regulations and their interpretation by bureaucrats at all levels." A young radio reporter in the Midwest, a woman, was succinct: "It's very difficult to get information from law enforcement—they have very strong censorship powers."

At a midwestern bureau of a wire service, a 40-year-old woman covering a state legislature complained that "many of the major decisions are made by powerful or influential legislators . . . at private meetings we are not allowed to attend." Another said, "All levels of government [are taking] an increasing amount of time to process [records] and make them available."

Of those journalists who saw external constraints as more salient than possible internal limits on autonomy, almost 35% mentioned a "hostile" public—a perplexing animosity from both news sources and the citizenry. For example, a desk editor for a mid-size newspaper in the South said journalists face "a hostile attitude from political leaders and a skeptical public." He added:

> I think those two combined tend to restrict journalists not so much in a legal sense, but in a sense of public opinion. It is almost like peer pressure, or community pressure. Right now there is a lot of pressure on journalists not to do the type of stories that could have been done a few years back. The political leaders make it hard for us, and the public, in large part, doesn't support us—which doesn't give us much ground to stand on when things get sticky and tough.

A television journalist at a mid-size newsroom lamented "the private sector's reluctance by everyday citizens to assist [the reporter] out of fear or a skepticism of journalistic process or ethics." At a large southern newspaper, a young reporter cited "the public attitude that is against prying too deeply." A TV reporter for a small station in the Midwest said, "People around here don't trust [journalists] . . . , so we don't get information we should be able to get."

For journalists in small communities, the constraints cited were sometimes self-imposed in anticipation of what might make the audience (or sources) "hostile." For example, one weekly editor in the Northeast, a 39-year-old woman, said: "The fact that this is a small town, and everybody knows each other . . . you have to be sensitive to people's personal lives and places in the community. You don't report everything you might unless it's a really wide-ranging story with major effects."

Contrary to conventional wisdom, only about 8% of journalists citing external constraints saw advertiser pressures as a threat to their autonomy. When they did see such a constraint, however, it was expressed strongly. A desk editor at a large metropolitan newspaper on the West Coast said, "Pressure from advertisers . . . keeps me from being able to report all the stories I'd like."

Another daily newspaper journalist in the West said there was intense pressure "... in hard times to avoid stories that might offend advertisers...." In the Northeast, a young television reporter in a small newsroom said it simply: "The wall between the newsroom and the sales department is coming down."

Professional Constraints

In addition to organizational and external limits, a small minority (8%) of journalists suggested that *professional norms*, such as objectivity, were a hindrance to their conception of autonomy. For example, a 41-year-old weekly newspaper reporter in the Northeast said, "[Objectivity] ... limits my freedom to do the story with what I think is the proper perspective." A 49-year-old wire service photographer at a large bureau in the Northeast said:

> As a journalist you do not share the same civil rights the average American has, and I'm very disturbed by that. For instance, it's inferred in this business that you can't have any feelings for anything you might conceivably cover, which, in general, is life.... This makes it look like any feelings we have take away from our objectivity.

A young newspaper reporter at a mid-size paper in the Northeast said constraints were sometimes an indirect result of "the nature of a beat" that has the journalist "talking with the same people week in and week out." Sometimes the constraints were seen as necessary. For example, a 46-year-old reporter working for a large metropolitan daily in the Northeast said: "We *could* be writing like the boys on [London's] Fleet Street. They obviously have a freedom that knows no bounds. I couldn't get away with writing the kinds of things they do." Only 6% of the respondents said they had no significant constraints. These journalists tended to be in upper level management at smaller media, with journalists from radio and weekly newspapers typically somewhat more likely to see no significant constraints.

PREDICTORS OF AUTONOMY

What are the characteristics of journalists who perceived they had the greatest clout in the newsroom? An intensive analysis attempted to test the relative strength of about 20 possible "predictors," ranging from gender to the size of the newsroom (see Table 3.5).[30] The statistical analysis suggests some obvious, but relatively weak, correlates of perceived autonomy, such as working for small organizations.

Journalists who worked for smaller media—particularly weekly newspapers and radio stations—that were still independently owned tended to see more personal discretion in their work. Those working for group-owned, privately held

TABLE 3.5
Predictors of Perceived Autonomy of Journalists

Predictors	Standardized Regression Coefficients	Simple r
Media sector		
Weeklies	.15**	.16
Magazines	−.10**	−.12
Radio	.16***	.15
Dailies	.02	−.08
TV	−.01	−.04
Journalism major	.02	.01
Education	.04	−.02
Additional journalism training	−.01	.01
Ideology (conservative)	.05	.07
Staff size	−.17***	−.19
Gender (male)	−.09**	−.06
Region		
South	−.09*	−.07
Northeast	−.10**	−.05
Midwest	−.06	.07
Supervise	.09**	.15
Union membership	−.08**	−.08
Income	.15**	−.04
Adversary role	.06*	−.01
Age	−.02	.03
Years in journalism	.02	.03
Public and group owned	.09	−.14
Group owned	−.02	−.05
Group owned, not publicly traded	.16*	.07
Independent news organization	.17*	.11
Comments from supervisors	.06*	.05
Race		
African American	.01	−.03
Asian American	−.03	−.07
Native American	.00	.03
Membership in journalism association	.04	.02

Note. $R^2 = .12$.
*$p < .05$. **$p < .01$. ***$p < .001$.

media were somewhat more likely to have a sense of autonomy than those at publicly traded corporations. As in 1982, in 1992 the size of the editorial staff on which a journalist worked was a predictor of perceived autonomy. The larger the staff, the less power the journalist felt, regardless of the ownership form of the employer.

Surprisingly, experienced senior journalists were no more likely than their "greener" colleagues to say they had control over their work. However, within various levels of experience, those making higher salaries were significantly more likely to see themselves as having greater efficacy to select and shape news stories.

Other significant, although slight, predictors of a sense of professional discretion were somewhat surprising. When years of experience and other key factors were accounted for, women journalists were a little more likely to have a sense of control over their work than were males, contrary to the findings from previous decades. Being politically conservative was also slightly related to a greater sense of autonomy. News magazine journalists tended to say they had less autonomy than did others. Working in the South or Northeast and belonging to a craft union were slightly related to thinking one had less clout with editors.

The characteristics of those journalists who saw themselves as having greater control over their work seemed, at least partly, to be those that were quickly fading from the scene. Small organizations of privately owned media may somehow be given new life by changing technology, but it is doubtful.

Overall, however, there was much that could not be explained about journalists' feelings of diminished freedom between 1982–1992. The larger lesson of this analysis is that journalistic autonomy in 1992 was an elusive factor—an increasingly precious prerequisite that depended more on highly individual circumstances than on commonly discussed factors, such as corporate ownership. All of the significant predictors combined explain only about 12% of the variance among journalists' perceptions of their autonomy. Although only speculative, a larger explanation for the perceived decline in autonomy likely rests with the fact that mass media, in a time of extended recessionary decline in advertising revenue, have fewer resources. If sociologists are correct in seeing the decisive component of organizational power as the allocation of resources, journalists' perceptions of powerlessness may be mostly a reflection of hard economic times.[31]

EXTENT OF COMMUNICATION WITH OTHERS

In 1992, news media were struggling to retain their particular niches, with the terms *reader-driven* and *market-oriented* commonplace in describing them. Thus, a look at the frequency with which journalists received others' reactions to their work was timely. In 1982, we found considerably more journalistic contact with audience members than was commonly assumed, and somewhat less feedback from supervisors than modern management theory recommends. The patterns in 1992 were roughly similar.

Among the overall sample of journalists—all job titles combined—the relative frequency of reaction from others in 1992 was similar to that of a decade previous. Feedback from the audience ranked slightly above peers in regularity, and supervisor–journalist contact in 1992 was about what it was in 1982 (see Table 3.6).

TABLE 3.6

Sources of Reactions to Journalists' Stories, by Medium (Means)

	Medium							
Reaction Type	Dailies (N = 633)	Weeklies (N = 160)	News Magazines (N = 58)	Wires (N = 58)	Radio (N = 99)	TV (N = 135)	All— 1992 (N = 1,143)	All— 1982–1983 (N = 993)
Audience	3.19[a]	3.57	3.12	2.38	3.36	3.27	3.22	3.33
People of same level	3.26	2.84	3.28	3.12	3.06	3.26	3.18	3.21
People above	3.22	2.77	3.26	3.33	3.12	3.00	3.13	3.12
News sources	2.90	3.04	2.72	2.69	2.81	2.64	2.86	3.08
People in other organizations	2.31	2.47	2.48	2.67	2.89	2.61	2.45	2.57

[a]4 = regularly; 3 = occasionally; 2 = seldom; 1 = never.

73

Surprisingly, regular reaction from news sources was somewhat less likely in 1992, despite a common perception among critics that sources were quick to attempt manipulation of the news. As noted earlier, a significant number of journalists cited an uncooperative, hostile public and official constraints as significant limits to their autonomy, which might suggest that regular "feedback" should have increased. Some critics, no doubt, would say that sources in 1992 were so successful at shaping the news they no longer needed to bother to react to journalists' work.

More reporters still said they regularly received comments about their work from audience members more than from peers, news sources, or their superiors. A little less than half of the reporters got regular audience comment. Among reporters for weeklies, audience reaction was somewhat more likely. Because of their remoteness from their widespread audiences, wire reporters were least likely to hear from their readers regularly (see Table 3.7).

For newspaper reporters, the likelihood of comment from supervisors was significantly greater in 1992 than in 1982, although only a little more than a third said they discussed their work regularly with a supervisor. This seemed to confirm the many discussions in trade journals about the increased accountability of editorial operations of newspapers. However, the pattern for broadcast journalists was the reverse, with significantly fewer talking to a supervisor regularly in 1992 than a decade previous.

Supervising journalists—desk editors and news producers, primarily—were roughly similar to reporters in how often they received reaction to their work. However, they were slightly less likely in 1992 to get reaction from anyone—colleagues, news sources, or audience—than they were in 1982 (see Table 3.8).

Despite the perception that modern managers keep tighter reins on their editorial staffs than in former times—seemingly confirmed in the drop in perceived autonomy among journalists—the degree of interaction in 1992 was only slightly greater than that found in 1982 (except for newspapers). About 45% of the supervisors said they met with individual reporters at least daily. Another 25% met with reporters at least several times a week.

JOURNALISTS' IMAGES OF AUDIENCES

Some of the most penetrating criticism of mass media in 1992 came from within journalism, emerging from household names such as Moyers and Bernstein. The thrust of their barbs was that journalistic pandering to a debased notion of audience preferences feeds on itself to create a "civic illiteracy" and an "idiot culture." Bill Moyers, television journalist, said, "Conventional wisdom says people don't want the kind of news that will bring them back to the public square."[32] It is publishers who underestimate the audience, Moyers said: "Those of us who are reporters can only hope this generation of publishers understands that what

TABLE 3.7

Reporters Who Regularly Received Comment About Their Work, by Source of Comment and Type of News Organization

Source of Comment	Medium						
	Dailies (%)	Weeklies (%)	News Magazines (%)	Wires (%)	Radio (%)	TV (%)	All (%)
Superiors							
1982–1983	29	28	41	42	49	42	35
1992	37	33	47	45	37	27	37
Peers							
1982–1983	38	41	20	42	46	45	40
1992	39	40	42	29	31	46	39
Journalists outside own organization							
1982–1983	15	16	17	33	17	16	17
1992	9	10	16	12	23	13	12
News sources							
1982–1983	48	32	33	21	33	36	39
1992	49	37	37	10	29	21	38
Audience							
1982–1983	48	56	40	13	50	55	49
1992	44	60	41	8	50	49	46

Note. 1992 Sample Sizes = Dailies, 383; Weeklies, 144; News Magazines, 45; Wires, 51; Radio, 91; TV, 92; All, 806.

TABLE 3.8

Supervisors Who Regularly Received Comment About Their Work, by Source of Comment and Type of News Organization

	Medium						
Source of Comment	Dailies (%)	Weeklies (%)	News Magazines (%)	Wires (%)	Radio (%)	TV (%)	All (%)
Superiors							
1982–1983	46	31	44	50	49	58	45
1992	45	25	56	31	44	40	41
Peers							
1982–1983	45	43	46	29	55	46	45
1992	39	44	52	35	37	36	40
Journalists outside own organization							
1982–1983	14	16	35	21	24	25	18
1992	7	9	15	10	30	10	11
News sources							
1982–1983	43	36	37	26	47	39	40
1992	31	45	28	17	33	23	32
Audience							
1982–1983	57	65	67	4	54	61	57
1992	48	66	44	17	50	52	50

Note. 1992 Sample Sizes: Dailies, 238; Weeklies, 89; News Magazines, 27; Wires, 29; Radio, 46; TV, 62; All, 491.

keeps journalism different is something intangible."[33] Carl Bernstein also impli-
cated the corporate media structures, but he went further, saying, ". . . The great
information conglomerates of this country are now in the trash business."[34] In
Bernstein's view, even the prestige press of America sometimes displays "a con-
tempt for the truth or the reality of most people's lives."[35]

Criticism that journalists underestimated their audience was also common in
1982, particularly from academics. David Altheide, a sociologist who has studied
television news organizations, long ago concluded that a major element of the
television news "perspective" is seeing the audience as "essentially stupid."[36] A
major study done for the Newspaper Advertising Bureau in 1982 suggested that
"far too many" newspaper journalists "express beliefs that the public is unsophis-
ticated and plebeian in its tastes."[37]

Our studies in 1982–1983 and 1992 asked journalists about their audiences.
In the 1982 survey, a majority (74%) agreed, either somewhat or strongly, that
their audiences preferred breaking news to analysis of trends. Slightly fewer
(69%) in the 1992 study thought the audience favored immediacy over analysis.

In 1982, about one third of our sample of journalists thought their audience had
little interest in reading about social problems such as racial discrimination and
poverty. Only 22% in 1992 thought the audience was uncaring about such
problems. More important, in the earlier study, only a small minority (16%) agreed,
either somewhat or strongly, that their audience was gullible or easily fooled. This
negative view was held in 1992 by a little more than 13% of the journalists.

Broadcast journalists in 1982 were somewhat more likely to see their audience
as more interested in breaking news than print journalists, and that was still the
case in 1992. Similarly, broadcast journalists were also slightly more likely than
their print colleagues to see their audience as gullible. Only journalists from
weekly newspapers were more likely than others to say their audience had little
interest in serious problems.

On balance, the typical journalist in 1992 was a little more likely to have a
congenial view of the audience than a decade previous. This view was nicely
illustrated in Anna Quindlen's spirited defense of audience interest in and media
coverage of the preliminary hearing of O.J. Simpson on charges of murder in
the summer of 1994. The New York Times columnist argued that it is the "tut-
tutters" among the critics—not journalists—who ". . . always talk about the
public as though it were a large hairy animal with poor hygiene and eating
habits." Although the audience may have been interested in the case because
of Simpson's celebrity status, Quindlen said, ". . . they may stay to learn about
suppression of evidence."[38] Although many will argue that the Simpson case was
a perfect example of segments of the press pandering to a less than idealistic
vision, our evidence suggests most mainstream journalists have a reasonably
high-minded image of the audience. Whether this view is reflected in the news,
of course, depends on many other factors.

JOURNALISTS' RATING OF THEIR ORGANIZATION

Some of the most visible critics of American news media, as suggested earlier, argued that there has been a serious decline in the quality of news. Charges of a journalistic preoccupation with "Whitewatergate" and "Troopergate"—both about President Bill Clinton and First Lady Hillary Rodham Clinton and allegations of misconduct occurring largely before they entered the White House—were often the focus of more dramatic criticisms. The conventional wisdom seemed to be that, during 1982–1992, mainstream news organizations yielded too easily to the sensationalist urges whetted by declining ratings and readership and stagnant advertising budgets. To what extent do journalists share those concerns?

For three decades, national samples of American journalists were asked to evaluate how well their news organization informed the public. In 1982–1983, almost 70% said their newsroom was either outstanding or very good, compared with little more than half the sample responding that way in 1971. The 1992 survey suggested a significant drop in the number of journalists who thought their newsroom was outstanding (see Table 3.9).

However, the general picture suggested that most journalists in 1992 rated their news organization as *very good* or *outstanding*, suggesting a better overall assessment of quality than in 1971, but less glowing than that of 1982. Those who tended to be the most positive were journalists for wire services, with the least positive assessments coming from television journalists.

To get beneath the simplism of a single, report card-type rating, the journalists in the 1992 study were asked to comment on their assessment of newsroom performance. Specifically, after asking a closed question about rating their newsroom on a range from *outstanding* to *poor*, they were asked, Why do you think [your newsroom] is doing a [poor . . . outstanding] job? The open-ended responses provide a compelling picture of the strengths and weaknesses of American journalism from the eyes of those closest to it.

TABLE 3.9
Journalists' Rating of How Well Their
Organization Informed the Public (Across Time)

	Respondent's Own Organization		
Rating	1971 (%)	1983 (%)	1992 (%)
Outstanding	14.9	17.9	12.5
Very good	38.1	49.1	50.2
Good	31.2	24.9	28.1
Fair	13.1	7.0	8.0
Poor	2.0	1.1	0.8
No opinion	0.7	0.1	0.6
Total	100.0	100.1[a]	100.2[a]

[a]Does not total to 100% because of rounding error.

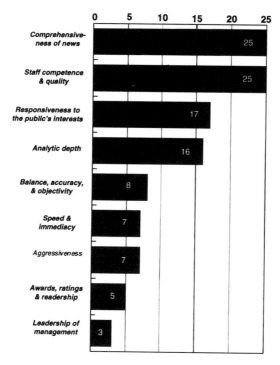

FIG. 3.6. Reasons given by journalists explaining why their newsrooms are judged
to be doing a good job (%).

The comments were rich in texture, and sometimes the narratives cited several
reasons a newsroom may be doing well or poorly. Summarizing them is not easy,
but several broad themes were common (see Fig. 3.6).

Reasons for Good to Outstanding Ratings

For journalists giving their newsrooms *good* grades, the primary reason was *comprehensiveness of news about the major institutions in their community, metropolitan, or regional area*, with one fourth of them mentioning it. Weekly newspaper
journalists were most likely to mention comprehensiveness (36%), followed by
daily newspaper staff (29%), radio (16%), and TV journalists (10%). Because
of their different roles, the local angle on comprehensiveness was not a factor
for wire service or news magazine journalists, although comprehensiveness of
global and national news was a common thread for wire service personnel.

A weekly newspaper editor in the Northeast, near retirement, rated his newsroom as *very good*, illustrating with the idea of comprehensiveness:

We keep track of everything that goes on in town hall, police and fire departments,
school system, [and the] social scene. We write not only factual stories but inter-

pretive stories. We try to stimulate public opinion and reaction. We get lots of letters. We present . . . many viewpoints and opinions.

A reporter on another northeastern weekly, in her late 30s, said her newspaper was *very good* because:

> . . . We have outstripped and scooped, on a continuous basis, the other papers in the area. My editor and publisher both are very strong on letting the public know what is going on in their government . . . and I know that's had an impact on the changes in the small towns around here. Also, we try to present all sides and not take advocacy positions, which I think many papers are doing.

A 48-year-old editor on a mid-size western daily newspaper said: "I think we provide very strong local coverage of what's going on and we're trying to provide a mix of national and international news as well. But the local news is our strong point." A 37-year-old managing editor on a mid-size southern daily said: "Our local news coverage provides the public with the important things they need to know about—government, politics, education, health, crime and other issues of the day—in a timely manner." At a large daily newspaper in the Midwest, a 37-year-old desk editor focused on the comprehensiveness of political coverage: "We give a real strong emphasis to local government and political news [and] do a lot of local news. I think our strength is informing about local events and political coverage. [We] pick up quite a bit of national and state politics as well." A 40-year-old television reporter working for a mid-size station in the Northeast described the comprehensiveness and depth of his newsroom's work. There was also the suggestion—common among the replies of the broadcast journalists— that the newsroom was very good despite a need for more staff:

> Our daily news coverage handles most of the most important stories in our region each day—which is our primary interest. We get into depth on important issues . . . that have an impact on people in our region, on issues that affect them. For the size of our staff . . . we do a very good job.

A 44-year-old radio reporter in the West saw his two-person newsroom as doing a good job:

> We work hard to bring [our listeners] as much information about government, and especially about the fire dangers and highway conditions that are important to the people in this county. We try to keep them up on issues of change that are facing them—like new shopping centers . . . and environmental issues. . . .

Finally, a 39-year-old wire service writer in the Northeast said his organization did a good job of informing the public because it ". . . provides an extremely wide range of coverage and a tremendous quantity of coverage."

Compliments on the *competence and quality of the staff* characterized the re-marks of one fourth of the journalists who praised their newsroom's performance. TV news people (27%) were slightly more likely to mention staff quality as the reason for excellence than were their colleagues on other media. Weekly jour-nalists (11%) were least likely to mention staff.

A young TV journalist in a small midwestern market said the staff made his station a good one: "I think we have the best reporting staff [and] the most experienced newsroom. And, I think we have a little better technology [than our competition]." A 28-year-old TV journalist on a small station in the West thought her newsroom did an outstanding job:

> We have the largest news staff in town . . . [an] experienced news staff with good sources. We have two newscasts a night that deal mainly with local and state-wide news. We're the only station in town that can get breaking news from across the state . . . [and] we will always have video no matter what.

A 38-year-old news director at a mid-size station in the Midwest said a com-petitive spirit, cited frequently by television journalists, was the key to his staff's very good performance: "I think we're very conscientious [with] a really strong work ethic [and] a lot of people on the staff who really care and go the extra mile to get information to the public. [We have] a very competitive spirit [and] don't want to be beaten by anyone."

Radio personnel typically work on small, often single-person, news staffs. As result, when staff competence was cited by journalists in radio (23%), they sometimes had themselves in mind. For example, this 46-year-old journalist, the only person reporting news at a southern radio station, said:

> I've been on the job for 13 years and have developed important sources. The people know who I am and I feel like they can trust what I say [and] . . . they depend on us to let them know what's going on in the community. I feel like we have the public trust.

Although multiperson radio news staffs were less common in 1992 than a decade previous, this response by a midwestern news director of a staff of four focused on their quality:

> We have an outstanding local news department, [with] dedicated, eager, enthusi-astic people who understand that news does not operate on a schedule and who have disseminating information to the public as a primary goal in life. . . . We are not as in-depth as an NPR-type newscast, and one of the filters that we employ [on world news] . . . is the immediate relevance of the information to the local listener. So for any listener to rely on us as the only source of news would be ludicrous. . . .

A mid-30s writer at a large daily newspaper in the West saw good writing as the key:

> We have a large-enough staff and talented enough staff to get enough of the issues that are affecting the public. The news room is committed to truth and telling people "stories." I think that is even a bigger factor. The approach we take is more important than the number of stories that we get.

A desk editor in his 50s at a large midwestern daily said the paper was good because:

> It's got "pros" on the staff—people who understand their function and role in the community. The newspaper has an institutional commitment to keep people informed [and] 110 years of history of being [an] efficient, reliable news purveyor.

For journalists at daily newspapers, comments about the quality of the news staff were sometimes linked to their autonomy, an important value, particularly for young reporters. At a mid-size southern daily, a 37-year-old reporter said her paper: "Gives its reporters almost total and complete responsibility for finding the news. They are also very conscious of social issues and develop special projects that focus specifically on those issues." Others mentioned the importance of having a news staff with a balance of younger and older, more experienced personnel. One 46-year-old reporter working at a large southern daily said her newspaper: "... Has a strong sense of purpose, and we have a lot of young reporters who still want to tackle the world, so they go after the tough stories. We have enough older reporters to bring some balance."

A 45-year-old news magazine subeditor, located in the Northeast, pointed to her staff: "There is professionalism [and a] dedication to gathering information—a responsibility that the journalists here feel, and a commitment to informing the public and being ethical." A 43-year-old wire service photographer in a southern bureau was succinct about why his organization was doing an excellent job: "The objectivity and the enthusiasm of the staff."

A keen sense of *responsiveness to the voices and needs of the audience* was mentioned by 17% of journalists as a primary strength of their newsroom. Journalists in radio news (26%) were more likely to mention this point, compared with those on weeklies (18%), television (15%), and dailies (13%). Because of their national scope, wire service and magazine journalists rarely cited responsiveness to audience as a factor.

"Talk Radio," which has developed into a considerable force since our study in 1982–1983 and now has its own trade magazine, *Talkers*, is a metaphor for some of the spirit of journalists' comments about their response to the audience. For example, a journalist in a one-person, midwestern newsroom illustrated the importance of "call-in" shows in affecting radio news selection:

> We concentrate our best on what we feel our audience is interested in. . . . We have a talk show where I try to guide our input on what our listeners want . . . [on] important issues in our area. I try to use that as a guide. We're very oriented to our listeners and try to keep a very open mind.

Another 55-year-old radio journalist in a small midwestern town said: ". . . There is a town newspaper, but we usually get the story out before they do. We also get feedback from our audience on a daily talk show we do. You get the feel for what is going on with the community and what they are interested in."

Newspapers, too, had a heightened concern for linkages to audience needs in 1992. Commenting on his outstanding newsroom, a young editor on a large weekly newspaper in the Midwest said:

> We have a presence in the community. We have developed many ties and contacts in the community—not just the business and government, but the general public—and . . . we have a good handle on what people expect from us and the things they care about.

At another midwestern weekly, a 39-year-old photographer said her newspaper did a good job because: ". . . We have the time to flesh out a story and stay with it. We have people who live within the communities that they report . . . so they get a feel for the chemistry of the people who live there. . . ."

A middle-aged reporter on a daily newspaper in a small city in the Southeast cited his good organization's "level of interest and diversity" and "efforts to be involved in the community," adding:

> [There is] extreme emphasis on balance [and] diversity of opinion of races, looking at the entire community. You would think [looking at the news pages from years ago] everyone was a white male in a suit. I have been in staff meetings where we have been told not to just parrot the words, but look for diversity . . . not just the white guys in suits. . . .

A 51-year-old writer on a large midwestern newspaper said: "We seem to know the needs of our readers. We somehow overcome our shortcomings every day." A young desk editor at a mid-size southern daily newspaper, who rated her staff's performance as *very good*, mentioned the role of research in linking the paper to the audience:

> . . . Reporters play a large role . . . in developing sources and finding out what people's concerns are. . . . Also in conducting surveys-polls and being familiar with their market and trying to accommodate the readers with articles, such as [about] senior citizens and various segments of the readership.

At a mid-size daily in the upper Midwest, a 39-year-old photographer expressed this in calling his paper *very good*:

We have . . . a strong commitment from the editors to report on stories of greatest interest to the most people. We . . . take minorities into account . . . [and] there is just a real .strong desire to do an outstanding job—to write from the average person's perspective. . . . We have a variety of things . . . to stimulate thinking.

"Town meetings" of journalists and their communities, particularly in the larger television markets, was a growing trend in 1992; they indicated the salience of the audience to the crafting of news.[39] That sensitivity was reflected frequently in the narratives about newsroom quality. A 33-year-old television journalist at a large southern station said for her news staff: ". . . Our main emphasis is on the people. We do a good job of going out and talking to the people that will be most affected by the story we're covering."

Another TV journalist, 37 years old, at a mid-size southern station blended audience responsiveness with projects of depth in explaining why his newsroom did a very good job: "We make an effort to find out what is important to our audience [and to] make it understandable. And we emphasize special projects so that our audience can get a better understanding of useful information." Still another TV journalist, 29 years old, at a large southern station reflected a multicultural consciousness in rating his organization as *outstanding*: "We try to address every aspect of our community and . . . address every race, every origin. We try to make our news easy to understand. It's just the way we come across to the public—the amount of personality we put into our newscast."

Analytic depth on issues of social importance was an attribute of newsroom success in the eyes of another 16% of our national sample of journalists. News magazine (50%), daily newspaper (20%), television (17%), weekly (12%), and radio journalists (10%) mentioned this as a factor in newsroom performance.

Of course, magazine journalists often focused on analytic qualities in rating their newsroom's work. One 47-year-old writer said the news magazine did an *outstanding* job because: "The stories try to analyze and interpret issues and events and identify their meaning and their future implications for the readers." Another magazine journalist, a 37-year-old woman, said: "We're doing a good job of selecting which national stories to cover, particularly those that have a Washington focus. . . . I think we do a very good job analyzing what is really going on beyond the headlines." A 63-year-old subeditor said his news magazine did an outstanding job by: "Combining a zeal for being on the scene getting the facts with an ability to quickly analyze the meaning of an event in a matter of days. We do it better than the competition."

Located in the West, a 33-year-old daily newspaper journalist focused on depth of reporting: "We cover things papers our size usually don't . . . putting national and international stories into contexts which are important to our readers." A 28-year-old southern desk editor at a mid-size daily, which did a *very good* job, said: ". . . We try to put analysis on national and world events because the readers have been seeing this on TV all day. So we try to tell them 'why.' " Another daily newspaper desk editor on a large southern paper seemed to think depth was only enough to get a *good* rating: "We are doing well at analysis and making complex issues simpler, but we don't cover mundane, breaking news—fires, etc.—well."

A 35-year-old desk editor at a large newsroom in the West also gave her newspaper a *good* rating. Her comments referred to investigative reporting, which was not mentioned very often: "I think we try to cover a broad range of issues, not just what the public wants to read about, but also what we feel the public should know, including some investigative-type stories." A young television reporter at a small station in the West said:

> We do a good job because we are able to get the basic stories of the day on the air and we do a fair amount of news analysis pieces. There's a commitment here in informing the public about social issues—such as education, social welfare, family issues—issues that seem to confront the listeners every day.

A few weekly journalists also mentioned analytic depth as a factor in the success of their newsroom. The editor of a large weekly in the Midwest, a 65-year-old woman, said, "We do a lot of analysis, and we cover a lot of school and municipal issues as well." An editor of a small weekly in the Midwest rated her paper as *outstanding*. She said, "We can go into more depth than the dailies." A 27-year-old reporter working on a small weekly in the Northeast said his paper was very good because: "We cover a broad range of important local issues [and] we try to find other angles and aspects that the other media do not pursue. . . . What we write about is taken seriously."

Radio journalists were least likely to cite analytic depth as a salient factor in their newsroom's success, but some did. One who mentioned depth was a 49-year-old news director at a two-person staff in the Northeast: "A major emphasis on news is an important part of our programming. In-depth analysis is part of our news, [and we] attempt to involve the public through daily live guests and call-in."

A variety of other factors relating to newsroom quality were voiced by small minorities of journalists. One significant theme was a characterization of *balance, accuracy, and objectivity* as the strongest attribute of quality by about 8% of the journalists. Wire service journalists (21%) were especially likely to mention this attribute, with television personnel (11%) also being a little more likely to say balance was the key to their evaluation than their colleagues in other media.

A 40-year-old wire service reporter in the Northeast rated the agency as *outstanding*, saying, "[We are] . . . very balanced in . . . reporting, almost to the extreme of having no apparent bias whatsoever." Another wire service reporter, a 31-year-old woman at a southern bureau, said: ". . . It's nuts and bolts journalism—just straightforward stories."

In a small western market, a television journalist said: "We have genuine integrity, and . . . we feel a sense of responsibility to the community. We pride ourselves on having accurate, honest and immediate news. . . . We bring a holistic quality to the news." Another TV journalist at a mid-size station in the Midwest said, "We're balanced, far-reaching, and I'd like to think, in touch with viewer concerns." A producer at a mid-size television station in the South said her station did a good job:

> We present objective, unbiased reports of area events, political events, public officials. We work very hard to cover all groups or segments of our area's population, ethnically, economically, and culturally. We try to be very fair on any controversial issue.

At a large western daily newspaper—rated as *outstanding*—a young desk editor said, "[Our newsroom] takes a very broad look at the news it must cover and . . . takes a very fair and balanced approach in presenting that news." The managing editor of the same paper agreed on the rating of *outstanding*, and said, "We provide an objective, broad and complete [view] both on national–international and local issues."

Another daily newspaper desk editor, 48 years old, at a mid-size paper in the Midwest said his newsroom was outstanding:

> Because we concentrate on the issues—environment, police and fire protection, and government's handling of money—that most directly affect our readers' lives, and we try to tell it straight-up without allowing anyone to embellish it from either side.

Speed and immediacy was a factor in effective newsroom performance for another 7% of the journalists, especially for those working at wire services (46%). Radio (9%) and television (6%) journalists also sometimes mentioned this factor. However, few newspaper and no magazine journalists focused on immediacy in their responses about newsroom quality.

The dimension of comprehensiveness, discussed earlier, was closely tied to speed and immediacy for wire service personnel. For example, a 34-year-old wire service writer linked comprehensiveness, accuracy, and staff quality to a strong sense of immediacy in assessing his agency's performance:

> It is on the front lines everywhere. It is connected everywhere—every corner of the country, world. If it [an event] has any impact, it may be immediately covered. [The agency] blankets and can inform people quickly and very accurately. By and large, it has very good reporters and editors.

A young, female wire service reporter said: "We are very quick in getting the news out, and we have very good editors who can spot holes in stories and make sure those holes are patched."

Based in a large midwestern bureau, a wire service reporter said it was his operation's "range of coverage [and] speed in getting it out" that was outstanding.

Radio journalists often mentioned immediacy, particularly in connection with their coverage of traffic and weather conditions. For example, a young journalist in a one-person operation in the Midwest said:

> Our severe weather coverage in the state . . . [is] outstanding and immediate. We fill a vacuum . . . in that area. . . . Management feels it is not quite as important to break news that is not as immediate and life threatening. In that regard, we fall behind the competition, but I believe the two situations do balance themselves out.

Another radio journalist in the South, a 23-year-old man in a one-person operation, thought he did an outstanding job. He said his station was able to "inform the public quicker and more thoroughly" than the local weekly newspaper. A 32-year-old television journalist in a mid-size southern newsroom rated it as *outstanding* because: "As news happens we do go live. We get the best news coverage available and warn the public of any danger." In the Northeast, a young woman who was news director at a small television station saw her newsroom as doing outstanding work, saying: "We have a larger staff than the other stations, therefore we can cover more news faster and bring it to the viewers quicker."

Another theme was *aggressiveness in challenging institutions and officials*, but it was mentioned by only a small minority of journalists. About 7% of our sample—mostly newspaper or TV journalists—pointed to aggressiveness, although their comments sometimes were in the context of coverage comprehensiveness.

A 46-year-old managing editor at a large daily newspaper in the Midwest said her newsroom did an outstanding job because:

> . . . We are watching everything: the elections, who's running. We let people participate in forums. We're constantly skeptical about politicians and public officials, and questioning and probing. We've broken a lot of stories and angles a lot of other media have missed . . . [and] we have an audiotext system . . . that people can call up and get updates [on the news].

A 35-year-old writer at a large Western daily said the reason the newspaper was very good at informing the public was:

> Aggressive, deep coverage of government and business. The paper is willing to look at a number of unusual issues of the community and state in depth. [We do] a good job of covering breaking news [but the paper] especially excels in developing stories [and is] willing to challenge the powerful institutions in government and business.

At a large daily newspaper in the Northeast, a 42-year-old writer praised his newsroom for being "skeptical, hard-hitting and aggressive in covering racial issues," but he felt the paper "diminishes the impact of its work" by not doing enough follow-up stories.

On the West Coast, the editor of a small weekly portrayed a classic view of journalism in describing her newspaper as *outstanding*:

> We are touching all the bases that I think we should be touching and getting related information about what is happening in our community. I think we are also challenging a lot of the institutions in our county and our state, and encouraging our readers to do so as well.

Another weekly newspaper editor, a 36-year-old in the Midwest, said: "We are pretty complete, [as we] cover all the traditional bases, talk to ordinary folk. We manage to get more than just the official line [and are] not afraid of controversy, stepping on toes."

Some television journalists also mentioned the aggressiveness of their news operations, but the tone was milder than that of their newspaper colleagues. A young producer at a mid-size southern station said: "We're aggressive. We stay on top of matters. We try to get to the bottom of everything, tirelessly." Another TV journalist, 28 years old, at a small western station said his newsroom did a very good job because: "We . . . are aggressive and community minded, and we have a reputation for delivering fair and honest news. . . . We break half the stories in the market." A 34-year-old news magazine subeditor added a slightly different twist to the idea of aggressiveness, saying his organization excelled by: "Taking a contrary view to publicly accepted wisdom, being extremely skeptical, and covering the news as exhaustively as possible."

About 5% of those who were favorable about their newsroom's performance pointed to awards, ratings, and readership as confirming their judgment. A few (about 3%) pointed to the leadership of newsroom management as directly responsible for the high quality of their media performance.

Reasons for Fair to Poor Ratings

Journalists who rated their newsrooms as *fair* or *poor*, a small minority, cited three main reasons: insufficient resources, not enough in-depth reporting on important issues, and news staffs that were professionally inadequate (see Fig. 3.7).

Almost half of the journalists in our study who were critical of their newsroom said the reason was *insufficient resources, staff, and news space* (47%). Broadcast journalists were more likely than their print colleagues to say their newsroom suffered from inadequate resources.

Radio journalists who gave their stations poor grades almost all said inadequate budgets and resources were devoted to news at their stations. For example, a young radio journalist at a one-person news staff in the South said, "The corporation does not want to spend any money to [get news] done." In the Northeast, a veteran reporter at a large radio station said his four-person staff—much larger

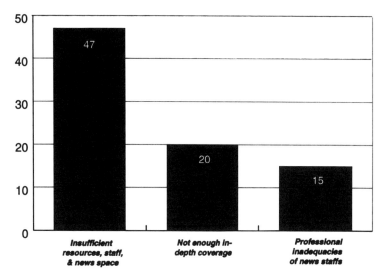

FIG. 3.7. Reasons given by journalists explaining why their newsrooms are judged to be doing a poor job (%).

than the typical radio operation—did not have "enough journalistic resources" and "the newscasts are too short."

Although still retaining his title as "news director," a 39-year-old southern journalist at a one-person radio staff described the demise of news at his station:

> . . . The emphasis has kind of turned away from local areas and gone to satellite music service, which takes up most of the [broadcast] time. . . . The amount of local news and local sports has been scaled back. . . . We do give the local mayor a half hour every couple of weeks. . . . We used to do public-affairs shows every week and those have been scaled back.

Television journalists also cited problems with inadequate support for their news staff. A young reporter at a large southern station said his newsroom only did a fair job: ". . . Because there are so many issues that go untouched, so much that goes unsaid, so little time to say it and so few resources to gather information."

Weekly journalists who gave their newspapers poor marks also frequently mentioned resources. The editor at a weekly in the West said, "We don't have the resources to be better [than fair]." At a small weekly in the Northeast, a journalist in his 40s said: "We don't have enough staff to cover all the things we should be covering and also the newshole space."

Journalists at daily newspapers were somewhat less likely than their broadcast and weekly newspaper colleagues to cite inadequate resources as a reason for poor newsroom performance. When they did, the feeling was sometimes bitter. At a large southern newspaper, a middle-aged writer said his paper did a poor job:

Because ... [of] the financial demands of [the corporation] our resources have dwindled year by year. We're now understaffed and we have a smaller newshole. We are an extremely profitable newspaper but [the corporation] sucks that out of us. ... More money goes to the corporation than goes back into our product.

At a large daily newspaper in the South, a 34-year-old reporter was less critical, but said: "We spend too much time and energy doing the wrong things. We're not focused on what's important. We try to do too much with too little staff."

About 20% of the journalists who rated their newsroom as *poor* or *fair* pointed to *not enough in-depth coverage*. Daily newspaper journalists who were critical were more apt to couch their reasons in these terms than were journalists for other media. For example, a 39-year-old writer working at a large southern paper said: "[Our] coverage is lacking in a number of areas. In-depth coverage is lacking, [and our] coverage area is too limited." A 36-year-old desk editor at a small daily in the South said: "I think that there are probably a lot of issues particular to this community that really don't get played up or get the proper emphasis. And, also, our ... staff is fairly lazy at looking at the big picture [of] ... things that affect this community."

At a wire service bureau, a 36-year-old reporter was critical of the agency's premium on immediacy, a quality many of his colleagues seemed to value: "[We] ... do a good job of breaking news, but ... a poor job of putting that news into perspective for readers. And, because [the agency] has a large international role in news, it has a leadership role that it doesn't live up to." A young producer at a small northeastern television station also focused on immediacy as a problem that explained why his newsroom was rated *fair*: "Because we don't cover enough news. Instead of reporting on what affects people on a day-to-day basis, we cover accidents, fires and staged press conferences."

Professional inadequacies of news staffs were most salient to about 15% of those who were critical of their newsroom's performance. A 35-year-old desk editor of a large daily newspaper in the West said, "I don't think their [reporters'] news judgment is very good." Another desk editor at a mid-size northeastern daily said: "I just think that there's not enough initiative taken either by management or the reporting staff to find out what is going on. I think there is a tendency to be lazy about journalism." A young reporter at a large southern daily newspaper said his newsroom's poor performance was because of: "Poor leadership [and] lack of focus. [We] lack agreement on what news is—of understanding what news is, not to mention understaffing."

At a large southern paper, a 37-year-old desk editor also pointed to news values as a problem: "[We] ... tend to overlook the common man a lot ... and concentrate on stories that appeal to the wealthy people of high standing." A 33-year-old female photographer at a weekly in the Midwest was critical because: "The newspaper caters too much to personal interest and what the owner perceives [to be of] importance. Too little attention is paid to objective reporting ... and to journalistic standards."

In the South, a young journalist at a large television newsroom said of his colleagues: "They are not as aggressive or as committed as they should be." At another large television operation in the South, a young journalist was critical: "I think because we are understaffed, because our leadership has eroded, and because our producers are too young. They are also inexperienced." A 35-year-old radio reporter at a three-person staff in the South gave a different perspective on professional autonomy in saying why his station only did a fair job of informing the public: "The freedom afforded the news department . . . allows for a lot of potential information to slip through the cracks. That is the drawback in that there are always some individuals who will not take the responsibility seriously." Small groups of journalists mentioned several other reasons for poor performance, ranging from problems with management to being overly concerned about ratings and readership.

The previous portrait of newsroom performance suggests that the most common threads of quality, in the eyes of journalists, were woven around comprehensive coverage, highly motivated staff who are acutely attuned to the needs of their audience, and a sense that there is opportunity to supplement timely information with analytic depth. Of course, that is not surprising. Looking more deeply, however, it is evident that those journalists who gave their newsroom the highest marks were much more likely to focus strongly on the thoroughness and comprehensiveness of news coverage. In addition, they were more likely to credit the leadership of their editors than those who rated their newsroom as *good* or *very good*. They sensed that their newsroom had an impact—that they went beyond comprehensiveness and analysis to make a difference in the lives of their audiences.

Unfortunately, as was seen earlier, the number of journalists rating their newsroom as *outstanding* declined between 1982–1992, suggesting that some of the quality in newsrooms also may have diminished.

Our analysis of the comments of those who did not think much of their newsroom's performance finds a lot of finger-pointing—at what journalists thought were inadequate resources being given to news. The group holding such negative views was not large, but their bitterness was evident. Their criticisms resonate with some of the explanations given by journalists about constraints on job autonomy.

JOB PERCEPTIONS: REWARDS AND SATISFACTIONS

Few could have predicted that the late 1960s and early 1970s would be such a heyday of American journalism, not only in the clout reporters had in their newsrooms and their communities, but in their salaries as well. At a median annual salary of $11,113, the buying power of journalists was greater than perhaps it will ever be again. The down side was the significant disparity in salaries paid to women in the field—about $4,000 less than their male colleagues.

The late 1970s brought a boom in employment, with the workforce growing rapidly. However, inflation took a great toll on the increasingly young press corps working in mainstream news media. In our 1982–1983 study, conducted at a time of considerable economic recession, a median salary of $19,000 (for the previous year, 1981) had the best-educated workforce in the history of the American press reading articles in trade publications about journalists surviving on peanut butter. The salary picture for 1991, from a survey done again in the midst a serious economic recession, was slightly better.

Annual Income of Journalists

The median income of full-time journalists increased from $19,000 in 1981 to $31,297 in 1991. The decline in the rate of inflation between 1981–1991 enabled the increase to exceed the rise in the Consumer Price Index (see Fig. 3.8). Still, the progress in salaries did not restore journalists' relative buying power to the level of the late 1960s. Using the Consumer Price Index as a base of constant dollars, the median journalist had about $4,000 less in purchasing power in 1991 than did one making a median salary of only $11,133 21 years earlier (see Fig. 3.9).

Not all journalists fared the same on salaries, of course, because there were considerable disparities among the various media. News magazine personnel had the most substantial median salary increases from 1981 to 1991, with a 90% increment bringing them to $66,071. Highly concentrated in urban areas with high costs of living, the real gains, no doubt, were substantially less. Daily newspaper journalists saw their salaries increase by 68% to a median of $35,180.[40] Broadcast personnel and weekly newspaper journalists realized much smaller gains in salary than those in other media (see Fig. 3.10).[41]

Geographic differences in salary were considerable. Journalists in the West leaped over their colleagues in the recession-battered Northeast to become the

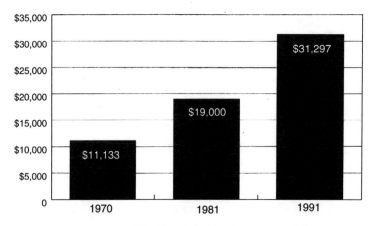

FIG. 3.8. Median income.

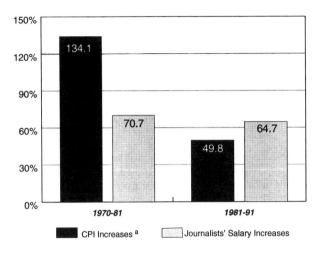

FIG. 3.9. Inflation vs. median salary increases.

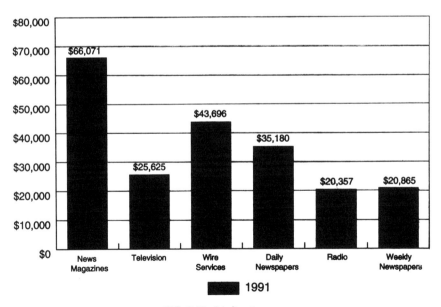

FIG. 3.10. Median income.

highest paid of the four large regions, at a median of $39,306. The South and North Central regions made greater overall gains than did the Northeast. However, these aggregate differences were deceptive. When statistically controlled for other factors, such as organization size and the media mix within the regions, the salary differences were quite small (see Table 3.10).

As in 1981, journalists 55 and older, with a 1991 median salary of $40,333, made gains over their younger colleagues. For the first time in 20 years, the seniors were the most highly paid age group. As of 1992, this age group was the target of "buy-out" programs at large media attempting to deal with a long

TABLE 3.10
Median Income in 1970, 1981, and 1991 by
Media Sector, Region, and Size of News Organization

	Median Income		
Factors	1970 (N = 1,328)	1981 (N = 939)	1991 (N = 1,115)
Media Sector			
News magazines	$15,571	$34,750	$66,071
Television[a]	11,875	17,031	25,625
Wire services	11,833	24,100	43,696
Daily newspapers	11,420	21,000	35,180
Radio[a]	9,583	15,000	20,357
Weekly newspapers	8,786	14,000	20,865
Region			
New England	11,274	30,000	33,461
Middle Atlantic	11,622	24,000	40,417
Total Northeast	11,532	27,000	36,136
East North Central	11,702	18,000	24,500
West North Central	9,600	15,933	30,147
Total North Central	11,187	16,999	26,964
South Atlantic	11,484	19,100	31,500
East South Central	7,846	16,033	28,370
West South Central	8,920	14,000	26,000
Total South	10,005	17,550	29,542
Mountain	9,118	15,933	35,833
Pacific	13,573	22,050	40,543
Total West	11,661	18,975	39,306
Size of News Organization			
1–10 editorial employees	8,632	15,000	20,319
11–25 editorial employees	9,866	15,985	24,342
26–50 editorial employees	11,657	21,000	28,167
51–100 editorial employees	10,892	23,960	32,574
Over 100 editorial employees	13,550	30,025	42,799

[a]Vernon A. Stone's survey of 1991 broadcast salaries reported these medians: Television—news directors = $45,000; executive producers = $34,000; producers = $21,000; reporters = $20,000; camera persons = $17,800. Radio—news directors = $17,810; reporters = $13,620. See "News Salaries Stand Still," Communicator (February 1992), pp. 14–15.

TABLE 3.11
Median Income in 1970, 1981, and 1991
by Gender, Age, and Years of Schooling

Factors	Median Income		
	1970 (N = 1,328)	1981 (N = 939)	1991 (N = 1,115)
Gender			
Male	$11,955	$21,000	$34,167
Female	7,702	14,984	27,669
Age			
Under 25	6,492	10,991	<15,000[a]
25–34	10,031	17,012	25,100
35–44	13,322	22,999	38,100
45–54	12,847	27,000	39,375
55 and older	12,000	22,000	40,333
Years of school			
High school graduate or less	10,992	16,000	27,857
Some college	10,164	18,022	28,750
Graduated from college	11,617	17,999	29,717
Some graduate training	11,424	21,000	36,667
Graduate degree	12,823	25,012	39,333

[a]Because the lowest salary category for 1991 was less than $15,000, an estimate of the median income could not be calculated.

recession in advertising revenues. Hence, the prospects for retaining the gains made by seniors are bleak (see Table 3.11).

One of the most significant findings concerning salaries in 1991 was the increasing parity of male and female journalists' income. Overall median salaries for women in 1991 were 81% of those for men, and the gender disparity nearly disappeared when years of experience in journalism was considered (see Fig. 3.11). Furthermore, when a variety of predictors of income were held constant (e.g., professional age, type of medium, and size of news organization), women journalists appeared to be even closer to parity with males on salaries, with less than 1% of the variation on salary being explained by gender (see Fig. 3.12).

Predictors of Income

Journalism is a field in which a few stars, such as network news anchors, make athlete-size salaries quite disproportionate to the modest earnings of most others. The factors that determine salary, though, are varied and complex. It is helpful to put them into a statistical "pot" to attempt to see their relative importance. For example, we already suggested that, in 1992, the geographic region of the country seemed to be an important factor in salary differences when, in reality, it was not. What, then, were the real predictors of who made the most money in journalism in 1991?

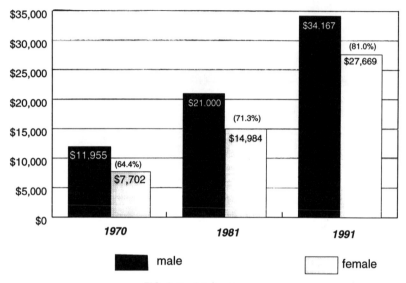

FIG. 3.11. Median income.

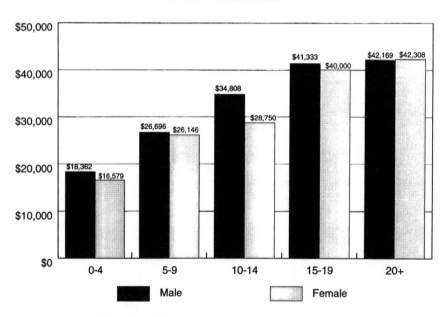

FIG. 3.12. 1991 median incomes by years in journalism.

For the most part, the answers are easy. Years of professional experience and the size of the employing organization were the strongest factors in 1991, as they were in 1971 (see Table 3.12). Working for a news magazine, as suggested earlier, and being a manager also meant higher salaries.

Beyond those somewhat obvious factors is a short list of weak, but significant, predictors of higher salaries. Working for a publicly traded corporation gave a slight edge. Being a member of a professional journalism group, such

TABLE 3.12
Predictors of Income Level of Journalists

Predictors	Standardized Regression Coefficients		Simple r	
	1982–1983 ($R^2 = .54$)	1992 ($R^2 = .55$)	1982–1983	1992
Professional age (number of years in news media)	.41	.37***	.49	.45
Media sector				
Weekly newspapers	−.01	−.28***	−.19	−.24
Daily newspapers	−.002	−.24***	.03	.03
Radio	.07	−.19***	−.11	−.20
News magazines	.27	.12***	.35	.31
Television	.15	−.13***	.02	−.11
Size of organization	.27	.26***	.43	.45
Managerial responsibilities	.15	.15***	.18	.17
Race				
Native American	—[a]	−.13**	—[a]	−.10
Asian American		−.05		.14
White		.02		−.11
African American		−.02		.04
Hispanic		−.01		.11
Publicly traded organization		.08***		.28
Member of journalistic association		.07***		.17
Gender (female)	−.10	−.07***	−.25	−.09
Editorial staff unionized	.14	.05*	.35	.21
Region				
Midwest	−.14	−.06*	−.14	−.17
Northeast	−.06	.05	.26	.20
South	−.03	−.03	−.08	−.12
Education level	.13	.05*	.17	.14
Group-owned medium	−.01	.00	−.003	.09
Age	−.02	.02	.37	.36
Majored in journalism	−.02	−.02	−.10	.01
Attended private school	—[a]	.00	—[a]	.13
Attended Ivy League school		.03		.13

[a]These predictors were not included in the 1982–1983 analysis.
*$p < .05$. **$p < .01$. ***$p < .001$.

as the Society of Professional Journalists, was slightly predictive of a larger salary.

More interesting are the factors that did not predict 1991 salaries. Chief among them was being in a craft union, such as The Newspaper Guild. In 1982, union membership was somewhat predictive of more money, but in 1992 the relationship was weaker. This likely reflected the general decline in the power of the labor movement in America because the number of journalists who belonged to a union in 1992 was 17%—the same figure as a decade previous.

A similar decline was seen in the power of education to affect salaries. Part of the explanation was the relative homogeneity of educational levels in the field—the B.A. degree predominated. However, even when other factors (e.g., attendance at elite, Ivy League institutions) were considered, education was only a marginal factor in earnings.

Another significant finding was on ethnicity and salaries. Except for Native Americans, whose salaries appeared lower, race had little impact on earnings. Asian Americans, African Americans, and Hispanics were slightly more likely to have lower earnings, but the impact of race was very, very small. Minority journalists, while still too few in number, appeared to have achieved some degree of equity on income. Most of the Native Americans in our 1992 study worked for media that were quite different from the mainstream news organizations making up the larger sample, so the finding of a salary discrepancy for them is problematic. (A more thorough discussion of minority journalists is contained in chap. 6, this volume.)

In 1971, Johnstone concluded that journalists' income was roughly equivalent to similar occupations. That certainly was not the case in 1982–1983, nor in the latest study. The 1991 median salary of $31,297 for full-time journalists was well below the income of comparably educated accountants, for example. In 1990, the average salary for nonsupervisory management accountants was $37,000. Internal auditors made $36,800. Insurance agents and brokers earned an average of $32,340 in 1991.[42] Technical writers and editors working for the federal government in 1991 earned a median salary of $36,897.[43] Attorneys with a median salary of $66,784 in 1991 earned a great deal more than journalists.[44]

In the field of public relations, the median salary for 1991 was $46,556—a figure that includes executive vice presidents of firms, as well as lower level creative personnel. However, even public relations account executives for corporate PR departments, at a median of $35,724, earned more than the typical journalist. Those working at public relations firms made somewhat less, at $28,132.[45]

It seems clear, then, that journalists' income during the inflationary years of the 1970s lagged more than did salaries in other comparable occupations. John Morton, well-known analyst of the industry, said, "No one in the history of newspapering has ever expected editorial people to act in their own economic best interest."[46] That may be changing.

JOB SATISFACTION

Modern notions about the importance of being satisfied with one's job would appear laughable to earlier generations of journalists. Many of them were driven to news work by forces almost beyond their control, with the intrinsic challenges of the field outweighing personnel practices that would seem cruel and unusual today.

Russell Baker, one of the craft's few remaining elders from the early Cold War period, remembered his early days at the Baltimore *Sun* of the 1950s as filled with a "loathing" for the executive editor and an "obsession" with money. "Yet," he said, "if we were sullen toward the company because of shabby pay, it also made us work better." Hard work could get a reporter a better job on a "more generous" newspaper. Some, however, took an easier route, Baker recalled in *The Good Times*: "The skimpy pay, even for the stars of the local staff, left reporters vulnerable to financial seduction by the politicians they covered." For Baker, however, a career in journalism in the 1950s was a romance as real as the smell of ink, the clack of manual typewriters, and the cries of "copy!"[47] The same was true for James Reston, whose recent book *Deadline* is an unabashed "memoir of love" about the journalism of an earlier era.[48]

Empirical Estimates of Job Satisfaction

In the first profession-wide study of job satisfaction among journalists in 1971, the Johnstone team of researchers concluded that news people were happier with their jobs than was the nation's labor force at large. By the early 1980s, the post-Watergate press corps had a youthful median age of 32 years, compared with 36 in the previous decade, and an outlook that seemed to mark the beginning of the end of a romantic view of the craft. Their feelings of job satisfaction were somewhat less sanguine than their elders. A decade later, in 1992, the trend was clear (see Fig. 3.13).

When asked a standard question (All things considered, how satisfied are you with your present job?), only 27% in 1992 said they were very satisfied. Although a majority in 1992 were at least fairly satisfied, the overall decline of job happiness was considerable (see Table 3.13).

Among the various media, journalists working for the wire services and weekly newspapers appeared to have had the highest rate of job satisfaction—36% of wire service and 34% of weekly journalists said they were very satisfied. Television journalists appeared to be least happy, with only 19% saying they were very satisfied.

Other Occupational Groups

The profile on journalists' job sentiments was somewhat less favorable than the picture of attitudes for other groups. For example, a national sample of 1,372 adult workers, conducted by the National Opinion Research Center in 1991, found 44%

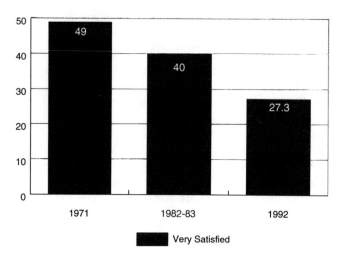

FIG. 3.13. Job satisfaction.

of them very satisfied with their work.[49] A Harris Poll studied a national sample of 1,000 American office workers in 1991, finding 43% of them very satisfied with their jobs.[50] Other surveys of the general workforce confirmed that general job satisfaction among the national workforce in 1992 remained high, although, not surprisingly, there was growing concern that pay and benefits were lagging.[51]

A national study of university professors conducted in 1988 found that 35% of them said they were very satisfied with their jobs—significantly more than in journalism.[52] Hence, the trend toward less favorable job sentiments among journalists was not simply a reflection of a larger disaffection among the general or professional workforce of the nation.

Journalists' Ranking of Job Factors

Social psychologists of work agree that the elements of job satisfaction are numerous, complex, and difficult to measure.[53] In an attempt to dig deeper, our survey asked journalists to rate the importance of several common factors (such as pay and autonomy) in their work.

TABLE 3.13
Job Satisfaction

Rating	1971 (N = 1,328) (%)	1982–1983 (N = 1,001) (%)	1992 (N = 1,156) (%)
Very satisfied	49	40	27
Fairly satisfied	39	44	50
Somewhat dissatisfied	12	15	20
Very dissatisfied	1	2	3

In rating pertinences to job satisfaction, a shift occurred during 1982–1992 (see Table 3.14). The editorial policies of their organization in 1992 were considerably more likely to be ranked by journalists as *very important*, with 69% saying that, compared with 57% in 1982–1983. This finding is consistent with the concerns journalists expressed when discussing the impact of tightened news policies on their autonomy.

Job security was also cited as important by more journalists, with 61% rating it as *very important*. The importance of fringe benefits also rose, but still only a minority of 35% said benefits were very important. The importance of a chance for advancement dropped as a factor in 1992—at a time when the reality was that opportunity for promotion was significantly less than it was a decade previous (see Table 3.15).

Substantial media differences emerged in 1992. Job security appeared to be the number one concern among daily newspaper, wire service, and radio journalists. These were obvious reflections of highly publicized employee layoffs and buy outs, as well as the continuing uncertainty of the survival of one of the major wire services (United Press International [UPI]). Job security was much less a worry among news magazine journalists, who tended to be more concerned about editorial policies and their autonomy on the job.

Pay was still at the bottom of most journalists' lists of explicit contributions to job happiness. That is, few journalists appeared willing to say salary was as important as other job aspects, even though other evidence (to be discussed later) contradicts them. Wire service and broadcast personnel, however, were somewhat more vocal about the importance of money than were their colleagues in other media sectors.

Having clout in public affairs—specifically, "the chance to influence public affairs," a new item in the most recent survey—was not something that most journalists said was an important reward on the job. This belies a growing view that news people enjoy throwing their weight around. In contrast, "the chance to help people" was one of the most important rewards—a consistent finding for three decades. As discussed later, when journalists were asked to explain

TABLE 3.14
Factors of Job Satisfaction, Percentage Saying *Very Important*

Factor	1982–1983 (N = 1,001)	1992 (N = 1,156)
Helping people	61	61
Job security	57	61
Editorial policy	57	69
Autonomy	50	51
Chance to advance	47	39
Developing a specialty	45	40
Fringe benefits	26	35
Pay	23	21

TABLE 3.15

Importance Journalists Assigned to Different Job Aspects, by Media Sector, with a Comparison Across Time of Total Sample Results

Job Aspects	Dailies (N = 627)	Weeklies (N = 155)	News Magazines (N = 59)	Wires (N = 56)	Radio (N = 99)	TV (N = 135)	1992 Total Sample (N = 1,131)	1982–1983 Total Sample (N = 996)	1971 Total Sample (N = 1,313)
Editorial policy	1.58[a]	1.66	1.90	1.66	1.54	1.57	1.60	1.40	—[b]
Job security	1.70	1.53	1.10	1.71	1.70	1.53	1.56	1.47	1.34
Importance of helping people	1.53	1.63	1.40	1.16	1.73	1.64	1.55	1.53	1.59
Autonomy	1.48	1.48	1.70	1.22	1.48	1.27	1.45	1.44	1.48
Fringe benefits	1.28	1.06	1.03	1.36	1.28	1.19	1.23	1.05	.97
Developing a specialty	1.26	1.14	1.08	1.23	1.06	1.30	1.22	1.28	—[b]
Chance to get ahead	1.15	1.17	1.13	1.24	1.39	1.46	1.21	1.32	—[b]
Chance to influence public affairs	1.17	1.23	1.33	.84	1.27	1.08	1.17	—[c]	—[c]
Pay	1.11	.88	1.03	1.32	1.14	1.20	1.10	1.07	1.06

[a]2 = very important; 1 = fairly important; 0 = not too important; mean scores for all respondents are reported in the table.

[b]Not reported in John Johnstone, Edward Slawski, and William Bowman, The News People (Urbana: University of Illinois Press, 1976), p. 229.

[c]Not reported in Johnstone et al. or in Weaver and Wilhoit, The American Journalist.

their answers to the closed-ended question on job satisfaction, the sense of having an impact on their audiences was a theme expressed often, but not in terms of having a direct effect on public policy.

NARRATIVES ABOUT JOB ATTITUDES

After responding to the structured questions about job satisfaction, journalists were invited to explain their answers in their own words. Specifically, they were asked: What are the most important reasons you say you are [very or fairly satisfied; somewhat or very dissatisfied] with your present job?

Specialists on job perceptions suggest that the reasons for positive and negative feelings about jobs may be quite different.[54] The journalists' responses to our open-ended questions reflected that difference—their reasons for job happiness were much more varied, and in quite a different order, than those for job dissatisfaction.

Satisfied Journalists' Reasons

Sources of satisfaction with journalism covered many different aspects, ranging from autonomy to having an impact on the community. The narratives given by journalists in our interviews usually had several factors tightly interwoven in them (see Fig. 3.14). Among those who liked their work, one fourth said *autonomy* was important. Journalists for all media, except television (12%), were about equally likely to mention it if they were satisfied with their work. Weekly journalists (36%) were the most likely to cite autonomy.

For example, a writer-reporter at a small-town weekly reflected on two frequently cited attributes, saying, "I have a lot of freedom to . . . 'cherry pick,' and I am very happy with . . . the people I work with." Another weekly journalist said: "I like the independence I have and the variety of activities I'm involved in. I like the feeling of having an influence in the community." A journalist at a large metropolitan paper combined several factors in what sounded like a "dream" job:

> I have an enormous amount of flexibility. Not only am I able to generate my own story ideas, but I regularly am assigned . . . pertinent or simply "fun" stories. I'm able to do a story that doesn't fall into my beats if I can show the editor that it's worth doing. I'm incredibly pleased with the editorial content of the paper and the way . . . it reflects the diversity of the city. . . . The salary is [also] great. . . .

An intrinsic *interest* or *challenge* of their jobs was mentioned by one fifth of the journalists who had positive feelings about their work. Television journalists (26%) were most likely to cite intrinsic interest or challenge, but their colleagues in radio (13%) were least likely to cite them. A daily newspaper reporter said, "It [the job] gives me the opportunity to write on issues I think are important.

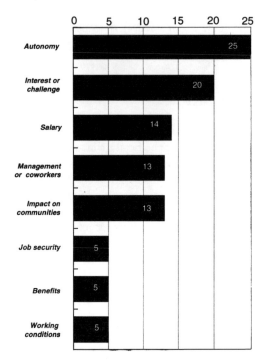

FIG. 3.14. Reasons journalists are "satisfied" with their jobs (% in each category).

..." A writer for another daily newspaper said: "I'm doing what I wanted to do 12 years ago when I got out of college. I'm getting to write sports, meet people, and inform people."

Fourteen percent of all journalists who liked their work mentioned their *salaries* as a factor, with news magazine personnel (29%) being most likely and weekly journalists (8%) least likely to praise their salaries. A reporter for a large, corporate-owned newspaper said: "I like the people I work with a lot and I like the chance to do different things . . . everyday. [The corporation] is a good organization to work for, the expectations are very high, the pay is good . . . more than I expected to be paid at a newspaper."

Management or *coworkers* were each mentioned positively by about 13% of the satisfied journalists. TV journalists (20%) were more likely to mention liking their colleagues than were journalists for other media. In fact, having excellent colleagues was the most frequent reason given by TV journalists who liked their job. A television reporter for a large station reflected the importance of colleagues, as well as autonomy: "I get to choose much of what I . . . do. [There's] . . . a lot of variety, the pay is good, great people to work with and a great place to work." A desk editor at a daily newspaper in a small state said: "[I am] challenged and have the ability to improve the news product and have the management supportive of me in the endeavor, . . . [making it] possible to directly inform [my state] of important matters." A television reporter said:

I have a good boss [who's] very understanding. And I think he's got a sense of what journalism is or should be. I believe now I cover the news the way it should be covered. Broadcast journalism in the last five years has become very soft. Coverage in most markets is now sensationalism or controversy.

Having an *impact on communities* or audiences was mentioned by about 13% of all those who liked their jobs, and was most likely to be cited by those in weekly newspapers (22%), as in this response by a weekly journalist from the Midwest:

We have received lots of recognition from our peers . . . [as] an award-winning paper [of] . . . regional, state and national awards mainly in community service. I think we are doing what a community paper should and that's pushing for change in the community, and being a leader in the community. We have been a watchdog of local government. . . .

Aspects of *job security, benefits,* or *working conditions* were each mentioned by about 5% of the journalists who were happy with their work. For example, a television sports director said, "I am at the top of what I can be, with job security and benefits." A reporter at a large daily newspaper added a different angle: "My husband works here too, and we have compatible schedules and days off. The pay is good and I understand my job responsibilities. And we have really good benefits."

Dissatisfied Journalists' Reasons

Disgruntled journalists spoke mainly about three problems: management policies, low salaries, and inadequate opportunity for advancement (see Fig. 3.15). Among journalists who were dissatisfied, half of them pointed to *management policies,* with only those on weekly newspapers (27%) being less likely to criticize their bosses. Television (56%) and daily newspaper journalists (55%) seemed most bitter at what they saw as the misplaced priorities of management.

A journalist at a small-market station said: "Management, the way things are in TV now, . . . really don't care about the worker as long as they make a profit. They buy TV stations, they come in and slash the budget to the bare bones, just to make a profit, and sell the station within three or four years." A reporter in a large television news department said, "Management style and corporate policy . . . [give] preference [to] putting profits before the public trust." Another cited a "cost-cutting" approach to news:

The motivation of the [television] company . . . is not necessarily to have a news organization as a public service: it's just to make money for them. Coinciding with the attitude of the owners, a certain apathy has developed in the news room. . . . When you cut corners, people get burnt out on not being able to do things right.

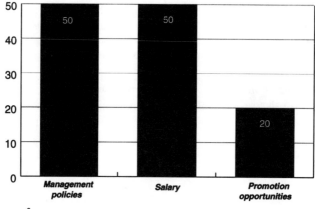

ᵃ Multiple responses are frequent and are accepted for this open-ended question

FIG. 3.15. Reasons journalists are "dissatisfied" with their jobs (% in each category).

Newspaper journalists sometimes portrayed their differences with management in terms of the pressures of "reader-driven" news values. For example, a reporter at a large daily said, "The repeated emphasis on color in story telling, in order to hang on to a shrinking readership, is daunting for someone whose real interest in life is reporting public affairs." Another said his newspaper "panders to the dumbest reader."

Some journalists pointed to other problems of management. An older journalist for a daily newspaper saw a subtle management policy affecting him:

> . . . I suspect that circumstances are being made less desirable in order to encourage older people to leave, and I think they [editors] would rather work with entry-level positions. . . . I don't feel that I've been valued nearly as much as when I was younger. My mental capacities aren't diminished any as far as I'm aware of, but I get the feeling I'm not considered worth spending time on.

A younger journalist at a medium-size newspaper offered another perspective: "I find that the newspaper and news room management here is insensitive and mean-spirited and confused by conflicting corporate goals." A television journalist combined several complaints:

> I don't think television is doing anyone a public service. Some events are altered for the shameless pursuit of ratings. . . . The owners of the station are interested in high profit . . . [so] they increase their margin . . . by giving it to their news department in the shin. Low salaries, no overtime, budget cuts. When the product comes off bad, it looks bad, and they don't give consideration in hiring new employees.

Nearly half of all the dissatisfied journalists complained about *salary*, with the heaviest concentration of comments among those on weekly newspapers (90%) and in radio news (57%). Television (36%) and daily newspaper (28%) personnel who were unhappy were not as likely to say salary was the problem, and salary was not a factor cited very often by either news magazine or wire service journalists.

Not surprisingly, complaints about salary tended to be terse and hardly literary. A weekly journalist was typical: "The pay stinks." Another young journalist at a weekly newspaper said: "The pay is very low, and it's not commensurate with my education or the hours I actually work . . . 50 to 60, so it's not really much incentive to work hard or work [such] long hours."

One fifth of the disgruntled journalists blamed lack of *promotion opportunities* for their feelings—a consistent factor for all media. A wire service reporter said, "[There's] not much chance of promotion in the near to medium term . . . [so] office politics tend to get out of hand." A radio journalist said: "Right now there is no opportunity to move up. When I came here seven years ago, there was room to move, but right now I feel like there's a roof over my head."

The snapshots of gratification in the work of journalists in 1992, then, were much more varied than were the sounds of the complaints. Clearly, those journalists who said they liked their work were apt to point to the intangible rewards of independence, collegiality, and accomplishment in their communities. In contrast, unhappy journalists focused on more concrete factors of salary, management, and promotion.

BACKGROUND PREDICTORS OF JOB SATISFACTION

Taking a step back to look at many of the individual journalists' responses simultaneously, we may see whether the statistical predictors of job satisfaction found in earlier research were still valid in 1992. Which circumstances of journalists were consistently predictive of job satisfaction over the last three decades? Did the ingredients of job satisfaction shift significantly in the new environment of corporate ascendance, long-term recession, and technological challenge?

Salary and Satisfaction

An intensive analysis of the possible relationships of a myriad of background factors to job satisfaction finds that, in 1992, annual income was a stronger predictor of job satisfaction for journalists in most media sectors than in previous decades. The exception to this was daily newspaper journalists, where factors other than salary—such as perceptions of how well the organization reported the news—appeared to be more important in job happiness.

For journalists who were 40 years and older in 1992, salary was the most important factor in job satisfaction. For younger journalists, too, salary was among the common denominators of job happiness—quite a different picture from their peers during the early 1980s, as the field was expanding rapidly and salaries were falling behind inflation (see Table 3.16).

Although salary's effect was modest—and was only one of several significant factors—the statistical finding essentially confirms the bitter comments about pay that were made by dissatisfied journalists. The comments about salary tended to be directed more toward the field generally than to the specific situations of the job holder. Although the statistical pattern did not include newspaper journalists, a senior newspaper reporter we interviewed captured the finding perfectly, saying the leading constraint on journalists was "probably the money," and adding, "it kicks out more from this profession than anything else . . . [and] causes people to leave . . . before they can do battle with the First Amendment."

Salary was a weak correlate of job satisfaction for journalists ages 40 and over in 1971, somewhat stronger in 1982, and even more highly relevant in 1992. In fact, in 1992, even for younger journalists, salary was a significant factor, although not as important as for their senior colleagues. Money, then, appeared to have become a worrisome subject for some in 1992, although a majority of

TABLE 3.16
Relative Strength of Several Predictors of Job Satisfaction
Among Journalists in Two Age Groups

Predictors	Standardized Regression Coefficients	Simple r
Journalists 40 or younger ($R^2 = .33$)		
Autonomy of story choice	.22***	.32
Getting ahead	−.09*	−.04
Pay important	−.14***	−.11
Gender (male)	−.09*	−.07
Rating of performance of the employing organization	.22***	.32
Supervisors' comments	.16***	.25
Audience's comments	.09*	.18
Helping people	.08*	.12
Salary	.18**	.13
Journalists older than 40 ($R^2 = .32$)		
Audience's comment	.17*	.21
Gender (male)	.12	.12
Short courses	−.14*	−.05
Helping people	.11	.12
Getting ahead	−.18**	−.06
Influencing public affairs	.15*	.12
Supervisors' comments	.16*	.18
Salary	.22*	.21

*$p < .05$. **$p < .01$. ***$p < .001$.

journalists still placed salary at the bottom of their list of hypothetical sources of job satisfaction. Journalists under age 40 who openly said that pay was important to them, a minority, were somewhat more likely to be among the dissatisfied group in our study. Those over 40, whose job satisfaction was more highly correlated with salary, were less likely to be explicit about the importance of income to their sense of job well-being than were their younger colleagues. Even younger journalists at news magazines, who were relatively well paid and happy in their work, sometimes linked dissatisfaction to salary. For example, one news magazine writer said, "The pay is much lower than in other fields that require the same level of expertise and education."

Many journalists, of course, saw salary as only one factor in a larger picture, as did this young reporter for a daily newspaper: "The newspaper industry has not kept up—at least this newspaper—in paying fairly or training news room professionals to grow. . . ."

Autonomy and Job Rewards

For younger journalists, those under age 40, a sense of control—the freedom to select the stories on which they worked—was important to job satisfaction. This was a consistent finding since the first national study in 1971. Another aspect of autonomy, getting an important story covered, was a factor for senior journalists in our 1982 study, but was not a predictor of their job satisfaction in the 1992 survey.

The importance of jurisdiction over their work was the most frequently cited factor among the comments made by journalists whose job satisfaction was high. For example, a reporter at a small daily newspaper who liked his work said: "I have a lot of autonomy. I dictate my own schedule, and I can write virtually anything I want. I assign myself. The editor is very receptive and strongly encourages new ideas."

A perception that autonomy was more limited in 1992 than in previous decades seemed to be a substantial factor in the decline of job satisfaction over the past two decades. Reflecting this, one young journalist at a large daily newspaper said that there was an "inability to act individually" that was so serious that even the assistant night editor had to "follow a chain of command" if a problem with a story arose. Another journalist for a daily newspaper said there was a disrespect for reporters: "[I'm] feeling like I waste a lot of my time on stories that aren't very important that I am told to cover."

Supervisors' Role

In the 1971 study, the Johnstone research team found that respect for an immediate supervisor was a substantial predictor of journalists' job satisfaction. Studies of other occupations have confirmed that the nature of supervisor–worker communication is critical to job satisfaction.[55] Our 1992 study looked at a more concrete aspect of supervision—the frequency with which journalists received comments from their editors. In the 1982 survey, as well as in the most recent study, frequent comments by supervisors enhanced the feeling of job satisfaction among their younger and older staff.

A young journalist at a large newspaper sensed the importance of feedback from the editor, saying, "Critically important in my satisfaction of my job is working with an excellent boss, and by that I mean sympathetic and also aggressive [in news]. . . ." A reporter at a mid-size daily said: "I do have a sense of autonomy. I have a boss who is fairly good about knowing when someone is overworked and watching out for them. [And] even though I am the low person on the 'totem pole,' . . . I do get to cover stuff fairly often."

Organizational Performance and Job Well-Being

A consistent finding between 1971–1992 was that younger journalists who thought their organization was doing a good job of informing its audience were more likely to have high job satisfaction. The same was true for journalists over 40 years as well, but esteem for the organization was not a significant factor for them in the 1992 study. The relationship was not as strong in 1992 as it was in 1982 and 1971 for the younger personnel, but the perceived success of the media outlet was still one of the most important predictors of job well-being for them. This was especially true for journalists on daily newspapers, where the job they saw the paper doing in news was the leading predictor of how satisfied they were.

The feeling that one's organization was on the "cutting edge" was an important factor in studies of the satisfaction of other professionals with their work, thus the finding for journalists was likely to be valid. A news magazine journalist's comments were exemplary: "Seeing how the news I write is immediately read and digested by our readers—whatever we publish definitely does have an effect—it forces one to take a certain pride in what you are doing." Another magazine journalist said:

> I am relatively secure, and [the job] is fairly interesting. I have a lot of good colleagues. I basically get along with my bosses, who are pretty smart. The working conditions are relatively good, and the organization I work for is respected by sources and by peers.

Other Factors of Job Satisfaction

The pertinence of economic values to job satisfaction in journalism was suggested indirectly in the finding, which first emerged in 1982, that younger journalists who placed a high priority on compensation had a tendency to be less satisfied. Also, those who placed high value on an altruistic role for the press tended to be happier with their jobs. Older male journalists were somewhat more likely to be happy with their jobs than were their female colleagues. Among younger journalists, it was the men who appeared to be slightly less satisfied with their work.

Changes Over Three Decades

The importance of autonomy on the job appears to have increased between 1971 and 1992 as an intrinsic factor of job satisfaction among younger journalists. Being part of a well-performing organization, and having a supervisor who regularly commented on their work, remained important elements of happiness for younger journalists. However, these factors were not as important for journalists who were over 40. Salary, influencing public affairs, and getting frequent comments from the audience seemed to matter more to older journalists' job satisfaction in 1992.

   These changes from 1971 to 1992 may have been related to an accommodation to the prevailing corporate culture of mass media. Unlike 1971, organization size—smaller meaning more happiness—in 1992 was no longer a predictor of job satisfaction. Ownership form—whether publicly traded corporation or privately owned independent—appeared to have had little to do with whether journalists liked their work.

COMMITMENT TO JOURNALISM

A substantial decline in relative job satisfaction among American journalists in 1992 was clear, but what does it say about the future of the profession? Jonathan Alter, a prominent news magazine writer whose beat is media and culture, saw journalists as "complainers by nature," and suggested the trend may not be of much significance.[56] Others have seen the growing disaffection as a vexing result of the ascendance of corporate culture and bad economic times. The Newspaper Guild's Linda Foley said news work has always been one of the few jobs where one could "make a difference," but that the "sense of mission" is disappearing.[57] Shelby Coffey, editor of the *Los Angeles Times*, said the attention given layoffs at his and other papers may have caused "a massive identity crisis." However, Coffey took a less foreboding view of its significance than some others in the field: "This can be a tense and exacting business, and there's no question that as you look across the field of journalism you would find individuals who at various points say, 'I want to do something else'."[58]

   In our early 1980s assessment, when a decline in job satisfaction was first noted, 11% of the respondents were planning to leave journalism—up from just 6% in 1971. In the 1992 study, the number of "defectors" was nearly double the figure of a decade previous. One fifth of the journalists in the 1992 national sample said they were planning to change careers (see Table 3.17).[59]

TABLE 3.17
Employment Aspirations of U.S. Journalists in 5 Years, by Age (Percentage in Each Grouping)

Age (years)	Employment Aspirations							
	Work in News Media		Work Outside News Media		Retire		Undecided	
	1982–1983	1992	1982–1983	1992	1982–1983	1992	1982–1983	1992
Under 25	80	76.6	10.4	21.3	—	—	9.6	2.1
25–29	84.8	73.6	11.2	23.6	—	—	4.0	2.7
30–34	81.4	74.9	10.2	22.7	—	—	8.4	2.4
35–39	87.9	74.9	7.6	21.1	—	—	4.5	3.6
40–44	84.2	70.7	13.2	25.9	—	—	2.6	3.4
45–49	91.9	83.8	6.5	15.2	—	—	1.6	1.0
50–54	85.1	79.2	10.6	13.2	—	5.7	4.3	1.9
55–59	71.2	65.2	11.5	23.9	7.7	10.9	9.6	—
60–64	75.0	43.3	—	6.7	25.0	46.7	—	—
65+	88.5	76.5	—	5.9	11.5	17.6	—	—
Total	82.6	73.8	10.6	21.0	1.7	2.3	5.1	2.9

It is important, then, to take a closer look at the characteristics of journalists who said they wanted to change careers. Furthermore, their reasons for defecting may shed some light on the professional "health" of the field.

Predictors of "Defection"

An intensive analysis of journalists who reported as a substantial part of their job reveals considerable change among those planning to leave the field. Among the defectors in 1982–1983, the more highly educated, altruistic, and experienced journalists—the "best and the brightest"—were present in disturbing numbers. That finding suggests a shift from the earlier decade. In the 1970s, job security and family-related matters had been more predictive of career plans than were professional attributes (see Table 3.18).

If there has been anything positive in the worrisome decline in career commitment among journalists, it has been that the threat of losing the "best and the brightest" appears to have subsided. In 1992, journalists with significant experience in the field were somewhat less likely to be among the defectors than were those at the beginning of their careers. Losing young talent may have posed long-term problems, but in 1992 there was a vast supply of new college graduates ready to assume their places in the field.

In 1992, educational background was no longer a predictor of leaving, and those who stressed professional values of public service were more likely to have career commitment. That was in contrast to the 1980s, when educational attainment, a sense of professionalism, and having significant journalism experience were warning signs of disaffection. In 1992, journalists who thought their organization was doing a good job of informing the public, those who placed higher value on job autonomy, and those who belonged to professional organizations were more likely to say they wanted to remain in the field than were their colleagues.

There was a tendency for women to be less likely than their male colleagues to want to stay in the field. This finding is statistically significant only for those who worked for newspapers, but women in the other media were also somewhat more likely than their male colleagues to say they wanted to change careers.

It was no surprise that, in 1992, job satisfaction and career plans were linked. What was a shock, however, was the increased salience of job satisfaction as a factor in defection in the 1990s. In previous decades, job complaints were more likely to be idle talk. In 1992, expressions of dissatisfaction were much more indicative of a real determination to change careers. This shift may have reflected the fact that fewer attractive opportunities were available inside the media field, or that fewer leave primarily to improve their salaries. Whatever the explanation, the "leavers" in 1992 were a larger and more unhappy group than they had been a decade previous.

TABLE 3.18

Comparison of the Importance of Various Factors That
Discriminate Between Reporters Who Planned to Change
Careers and Those Who Wished to Stay in Journalism[a]

Factor	1971[b]	1982–1983	1992
Education and background			
Education level	—	−.24	.09
Journalism major	—	.24	.10
Journalism minor	—	.31	−.07
Age	—	−.15	.25
Married	.33	−.14	−.17
Have children	.16	−.12	−.04
Gender (male)	—	—	.27
Organizational characteristics			
Print journalist	—	−.25	.07
Group owned	—	.30	−.04
Size of organization	−.16	.25	.04
Guild organization	−.15	−.03	.04
Peer feedback	—	.18	.08
News source feedback	—	.22	−.24
Years in journalism	—	−.24	.37*
Income	—	.14	.03*
Job sentiments			
Evaluation of organization	—	.04	.20*
Perceived autonomy	—	−.33	.11*
Job satisfaction	.36	.38	.73*
Professional factors			
Stress on professional values[c]	—	−.40	.18*
Stress on nonprofessional values[d]	.18	—	−.07
Stress information-disseminator role[e]	.11	.32	−.10
Membership in journalism organizations	.18	.21	.28*

[a]Discriminant analysis was used to determine the "power" of the various factors to discriminate between reporters who were "defectors" and "stayers." The coefficients are analogous to beta weights in regression analysis. A positive number means the factor is characteristic of "stayers." A negative number means the factor is associated with "defectors."

[b]Data for 1971 are from Lee B. Becker, Idowa A. Sobowale, and Robin E. Cobbey, "Reporters and Their Professional and Organizational Commitment," reprinted in G. Cleveland Wilhoit and Harold de Bock, eds., Mass Communication Review Yearbook, Vol. 2 (Beverly Hills, CA: Sage Publications, 1981), pp. 339–350.

[c]This variable is the sum of the respondents' rating of the importance of helping people, organization's editorial policies, and autonomy on the job. These are three of the four items used by Becker et al., p. 344. The fourth item, "freedom from supervision," was not included in the 1992 survey.

[d]This variable is the sum of the respondents' rating of the importance of pay, fringe benefits and job security, and the chance to get ahead. These are the same items used by Becker et al., p. 344.

[e]This variable is the sum of the two variables that loaded highly on the information-dissemination journalist role, as identified in the 1982–1983 study. These two variables are the respondents' rating of the importance of concentrating on news that is of interest to the widest possible audience and getting information to the public quickly. See David H. Weaver and G. Cleveland Wilhoit, The American Journalist (Bloomington: Indiana University Press, 1986), p. 115.

*$p < .05$.

Reasons for Leaving the Field

Journalists who said they planned to leave the field were asked why in 1992. One might have expected their open-ended answers to be similar to the portrait of job dissatisfaction discussed earlier, but there were substantial differences. When journalists were asked about general job dissatisfaction, the dominant complaint was about pay, with half of the disgruntled respondents mentioning it. Among those who actually decided to leave the field, however, salary was only one of five main reasons given, being cited by only 20% of the defectors (see Fig. 3.16).

Exasperation about pay was sometimes worded simply. For example, a magazine writer said, "[I am leaving] mainly because I don't think it pays very well." Sometimes, however, pay was linked to other complaints, such as long hours, cited by about 15% of the "leavers."

A young woman reporter at a small daily newspaper in the Midwest said, "[I'm leaving] because the hours are long and the pay is poor." However, newspaper journalists in 1992 were somewhat less likely than their colleagues in other media to mention pay—unlike a decade previous. When they did mention pay, it was frequently one of several factors. A reporter in her early 30s at a large

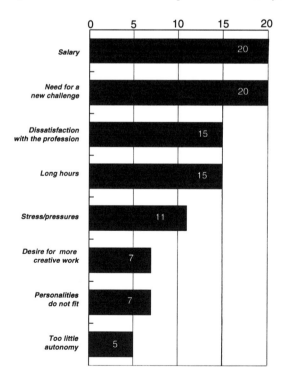

FIG. 3.16. Reasons for leaving the field (% in each category).

southern daily said: "First of all, [in another job] my hours wouldn't be as erratic or unpredictable. Secondly, the stress level would be somewhat reduced, and, the last thing would be pay, [but] it is not the most important reason."

A desk editor on a large paper in the West said, "I want to try and have a little more normal schedule and make a little more money." Another writer on a large daily in the West said he wanted more "independence and financial reward."

Journalists on weekly newspapers who wanted to change careers were more likely to focus on pay than were colleagues in other media. A 31-year-old woman at a small weekly newspaper in the South said:

> Poor pay is a big concern. I feel like it's become a young person's job because it's so time consuming. The older you get, you see you'd like to do other things, like living. Mainly salary, though; if I felt I was compensated for the work I do I wouldn't be as eager to leave.

Another journalist, 27, working at a small weekly in the Northeast said low pay was the main reason she was leaving, but that staff cutbacks had added more work to her position and that the community had become "hostile" to the paper. A young journalist at a television station in the Midwest said he could ". . . make more money outside the news business," adding:

> I would be more financially stable for future family plans. . . . I love photography and the news, but lately companies that own stations in smaller markets aren't giving [them] the money they need. They're not looking at news. They're looking at profits.

Other major factors cited by those who decided to leave the field ranged from the need for a new challenge to problems of stress. Expressions of a need for a new challenge, cited by 20%, tended to come from those who had significant experience. A writer on a large western newspaper, age 36, said: "I just think that after 10 years, you've done all you can do . . . and it's time to move on to something else. There's a limited scope in the work you can do as a daily reporter—not enough detail and scope in the writing." The managing editor of a small midwestern daily, a 46-year-old woman, said: "I feel like I've done every-thing. . . . I've discovered everything I can here and I need a new challenge." A 43-year-old news magazine writer said: "I have done it for 21 years and I am sick of it. Also, there is nothing left for me to do in formal journalism . . . as I don't want to become an editor. That's not interesting. I am a writer." A 39-year-old reporter on a weekly newspaper in the West said: "First, [I want] an opportunity to try a new challenge. Second, more money is available outside the journalistic profession—at least in this market."

Sometimes the need for a new challenge was linked to a general dissatisfaction with the profession, cited by 15% as a reason for leaving the field. For example, a TV journalist in a small northeastern newsroom, age 40, said: "It boils down to [the fact that] I am looking for some new challenges in my life and I am not particularly happy with the philosophical direction that the news media, in general, are taking."

Some TV news journalists who wanted to change careers suggested their general dissatisfaction with the profession was related to problems caused by budgetary retrenchment. A 28-year-old woman reporter on a mid-size TV station in the South said:

> Local TV is not what it was when I first began. Stations are not making the kind of money they once did . . . [and] not doing quality work, [and instead] are doing quantity. [They are] not covering stories in depth as we used to. Stations don't want to spend the money, so travel is limited . . . [and they are] going to less experienced personnel because they can hire them cheaper.

A woman photographer in her early 40s who worked for a large newspaper in the Northeast said: "I think the news media have been corrupted by the corporate system and bottom-line thinking. As a print journalist, I think that electronic journalism . . . is more invasive than we have traditionally done things. I don't like that." A desk editor on a large newspaper in the South said: "I have been in this business for 16 years, and I have become very disenchanted with what the media stand for and how the media are perceived by the public."

In the Northeast, a 44-year-old writer working for a daily newspaper was frustrated with the profession, saying, "I'm tired of the negative, [as] the news media have gone beyond where . . . [we are] supposed to." Some expressed a general pessimism about the field, as did a 42-year-old desk editor on a large southern daily newspaper: "Well, I think it is a dying profession." Another desk editor, a 41-year-old woman at a small daily in the Northeast, complained about the field's superficiality: ". . . I think the genre of journalistic writing is more limited than I feel satisfied with. I'd rather work with something that allows a little more depth." That comment also suggests another reason for leaving journalism; the need for more creative work, mentioned by about 7% of the "defectors." A 43-year-old writer at a mid-size newspaper in the Northeast said she wanted "more freedom creatively." An editor at a news magazine in the Northeast said she had become interested in book-length work, adding: "One of the appealing aspects of the medium of journalism is that you see your work very quickly, but your work seems so disposable. I want to make a more considered and permanent contribution."

The problem of job stress, or difficulties with deadline pressures, was seen as a primary reason for leaving the field by about 11% of the respondents. A 58-year-old journalist in the graphics department of a large daily newspaper in the West said: "The pressure of the work is constant. The fact that graphics are a major component of the page holds up the press work, and the deadline pressure is strong." However, this journalist added that he was also disillusioned by the news media's reflection of "secular humanism" that has "an almost anti-church effect. . . ."

At least eight other reasons for leaving were cited by small groups of journalists. About 7% felt their personalities did not fit journalism. About 5% wanted more autonomy on the job. A smattering felt blocked by limited promotion. Family difficulties, age, and health problems (repetitive stress injury, typically) were also cited.

In summary, the pattern of disgruntlement among those who planned to leave the field in 1992 was a much more tangled web than it was a decade previous. Salary, the dominant reason for leaving in 1982–1983, was only one of a half-dozen factors recounted for us by a majority of the defectors. Although salary still dominated the reasons journalists gave for being unhappy on the job in 1992, by the time they made a decision to leave, other factors had risen to the top in their minds. A need for a new challenge, general disillusionment with the field, and diminished autonomy tended to be as important in 1992 as salary was for a smaller pool of defectors a decade previous.

CONCLUSIONS

Significant decline in the perceived autonomy of journalists, as well as diminished overall job satisfaction, occurred between 1971 and 1992. These changes may have been unique to journalism. Other comparable occupational groups did not appear to reflect a similar erosion of job satisfaction. The causes of change are complex, of course, and cannot be determined fully with surveys. However, some suggestions are possible.

Changes in perceived autonomy were said by journalists to be largely a result of internal, organizational factors that had to do with declining resources. Those journalists in smaller, privately owned media—an endangered species—tended to see themselves as having greater clout in the newsroom than their colleagues in other media sectors. As an explanation, though, ownership type was far less important in 1992 than a host of diverse factors related to the general economic recession of the industry.

The diminished autonomy was a substantial factor in declining job satisfaction, especially for younger journalists. However, corporate ownership—the popular explanation for all change in journalistic behavior—was *not* a significant factor in the erosion of overall satisfaction. These changes occurred in the 1980s, during which time journalistic salaries recovered somewhat from the ravages of inflation and the gender gap in salary almost disappeared. Still, other comparable occupations were compensated notably better than were journalists.

But salaries apparently explained very little of the attitudinal change that occurred in the profession. The sources were much deeper. Journalists in 1992 appeared to want to lead normal lives. They were less willing to suffer the dislocation and unpredictable schedules that were accepted by an earlier generation, especially in a competitive environment in which newsrooms were expected to do much more with fewer resources, and where there was little hope of professional advancement in an era of stalled growth. As noted earlier, a serious decline in relative job satisfaction, then, was clear. But what does it say about the future of journalism? Our study found that more than 20% of those surveyed wanted to be working somewhere else outside the news media—double the figure of 1982. However, the group of "defectors" no longer had a disproportionate number of the "best and the brightest," as had been true in 1982–1983. Ironically, then, the discontent may not have posed as great a problem for the quality of personnel in the field as it did earlier, when the more experienced, highly educated, and altruistic journalists were more likely to want to leave the field. An exception was that women—who were still in the minority after making substantial gains in their ranks during the 1970s—were more likely in 1992 to want to change careers. That was a particular problem for newspapers, where the trend was more strongly substantiated in our study.

The reasons for the trend of rising unhappiness in 1992 raise critical concerns about the quality of *news* the public receives. A perceived decline in the organizational incentives and resources to cover the news adequately—evident in the open-ended responses of the journalists in our sample—is a serious matter. The constraints cited were more likely to be a result of a general anemia in the advertising industry than of a pervasive corporate culture so often cited by the critics, but the result was the same. Many journalists in 1992 felt quite strongly about these constraints. Combined with the feeling by a sizable minority of journalists that the public was hostile to their efforts anyway, the outlook was scary. The sense of public service that had long been an attraction for journalists was, indeed, threatened in 1992.

Journalists' overall assessment of how well their newsroom was performing showed a mixed picture. The typical journalist thought newsroom performance was either very good or outstanding, and was more likely to feel that way in 1992 than in 1971. Overall, however, there was a noticeable drop since 1982 in the percentage of journalists rating their news organization as *outstanding*, and a slight drop since 1971. Journalists for the wire services were the most positive. The least favorable ratings on informing the public were from television journalists.

Analysis of open-ended comments about newsroom performance suggests that comprehensiveness of news coverage—the classic surveillance function—and a highly qualified staff that is attuned to the authentic needs of the audience were the main conditions journalists listed for high-quality journalism. Also closely linked was the opportunity to provide analytic depth to the news about important issues—the familiar interpretive function. The most significant finding, however, is that the higher the rating journalists gave their newsroom, the greater was the focus on thoroughness and comprehensiveness of news coverage and the likelihood that leadership by editors was cited as a factor. More important, those giving the highest marks were more likely to link comprehensiveness to the idea that their organization's work had an impact on the audiences, expressed—often altruistically—in terms of people's individual, personal lives.

In contrast, the "checking" function of the press—an aggressive challenging of other powerful institutions and officials—may have declined. Keeping an eye on powerful institutions was still an important part of newsroom excellence in 1992 for a significant minority—typically journalists from the larger daily newspapers and, to a lesser extent, television newsrooms. But dearth of aggressive journalism as a perceived characteristic of newsroom excellence was cause for concern. It appeared that the spirit of "progressive reformism," which sociologist Herbert Gans identified in the late 1970s as the dominant "ideology" of American journalism, was becoming all too rare.[60] Seen against a backdrop of the significant decline in the number of journalists who rated their organization as *outstanding*, the suggestion was that the public service dimension of journalism was changing, if not eroding.

In summary, our analysis of job conditions and satisfactions of U.S. journalists in 1992 reveals these major findings:

1. The typical newsroom of mainstream journalism was still reflective of a "young people's profession"—compared with others such as law, medicine, and college teaching—but not as much as in the early 1980s. The age and experience profile in 1992 was more similar to that of the early 1970s.

2. The typical reporter in 1992 was 34 years old, with 10 years of journalism experience—older than in the 1980s.

3. Supervisory personnel were also older than were their counterparts in the 1980s, with lower level managers (e.g., desk editors, assignment editors, and news producers) typically about 37. Upper level managers (e.g., managing editors, editors, and news directors) were only a little older, at 38.

4. Of those with supervisory responsibility, one third were women in 1992— up from 28% a decade previous and matching the percentage of women in the workforce, 34%, similar to a decade previous.

5. The extent of autonomy perceived by journalists diminished considerably between 1971–1992. Although internal organizational factors (led by declining resources devoted to news) were seen as the major reasons, significant numbers of journalists cited external forces (such as official constraints) as affecting their discretion.

6. The amount of feedback from others inside and outside the newsroom in 1992 was roughly similar to that of a decade previous, although regular reaction by news sources was down slightly, and supervisor–journalist interaction was seen to have increased somewhat.

7. The typical journalist had a favorable image of the audience's appetite for information important for citizenship. That image was slightly more congenial to the audience in 1992 than in 1982.

8. A majority of journalists rated their newsroom's performance as either *very good* or *outstanding*, but significantly fewer saw outstanding performance than a decade previous.

9. Associated with good performance in the eyes of journalists were comprehensive coverage, highly motivated staff acutely attuned to the needs of their audience, and a sense that there was opportunity to supplement hard information with analytic depth.

10. The minority who gave their newsroom fair to poor marks tended to cite inadequate resources as the reason.

11. Salaries improved slightly between 1982 and 1992, enabling journalists to recover some of the buying power lost during the inflation of the late 1970s. Considerable progress was made toward parity of male and female salaries as well. Still, journalistic salaries were less than those of other somewhat comparable occupations.

12. A serious decline in job satisfaction since 1971 was evident, although a majority of journalists were still at least fairly satisfied with their work in 1992. The erosion of job satisfaction was somewhat unique to journalism, as other professional groups did not show a similar trend.

13. An altruistic expression of "helping people" was still the top-rated source of job satisfaction for most journalists, but the importance of newsroom policies and fringe benefits was rated much higher in 1992 than in 1982.

14. A leading predictor of diminished job satisfaction was the erosion of job autonomy, particularly for younger journalists, although salary was the biggest complaint given by the journalists. In actuality, salary seemed to be a better predictor of happiness among more experienced journalists than for their younger colleagues. Both groups seemed happier if they got lots of feedback from their supervisors.

15. Plans to change careers were on the minds of 2 of 10 journalists in 1992—a 20-year high. The only bright spot was that the defectors were no longer disproportionately the "best and the brightest," as appeared to be the case in 1982. Of concern, particularly to newspapers, was the tendency for women to want to leave the field in greater numbers. The reasons for leaving were much more complex in 1992 than a decade previous, when salary was the key for many. Money was still a factor in 1992, but disillusionment and doubts about the future of the field were just as important.

NOTES

1. Alice Rivlin, Distinguished Lecturer Series, Institute for Advanced Study and the Society for Advanced Study, Indiana University, Bloomington, September 1992.
2. Jon Katz, "The Capital Gang Bang: The Failure of the Washington Press Corps," *Rolling Stone*, August 19, 1993, pp. 37–39.

3. H. Brandt Ayers, "The Death of Civility," *The New York Times*, July 16, 1994, p. 11.

4. John C. Busterna, "Trends in Daily Newspaper Ownership," *Journalism Quarterly*, 65 (Winter 1988), pp. 831–838.

5. Ben H. Bagdikian, *The Media Monopoly* (Boston: Beacon Press, 1987), p. 21.

6. William Glaberson, "Times Co. Acquiring Boston Globe for $1.1 Billion," *The New York Times*, June 11, 1993, p. 1.

7. James D. Squires, "Plundering the Newsroom," *Washington Journalism Review*, December 1992, pp. 18–24.

8. Douglas Underwood, *MBAs in the Newsroom* (New York: Columbia University Press, 1993).

9. Doug Underwood, "When MBAs rule the newsroom," *Columbia Journalism Review*, March/April 1988, pp. 23–30.

10. Doug Underwood and Keith Stamm, "Balancing Business With Journalism: Newsroom Policies at 12 West Coast Newspapers," *Journalism Quarterly*, 69 (Spring 1992), pp. 836–846.

11. Keith Stamm and Doug Underwood, "The Relationship of Job Satisfaction to Newsroom Policy Changes," unpublished manuscript accepted for publication in *Journalism Quarterly*, 1993.

12. David Pearce Demers, "Structural Pluralism, Intermedia Competition, and the Growth of the Corporate Newspaper in the United States," *Journalism Monographs*, 145 (June 1994), p. 6.

13. Russell Baker, *The Good Times* (New York: Penguin Books, 1990), p. 40.

14. Russell Baker, Speech at the 75th Anniversary Celebration of the Pulitzer Prizes, Columbia University, New York, September 22, 1991.

15. Baker, *The Good Times*, p. 40.

16. Baker, *The Good Times*, p. 40.

17. Pete Dexter, *The Paperboy* (New York: Random House, 1995), pp. 17–21.

18. Dexter, *The Paperboy*, pp. 17–20.

19. Dexter, *The Paperboy*, pp. 17–20.

20. Russell Baker, Speech at the 75th Anniversary Celebration of the Pulitzer Prizes, September 22, 1991.

21. William Strauss and Neil Howe, *Generations: The History of America's Future, 1584 to 2069* (New York: William Morrow, 1991), p. 441.

22. Strauss and Howe, *Generations*, pp. 295–346.

23. Anna Quindlen, "A Good Fire," *The New York Times*, July 16, 1994, p. 11.

24. Quindlen, "A Good Fire," p. 11.

25. Elizabeth Chang, "The Buyout Boom," *American Journalism Review*, July/August 1993, pp. 17–21.

26. Bill Green, "The Fake Pulitzer Story: 'How Did It All Happen?'" *Louisville Courier-Journal*, April 26, 1981, p. D3.

27. Eugene Patterson, "The Press: A Few Problems to Solve," convocation address to the Indiana University School of Journalism, Bloomington, September 6, 1983.

28. Ken Auletta, "Opening Up The Times," *The New Yorker*, June 28, 1993, pp. 55–71.

29. Auletta, "Opening Up The Times," p. 70.

30. Three questions were used to form an autonomy scale: 1. If you have a good idea for a subject which you think is important and should be followed up, how often are you able to get the subject covered? 2. How much freedom do you usually have in selecting the stories you work on? 3. How much freedom do you usually have in deciding which aspects of a story should be emphasized? A reliability cooeficient of .74 was obtained. A multiple-regression analysis was conducted using 43 variables in a listwise deletion approach.

31. Lee Clarke, "New Ideas on the Division of Labor," *Sociological Forum*, 4 (June 1989), pp. 281–289.

32. Bill Moyers, "Old News and the New Civil War," *The New York Times*, February 22, 1992, p. C1.

33. Moyers, "Old News and the New Civil War."

34. Carl Bernstein, "The Idiot Culture," *The New Republic*, June 8, 1992, pp. 22–28.

35. Bernstein, "The Idiot Culture."

36. David L. Altheide, *Creating Reality: How TV News Distorts Events* (Beverly Hills, CA: Sage Publications, 1974), p. 49.
37. Judee K. Burgoon, Michael Burgoon, and Charles K. Atkin, *The World of the Working Journalist* (New York: Newspaper Readership Project, Newspaper Advertising Bureau, September 1982), p. 79.
38. Anna Quindlen, "Order in the Court," *The New York Times*, July 13, 1994, p. A11.
39. Associated Press, "Some Stations Cut Violent News Images," *The [Bloomington, IN] Herald Times*, July 16, 1994, p. 9.
40. Daily newspaper salaries appear to have kept up with the rises in the Consumer Price Index since 1991, but barely. Senior reporters with 5 years experience on small dailies (20,000–30,000 circulation) had a median salary of $28,078 in 1994. Those on larger papers (101,000–150,000) had a median salary of $36,083. City editors averaged $33,540 and $49,488 for small and large daily newspapers in 1994, respectively. See E. Donald Lass, "Pay Raises in 1994 Lagged Those of the Year Before," *ASNE Bulletin*, March 1995, pp. 34–35.
41. Recent salary data from media industry sources suggest that salaries for broadcast journalists rose at an average rate slightly exceeding inflation through 1994. The average salary for television reporters in 1994 was $24,154, for news producers $22,909, for executive producers $37,516, and for news directors $52,782. Radio reporters in 1994 averaged $16,387, and radio news directors $23,182. See Bob Papper and Andrew Sharma, "Salaries Going Up," *RTNDA Communicator*, May 1995, pp. 14–19; and Vernon A. Stone, "Pay Gains Top Cost of Living," *RTNDA Communicator*, February 1994, pp. 68–70.
42. U.S. Department of Labor, Bureau of Labor Statistics, *Occupational Outlook Handbook*, Bulletin 2400, May 1992, p. 17. The mean salary for all full-time U.S. journalists was $31,500, slightly less than the figures for the median that were used consistently in our reports on journalists.
43. *Occupational Outlook Handbook*, Bulletin 2400, p. 172.
44. Associated Press, as reported in the *Sunday [Bloomington, In.] Herald Times*, August 8, 1993, p. A12.
45. "Seventh Annual Salary Survey," *Public Relations Journal* (August 1992), pp. 10–21.
46. Chang, "The Buyout Boom," p. 21.
47. Russell Baker, *The Good Times* (New York: Penguin Books, 1990), pp. 140–149.
48. James Reston, *Deadline: A Memoir* (New York: Random House, 1991), p. ix.
49. National Opinion Research Center, "General Social Survey, 1990." Question: On the whole, how satisfied are you with the work you do?
50. The Harris Poll, "Steelcase World-wide Environmental Index," 1991.
51. International Survey Research Corporation, "Employee Satisfaction Surveys" (Chicago, IL: 1984–1992).
52. Susan H. Russell et al., *Profiles of Faculty in Higher Education Institutions, 1988* (Washington, DC: National Center for Education Statistics, U.S. Department of Education, August 1991), p. 75.
53. C.J. Cranny, Patricia Cain Smith, and Eugene F. Stone, *Job Satisfaction: How People Feel About Their Jobs and How It Affects Their Performance* (New York: Lexington Books, 1992), p. xvii.
54. Cranny, Smith, and Stone, *Job Satisfaction*, p. xvii.
55. J. David Pincus, "Communication Satisfaction, Job Satisfaction, and Job Performance," *Human Communication Research*, 12 (Spring 1986), pp. 395–419; and Charles A. O'Reilly, III and John C. Anderson, "Trust and the Communication Performance Appraisal Information: The Effect of Feedback on Performance and Job Satisfaction," *Human Communication Research*, 6 (Summer 1980), pp. 289–298.
56. "The American Journalist in the 1990s," a conference at the Freedom Forum World Center, Arlington, Virginia, November 17, 1992.
57. Chang, "The Buyout Boom," p. 21.
58. Chang, "The Buyout Boom," p. 21.

59. A careful national study of 627 daily newspaper journalists by Kristin McGrath for the Associated Press Managing Editors Association in 1993 found similar figures on job satisfaction and career plans. See APME *Journalist Satisfaction Study* (Minneapolis, MN: MORI Research Inc., September 1993), pp. 5–9.

60. Herbert G. Gans, *Deciding What's News: A Study of CBS Evening News, NBC Nightly News, Newsweek, and Time* (New York: Vintage Books, A Division of Random House, 1979).

Professionalism:
Roles, Values, Ethics

Professionalism is a term journalists often use to describe the excellence to which they aspire, and some see journalism as a profession. A careful survey of newspaper personnel in 1992–1993 concluded, ". . . Journalism, in the minds of journalists, is a profession built on and emerging from a craft."[1] Yet the larger meaning of *profession*—as the autonomous practice of work that is based on strict educational requirements and licensing—has never fit the field well. Few analysts of the professions regard journalism as even close to that definition.

Louis Menand's recent essay in *The New York Times Magazine*, "The Trashing of Professionalism," took a new look. Journalism, Menand argued, is now similar enough to the major professions that the public views journalists with the same disdain it holds for lawyers, doctors, and professors. What it lacks in licensing and strict degree requirements, journalism makes up for in *disinterestedness*—the core value that Menand saw as common to all "true" professions. "A good journalist is supposed to be someone who gets the story without, as they say, fear or favor," said Menand.[2]

Advocates of "public journalism"—creating a journalistic "public square" by framing the news from the citizens' point of view—also abhor the stance of disinterestedness that they, too, see dominating traditional journalism. Davis Merritt, an editor who has done much to advance the civic approach, said "determined detachment" is the "operating axiom" of contemporary journalism, and that it "breeds a dangerous arrogance, a self-granted immunity that smacks of a priesthood."[3]

Others also see professionalization as bad for journalism, but for different reasons. A main concern is its potential effects on the diversity and robustness of news. John Merrill, an educator and longtime critic of attempts to professionsionalize journalism, said, "It seems clear to me that this tendency, if carried very far, would stamp out unusual or eccentric concepts and, ultimately, also the journalists who embrace them."[4] Some fear that has happened already.

Theodore Glasser, a media scholar, argued that professionalism—particularly as taught in schools of journalism—stifles diversity. He said, "Professionalism implies standardization and homogeneity; it accounts not for differences among journalists but for what journalists have in common." The result is that ". . . professionals typically operate with assumptions and attitudes that can be fairly described as ethnocentric."[5]

To illustrate the effects of a professional mentality on serious journalism, Glasser and James Ettema dissected some of the best, recent investigative reporting. After careful reading of such classics as the *Philadelphia Inquirer* series on "The Great Tax Giveaway" by Donald L. Barlett and James B. Steele, researchers Glasser and Ettema concluded that professionalism enables journalists to mask a cynical agenda with what seems to be strictly the "facts." For example, in writing about the Tax Reform Act of 1986 and its tax exemptions for thousands of influential individuals and businesses, Barlett and Steele compared the words of legislators to their actual deeds, thereby creating "villains and victims," said Glasser and Ettema. "Such 'objective' vocabularies for the description of conduct transform moral claims into empirical claims and allow journalists to maintain their pretense of dealing in facts and not values," they argued.[6]

So, whether the image of journalism is as an elitist, homogeneous "priesthood," or of reporters as "factitioners" of cynicism, the shadow of professionalism seems to dominate the canvass of many of the critics. At the same time, the massive news coverage of the arrest and trial of O.J. Simpson resurrected the argument *for* nurturing a professional character in journalism.

Steven Brill, editor of *The American Lawyer*, said the Simpson case exposed the fault lines of journalism's weak professional culture. "Here's a new lawyer joke," said Brill: "Question: Why should lawyers love the press? Answer: Journalism is the only profession that makes lawyers look good." In the public's mind, Brill claimed, "Lawyers don't come close to the press when it comes to unaccountability and self-righteousness in pursuit of self-interest and money. . . ."[7] For Brill, it was the "zoo" of journalists, cameras, and satellite trucks outside the Simpson courthouse in 1995 that became the public's defining image of journalism as a nonprofession. "Yet lots of us," said Brill, "do think we constitute a profession, with standards of conduct, honor and purpose that should be . . . every bit as high as those of the law."[8]

Others in the elite, mainstream press also seemed embarrassed by the spectacle of the Simpson case. Frank Rich, a columnist for *The New York Times*, captured the widespread frustration of many: "O.J. permeates the airwaves, journalism, most overheard conversations. O.J. is now the nation's weather, and it's raining all the time."[9]

As both Brill and Menand suggested, however, it is not just journalism that is floundering in the 1990s. Profound difficulties plague *all* the established professions, and journalism is often at odds with them. Nowhere is this clearer than in the law. Protruding from the colossus of the Simpson trial coverage are as many problems in the judicial system as there are doubts about the capacity of journalism to control its own excesses. Yet journalism is no match for the bar in defending itself. With its vast array of powerful university law schools and big national professional bodies skilled at public relations, the bar is likely to be tarnished only temporarily by the Simpson case. In contrast, journalism may be the long-term loser.[10]

This chapter suggests that, contrary to many of the critics, journalism's major problems may stem from too little professionalization, not too much. In a nutshell, the fragile intellectual-institutional grounding of journalism seems unable to keep up with the dazzling changes in the technological platform from which news is reported. Looking back just a quarter of a century, the reasons for the lag become clearer.

In a landmark sociological study in 1971, *The News People*, John W. C. Johnstone and his colleagues found the field a mixed picture of institutional contradictions. Although the Johnstone team concluded that journalism *was* a profession in an "abstract formal sense," the actual behavior of journalists defied the traditional notions of a profession.[11] Journalists valued public service, autonomy, and freedom from supervision. They leaned toward altruism, at least in ranking economic rewards as less important than public service. But in their nurturance of the field, journalists were unlike other professionals. Their rate of membership in professional groups was remarkably low, and the influence of those associations on the professional styles of their members was negligible.[12]

A decade later, our national study of journalists in 1982–1983 found the professional culture of journalism still quite weak compared with the fields of accounting, law, and medicine. The one sign of strengthening professional identity was an increase of membership in national associations during the 1970s. About 20% of all journalists belonged to a national professional group, compared with 13% in the earlier study. In addition, journalists in the 1980s were more highly educated than in any previous time, with a large majority having a bachelor's degree. A slight majority either majored or took courses in schools of journalism–mass communication.

Although they professed a distinctly professional spirit of public service, there was deep division among them on many questions of journalistic practice. Most appeared to subscribe to seemingly contradictory conceptions of their role (i.e., they were both "objective" informers and "subjective" interpreters). As an occupation, mainstream news journalism hardly fit the traditional lines of a profession, except in the loose sense that journalists reflected a professional "mood." Despite widespread perception of considerable individual autonomy, the dynamics of the newsroom appeared to be the cauldron in which news values and attitudes were shaped most directly.

This chapter analyzes a wide range of survey questions about organizational memberships, roles, ethics, and values. It suggests the field's already weak professional culture eroded further in the 1980s. Despite the highest levels of education in the history of journalism, improved salaries, and lingering idealism among journalists, the press corps in 1992 seemed plagued by self-doubts and stung by public criticism.

THE JOURNALIST'S PROFESSIONAL COMMUNITY

Despite its robust defiance of an orthodox, sociological type of professionalism, there is value in analyzing journalism from that perspective.[13] One of the best recent studies focused on the relative impact of the media organization and the individual journalist on professionalism. Randal Beam, a media researcher and former newspaper journalist, studied the extent of professionalism at 58 daily newspapers in 1990. He looked at news policies, how they were established, and the extent to which they matched the expectations of national professional groups. Beam concluded that the news organization, as opposed to the individual journalist, was the source of professional values and behavior.[14] Furthermore, there was considerable variation across organizations on the extent to which expectations of journalistic behavior and standards of work reflected those of the occupation at large. The key factor appeared to be the size of the organization, as opposed to the type of ownership. Larger media were more likely to reflect *appropriate* behavior, as defined by national journalism associations. Within the newsrooms, individual involvement in national journalism groups appeared to be unrelated to professionalism.[15] That is not surprising, as a look at organizational memberships and the readership of professional literature among journalists will suggest.

Professional Group Memberships

The professional "community" of news journalism was more diverse in 1992 than in 1982–1983. Memberships in 55 national groups—ranging from the Society of Professional Journalists (SPJ) and the Radio-Television News Directors Association (RTNDA) to the National Lesbian and Gay Journalists Association— were claimed by the journalists in our sample. In 1982, 35 organizations were listed.

Increased diversity of professional memberships suggests that the field was grappling with both social and technological change, but the overall decline in membership, first noticed in 1982–1983, continued. Only 36% of the workforce in 1992 belonged to any professional group, down significantly from 1971 (see Fig. 4.1). Furthermore, the rise in identification with national journalism groups,

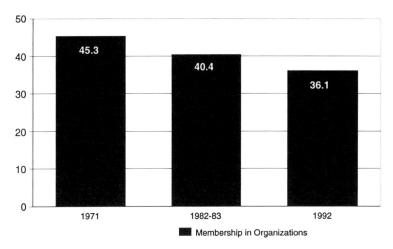

FIG. 4.1. Membership in professional organizations (percentage of all journalists saying they belong to one or more).

which marked the growing workforce in 1982, was reversed. In 1992, SPJ, while still the largest association, had only about 7% of all journalists on its rolls (compared with 17% in 1982–1983).[16] Other important national groups, such as RTNDA (2%), appeared to have about the same allegiance as earlier. The Investigative Reporters and Editors Association (IRE) was up slightly, with about 3% of all journalists belonging.

Still, the splintering rolls of the major national professional groups is perplexing. No doubt, shrinking journalistic salaries in the early 1980s made professional membership dues harder to pay, perhaps a factor in dropping membership. If so, the slightly improved salary picture in the early 1990s was not enough to reverse the trend. The decline almost certainly signaled the erosion of an already weak institutional fabric, especially compared with other fields. For example, accounting experienced a growth in national organizational membership during 1982–1992. By 1992, about 78% of all accountants were members of the American Institute of Certified Public Accountants—up from 70% just 10 years previous.[17] Half of all attorneys in the country were members of the American Bar Association.[18] About 45% of all physicians belonged to the American Medical Association.[19]

Of the other major fields, only the professoriate comes close to journalism in its thinness of professional identity. In 1992, just a small minority of professors belonged to the American Association of University Professors, the oldest and largest academic professional group. However, a majority of college and university faculty were members of professional groups for specific disciplines, such as the Association for Education in Journalism and Mass Communication, the International Communication Association, or the American Political Science Association.

Which Journalists "Belong"?

The portrait of the typical journalistic "joiner" of professional groups in 1992 was a little different from that of a decade previous. More experienced journalists were still more likely to have ties to such groups than their junior colleagues. However, having supervisory duties was no longer associated with belonging. Print journalists, particularly those on weekly (45%) and daily (37%) newspapers, were more likely to join professional groups than were their broadcast colleagues, as Table 4.1 indicates.

Journalists at the more prominent, national media in 1982 tended not to be members of professional organizations. In contrast, journalists at larger media in 1992 were at least as likely to belong to professional groups as their colleagues at smaller organizations. In 1982, journalists at smaller media were more likely to join professional groups than were those at large organizations. Still, one might expect that persons in prominent, larger media would be much *more* interested in professional leadership than their colleagues in smaller or less prominent media. That was not the case in journalism—a consistent finding over three decades.[20]

Surprisingly, having a journalism or communications degree was no longer predictive of membership in a professional group in 1992. Although the journalism school link was only modest in 1982, it appeared at a time when the quality of journalism graduates was being celebrated, and they were an increasingly large proportion of the new hires. The only "silver lining" in the present finding is that those who feared journalism schools would foster a narrow professionalism may be wrong.

Trade unions, primarily The Newspaper Guild (TNG) and the American Federation of Television and Radio Artists (AFTRA), held their own during 1982–1992, with 17% of our sample claiming membership. Union membership in 1992 was the same as in 1982–1983, the end of a decade in which the extent of union representation failed to keep up with the growing workforce. In 1971, 29% of all mainstream news journalists were members of a labor group.

TABLE 4.1
Membership in Professional Associations by Medium
(Percentage Saying One or More)

Medium	%	N
Daily newspaper	36.6	634
Weekly newspaper	44.7	161
News magazine	34.4	61
Wire service	31.0	58
Television	33.6	137
Radio	28.0	100
Total	36.2	1,151

Readership of Professional Journals

Journal and trade publication reading among news personnel in 1992 reflected the considerable breadth of the news media. When asked to name professional publications they read either regularly or occasionally, journalists mentioned 48, ranging from *Editor & Publisher* to the *RTNDA Communicator*. More striking was the decline of readership that occurred.

In 1982–1983, we found that the oldest trade magazine in the field, *Editor & Publisher* (*E&P*) was read at least "sometimes" by about 60% of journalists. A decade later, that figure was about 40%. Some of the drop may have reflected a changing field and the image of *E&P* as an old-line "print" publication. However, other journals that focus more squarely on essays about vital professional issues also lost readership among journalists. *Columbia Journalism Review* and *The Quill* both reached about half of all journalists in 1982. In 1992, only one third said they read *CJR*, and only 10% saw *The Quill*, at least occasionally. *CJR* is an independent journal of Columbia University's Pulitzer School of Journalism. *The Quill* is a publication of SPJ, and its readership decline in 1992 reflected the shrinking membership rolls of SPJ. The *American Journalism Review*, a publication of the University of Maryland's College of Journalism, passed *The Quill* in readership among journalists, with 22% seeing it at least occasionally. Still, *AJR* was down from having reached 43% of news personnel in 1981–1982 (see Table 4.2).

The picture was not much different when looked at by media sector. In 1992, a little less than half of the journalists at daily newspapers saw *E&P* at least occasionally (compared with 79% in 1982–1983). Only 19% read it regularly. About one third of all broadcast journalists read *Broadcasting and Cable* (15% said "regularly"). *Publisher's Auxiliary* was read by 27% of the weekly newspaper personnel (19% said "regularly").

TABLE 4.2
Readership Among All Journalists of Professional Journals and
Trade Publications (Percentage Naming Each Publication)[a]

	Frequency of Readership		
Publication	*Regularly*	*Occasionally*	*Never*
Editor & Publisher	13	26	61
Columbia Journalism Review	12	21	67
American Journalism Review	8	14	78
The Quill	4	6	90
News Photographer (NPPA)	4	1	95
Broadcasting and Cable	3	4	93
Publisher's Auxiliary	3	1	96
ASNE Bulletin	2	1	97
News, Inc.	2	3	96
Presstime	2	1	97

Note. N = 1,156.
[a]About 40 other publications were mentioned, with 1% or less readership.

CJR was the leading journal among wire service and news magazine journalists in 1992. The journal reached 64% of wire personnel (26% said "regularly"). About half of news magazine journalists read *CJR* (15% said "regularly").

Some of the apparent decline in readership of the dominant professional sources may have resulted from a change in the question used in the latest study. Instead of providing a list of journals, the respondents in 1992 were asked to name the professional journals and trade publications they read. This approach got at the real impact of the journals better, but in so doing, may have exaggerated the apparent decline in reach.

The unmistakable point, though, is that a common body of professional literature reached only a minority of journalists. Other professions, except for the professoriate, had a *single* journal that reached far larger numbers of their practitioners than did journalism. There is little doubt that a majority ignored important literature that could nurture a critical mass of intelligent thinking on timely questions of journalistic practice. This is additional evidence of a weak (and likely a weakening) institutional structure. It was consistent with other trends—notably the drop in membership of professional associations in the field.[21]

On the other hand, journalists in 1992 reported on media problems much more frequently. For example, our study of *The American Journalist* in 1982 received only minor press coverage. In contrast, the 1992 study's preliminary results attracted considerable attention in major national media. Specific media controversies, such as the rigged crash test of a truck for NBC's *Dateline* in 1993, received massive coverage. *The New York Times* and other elite newspapers and magazines consistently reported on the changing technology of news and issues of journalistic practice. ABC's *Nightline*, the *McNeil-Lehrer Newshour*, and the network evening newscasts occasionally covered media problems. CNN's *Reliable Sources* was devoted entirely to media criticism. Another source of ideas and criticism was the frequent C-SPAN cable network coverage of various professional meetings and conferences on journalism. Overall, however, the combined reach of mass media reports on media problems and professional journals left a wide swath of journalists who were not likely to be reached consistently by intelligent criticism.

Friends of Journalists

A classic tune by the Beatles in the 1960s sang of "a little help from my friends." If an indicator of professional identity, as some assume, is the amount of socializing journalists do with other news people, in 1992 the field was stable. When asked how many of their social friends were newsroom colleagues, the estimates were similar from 1971–1992. About one third of the typical respondent's social friends were other journalists, both in 1992 and the earlier studies. As with organizational memberships, the patterns of journalistic friendship changed somewhat. Younger journalists in 1992 were still more likely to have more newsworkers as friends, but not as much so as a decade previous. Women in the newsroom in 1992 were a little more likely to have other journalists as friends than were their male colleagues. But having a journalism degree no longer was related to more socializing with fellow journalists.[22]

Overall, the institutional structure of journalism in 1992 appeared weaker than it was a decade previous. The thinness of the base of shared literature and professional leadership left the field vulnerable. Perhaps never has the gap been wider between the public's conception of an appropriate role for the mass media and journalists' own views of their purpose. The next section attempts to look closely at how journalists viewed the purposes of news work in 1992.

JOURNALISTIC ROLE CONCEPTIONS

Perhaps it's only a romantic view, but, for many journalists, a "love of the game" seems to have played a part in driving them to their "profession," much the same as in baseball. The baseball strike of 1994 convinced many fans that the sport is an industry driven by greed, not a love of the game. Unfortunately, the public mood about journalism in 1992 seems to have been just as bitter. As Louis Menand pointed out, the disenchantment with journalism is tinged with irony. It is the journalist's love of the craft, a loyalty to the story, that fuels widespread disdain. In the public's view, said Menand, "Journalists care only about getting the story; they can't see how they're trampling the lives of other people to get it."[23]

A larger irony is that altruism, the feeling that one's work contributes to human betterment, has always attracted and sustained many journalists. Querying almost any reporter, except those of the small minority of highly paid and visible "stars," elicits a comment about how no one chooses journalism for the money. The previous chapter showed that the idea of helping people was one of the most important sources of satisfaction on the job for our 1992 respondents. Yet the characterization of contemporary journalists as disinterested and detached seemed to stick in the public mind.

How did journalists view these questions? What did they see as their most cherished professional values? What was their view of news journalism's basic purposes? Did their attitudes change over the last several decades?

A Quarter Century of Attitudes About Journalistic Roles

Convulsive debate and civil unrest about the Vietnam war were the backdrop against which the Johnstone team carried out its large-scale national study of journalists in 1971. At that time, the lines between personal feelings about the war and the job of reporting the wrenching struggle to end it became harder to draw for many journalists. The symbols of resistance—black arm bands and antiwar buttons—began appearing in newsrooms. Wes Gallagher, the venerable chief executive of the Associated Press at the time, seemed to some journalists as if he were manning the barricades of outmoded traditions as he implored them to guard the fundamental values of "objectivity."[24]

A Benchmark Study

It is hardly surprising, then, that the 1971 study by Johnstone found evidence of two "pure" ideological types among working journalists. The cleavage in values reflected old arguments about objectivity, detachment, involvement, and advocacy, which were made salient again by widespread public protest of the war. Johnstone and his colleagues characterized the competing belief systems as a *neutral*, "nothing-but-the-truth" orientation versus a *participant*, "whole-truth" mentality. However, the surprise was that fewer than one in five journalists could be classified as hard-line proponents of a single view. Most adhered to some parts of both "ideologies."[25]

By the time we were in the field in the winter of 1982–1983 for a revisit of the decade-old Johnstone study, the "Watergate" scandal had toppled the Nixon presidency, and the movie *All the President's Men* made Woodward and Bernstein the most famous print journalists of their generation. Journalism seemed to have gained a lasting respectability. By the end of the 1980s, however, Andy Warhol's notion about the fleetingness of fame was being realized by an entire field of journalists as the public began to sour on them. Media coverage of 444 days of the Iranian hostage crisis—from 1979 to 1981—signaled the impact that satellite-based global communication technology had on politics and diplomacy.[26] The crisis was also a metaphor of sorts for what the Johnstone team had labeled a *participant ideology*—with journalists appearing to be the unwitting "tools" of terrorism. *Time* aptly summarized the emergent view of journalists during the period: "They are rude and accusatory, cynical and almost unpatriotic."[27] The romantic image of journalists following the trail of the abuses of power in the Watergate scandal was fading, even among leading editors. Michael J. O'Neill, then editor of the *New York Daily News*, deplored the rise in journalism of an "adversarial mindset" in his 1982 presidential address to the convention of the American Society of Newspaper Editors.[28]

Another Study in an "Adversarial" Age

In our 1982–1983 survey, we added questions about adversarial stances toward government and business to the battery of role questions developed by the Johnstone team. The expanded list of items was subjected to factor analysis, a complex statistical procedure, to determine whether patterns, or clusters, of roles would emerge, and whether they would resemble the neutral and disseminator stances found by Johnstone.

Given the tenor of the times, we expected a complex picture of journalistic roles. Hugh Culbertson, a journalism professor at Ohio University, studied 285 editors and writers on 17 newspapers in 1982; he found three, as opposed to the earlier two, role conceptions. Our analysis also suggested adversarial, interpretive, and disseminator clusters of attitudes about journalistic purpose. The surprise, however, was twofold. First, contrary to the critics, the adversarial conception was hardly dominant, with only 17% of the sample considering the role as central to their work. Second, the pluralism of the journalistic mindset was significantly greater than a decade earlier, with about a third of all journalists fully embracing both the interpretive *and* the disseminator roles. Only about 2% of the respondents were exclusively one-role-oriented, compared with 18% in 1971.

In a Climate of Cynicism, a Third Look

Our most recent interviews of journalists were done in the summer of 1992. The only thing 1992 seemed to have in common with the period of our 1982–1983 study was that another economic recession had upset the advertising revenue base of the field. The journalistic glory of Watergate was a distant memory, and Rush Limbaugh, a major figure in the emergence of "talk" radio in the 1980s, was drawing national attention to his conservative criticism of the "liberal" press. It was also a time when some within the mainstream press worried that the widespread cynicism in American society—reflected in talk radio's shrillness, as well as in voter apathy—was, indeed, partly the fault of journalists. Davis Merritt, a newspaper editor, and Jay Rosen, a scholar, argued for a change in the nature of reporting and a shift to "public journalism." In their view, ". . . Opinion polling, the commercial success of the news media, and the professionalization of journalism all conspired to bury the issue of how we imagine—how we create—this 'thing' we call the public."[29]

In that context, the journalists in our 1992 national sample were asked about numerous conceptions of "things the media do or try to do today." Specifically, each journalist responded to 12 questions such as this: "How important is it for the news media to investigate claims and statements made by the government?" Responses included *extremely important, quite important, somewhat important*, and *not really important*. Most of the questions were identical to those asked in the previous studies, allowing us to compare journalists over three decades. As in the two earlier studies, each of the questions about roles was considered individually. Then we aggregated them into larger clusters of functions to assess other, possibly broader, changes in the core philosophies of U.S. journalists.

Journalistic Roles in the 1990s

Two journalistic roles were rated as *extremely important* by a majority of journalists in the 1992 study: getting information to the public quickly (69%) and investigating government claims (67%). Compared with 1971, journalists in 1992 were more likely to rank providing information quickly as *extremely*

TABLE 4.3
Importance Journalists Assigned to Various Mass Media Roles

Media Roles	Percentage Saying Extremely Important		
	1971[a]	1982–1983[b]	1992
Investigate government claims	76	66	67
Get information to public quickly	56	60	69
Avoid stories with unverified content	51	50	49
Provide analysis of complex problems	61	49	48
Discuss national policy	55	38	39
Concentrate on widest audience	39	36	20
Develop intellectual/cultural interests	30	24	18
Provide entertainment	17	20	14
Serve as adversary of government[c]	—	20	21
Serve as adversary of business[c]	—	15	14
Set the political agenda[d]	—	—	5
Let people express views[d]	—	—	48
	N = 1,313	N = 1,001	N = 1,156

[a]Data are from John Johnstone, Edward Slawski, and William Bowman, *The News People*, p. 230.
[b]Data are from David Weaver and G. Cleveland Wilhoit, *The American Journalist*, p. 114.
[c]Not asked in the 1971 survey.
[d]Not asked in the 1971 or 1982–1983 surveys.

important, especially those working for television and wire services (see Table 4.3). This change reflected a premium on immediacy that was driven by continuing innovations of cellular, satellite, and other mobile technologies. The traditional "watchdog" role (i.e., investigating the claims of government), which dropped in salience in the early 1980s, was unchanged in relative importance in 1992, and was ranked about the same by staff on all media except radio. News staffs in radio (as was seen in chap. 3, this volume) shrunk during 1982–1992, hence the radio journalists in our study appeared to reflect a hard reality of those constraints as they considered the "watchdog" role as less salient in 1992.

Identification with the analytical role of news media—providing analysis of complex problems—also remained about the same during 1982–1992, but there was a significant drop since 1971 in those rating it as *extremely important*. News magazine and daily newspaper personnel were much more likely than those in other media to see the analytic role as highly salient.

Only about a fifth of all journalists in 1992, significantly fewer than 10 or 20 years previous, agreed that reaching the widest possible audience was extremely important. During 1982–1992, new media and emerging technologies chipped away at news audiences, particularly in television. The breadth of the geographic areas served by some major newspapers was reduced to enhance cost-effectiveness to advertisers and reduce circulation costs. Particularly for large urban newspapers and major network newscasts, audiences in 1992 were somewhat diminished. These and other factors appeared to underlay the major shift in journalists' somewhat diminished perception of the importance of *mass* appeal for their stories, although broadcast journalists (32%) were still more likely than their print colleagues (20%) to value a wide audience.

Journalistic Functions in the 1990s

Using factor analysis, the individual responses to the battery of separate questions were aggregated into broader, attitudinal clusters: interpretive/investigative, disseminator, adversarial, and populist mobilizer.[30] Despite the enormous changes in the journalistic environment during the 1980s, the portrait of core functions in 1992 was fairly similar to that of 1982–1983. Some subtle, but significant, changes appeared within the functions, however, and an emerging "new" function was apparent. Each function, or core "belief system," and its implications are discussed next, beginning with the interpretive orientation (see Fig. 4.2).

The *interpretive/investigative function* remained the larger perception of American journalists in 1992. As in 1982–1983, most of them in 1992 perceived the interpretive goal as an essential of journalistic life. This approach was a blending of three important roles: investigating government claims, analyzing and interpreting complex problems, and discussing public policies in a timely way (see Table 4.4).

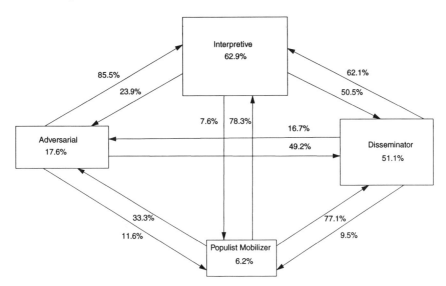

FIG. 4.2. Journalists' perceptions of functions. Note: Percentages in boxes indicate the proportions of journalists who rate each function as very important (the top quartile of each scale). Percentages along the arrows indicate the overlap in the proportions of journalists who strongly endorse both roles. For example, 85.5% of those journalists who consider the adversarial role very important also consider the interpretive role very important.

TABLE 4.4
The Interpretive Function: Percentages of Journalists of Various
Media Who Saw the Dimensions as Extremely Important

Media Type	Investigating Official Claims (%)	Analyzing Complex Problems (%)	Discussing National Policy (%)	N
News magazines	82	66	57	61
Wire service	76	55	50	58
Dailies	70	54	44	635
Weeklies	62	39	28	162
TV	62	37	26	137
Radio	46	25	22	101
Total	67	48	39	1,154

Journalism's majority culture, then, framed its basic purpose in terms resonant with the old recommendations of the Hutchins Commission on Freedom of the Press in 1947. Although few had likely heard of it, and fewer still had ever read the report, most journalists in 1992 appeared to have a "belief system" that reflected the Commission's goal of investigating "the truth about the fact[s]" and providing "a context which gives them meaning."[31] The Commission would undoubtedly view with raised eyebrows the somewhat diminished salience of the analytic fiber of the interpretive role we found in 1982 and 1992.

This majority acceptance of an interpretive function was seen by some as a possible source of public disenchantment with the press. Stephen Bates, a media scholar, argued that, although the "men of the Hutchins Commission would be pleased" with the attitudes of present-day journalists, the interpretive role requires too cozy a relationship with intellectuals and other elites. Bates added, "Journalists of the 1990s, trying, as journalists always have tried, to make a difference with their reporting, are becoming what journalists of the 1940s reviled: backstage activists, professional experts, undemocratic elitists—or, one might say, democratic realists." The contrast is stark, in Bates' view: "Reporters of 50 years ago saw their job as providing information to the masses."[32] The irony in the portrait of the majority culture of the interpretive function is, however, that there was still a strong streak of the disseminator mentality in 1992.

The *disseminator function* was essential for a slight majority in 1992, just as it was in 1982–1983. The modest changes in the contour of this role in 1992 were significant, however. The disseminator view in 1992 was a meshing of two key roles: getting information to the public quickly, and avoiding stories with unverifiable "facts" (see Table 4.5).

In 1982, the statistical clustering of the disseminator "factor" included the importance of reaching the widest possible audience (as it had for Johnstone in 1971). But the audience element was no longer part of the "mindset" of those journalists stressing the information function in 1992. However, the importance

TABLE 4.5
The Disseminator Function: Percentages of Journalists of Various
Media Who Saw the Dimensions as Extremely Important

Media Type	Getting Information to Public Quickly (%)	Avoiding Unverifiable Facts (%)	N
Wire service	81	55	58
TV	80	49	137
Dailies	70	50	635
News magazines	67	32	61
Radio	67	50	101
Weeklies	53	48	162
Total	69	49	1,154

of avoiding unverifiable stories was, again, a value for disseminators in 1992 (it had not been a significant element in 1982–1983, unlike the 1971 study). This may have reflected the resurging concern about stories based on anonymous sources among those journalists who identified strongly with the disseminator role.

The *adversary function* was very much a minority "mindset" among journalists in 1992. An adversarial orientation was a tightly correlated melding of two items: being constantly skeptical of public officials as well as business interests (see Table 4.6).

The field's position on the adversary function is a persistent puzzle. Despite continuing charges by many critics that modern journalism is led by a "generation of vipers," the adversary stance was highly salient only for a small minority of journalists in 1992, just as it was a decade previous.[33] Most journalists do not admit to placing a premium on sustained skepticism of those in power. Not even the more visible, "national" journalists in the larger urban areas of the Northeast—where the critics tend to place them—see themselves as seriously adversarial. It is true that fewer journalists in 1992 (about 20%) completely rejected

TABLE 4.6
The Adversarial Function: Percentages of Journalists of Various
Media Who Saw the Dimensions as Extremely Important

Media Type	Adversary of Officials (%)	Adversary of Business (%)	N
News magazines	32	33	60
Dailies	26	17	629
Wire service	23	11	56
TV	17	9	137
Weeklies	11	8	161
Radio	8	7	101
Total	21	14	1,144

the adversarial approach than was the case in 1982, when about a third found no importance at all in an adversary function.

Given that some critics both within and outside the field appear to accept characterizations like House Speaker Newt Gingrich's that journalists are "out to get everybody," our finding represents either the ultimate denial, mass lying, or a misunderstanding. Whatever the explanation, other data have been consistent with the thrust of our survey findings. The Times Mirror Center for The People & The Press found in early 1995 that 68% of journalists for "national" media and 81% of "local" journalists "strongly denied" focusing on the misdeeds and personal failings of "public figures."[34]

Another significant finding is the emergence of a new cluster of roles that may be the harbinger of change in the field. The populist mobilizer function, while held strongly by only about 6% of our sample, consists of a provocative group of four notions: developing interests of the public, providing entertainment, setting the political agenda, and letting ordinary people express views (see Table 4.7).

Until the early 1990s, the query (in all three surveys) about the importance of journalists providing entertainment was not a "building block" of any core value. In the minds of a small minority, the importance of "entertaining" in 1992 was linked to the two items added to the latest survey—the importance of setting the political agenda of the public, and developing the intellectual-cultural interests of the audience—to make up a "new" populist role. The logic was that journalists attract attention through interesting, entertaining stories. Once having the audience's attention, the public's intellectual-cultural interests may be developed and channeled through an agenda-setting role that is independent of officials. A fourth value, giving ordinary people a chance to express their views on public affairs, was also linked to the populist mobilizer role, but not as strongly as the other microroles. If our analysis is right, the new role is tantalizing evidence that the spirit of the "public journalism" movement may have established a foothold among the core values of a tiny minority of journalists.

TABLE 4.7
The Populist Mobilizer Function: Percentages of Journalists of Various
Media Who Saw the Dimensions as Extremely Important

Media Type	Allow Public to Express Views (%)	Develop Cultural Interests (%)	Entertainment (%)	Set the Political Agenda (%)	N
Weeklies	58	17	17	3	162
Dailies	52	18	16	5	635
Radio	46	19	10	4	101
TV	39	18	7	4	137
News magazines	27	32	10	5	61
Wire service	26	14	14	2	58
Total	48	18	14	5	1,154

Pluralism Is the Key

Perhaps more significant was the 1992 study's strong showing again that a majority of journalists are *pluralistic*. That is, most journalists strongly endorsed a combination of two, and sometimes three, of the core roles. At least superficially, then, most journalists saw themselves as serving seemingly *contradictory* functions (see Fig. 4.2). About a third of them fully embraced both the interpretive and disseminator ideas—a similar pattern to that of the 1982–1983 study. More important, this third wave of data suggests that, for most journalists, the interpretive stance—what the Johnstone group in 1971 called the *participant role*—did not extend to a full acceptance of an adversary function. Similarly, the disseminator role did not necessarily mean a neutral stance for a majority of those seeing the information function as a core role. However, as we noted earlier, those favoring the disseminator stance in 1992 were more cautious about unverified sources than they were a decade previous.

THEORETICAL "CAUSES" OF ROLE CONCEPTIONS

Explaining the professional attitudes, or the behavior, of journalists is easy or difficult, depending on where you stand. Critics find it easy, although they are often contradictory. Scholars tend to find it hard indeed. That is the case with the present work, representing broad-scale surveys over three decades. Nevertheless, some modest possibilities of broad "predictors" of orientations toward the three larger media functions emerge from this work. (Because the populist mobilizer orientation consists of such a small sample, the comparative statistical analysis of the predictors does not include it.)

Three categories of factors are considered, allowing us to "explain" about half of the variance in attitudes on core roles. Organizational context, individual background, and external factors are the categories of possible "causes" (see Table 4.8).

Since 1971, the organizational context has increased substantially in the leverage it has on individual perceptions of journalistic role. At that time, the Johnstone team concluded that factors in the external environment, as opposed to the more formal job circumstances, were dominant in journalistic images of role and purpose.[35] In 1982–1983, organizational status appeared more relevant, with 5 of 12 factors affecting role conceptions being related to organizational status. Of the 14 factors that appeared to be associated with the broad perceptions of the journalistic role in 1992, 8 of them had to do with various aspects of the organizational context of the journalist's work.

Organizational Context

Ownership, which was not a factor in the earlier studies, emerged as a "predictor" in the 1992 analysis. Knowing that a journalist worked for a large, publicly traded corporation predicted a strong endorsement of the interpretive function. Some

TABLE 4.8
Predictors of Professional Values Among Journalists

Variables	Interpretive Values (R² = .24)		Disseminator Values (R² = .07)		Adversarial Values (R² = .17)	
	Standardized Regression Coefficients	Correlation Coefficients	Standardized Regression Coefficients	Correlation Coefficients	Standardized Regression Coefficients	Correlation Coefficients
Organizational context						
Income	.11	.19	—	—	.07	.15
Print medium	.15	.28	—	—	.09	.21
Ownership—publicly traded	.26	.16	—	—	—	.15
Reporter	.07	.13	—	—	.13	.05
Supervisor—lower level	—	—	—	—	.10	.21
Staff size	.08	.27	.08	.04	.07	.15
Importance of autonomy	.13	.18	—	—	.10	.15
Importance of job security	—	—	.06	.08	—	—
Influence of audience research	—	—	.07	.10	-.10	-.16
Importance of journalism training	—	—	.09	.12	—	—
Individual background						
Private college	.07	.18	—	—	—	—
Being conservative	-.12	-.26	.07	.07	-.09	-.19
External factors						
Amount of comment from news sources	.07	.11	—	—	.09	.14
Influence of friends	—	—	—	—	.08	.08

critics would suggest that large corporations, for which many journalists worked in 1992, would nudge their newsrooms toward a somewhat more conservative disseminator role. That did not appear to be the case in 1992, however.

The adversarial function was also considerably more highly salient among journalists working in larger organizations, particularly the print media. Type of ownership of the media, however, was not related to the adversarial function.[36]

Journalists who made higher salaries were more likely to be among those who tended to be interpretive or adversarialist. But the tendency for disseminator-oriented journalists to be less well paid was considerably less in 1992 than in 1982–1983. Reporters were a little more likely to subscribe strongly to the adversary and interpretive functions than were other journalists. Lower level editors were also slightly more likely to be adversarialist than were their upper level colleagues. Reporters, lower editors, and upper management did not differ much in their patterns of acceptance of the disseminator role.

In the 1982–1983 study, there was a tendency for supervisors to be somewhat less likely than their reporting staffs to be either interpretive or adversarial. The overall picture in 1992 was that the gap between editors and reporters on the broad purposes of journalism—always somewhat small—was even less pronounced.

Salience of professional autonomy and job security were factors in the latest study, just as they also were in the previous studies. The greater the importance of autonomy to the journalists, the greater the tendency to identify strongly with the interpretive or adversarial functions. However, in 1982, autonomy was related to the interpretive function, but not to being adversarial.

Feelings about the importance of job security were pertinent in 1992. In all three studies, those journalists who said job security was of higher importance to them were somewhat more likely to be strong on the disseminator function. The perceived importance of journalism training—which is a blend of on-the-job and previous college experiences—also related to the disseminator perspective. Journalists who valued highly their journalism training as a referent when they considered aspects of newsworthiness also tended to be disseminator-oriented.

Although none of the "predictors" was particularly strong, the cumulative impact of the various aspects of the organizational context suggests it was more important in the makeup of role orientations in 1992 than in the previous studies.

Individual Background Characteristics

The 1971 study found that educational experiences were among the most powerful predictors of journalistic role.[37] A decade later, in 1982, educational levels among journalists were higher and more homogeneous, so the effect of schooling was somewhat less. Still, in 1982–1983, having fewer years of schooling suggested the journalist was likely to hold strongly to the disseminator function.

In the 1992 study, the impact of education was even less and in a slightly different direction. Graduating from a private college or university was a modest "predictor" of strong interpretive leanings in 1992. In contrast, having a journalism degree was not a "predictor" of journalistic role orientation, suggesting that such programs do not have the homogenizing effects some critics claim, at least not on perceptions of which roles are most important.

Political leanings were related to core roles in 1992. Journalists who said they were politically liberal were somewhat more likely to be interpretive or adversarial in orientation. Journalists who were politically conservative were more likely to endorse the disseminator role. That was consistent with our earlier study.

External Factors

Two items on interaction with news sources and friends had a small effect on journalistic role orientation. The more frequently news sources were said to comment on the journalist's work, the more likely the interpretive and adversary roles were endorsed. Additionally, the more the journalist valued the input of personal friends on what makes news, the more likely the adversarial role was dominant.

Some factors that appeared to be unrelated to attitudes about journalistic role are worth noting. Geographic location of the media, a predictor of journalistic core roles in the 1982–1983 study, was no longer a factor in 1992. Being a journalist in the South or North Central regions no longer suggested a tendency to avoid either the interpretive or adversarial roles. Professional memberships, which were on the decline in 1992, were not an influence on role orientations. That was consistent with the two previous studies. It appears, then, that the organizational context became more important during 1971–1992 in affecting expression of professional values among journalists. Still, at least half of the complicated complexion of journalistic roles was *not* explained by our findings.

PROFILES OF JOURNALISTS EMBRACING DIFFERENT ROLES

What can we say about the profiles journalists who "leaned" toward the various conceptions, given that most of them perceived more than one core function as extremely important?

Interpreters: Who Were They?

In a nutshell, they might be called *source-interactive, somewhat liberal pundits*.

The dominant, interpretive function was most salient among those who worked for the larger, corporate (publicly traded) media, particularly news magazines and daily newspapers. Wire service personnel also tended to identify with this perspective. Weekly newspaper and broadcast news personnel, particularly those in radio, were less likely to place as much importance on interpretive journalism as were their other colleagues.

Journalists who said job autonomy was very important to them—particularly those who graduated from private institutions and whose salaries were higher— were a bit more likely than others to consider the interpretive stance as highly salient. That portrait is roughly similar to the one Johnstone found in 1971, except that he found the younger, less experienced journalist was more likely to be "participant" (interpretive) in orientation. In 1982–1983, education and salary appeared to have less of an impact on the interpreter role than in 1992.

The term *source interactive* may be puzzling at first glance. Of course journalists interacted with sources—that was their job. However, this was a slightly different slant. Interpreters were more likely to say they got frequent comments about their work from news sources than were their colleagues who identified strongly with the other functions of journalism. We found the same characteristic in our 1982 study. Regrettably, we have no evidence whether the tone of the feedback was positive or negative, nor whether the feedback was a result of the nature of the news stories produced by the journalists.

Unlike in 1982, interpreters in 1992 tended to see themselves as more liberal politically. At that time, a liberal bent was associated with the adversary stance, but not the interpretive role.

Disseminators: Who Were They?

In a few words, they tended to be *audience-oriented, somewhat conservative and cautious immediacy-seekers*.

The second most salient press function, information dissemination, seemed to be a "streak" among a great variety of journalists, making a "typical" portrait somewhat faint. They were about as likely to be working for larger media as smaller organizations and for all types of ownership.

Other factors related to disseminator leanings were feelings about journalism training and the role of audience research. Those who said their journalistic training was a key determinant of newsworthiness, or who thought audience research played a significant role on newsroom decisions, were somewhat more likely to be disseminator in outlook.

One of the most significant characteristics of "disseminators" had to do with cautiousness. They tended to be considerably less accepting of controversial reporting practices, such as posing as someone else or using unauthorized documents, than were their colleagues who were more strongly interpretive or adversarial. Disseminators were also slightly more apt to be politically moderate to conservative—a consistent pattern in all three studies.

Adversarialists: Who Were They?

In broad strokes, adversary journalists might be labeled *investigative, friend-oriented, moderate-to-liberal skeptics*.

Clearly, most "adversarialists" were also interpretive in approach, and were especially likely to feel strongly about the government "watchdog" responsibility of journalism.[38] Their strong affinity for the interpretive function obviously made them largely reflective of the characteristics associated with the previous portrait of the interpreters. Somewhat like the "interpreters," adversarial journalists tended to be moderate-to-liberal "leaners," and placed great value on job autonomy. They also tended to work for the larger print media.

A few unique tendencies typified the adversarialists. They spent most of their time reporting, but were also found occasionally among lower level editing jobs. Those in upper level management did not show up in the ranks of the adversarialists very often.

Audience research appeared to be an issue for adversarialists. They tended to see audience research as having less influence on newsroom decisions than did "disseminators," who seemed to think that audience research was more salient in their newsrooms.

The label *friend oriented* in the thumbnail sketch of adversarialists is an ironic twist. They tended to think of their friends and acquaintances as more influential on their notions of what was newsworthy than did their colleagues who were strongly "interpretive."

In a sense, the adversary mentality was a bit like a gene that requires the right kind of nurturance to result in behavior. It was not dominant most of the time, even among the big-city newspaper journalists. A scene from Ron Howard's hit movie *The Paper* captured the tone, as the executive editor of the "New York Sun" reminded his "metro editor" Henry Hackett (played by Michael Keaton)—who, at the moment was in an adversarial mode—of the newspaper's role: "They [sources] talk, you write, and we print."

Adversarialists, too, were almost as likely to be in the smaller media, if the conditions were right. As was seen earlier, journalists on big staffs also tended to be tuned in strongly to the disseminator role.

Populist Mobilizers: Who Were They?

Very tentatively, they were *small-media, community-oriented idealists.*

This was such a small group (about 6%) that statistical analysis cannot yield a valid portrait. Some very tentative suggestions are that radio, weekly, and daily newspapers—likely the smaller ones—made up the newsrooms in which "mobilizing" journalists worked (see Table 4.7). This was supported in open-ended comments about job satisfaction from the earlier chapter, particularly from radio journalists in all-news and "talk" radio formats, and from weekly and smaller daily newspaper personnel. The idea of connecting to the local communities and giving "voice" to them was a theme in some of those comments.

One of the most interesting aspects of the mobilizing function was the element of giving voice to ordinary people—considered a strong value by about half of the journalists from weeklies, radio, and daily newspapers. It was expected that news magazine and wire service journalists, considering their national scope, would be less likely to see giving "voice" as a high value. It was surprising that television journalists were less likely to see this as salient. Even more surprising was the reticence of television journalists to accept the entertainment role as highly important, especially given trends in television news toward entertainment values during 1982–1992.

However, daily newspaper journalists were also more reticent in 1992 than they were a decade previous to accept the entertainment label, as were personnel in all other media, except wire services. Perhaps this was an indication of wishful thinking, making the finding of questionable validity. In contrast, sympathy for interesting and entertaining journalism was linked, for the first time, to a mobilizing conception of the news, perhaps a sign that journalists were striving to "use" entertainment in a positive way.

Finally, despite the clear, statistical linkage of an "agenda-setting" notion to a populist mobilizing role conception, there was a striking consistency in the smallness of the groups of journalists in all media who saw it as a high value. If the notion of agenda setting *was* linked to a mobilizing mentality, as we maintain, that is a positive sign. It may also mean that journalists simply refused to admit to the characterization of critics that they were only too willing to "throw their weight around" in affecting public affairs.

NEWS VALUES

Nothing in the field is more important than decisions about what is worthy of publication or broadcast. Dissatisfaction with the press, both within and outside the mass media, often is about news values and selection. For example, a Times-Mirror study in early 1995 found that 71% of American "opinion leaders" and 66% of the general public felt the news was "too focused on misdeeds." Although journalists largely disagreed with that opinion, the gap between the public's conception of news and their own seems to be widening.[39]

Among journalists and scholars, notions about what makes something newsworthy are many: conflict, prominent sources, events that affect large numbers of people, pseudoevents staged by publicists and "handlers." The list is long. Scarcely anyone believes, as some once claimed, that journalists simply "hold up a mirror on the world." However, an important element of newsworthiness often rests with journalists, as well as newsroom interaction and the larger newsgathering context.

In our 1982–1983 study, when respondents were asked about the importance of many factors to determining newsworthiness, journalistic training—largely on the job, but including college experience and campus media—was the source most often ranked as influential. The term *journalistic training* covered a lot of ground, but it did not overlap with more concrete items about contacts with supervisors and staff peers. Both supervisors and peers were important referents of newsworthiness in the minds of our respondents in 1982. Of the nine aspects asked about at that time, nonjournalistic friends and acquaintances were the least likely influences, although about 2 in 10 journalists did mention them as important.

As a follow-up to our 1982–1983 study, we asked journalists in 1992 how influential a number of factors were in determining what was newsworthy in their day-to-day work. Overall, the influences on newsworthiness were fairly similar to those of a decade previous (see Table 4.9). A noteworthy exception was the perceived influence of friends, which outranked wire service budgets in importance as a factor in newsworthiness. A new question about public opinion polls also found them to be considered influential by a slightly larger minority than wire budgets, which was the last item on the list in 1992.

In our 1982 study, various referents of newsworthiness were combined into clusters of items that correlated strongly. Using similar categories for the 1992 results suggests some media differences in the extent to which each of the elements was important to newsworthiness. Also, for each of the categories, other important characteristics of journalists were used to determine which were the most important in "predicting" why the category was salient to newsworthiness. These results are discussed here within the overall hierarchy of the factors, as ranked by the overall sample of journalists.

Journalistic Training

Just as in 1982, the long-term notions acquired from newsroom training and college experiences in 1992 were the leading referents of newsworthiness in the eyes of journalists in all media. Broadcast and wire service personnel, however, tended to rank journalistic training even more highly than their colleagues in other media.[40]

More experienced journalists—and especially those who had degrees or courses from schools of journalism—were more likely to see a strong connection between journalistic training and their notions of newsworthiness. Women and those who worked on smaller staffs were slightly more likely to value journalistic training's influence on how they defined news.

Lower level editors were less likely than their staffs to see their journalistic training as important to newsworthiness. Journalists in the Midwest and Northeast seemed less likely to say it was important to newsworthiness than those in other regions of the country.

News philosophy was related to salience of journalistic training. Journalists who valued highly the disseminator function were more likely to see a connection between their journalistic training and their notions of newsworthiness.

Media Staff

Editors and peers in the newsroom were the second most important influence on what made news for journalists in all media except radio. In radio news, where the typical news staff was one person, there may have been less opportunity for peer influence on newsworthiness.[41]

TABLE 4.9

Factors Influencing Concept of Newsworthiness, by Medium

Factor				Percentage Saying Very Influential				
	Daily	Radio	Weekly	News Magazine	Wire	TV	Total 1992	Total 1982
Journalistic training	72	76	71	67	79	79	73	77
Supervisors	53	38	52	51	62	50	51	58
Sources	33	65	50	37	18	53	40	53
Staff peers	41	25	49	51	41	34	41	43
Readership/audience research	30	43	53	17	19	40	35	42
Local competing news media	23	40	26	11	31	26	25	36
Network news and prestige papers	25	41	13	21	29	39	27	28
Wire service budgets	22	23	2	7	61	21	20	22
Friends	25	16	23	26	12	28	23	19

Note. Daily, $N = 635$; Radio, $N = 101$; Weekly, $N = 162$; News magazine, $N = 59$; Wire, $N = 58$; TV, $N = 134$; Total 1992, $N = 1,149$; Total 1982, $N = 991$.

Just as we found in 1982, in 1992 journalists who rated their organizations as *excellent* were somewhat more likely to value media staff for cues on the definition of news. This was consistent with the open-ended narratives, discussed in chapter 3 (this volume), that pointed to staff colleagues as the key to newsroom excellence.

Some new factors emerged in the 1992 study. Younger journalists—those with degrees from private universities—and personnel who worked in newsrooms with an ombudsman were more likely to see media staff as important to their ideas about newsworthiness. Editors and news directors were also slightly more likely to see media staff as more important in determining newsworthiness than were lower level editors.

Geography was not a factor in 1982, but was related in 1992. Journalists working in the South were more likely to point to media staff as being influential as cues to newsworthiness than were those in other regions.

Audience/Sources

Weekly and daily newspaper personnel tended to rate news sources, audience research, and public opinion polls as the third most influential referents of newsworthiness. Broadcast personnel ranked this cluster much higher in importance than did other journalists. Particularly for television journalists, the salience of ratings made this category as important to news determination as supervisors and colleagues in the newsroom. Magazine and wire journalists tended to see this cluster as their least important referents for newsworthiness.[42]

Journalists at smaller organizations—and particularly those who worked for privately owned, independent media—were most likely to see audience/sources as important to how they defined news. That was similar to what was found in 1982.

Some new characteristics of audience/source orientation appeared in the 1992 study. Women and minority journalists appeared to be somewhat more sensitive audience/source referents to newsworthiness than were others. Having a major or minor in journalism was also related to greater salience of this factor.

Journalists who were high on a "populist mobilizer" stance, or being a disseminator in approach, were more likely to consider audience/source referents important to news concepts. However, adversarialists were somewhat less likely to be oriented to this factor. Top editors and news directors were a bit more oriented to audience/source referents than were lower level managers. Interestingly, southern journalists were also tuned in to cues from audience/sources somewhat more highly than were their colleagues in other regions.

Friends

The perception of the importance of friends to their definition of news became stronger for all journalists during 1982–1992. This was especially true for daily newspaper, news magazine, and wire service journalists, who ranked personal friends as almost as important to defining news as the category of audi-ence/sources. Television and weekly newspaper journalists ranked friends as the fourth most important influence. Radio journalists saw friends as less important than did their colleagues.[43]

Journalists who were particularly sympathetic to a "populist mobilizer" role were considerably more likely to be tuned in to friends as important referents to what was news. Journalists working for privately owned, independent media were slightly more likely than others to say friends and acquaintances were more influential referents. And journalists in the South were more sensitive to friends as influential influences on their ideas about news.

External Media

The news budgets of television networks, prestigious newspapers, and the wire services were ranked last as agenda setters of newsworthiness for journalists in all media except radio and the wire services. Both radio and wire service personnel saw other media as their second or third referent for newsworthiness. The com-petitive context for radio, and its dependency on other sources for news, both enhanced the importance of external media for newsworthiness. Of course, wire services depend on their affiliated media for a supply of stories to supplement their bureaus, so the findings for both radio and wire journalists reflected their special needs.[44]

Women journalists and personnel at smaller operations were a bit more likely to pay attention to external media on questions of newsworthiness than were some of their colleagues. Not surprisingly, younger journalists seemed more likely to take cues about newsworthiness from external media than were their elders, except for lower level management, who also kept their eyes on other media for cues about news.

In summary, journalists perceived organizational context and journalistic training as the most influential factors affecting newsworthiness. These 1992 findings were consistent with those from a decade previous.

One of the most significant 1992 findings was not only similar to 1982, but also reflected those discussed in the previous chapter. Journalists who saw them-selves working in an excellent newsroom serving its audience well were much more likely to be tuned in to "media staff" for cues on newsworthiness. The reason that many of our respondents said their newsroom was doing an excellent job was because of the talent and resourcefulness of their colleagues, including editors. It makes sense, but it is also comforting evidence of a consistency between the open-ended comments and the closed questions on different aspects of the journalistic life.

There appeared to be more media differences in 1992 than in 1982–1983, largely because of shrinking news staffs in radio and the increasing salience of audience ratings for television journalists. Another noteworthy change was the rising importance of friends as referents for newsworthiness, particularly in daily newspapers and news magazines. There was no evidence that the number of nonjournalistic friends increased from 1982 to 1992, at least in comparison with the friendships with journalists. The change may reflect a decline in the perceived influence of external media sources on newsworthiness, more than any enhancement in the role of friendships.

Another significant finding in 1992 was the pertinence of journalism education and courses to the salience of journalism training as a factor in the determination of what was news. That was not the case a decade previous. Also, journalists working in the South were more sensitive than those of any other region to all the newsworthiness referents.

Staff size was a consistent correlate of the referents. Those on smaller staffs were more likely to consider all the factors as highly influential than were journalists in bigger operations. The same was true for those who were strongly populist or disseminator in news philosophy. The implication is that interpreters and adversarialists were somewhat more "inner-directed" in their notions about newsworthiness than were their other colleagues.

Some factors that did not appear to say much about style of determining newsworthiness were significant. Ownership type appeared to play very little role. The single influence it seemed to have was a bit of a surprise, with privately owned, single media being the setting where audience/source referents were more important to news. The critics might have predicted such a relationship for corporate groups, but not for the independent media. There did not appear to be much of a gap between reporters and editors on referents for news. Editors were a little more likely to pay attention to external media when thinking about news than were reporters, but that was not surprising. They were not quite as likely to see their journalism training's pertinence as were their reporters. Executive editors and news directors were even more sensitive to media staff than were reporters in thinking about news values.

ETHICS IN JOURNALISM

Ethical and moral development for journalists has been in some journalism school curricula for at least half a century, long before the topic of applied ethics for professionals became fashionable in universities in the early 1980s. In 1924, Nelson A. Crawford, head of the Department of Industrial Journalism at Kansas State Agricultural College, published The Ethics of Journalism with the distinguished house of Alfred A. Knopf. His aim was to contribute to a "professional consciousness" and an ethical philosophy that was "realistic, discerning, intellectually honest, and applicable to the press as a social institution."[45] Crawford wisely realized that the goal was ambitious, but he could never have imagined that a recent textbook on media ethics, written by Conrad Fink, would be saying, ". . . Everywhere are signs of ethical deterioration."[46]

In our book on the 1982–1983 national study, we wrote that concern about journalism ethics was at an historic peak. The high-water mark, we thought, was the ill-fated Pulitzer Prize awarded to Janet Cooke, then of the *Washington Post*, for what turned out to be a fabricated story about the drug-infested world of an imaginary 6-year-old child. The same year, *Absence of Malice*, a classic motion picture written by former journalist Kurt Luedke, dramatized other ethical dilemmas of the press.

The 1990s also saw no shortage of work for media ethicists. Soon after we completed fieldwork for the 1992 study, the rigged crash test of a GM truck for *Dateline NBC* exploded in a firestorm of adversarial zeal to become an ethical catastrophe for journalism. The trial of William Kennedy Smith on charges of rape and, later, the O.J. Simpson trial brought charges that even the elite press was falling victim to the tawdry ethical standards of the "supermarket tabloids." Oliver Stone's controversial movie *Natural Born Killers* later portrayed television journalists gleefully making a Faustian bargain with criminals for "good visuals."

The rising tide of concern about media ethics seems to resonate with the present generation of journalists. In a careful survey of newspaper journalists done in 1992–1993, ethics topped a long list of topics on which they wanted inservice training. More than 80% of the 650 journalists in the sample mentioned ethics as a priority.[47]

There is debate among thinkers on whether, and how, ethics can be taught. Learning to be ethical may be as complex as learning to be prejudiced. Stealing a line about prejudice from Rodgers and Hammerstein's classic *South Pacific*, "it must be carefully taught." The song, of course, suggests it is taught from infancy, and so the same may be with ethics.

In that spirit, our two national studies asked journalists to consider the influences of their past or present circumstances on their ethical bearing. Specifically, the respondents were asked about the influence of a set of factors—ranging from family upbringing to their publisher or general manager—in shaping their ideas in matters of journalism ethics. The results suggest similar patterns of perceived influences over the two studies (see Table 4.10).

In both studies, day-to-day newsroom learning was the factor cited most frequently as either "extremely" or "quite" influential in matters of journalism ethics. Family upbringing was the second most cited influence in both studies, exceeding the perceived importance of senior editors or senior reporters. Editors and reporters were cited less frequently in 1992, with the figure for senior reporters being significantly less.

Journalism school teachers were mentioned by about half the respondents in both studies. However, the biggest change was in the perceived importance of college teachers, in general, as influential shapers of ethics. In 1982, they were mentioned by half the respondents—a figure similar to that for journalism school teachers. Now that ethics is much more widely taught across university curricula, it was a surprise to see the figure drop to 21% for college teachers in 1992. High

TABLE 4.10
Sources of Influence on Ethics

| | Percentage Saying Influential | |
Source	1982–1983	1992
Newsroom learning	88	88
Family upbringing	72	74
Senior editor	61	58
Coworkers[a]	57	—
Journalism school teachers	53	49
Senior reporter	52	45
College/university teachers	50	21
Religious upbringing	35	36
Publisher	25	17
High school teachers	24	17

Note. 1982–1983, $N = 1,000$; 1992, $N = 1,155$.
[a]Not asked in 1992.

school teachers, frequently cited as a major influence on journalism as a career choice, also declined slightly as an influential "shaper" of ideas about journalism ethics. Publishers and general managers were also mentioned as influential somewhat less often in the latest study.

More than 90% of the journalists, in both studies, said they were brought up in a religious denomination. In the 1992 survey, more than a third said religious beliefs, in general, were "very important," and another third said "somewhat important" to them. Still, only 36%—similar to a decade previous—said their religious upbringing was influential as a source of ethical orientation in journalism.

INFLUENCES ON ETHICS

Intensive analysis of the sources of ethical influence suggested that the items could be grouped into three clusters: newsroom context, family and religion, and teachers.[48] These clusters were used to search for different patterns of influence on ethical orientations among journalists. The purpose was to see what factors were associated with a tendency of journalists to see themselves as relying on a particular set of factors in matters of journalism ethics.

Newsroom Context

The cluster of newsroom-related factors—journalism training, editors, reporters, and publishers—appeared to be the most frequently cited overall factor as a perceived influence on ethics. No significant differences in its importance appeared among journalists for different media—a finding similar to that of 1982.[49]

Journalists who saw the disseminator, populist, or adversarial functions as important were somewhat more likely to rate the newsroom context as *influential* than were their colleagues who were interpretive in news philosophy. Smaller staffs were a bit more conducive to the newsroom context being seen as an important influence on matters of ethics. That was consistent with our finding that journalists on smaller staffs were also more likely to say their colleagues were influential on their ideas about newsworthiness. Those who worked in a newsroom they regarded as doing an excellent job informing the audience also tended to cite newsroom influences on ethics more often.

Unlike 1982, having an ombudsman in the newsroom in 1992 did not increase the likelihood that newsroom context had an ethical influence. Education also seemed to soften the newsroom's influence in 1992. The more years of schooling the journalist had, the less likely the newsroom was seen as influential in matters of ethics.

Family and Religion

The perceived impact of the newsroom context on ethics was no surprise. That journalists saw family and religion as important as they did, however, certainly did not fit the secular, hardened image of them that abounded in 1992. A decade previous, age was related to the salience of family and religion as ethical referents, with older journalists somewhat more likely to see them as having an ethical influence. That was still true in 1992. However, ownership form was no longer a factor. In 1982–1983, journalists working for privately owned, independent newsrooms were somewhat more likely to cite family and religion as ethical influences.

Geography emerged as a factor in the 1992 study. Journalists working in the South were more likely to see family and religion as important to their ethical orientation than journalists in other regions. Those who leaned toward the populist mobilizer function also tended to cite family and religion, whereas interpreters were apt not to see them as influences on their ethical orientation.[50] Lower level editors were slightly less likely than their staffs to mention family and religion in matters of ethics.

Teachers

Smaller organizations were somewhat more likely than larger to have journalists on their staffs who thought of teachers as influential on their ethics. That was the case in 1982 as well. Weekly newspaper and radio news personnel in 1992 were slightly more likely to rank teachers as influential.[51]

Education, of course, was related to the remembrance of teachers as an ethical influence. As was the case in 1982, those who had journalism–mass communication degrees or took those courses as a minor were more likely to cite teachers in 1992. Women journalists were more likely than male graduates to cite their teachers as an ethical influence. Liberal arts teachers, as was seen earlier, were cited significantly less frequently in 1992, even by journalists who had only liberal arts degrees, than a decade previous. Of particular significance was the finding that journalists working in newsrooms they regarded as excellent were more likely to see teachers as having influenced their ethical orientations.

In conclusion, this analysis of ethical influences finds that, in 1992, journalists saw the newsroom environment as the most powerful force in shaping their ideas about ethical matters. The same appeared to be true 10 years previous. However, an interesting wrinkle emerged for the larger media. Although journalists who worked for them still considered the newsroom environment as important in ethical matters, they appeared *less* likely to see it as influential than a decade earlier.

The implication is that the present trend toward writing, or revising, formal codes of ethics for newsrooms is in the right direction. This is especially important for larger newsrooms. Our study suggests that newsroom environments of larger organizations became less salient as an ethical force during 1982–1992. David Hawpe, editor of the Louisville *Courier-Journal* and head of an APME committee to revise the Associated Press code of ethics, said there "... is a need for an ongoing conversation about ethics," and that writing codes is a way of doing that.[52] Not everyone agrees that codes should be written, of course. As Hawpe suggested, however, anything that enhances conversation about ethics within the newsroom environment is important. Nothing makes this clearer than the deep divisions that existed in 1992 among journalists on the appropriateness of various controversial reporting practices, dealt with in the next section.

ETHICAL PERCEPTIONS OF REPORTING PRACTICES

News ethics, of course, covers a broad landscape, but nothing is more central than specific reporting practices. The tactics of journalists in obtaining information sometimes reflect their basic role orientations, as well as a zeal for a "good story." A scene from *The Paper* is revealing. In this film, the "metro editor" Henry Hackett badgers an informant in verifying that police lacked evidence to hold two African-American murder suspects. Clearly the fictitious journalist, played by Michael Keaton, is driven by a sense of justice for the suspects, but his desire for a "hell of a story" is just as great. The film nicely portrays an ethical dilemma forged by an adversarial mood, strong "disseminator" tendencies, and a passion for "the story." Should a news source ever be badgered? It depends, of course. This section looks at the most basic level of tolerance for a number of such reporting practices.

In our two surveys, journalists were asked to think about 10 reporting situations, ranging from the possibility of paying for confidential information to undercover reporting. The interviewees indicated whether, given an "important

TABLE 4.11
Journalists' Acceptance of Various Reporting Practices

Reporting Practice	Percentage Saying May Be Justified	
	1982–1983[a]	1992
Getting employed in a firm or organization to gain inside information	67	63
Using confidential business or government documents without authorization	55	82
Badgering unwilling informants to get a story	47	49
Making use of personal documents such as letters and photographs without permission	28	48
Paying people for confidential information	27	20
Claiming to be somebody else	20	22
Agreeing to protect confidentiality and not doing so	5	5
Using hidden microphones or cameras[b]	—	60
Using re-creations or dramatizations of news by actors[b]	—	28
Disclosing the names of rape victims[b]	—	43

Note. 1982–1992, N = 1,001; 1992, N = 1,156.
[a]Data from David Weaver and G. Cleveland Wilhoit, *The American Journalist*, p. 128.
[b]Not asked in 1982–1983 survey.

story," the reporting practices "may be justified on occasion," or would not be approved "under any circumstances."

We understand that the question captures only a sliver of information, but it is important information. In journalistic life, the situations to which the various practices pertain are usually immensely complicated. An entire survey could be devoted to each one. The question used was not designed to measure preference. Instead, it sets up "worst case scenarios" on which a journalist may say, in effect, "here is a practice that I could never see myself, nor any other journalist, doing."

The results show some significant changes in how the lines have been drawn on these practices during 1982–1992 (see Table 4.11).

Disclosing Confidential Sources

If there is a bedrock principle among journalists, it is that a commitment to a source's anonymity must be honored at all costs. Almost all journalists (95%), in both the 1982–1983 and 1992 studies, said divulging the name of confidential sources was not approved under any circumstances. So, rulings by federal and state courts that have undermined journalists' claim of a constitutional right of source privilege have not shaken their belief that a promise of confidentiality must be honored. In 1992, the U.S. Supreme Court ruled that the First Amendment did not shield editors at the *Minneapolis Star Tribune* and *St. Paul Pioneer Press* from a lawsuit for breaking a reporter's "contract" not to disclose a source who "leaked" damaging information about a political opponent.[53] Most editors believe as strongly as reporters in the confidentiality principle. For example, in 1993, Paul Tash, executive editor of the *St. Petersburg Times*, escorted Tim Roch, a reporter, to jail to serve 30 days for refusal to divulge his source in a Florida case. Tash said, "... I'm quite proud of Tim for his courage and his commitment to this very important principle."[54]

Using False Identification

Masquerading as someone else may be relatively innocent for a reviewer of restaurants, but what about the willful use of a false identify by a reporter? In their classic book about the *Washington Post*'s Watergate investigation, Carl Bernstein and Bob Woodward said they "dodged, evaded, misrepresented, suggested and intimidated" in gathering evidence on one of the most important stories of the century.[55]

Some media, such as *The New York Times*, forbid false identification in all circumstances. Others weigh the importance of the evidence and whether it may be obtained without the deceit.[56]

Few voices, either inside or outside the press, criticized celebrated Chinese dissident Harry Wu for posing as a Chinese-American business man in his former homeland to report on prison-labor exploitation for CBS's *Sixty Minutes* in 1992. Using a hidden camera, Wu recorded a Chinese official saying prisoners were beaten to maintain quality control of goods for export. The CBS reporting led to appearances in Congress for Wu, who became a naturalized U.S. citizen in 1994.[57] Rarely, however, does such reporting go unchallenged when the subject is within our own borders.

In our 1982–1983 study, conducted in the afterglow of Watergate, only a small minority (20%) of journalists felt that claiming to be somebody else might be justified under any circumstances. Weekly and daily newspaper journalists were significantly less likely to accept such a practice than their broadcast and news magazine colleagues.

Overall, the 1992 study found a similar consensus against misrepresentation, with only 22% saying it might be justified. Television and news magazine journalists were somewhat more likely to tolerate masquerading than were their colleagues. Compared with 1982, in 1992 a larger number of weekly newspaper journalists, but fewer radio personnel, said the practice might be justified (see Table 4.12).

Paying for Confidential Information

Recent abuses of "checkbook" journalism obscure the fact that it has been a long-standing problem. After Watergate, a former aide to President Richard Nixon, John Ehrlichman, claimed, "There are various types of raconteurs who are paid money by publishers, news syndicates and the networks." These persons

TABLE 4.12
Opinion on Using False Identification, by Medium

| Medium | Percentage Saying May Be Justified | | | |
| | 1982–1983 | | 1992 | |
	%[a]	N	%[b]	N
Television	31	121	31	137
News magazines	30	62	34	61
Radio	25	119	13	101
Daily	19	463	20	635
Wire	15	47	21	58
Weekly	12	183	22	162
Total sample	20	995	22	1,154

[a]$p < .001.$ [b]$p < .02.$

"peddle" their "secrets never before revealed to the highest bidder."[58] A celebrated example at that time was Mr. Nixon, who sold "news" interviews to CBS's *Sixty Minutes* in 1984.

Some felt the problem reached epidemic proportions in the early 1990s, with the O.J. Simpson case, allegations about Olympic skater Tonya Harding's involvement in an attack on a fellow skater, and the caning of American teenager Michael Fay in Singapore on charges of vandalism. "Tabloid" newspapers and television shows apparently paid sources openly in those cases. *Hard Copy* was said to have paid $100,000 for interviews in 1994 with Michael Jackson's former bodyguards for information on child molestation charges against the famous singer.[59]

Lou Prato, writing in *American Journalism Review*, said, "The practice of paying sources has become so rampant in television that it now threatens the fundamental credibility of TV news."[60] However, some media have gone to extraordinary lengths to avoid the temptation. In 1993, a *Kansas City Star* reporter paid $30 for a load of asphalt mix that was stolen by municipal employees and sold illegally at a private service station. The paper's editors refused to run the story because they saw the payment as an "ethical mistake."[61]

In our earlier interviews, about 27% said paying for sources may be justified. In 1992, the figure dropped significantly, with only 20% of our 1992 sample saying the practice was justifiable. Those tolerant of the practice were a smaller minority in 1992, compared with 1982–1983, in all media except weekly newspapers (see Table 4.13). Journalists on daily newspapers were the least likely group in 1992 to accept paying for information, but there was striking consensus among journalists of all media opposing the practice under any circumstances.

Whether journalists' personal opposition can help to curb the practice is, of course, in question. Diana Olick, a reporter at KIRO in Seattle, said the competitive pressures are immense, adding, "If you want to play, you're gonna have to pay."[62]

TABLE 4.13
Opinion on Payment for Confidential Information, by Medium

| | Percentage Saying May Be Justified | | | |
| | 1982–1983 | | 1992 | |
Medium	%[a]	N	%[b]	N
News magazines	35	62	25	61
Television	32	121	25	137
Wire	30	47	22	58
Daily	26	463	17	635
Radio	26	119	23	101
Weekly	23	183	24	162
Total sample	27	995	20	1,154

[a]$p > .05.$ [b]$p < .01.$

Badgering Sources

Scarcely anyone aware of the hitting feats of baseball-great Mickey Mantle and who watched him at a press conference in the summer of 1995, several weeks after his liver transplant, will ever forget it. Live on CNN, a reporter badgered the sick, old hitter about whether he had received preferential treatment in getting a liver donation so quickly. It was a legitimate question, but the tone of the query struck some as inappropriate. The award-winning CBS *Sixty Minutes* news magazine show, in its 26-year history, has shown many sources being goaded, often at the hands of Mike Wallace, a master of the tactic. His "badgering" image was certainly one of the more visible ones when we designed the 1982–1983 interviews on this topic.

Journalists then were deeply divided on the tactic. Our 1992 results show that American journalists were still deeply divided on the acceptance of badgering unwilling informants. About half said the practice may be justified, just as we found a decade previous. Print journalists were somewhat more likely to tolerate the practice than were broadcast personnel—similar to the pattern in 1982–1983 (see Table 4.14). Among daily newspaper journalists, a significant rise in acceptance appeared; in radio, there was a substantial drop.

Using Personal Documents Without Consent

In an age of electronic mail, the meaning of personal documents may be changing. We know of no cases of "computer-hacking" journalists breaking into private files, but it may be just a matter of time. However, the amount of personal information available in the databases of both private and public agencies has changed the nature of privacy questions facing the press.[63]

TABLE 4.14
Opinion on Badgering Sources, by Medium

| | Percentage Saying May Be Justified | | | |
| | 1982–1983 | | 1992 | |
Medium	%[a]	N	%[a]	N
Wire	68	47	53	58
News magazines	67	62	59	61
Television	52	121	46	137
Daily	47	463	55	635
Radio	43	119	28	101
Weekly	38	183	36	162
Total sample	48	995	49	1,154

[a]$p < .0000.$

In 1982, the notion of "personal" documents had a more quaint meaning. For example, a respected book on ethics tells of a classic case of a West Coast newspaper that wanted a photograph of a murdered man. The family refused, so a reporter stole one, published it, then returned it to the distraught family.[64] On the surface, it does not appear that this sort of privacy invasion occurs very often. However, the difference in responses to the question in our two national studies about the use of personal documents was striking.

Almost half of the 1992 sample said making use of personal documents without permission may be justified. In 1982, only about one in four said that (see Table 4.15). Radio and weekly newspaper journalists in 1992 were the least likely to accept use of unauthorized documents, although substantially more of them were tolerant of the practice than in the earlier study. Slight majorities of daily newspaper, news magazine, and wire service journalists said the use of unauthorized personal documents may be justified.

TABLE 4.15
Opinion on Unauthorized Use of Personal Documents, by Medium

| | Percentage Saying May Be Justified | | | |
| | 1982–1983 | | 1992 | |
Medium	%[a]	N	%[a]	N
Wire	49	47	53	58
Daily	33	463	54	635
News magazines	32	62	54	61
Television	26	121	45	137
Weekly	21	183	31	162
Radio	12	119	28	101
Total sample	28	995	48	1,154

[a]$p < .000.$

The changing form of documents may have been in the back of journalists' minds in the most recent study, when they answered our question about unauthorized personal documents. If so, the escalating concerns about personal privacy among the general public seem to take a back seat to a feeling among journalists that the privacy movement threatens a larger value of "the public's right to know."[65]

Using Unauthorized Confidential Documents

Government secrecy and the handling of classified documents is a continuing problem for many journalists at the national level. In 1995, *The Wall Street Journal* used a confidential Philip Morris internal document in a story that suggested that a company "task force"—disbanded in 1992—had conceded the chemical similarity of nicotine to cocaine. The company told the newspaper that the report was written by a "non-scientist" whose views did not represent those of Philip Morris.[66]

The hazards of such reporting on cigarette interests became clear in 1986 when Walter Jacobson, then news anchor and commentator on the CBS-owned WBBM-TV in Chicago, lost a $3 million libel suit to the Brown and Williamson Tobacco Company. Jacobson used a confidential Federal Trade Commission document to claim that the company sold Viceroy cigarettes to youth by linking them to "pot, wine, beer and sex." The marketing strategy had been conceived in a confidential document from an advertising agency that the cigarette company had fired.

The U.S. Supreme Court refused to overturn the lower courts in finding that Jacobson and CBS had shown "actual malice" because the news operation destroyed critical documents in the case that might have shown the story to be false. This was a case of the use of unauthorized documents that clearly turned sour for journalism.[67]

In the movie *The Paper*, the use of unauthorized business documents takes the ironic twist of a journalist stealing from another. "The Sun" metro editor Hackett goes for an interview at another, more "prestigious" New York paper. During his interview at "The Sentinel," Hackett steals an exclusive story by reading notes on "editor" Paul Bladden's desk. In a review of the film, Bill Hoffman, a real reporter and film critic for the *New York Post*, one of the papers on which the script is based, asked rhetorically, "Would any of us ever do something so dastardly?" His answer: "You bet your sweet ass we would! And we'd brag about it, too!"[68]

No single survey question, nor even a battery of them, could capture the situational complexity of the Pentagon Papers or the Jacobson case, much less the problem dramatized in the movie. Nevertheless, just as on the question about personal documents, the responses to our question on unauthorized government and business documents showed a striking change in tolerance.

In 1982–1983, a slight majority said that, given an important story, the use of an unauthorized business or government document may be justified. Ten years

TABLE 4.16
Unauthorized Use of Confidential Documents, by Medium

| Medium | Percentage Saying May Be Justified | | | |
| | 1982–1983 | | 1992 | |
	%[a]	N	%[a]	N
Wire	68	47	93	58
News magazines	67	62	90	61
Daily	62	463	89	635
Television	55	121	77	137
Weekly	46	183	67	162
Radio	33	119	57	101
Total sample	56	995	82	1,154

[a]$p < .0000$.

later, the majority was much larger. In 1992, more than 80% of American journalists said the practice may be justified (see Table 4.16).

A majority of journalists in all media have some tolerance for unauthorized documents, but in 1992 those who worked in print tended to be the most likely to justify using them. A majority of television, weekly newspaper, and radio personnel said use of unauthorized business and government documents may be tolerated, but in smaller numbers than their print colleagues.

"Undercover" Reporting

One of the most controversial cases of reporting had a unique twist in that a newspaper opened its own undercover business. Several years before our 1982–1983 survey, the Chicago *Sun-Times* made the "Mirage Bar" a journalistic euphemism for undercover reporting. In documenting corruption among city inspectors and other public officials who were taking bribes from local businesses, the newspaper set up its own bar, staffed by journalists. It was strictly legal, and each violation of the law was reported directly to authorities. The resulting 25-part series, nominated for the Pulitzer Prize, contained sophisticated documentation of official wrongdoing, but the entrapment and deception led to considerable controversy within the field.[69]

Not all such reporting leads to such controversy. The *Indianapolis Star* permitted one of its reporters to get a job with an operation that claimed to raise money for volunteer fire department charities for handicapped children. The reporter was able to document that none of the money ever reached the children. Lawrence "Bo" Connor, then managing editor of the paper, said in 1984 that, at one level, undercover investigations may violate an "unwritten" code, but that "when you are dealing with a rat" there may be "no other way to get that story."[70]

TABLE 4.17
Opinion on Using Undercover Employment, by Medium

| | Percentage Saying May Be Justified | | | |
| | 1982–1983 | | 1992 | |
Medium	%[a]	N	%[b]	N
Television	78	121	65	137
Wire	77	47	55	58
News magazines	71	62	67	61
Daily	68	463	63	635
Radio	64	119	60	101
Weekly	58	183	62	162
Total sample	67	995	63	1,154

[a]$p < .02.$ [b]$p = .340.$

Tolerance of such undercover work in 1992 was down slightly, with 63% saying it may be justified, compared with 67% a decade previous. The most substantial drop in acceptance was among television and wire journalists (see Table 4.17).

Using Hidden Cameras and Microphones

The tools of undercover and investigative reporting are sometimes hidden cameras and microphones. Some of the more controversial cases of undercover reporting have involved them. In 1993, ABC News used hidden cameras to record the mishandling and selling of adulterated meat in a large supermarket chain.[71] The same year, after hundreds of poisonings from beef tainted by E. Coli bacteria, CBS's 48 Hours got an employee of Federal Beef Processors Inc. to wear a hidden camera inside a South Dakota plant. "Bum Steer" aired in 1994, using the hidden video that showed workers dealing with contaminated meat. The company is suing the network for trespass, bribery, invasion of privacy, and exposing trade secrets.[72] Obviously this is risky business.

Local operations also sometimes use hidden video. The "Target 7" unit of WXYZ-TV in Detroit is a noted example. The team's hidden cameras were important in showing black-marketed school supplies, weapons being sold at a gun show to underage children, and on-the-street trading of food stamps for cash. Shellee Smith, head of the investigative unit, said, "With the hidden camera, viewers can see the corruption with their own eyes."[73]

A majority of journalists in all media in 1992, except weekly newspapers, said hidden cameras and microphones may be justified in an "important story" (see Table 4.18). The numbers approving such tactics were roughly similar to those who tolerated undercover reporting, except in television and weekly news-

TABLE 4.18
Opinion on Using Hidden Microphones or Cameras, by Medium

Medium	Percentage Saying May Be Justified 1992	
	%[a]	N
Television	90	137
Wire	59	58
News magazines	63	61
Daily	58	635
Radio	59	101
Weekly	45	162
Total sample	60	1,154

[a]$p < .0000$.

papers. Not surprisingly, it was television journalists who were most likely to approve of the practices (90%) and weekly journalists who were least likely (45%).

Using Re-creations of News Events

Using actors to do video renditions of news events is not a frequent tactic of television news. For the most part, syndicated "reality-based" programs such as *Highway Patrol* are the most frequent users of the technique. One of the most controversial examples of the tactic's use, however, was a 1989 ABC News reenactment of alleged spying by an American diplomat, Felix S. Bloch. The network showed two still photographs of a man resembling Bloch giving a brief-case to another person. An ABC correspondent narrated "voice over" for the photos: "It was not until earlier this year that Bloch was videotaped handing over a briefcase to a known Soviet agent on the streets of a European capital." The photographs were staged, and the network aired them with no indication to viewers that the photos were not authentic. The network admitted later that its producers had made a "terrible mistake" in not labeling the photographs, but said such reenactments were comparable to sketches used in illustrating court proceedings when cameras were prohibited.[74] The allegations against Bloch were reported widely in the press, but it was the reenactment that was the most controversial of the stories.

Our sample of journalists was asked whether "using re-creations or dramatizations of news by actors" may be justified. In 1992, only 28% said that the practice may be tolerated. (This question was not asked in 1982–1983.) The gap between print and broadcast journalists, while not surprising, was considerable. About 40% of both television and radio journalists said re-creations of news may be justified (see Table 4.19).

TABLE 4.19
Opinion on Using Re-Creations of News by Actors, by Medium

Medium	Percentage Saying May Be Justified 1992	
	%[a]	N
Television	42	137
Wire	21	58
News magazines	23	61
Daily	22	635
Radio	42	101
Weekly	36	162
Total sample	28	1,154

[a]$p < .0000$.

Disclosing the Names of Rape Victims

When this topic is mentioned, it is likely that the televised image of the blue circle hiding the face of Patricia Bowman comes to mind for many. In 1991, the CNN-televised trial of William Kennedy Smith, a nephew of Senator Ted Kennedy, on charges of raping Bowman put the issue of disclosing the identity of such victims, long discussed in classrooms and newsrooms, on the public's agenda. When NBC News and *The New York Times* eventually decided to publish the victim's name, considerable debate took place, although the tabloid press, in Europe and America, had made the name public much earlier. A verdict of "not guilty" for Smith did little to resolve the issue of whether the prestige media should have disclosed the victim's identity.[75]

The year before the Smith trial, a midwestern editor had jarred the field by questioning the policy of most newspapers not to disclose the names of rape victims. Geneva Overholser, then editor of the *Des Moines Register*, wrote in a column that the protectionist aims of withholding names may, in fact, perpetuate the stigma of being a victim and mute the public outrage about such crimes. As a result, a victim came forward to tell her story, and a Pulitzer Prize-winning series was published by the paper in 1990.[76]

We asked our national sample in 1992 whether disclosing the names of rape victims may be justified. The results suggest a wider division than might be expected, as 43% of our respondents said publishing the names was justifiable, given an important story. Print journalists were more likely than their broadcast colleagues to think the names might be published (see Table 4.20).

As in all the reporting practices asked about in the 1992 study, gender made no difference on the journalists' response. Women and men were equally divided on the question of disclosing names in cases of rape.

Overall, then, the 1992 results suggest, as they did in the 1982 study, deep divisions within the field on half of the reporting practices posed in the questions.

TABLE 4.20
Opinion on Disclosing Names of Rape Victims, by Medium

Medium	Percentage Saying May Be Justified 1992	
	%[a]	N
Television	34	137
Wire	59	58
News magazines	45	61
Daily	47	635
Radio	28	101
Weekly	38	162
Total sample	43	1,154

[a]$p < .0001$.

However, differences among media were largely predictable ones, showing radio and weekly newspaper journalists to be more reluctant to "justify" the tactics. The gaps between print and television journalists appeared related to medium-specific practices, such as hidden video.

Did overall tolerance for the practices rise or drop during 1982–1992? It is about the same, except in one important area. Our study found that tolerance of the use of unauthorized personal, business, and government documents rose, despite legal questions about them and increasing public concerns about privacy.

CORRELATES OF ETHICAL PERCEPTIONS

What characteristics were typical of journalists in 1992 who were cautious or aggressive about the use of the various reporting practices? Combining the responses to all 10 permitted a look at the extent of overall tolerance and the factors related to it.[77]

Intensive analysis suggests that the degree of tolerance was not strongly related to either situational or personal characteristics. That was similar to the findings in 1982–1983. Then the basic difference in tolerance was generational and related to the staff size of the organization. Older, more experienced journalists were somewhat more likely to be cautious about the various reporting practices. The smaller the organization in which the journalist worked, the less likely the tactics were seen as justifiable.

In 1992, older journalists were still slightly more likely to reject the reporting practices than were their younger colleagues.[78] However, size of the news staff was no longer related to degree of acceptance of the reporting practices (see Table 4.21).

But some significant new patterns emerged in the 1992 study. Philosophy about journalism functions, political leanings, educational level, and media ownership

TABLE 4.21
Predictors of Justification of Various Reporting Practices

Variables	Standardized Regression Coefficients (betas)	Correlation Coefficients
Organizational context		
Ownership—publicly traded corporation	.06	.07
Group, but privately owned	−.26	.03
Independently owned	−.31	−.10
Radio	−.14	−.10
Weekly newspaper	−.09	−.13
Job security's salience	−.18	−.09
News functions		
Disseminator function	−.10	−.12
Adversarial function	.12	.21
Interpretive function	.15	.23
Individual background		
Age	−.12	−.11
Education level	.10	.17
Political leanings (conservative)	−.09	−.16
External factors		
Family and religion ethical salience	−.07	−.09
Comments from news sources	.08	.10

$R^2 = .13.$

were related to tolerance of reporting tactics. Journalists who were strongly adversarial or interpretive in their news philosophy were also more likely to be tolerant of the practices. However, those who valued the disseminator function most highly tended to be less likely to say the tactics may be justified. Political thinking was a factor too. Journalists who were more politically conservative were less likely to accept the controversial practices than were their more liberal colleagues.

Other new "predictors" in the 1992 study were educational level and employer ownership. The more years of schooling a journalist had, the more likely the tactics were considered justifiable. The relationship of education to tolerance seemed independent of whether the journalist attended private schooling or got a journalism degree. Journalists who worked for a privately owned, independent organization tended to be more reluctant to accept the reporting practices than were those working at publicly traded, corporate media, who were slightly more tolerant of the tactics.

If job security was very important to the journalist, it was a bit more likely that the controversial reporting practices were rejected. News sources appeared to be a factor too. Journalists who said they got a lot of feedback from sources were more likely to be tolerant of the reporting approaches.

Based on our separate sample of minority journalists, there were modest differences in the responses to the various news practices. African-American and

Asian-American journalists were more likely to be tolerant of some of the reporting tactics than were their White colleagues. Native Americans were considerably more likely to be reticent about a majority of the reporting situations, with Hispanic journalists being closest to Whites in their profile (see chap. 6, this volume, for a more detailed analysis of these responses).

As discussed earlier, those working in radio and weekly newspapers in 1992 were less likely to accept the reporting practices (although weekly journalists seemed somewhat less reticent about the tactics compared with 1982). No other media differences registered when the overall reactions to the items were aggregated to look at general tolerance.

Some of the most interesting aspects of the portrait of reporting-practice tolerance were several things that did not appear. There was no cleavage between reporters and editors on these practices. That was also true in 1982–1983. And, both men and women journalists appeared to have similar profiles on their acceptance of the various reporting practices (see chap. 5, this volume, for a more detailed analysis of the responses based on gender).

The most significant "missing links" in the findings about reporting tolerance were the referents to ethical "thinking" discussed earlier. Among the four categories of potential influences on ethical bearing, only the family and religion factor was associated with degree of tolerance. The more importance the journalist placed on family and religion as referents to ethical orientation, the more likely the reporting practices were rejected. Newsroom context and teachers were not related to the degree of tolerance of the various practices. In an indirect way, these results suggest that newsrooms and classrooms may need to do more to prepare journalists for the ethical dilemmas posed by the controversial practices.

As in 1982–1983, we found no geographic differences in tolerance in 1992. Journalists in the various regions of the country had roughly similar tolerance of the practices, including the Northeast—the region where some would expect greater acceptance of the controversial methods.

What type of journalist, then, was most apt to be more cautious about the reporting practices? It tended to be those who were older, disseminator-oriented, more conservative politically, and family- and religious-oriented in factors they thought influenced their ethics, with slightly fewer years education and a bit more concern for job security than their colleagues. What about those who were more likely to think these reporting methods may be justified? They tended to be younger, more liberal and adversarial, with more years of schooling, to get more feedback from news sources, and to work for a publicly traded corporation.

CONCLUSIONS AND SUMMARY OF FINDINGS

The institutional culture of journalism, never particularly strong, was weaker in 1992 than a decade previous. Compared with other fields, such as accounting, law, university teaching, and medicine, U.S. journalism's formal trappings of institutional vitality were on the decline between 1971 and 1992. Membership in professional organizations and exposure to a common body of critical literature dropped from 1982 to 1992.

Other fields have deep troubles, but their professional associations and institutional fabric are relatively firm. Some will argue that journalism should not be compared with them in the first place. After all, journalism does not have— nor should it—the formality that comes with required education, certification, and licensing. Still, the immense problems wrought by technology and a more complicated, uncertain society require an intellectual leadership that can only be nurtured by stronger and more broadly supported professional associations.

Educational institutions bear some responsibility for the field's difficulties. Although journalism and communication education reaches a slight majority of journalists—either as a major or minor field of study—it fails at inspiring its graduates to participate in building a stronger institutional foundation for the field. Those with journalism education are no more likely to be members of professional associations than are liberal arts graduates. Journalism schools often fail to make accessible important literature on professional practice for journalists. Their principal success is in being considered an influential source on matters of ethics. Journalism school alumni tend to see an important connection of journalism education to their overall "journalism training" and its contribution to their conceptions of news. But the critics who fear that journalism schools are creating a homogeneous and narrow conception of journalistic practice are badly off the mark.

Although the majority culture of journalism in 1992 was interpretive, the overwhelming finding was that the typical journalist was *pluralistic* in news philosophy. That was also true in 1982, but it was even more pronounced in 1992. This chapter drew tentative sketches of those who lean toward various media functions, but many journalists cannot be described simply as interpreters, disseminators, or adversarialists. They are often strongly oriented toward two of the functions, and sometimes three. Although fewer than one in five strongly endorsed an adversary approach, most journalists (about 80%) see some importance for it. Also, the 1992 analysis found an emerging core role, a *populist mobilizer* function, somewhat resembling the goals of the "public journalism" movement.

A description of the journalistic role given more than a decade ago by Martin Linsky seems even more appropriate today: "It is not adversarial, it is not symbiotic, it is not independent, it is not under the tent." Instead, he said, "It's a marble cake. It's a combination of all these things."[79]

Journalistic life in the 1990s, even more so than in the 1980s, attempts to blend the classical *critical* role of the journalist—as interpreter-investigator—with the technical requirements of disseminating great volumes of *descriptive* information.[80] In 1992, the disseminator function—even more focused on immediacy and speed than a decade previous—was a very strong streak in more than half of the interviewed journalists. Add to that a sturdy "minority" function of adversarity and it seems to be a contradictory mix, or a "bifurcated professional existence," as Bernard Cohen called it more than 30 years ago.[81] However, journalists seem to view the functions as complementary, or as Linsky so aptly put it: "At 9 o'clock it's adversary, at 10 o'clock it's symbiotic, at 11 o'clock it's independent and at 12 o'clock the politicians are manipulating the press. It goes back and forth, it's all over the place."[82]

Within a "belief system" of seemingly contradictory roles, there was evidence of purpose and a spirit of public service among journalists in 1992. Yet, as suggested earlier (chap. 3, this volume), there was considerable frustration about diminished resources and declining autonomy, such that an erosion of the traditional altruism of journalism was perhaps in the offing. Even so, the ethic of "disinterestedness" that Louis Menand saw as contributing to the public's disgust with journalism was not easily found among our respondents.

The kind of "determined detachment" seen by Davis Merritt and Jay Rosen was also hard to find. The pluralistic makeup of the dominant "belief systems" of journalists complemented the open-ended comments (from chap. 3, this volume) about the somewhat altruistic sources of job satisfaction. Themes of public service and commitment underlay both job satisfaction and journalistic roles. In the main, there was the same kind of commitment by journalists to making democracy work and to bettering their community that Herbert Gans saw two decades ago when he described them as "progressive reformists" who very much wanted the society to "work."[83] As we saw in chapter 3, however, the progressive reformist spirit was not reflected as often in newsroom performance (in terms of aggressive, in-depth reporting) as many journalists might have liked.

The venerable Walter Cronkite always ended his newscasts for CBS with, "And that's the way it is." The evidence in this chapter is based on journalists *saying* "that's the way it is" with their thoughts and work. Real life may be different. Later in the book, we directly analyze some of our respondents' "best work." This offers some behavioral evidence of a pluralism of roles for American journalists. It also suggests that, once the newsroom has done its work, the disseminator function may be more prevalent in the actual "copy" than journalists realize.

Of the various factors that shaped the professional values of journalists in 1992, the newsroom environment was the most important. The day-to-day interaction with editors and colleagues was perceived by journalists as the most powerful force over their conceptions of values, ethics, and professional practice. On balance, the newsroom environment was even more powerful in 1992 than ever. Although there were some philosophical differences between reporters and editors, and between younger and older journalists, the gaps were not nearly as pronounced as some might think, even on such things as controversial reporting practices.

Ownership form in 1992 was more important to the contour of professional values than a decade previous, but not in predictable ways. Journalists working for publicly held, corporate media were somewhat more likely to be interpretive in philosophy. The minority of journalists who worked for privately owned, independent media were more apt to perceive audience and source feedback as greater influences on their conceptions of newsworthiness. Ownership form had no relationship to perceptions of the relative importance of various ethical referents, but it did affect the tolerance of controversial reporting practices. Journalists at publicly owned groups were somewhat more likely to be tolerant of such tactics as undercover reporting.

In 1971, the landmark Johnstone study concluded that journalism was replete with profound contradictions, but it met the abstract criteria of a profession. In 1982–1983, our study also found contradictions, but we described journalists at that time as educated, altruistic, and principled. Yet they were deeply divided on many questions of journalistic practice. All those things were still true in 1992. Overall, however, the institutional forms of professionalism eluded the field much more in 1992 than a decade earlier. A professional "mood" remained in 1992, but the power of its expression rested almost exclusively within individual newsrooms.

NOTES

1. Brian Buchanan, Eric Newton, Richard Thien, G. Donald Ferree, Jr., and Edward C. Pease, *No Train, No Gain: Continuing Training for Newspaper Journalists in the 1990s* (Arlington, VA: The Freedom Forum, 1993).
2. Louis Menand, "The Trashing of Professionalism," *The New York Times Magazine*, March 5, 1995, pp. 41–43.
3. Davis Merritt and Jay Rosen, "Imagining Public Journalism: An Editor and Scholar Reflect on the Birth of an Idea," *Roy W. Howard Public Lecture in Journalism and Mass Communication Research*, No. 5 (Bloomington: Indiana University, April 13, 1995), pp. 8–9.
4. Everette E. Dennis and John C. Merrill, *Media Debates: Issues in Mass Communication* (New York: Longman Publishing Group, 1991), p. 205.
5. Theodore L. Glasser, "Professionalism and the Derision of Diversity: The Case of the Education Journalist," *Journal of Communication*, 42, 2 (Spring 1992), pp. 131–140.
6. James S. Ettema and Theodore L. Glasser, "The Irony in—and of—Journalism: A Case Study in the Moral Language of Liberal Democracy," *Journal of Communication*, 44, 2 (Spring 1994), pp. 5–28.
7. Steven Brill, "A New Code for Journalists: A Challenge to the Press to Live by the Code," *The American Lawyer*, December 1994, pp. 5–7, 85.
8. Brill, "A New Code," p. 5.
9. Frank Rich, "The Longest Year," *The New York Times*, June 15, 1995, p. A17.
10. David Margolick, "For Good or Ill, the Simpson Case Has Permeated the Nation's Psyche: Today Marks First Anniversary of the Murders," *The New York Times*, June 12, 1995, p. A12 is a nicely balanced summary of the impact of the trial. Significantly, he concluded: "The first casualty of the case could be the courtroom camera."
11. John W. C. Johnstone, Edward J. Slawski, and William W. Bowman, *The News People: A Sociological Portrait of American Journalists and Their Work* (Urbana: University of Illinois Press, 1976), p. 102.
12. Johnstone et al., *The News People*, p. 111.
13. Jack McLeod and Searle Hawley in 1964 did one of the first studies of journalistic professionalization. They defined professionalism in terms of advanced training, originality and initiative,

being respected by others in the field, doing valuable work for the community, having an influence on public opinion, freedom from close supervision of work, and having an influence on important decisions and one's news organization. See "Professionalization Among Newsmen," *Journalism Quarterly*, 41 (Autumn 1964), pp. 529–538, 577.

In 1978, Swen Windahl and Karl Erik Rosengren criticized previous studies as being too narrow. They followed a definition of *professionalism* proposed by Peter Blau and W. R. Scott in *Formal Organizations: A Comparative Approach* (San Francisco: Chandler Publishing Co., 1962). That definition included adherence to universalistic norms, the importance of expertise, neutral relations with clients, achieved status rather than ascribed, and altruism. They also argued for measuring professionalism at two levels—individual and collective. See "Newsmen's Professionalization: Some Methodological Problems," *Journalism Quarterly*, 55 (Autumn 1978), pp. 466–473.

14. Randal A. Beam, "Journalistic Professionalism as an Organizational-Level Concept," *Journalism Monographs*, 121 (June 1990).

15. Randal A. Beam, "The Impact of Group Ownership Variables on Organizational Professionalism at Daily Newspapers," *Journalism Quarterly*, 70 (Winter 1993), pp. 907–918.

16. The drop in The Society of Professional Journalist membership is confirmed by SPJ's records. In 1992, SPJ membership was 14,188 (of which about 25% was students), with SPJ having lost about 10,000 members over the decade. Telephone conversation with Ernie Ford, SPJ Executive Director, November 13, 1992.

17. Telephone conversation with Steve Green, information officer of the American Institute of Certified Public Accountants, November 13, 1992.

18. Telephone conversation with Mary Wahan, American Bar Association, November 12, 1992.

19. Lynn Harvey, American Medical Association, in a personal communication to Douglas Freeman, Medical Sciences Librarian, Indiana University, November 4, 1992.

20. A multiple-regression analysis of 12 items found these significant predictors of belonging to a professional journalism group: professional age (beta = .15, r = .06), being a supervisor (beta = .05, r = .06), age (beta = −.11, r = .03), and organizational prominence (beta = −.06, r = −.04).

21. Precise comparative figures are not available, but most accountants receive the *Journal of Accountancy*, 41% of all attorneys read the *ABA Journal* (most are "heavy" readers), more than half of the physicians in the United States receive the American Medical Association's *American Medical News* (which deals with nonresearch, professional issues), and 38% of all doctors read the *Journal of the American Medical Association* (a major medical research journal). These figures are from telephone information obtained from the associational headquarters of the previously cited groups, June 1995.

22. A multiple-regression analysis of 12 items found these significant predictors of percentage of friends in journalism: professional age (beta = −.05, r = −.15), being a supervisor (beta = −.06, r = −.08), age (beta = −.11, r = −.16), and being male (beta = −.06, r = −.08).

23. Menand, "The Trashing of Professionalism," p. 42.

24. Jerry Bruck, "I.F. Stone's Weekly," Film, 1973.

25. Johnstone, Slawski, and Bowman, *The News People*, p. 102.

26. Stephen Engelberg, "Hostage-Taking Is a Weapon of War Whose Time Is Now," *The New York Times*, June 25, 1995, section 4, pp. 1, 3.

27. "Journalism Under Fire," *Time*, December 12, 1983, pp. 76–93.

28. Michael J. O'Neill, "A Problem for the Republic—A Challenge for Editors," address to the American Society of Newspaper Editors, May 5, 1982. Reprinted in *The Adversary Press* (St. Petersburg, FL: Modern Media Institute, 1983), pp. 2–15.

29. Davis Merritt and Jay Rosen, "Imagining Public Journalism," p. 20.

30. Factor analysis, a statistical procedure for locating clusters of common elements in the results of a set of questions, yielded four factors. The factor loadings: adversarial = .89 for both items; interpretive = .51, .72, and .63; disseminator = .59 and .70; populist mobilizer factor (consisting of two old and two new questions) = .53, .55, .57, and .63. The four factors "explained" 55%

of the common variance. The various items in each cluster were combined to form four scales, with each question weighted equally. The scales were used in regression analysis to look for "predictors" of all the functions (except the "populist mobilizer" group, which had a very small number).

31. The Commission on Freedom of the Press, A Free and Responsible Press (Chicago: The University of Chicago Press, 1947), pp. 21–22.

32. Stephen Bates, Realigning Journalism with Democracy: The Hutchins Commission, Its Time, and Ours (Washington, DC: The Annenberg Washington Program in Communications Policy Studies of Northwestern University, 1995), pp. 30–31.

33. We are quite aware that we are reporting journalistic self-perceptions, and that behavior may be different. That point is addressed later in this chapter and in the book. See Paul Starobin, "A Generation of Vipers," Columbia Journalism Review, March/April 1995, pp. 25–32.

34. The People, The Press & Their Leaders, p. 27.

35. Johnstone et al., The News People, p. 129.

36. In a separate hierarchical regression analysis, Wei Wu, a doctoral student at Indiana University, confirmed the tendency of adversarialists to work for larger media. See "Predictions of the Endorsement of the Adversarial Role by U.S. Journalists in 1992," unpublished J600 paper, April 1994, p. 6.

37. Johnstone et al., The News People, p. 124.

38. Wei Wu, a doctoral student at Indiana University, confirmed this connection in a hierarchical regression analysis. The beta of .24 ($p = .001$) suggests a comparatively strong link between investigating government claims and the adversarial role. Overall, however, the factor analysis confirmed that the investigative item was clustered with the interpretive function. Wei Wu, "Predictors of Political Learning and the Adversarial Role by U.S. Journalists in 1992," unpublished J600 paper, April 1994.

39. The Times Mirror Center for The People & The Press, The People, The Press & Their Leaders, 1995 (Los Angeles: Times-Mirror, 1995), p. 27.

40. A multiple-regression analysis of 28 variables revealed these "predictors": journalism education (beta = .15, $r = .14$), Midwest (beta = −.17, $r = −.11$), disseminator function (beta = .08, $r = .10$), journalism experience (beta = .18, $r = .07$), staff size (beta = −.09, $r = −.05$), lower level editors (beta = −.08, $r = −.09$), male (beta = −.07, $r = −.05$), interpretive function (beta = .08, $r = .05$), and Northeast (beta = −.09, $r = −.05$).

41. In a multiple-regression analysis of 28 items, these "predictors" emerged: rating of the organization (beta = .19, $r = .20$), radio (beta = −.18, $r = −.13$), age (beta = −.15, $r = −.12$), South (beta = .12, $r = .11$), upper management (beta = .08, $r = .11$), private education (beta = .07, $r = .08$), and ombudsman (beta = .06, $r = .07$).

42. A multiple-regression analysis of 28 items found these "predictors": staff size (beta = −.15, $r = −.16$), journalism education (beta = .11, $r = .10$), education level (beta = −.09, $r = −.11$), privately owned, independent media (beta = .24, $r = .06$), publicly traded media (beta = −.28, $r = −.07$), being White (beta = −.08, $r = −.10$), being male (beta = −.06, $r = −.06$), populist mobilizer (beta = −.20, $r = .13$), disseminator (beta = .05, $r = .13$), adversarialist (beta = −.10, $r = −.13$), TV (beta = .34, $r = .13$), radio (beta = .27, $r = .13$), and South (beta = .18, $r = .11$).

43. A multiple-regression analysis of 28 items found these "predictors": populist mobilizer (beta = .11, $r = .14$), radio (beta = −.16, $r = −.15$), South (beta = .16, $r = .14$), privately owned, independent media (beta = .37, $r = .07$), and group-owned, private media (beta = .29, $r = −.05$).

44. A multiple-regression analysis of 28 items found these "predictors": age (beta = −.10, $r = −.17$), South (beta = .08, $r = .10$), populist mobilizer (beta = .13, $r = .12$), being male (beta = −.11, $r = −.10$), staff size (beta = −.14, $r = −.07$), lower level management (beta = .06, $r = .07$), and working for a weekly newspaper (beta = −.29, $r = −.17$).

45. Nelson Antrim Crawford, The Ethics of Journalism (New York: Alfred A. Knopf, 1924), pp. 114, viii.

46. Conrad C. Fink, Media Ethics (Boston: Allyn & Bacon, 1995), p. xiii.

47. Brian Buchanan et al., *No Train, No Gain*, p. 15.
48. We used clusters that were based on the factor analysis of the 1982–1983 data set. At that time, the items loaded on three factors, just as logic would predict: *newsroom context* = senior editor (a loading of .72), senior reporter (.72), publisher (.44), and newsroom learning (.39); *teachers* = journalism school teachers (.55), university teachers (.85), and high school journalism teachers (logic, but no loading); *family and religion* = religious upbringing (.78) and family upbringing (.54). Each of the three sets was used as a dependent variable in regression analysis with 28 "predictors."
49. A multiple-regression analysis of 29 items found these "predictors": populist mobilizer (beta = .12, r = .19), disseminator orientation (beta = .11, r = .14), adversarialist (beta = .08, r = .08), education level (beta = −.07, r = −.07), rating of organization (beta = .06, r = .09), and staff size (beta = −.13, r = −.08).
50. A multiple-regression analysis was conducted with 28 items, with these "predictors" emerging: South (beta = .19, r = .12), age (beta = .10, r = .11), populist mobilizer (beta = .11, r = .10), interpreter (beta = −.09, r = −.06), and lower level editors (beta = −.06, r = −.06).
51. A multiple-regression analysis of 28 items found these "predictors": staff size (beta = −.11, r = −.10), journalism education (beta = .10, r = .08), education (beta = −.09, r = −.09), rating of organization (beta = .09, r = .09), populist mobilizer (beta = .07, r = .07), weeklies (beta = .24, r = .07), and radio (beta = .23, r = .07).
52. Alecia Shepard, "Legislating Ethics," *American Journalism Review*, January/February 1994, p. 38.
53. Lyle Denniston, "The High Cost of Burning a Source," *American Journalism Review*, May 1992, p. 51.
54. Conrad Fink, *Media Ethics*, p. 76.
55. Carl Bernstein and Bob Woodward, *All the President's Men* (New York: Simon & Schuster, 1974), p. 224.
56. Conrad Fink, *Media Ethics*, p. 77.
57. Elaine Sciolino, "China's Prisons Forged Zeal of U.S. Crusader," *The New York Times*, July 10, 1995, pp. A1, 4.
58. *USA Today*, March 21, 1984, p. 4.
59. Ernest Sander, "A TV Tabloid Vows to Clean Up Its Act," *American Journalism Review*, May 1994, p. 15.
60. Lou Prato, "Tabloids Force All to Pay for News," *American Journalism Review*, September 1994, p. 56.
61. Alecia C. Shepard, "Legislating Ethics," p. 37.
62. Lou Prato, "Tabloids Force All to Pay," p. 56.
63. "Privacy and the Need to Know," *Presstime*, October 1992, pp. 18–21.
64. William Rivers, Wilbur Schramm, and Clifford Christians, *Responsibility in Mass Communication*, 3rd ed. (New York: Harper & Row, 1980), p. 197.
65. "Privacy and the Need to Know," *Presstime*, p. 18.
66. The Associated Press, "Report: Philip Morris Knew Nicotine Threat," *The (Bloomington, IN) Herald-Times*, December 9, 1995, p. A3.
67. *Brown and Williamson Tobacco Corp. vs. Jacobson* (1983) as discussed in American Bar Association, "The First Amendment: A Journalist's Guide to Freedom of Speech," Videotape, Chicago, IL, 1992.
68. Bill Hoffman, "Nice Try!" *American Journalism Review*, May 1994, p. 45.
69. Edmund B. Lambeth, *Committed Journalism*, 2nd ed. (Bloomington: Indiana University Press, 1992), pp. 41–42.
70. Personal interview with Lawrence Connor, Indianapolis, Indiana, October 12, 1984.
71. Conrad Fink, *Media Ethics*, p. 80.
72. Lyle Denniston, "Going Too Far with the Hidden Camera," *American Journalism Review*, April 1994, p. 54.
73. Shellee Smith, "Shoptalk," *Scripps Howard News*, May/June 1995, p. 15.

74. Steve Weinstein and Diane Haithman, "ABC News Draws Criticism of Spy Case Re-creation," *Los Angeles Times*, July 26, 1989, section 6, p. 1.

75. Fink, *Media Ethics*, p. 253.

76. Fink, *Media Ethics*, p. 252.

77. In our study in 1982, we used a Guttman scale of selected items from the set of reporting practices: *using confidential business or government documents* (1), *using personal letters and photographs* (2), and *getting employed in an organization to gain inside information* (3). In the 1992 study, we decided to create a Likert-type scale using all 10 of the items in the battery of reporting practices, with each item weighted equally. The Likert-type "tolerance" scale was then used as a dependent variable in a multiple-regression analysis with 36 independent variables.

78. In a separate, hierarchical, multiple-regression analysis, Sandra Borden, a doctoral student at Indiana University, also found age was a "predictor." She looked at six of the more controversial of the items, and found a beta of −.16 in an unpublished J600 paper, "Does the Extent to Which Journalists Identify with Outsiders Affect Their Willingness to Sacrifice the Autonomy of Others?", May 1994.

79. Martin Linsky, in a symposium, in *The Adversary Press* (St. Petersburg, FL: Modern Media Institute, 1983), p. 29.

80. This interpretation draws on Carey's argument that the contemporary journalist has been "de-intellectualized" to the role of mere translator in service to the institutions reported on. See James Carey, "The Communications Revolution and the Professional Communicator," *Sociological Review Monographs*, 13 (January 1969), p. 32.

81. Bernard C. Cohen, *The Press and Foreign Policy* (Princeton, NJ: Princeton University Press, 1963).

82. Linsky, in *The Adversary Press*, p. 29.

83. Herbert J. Gans, *Deciding What's News: A Study of CBS Evening News, NBC Nightly News, Newsweek, and Time* (New York: Vintage Books, 1979).

Chapter 5

Women Journalists

Drawing on data from our 1982–1983 study of U.S. journalists, Sue Lafky concluded that, "the status of women in journalism in many ways reflects the status of women in the workplace as a whole."[1] During the past few decades, women have entered the U.S. workforce in dramatic numbers.[2] In 1960, there were about 23 million working women who made up about one third of the nation's workforce. By the mid-1980s, there were nearly 50 million women—about 45% of all workers—holding jobs in the United States.[3] By 1991, the U.S. Bureau of Labor Statistics estimated nearly 57 million women working in the country— 45.4% of the civilian workforce.[4]

From 1971 to 1983, the proportion of women in journalism also increased notably—from about one fifth[5] to just over one third.[6] This growth was accompanied by an increase in women in U.S. college and university journalism programs,[7] where women outnumbered men for the first time in 1977 after about four decades of a 60:40 ratio favoring men.[8]

But U.S. journalists in 1992 were no more likely to be female than a decade previous, as noted in chapter 1 (this volume), despite dramatic increases in women journalism students in U.S. universities and an emphasis on hiring more women in journalism in the 1980s. Table 1.5 in chapter 1 showed that the overall percentage of women journalists in 1992 was 34—virtually the same as in 1982–1983. Although 45% of all full-time journalists hired in the 4 years before our 1992 study were women, the negligible growth in full-time journalism jobs during the 1980s meant that not enough women in absolute numbers were hired to make a difference in the overall workforce percentage, considering the number leaving journalism.

When compared with the total U.S. labor force, the percentage of women in journalism in 1992 lagged behind by more than 11 points, and was at about the same level as the percentage of women in the total U.S. labor force in 1971 (34%). But when compared with some other professional occupations, women were better represented in journalism. In 1992, only about 27% of U.S. college faculty were women, 22% of attorneys, 9% of dentists, and 18% of physicians.[9]

Women journalists in 1992 had worked in journalism 3 years less than men, had somewhat lower incomes, were about a year younger than men, were less likely to be married, and were more likely to identify with the Democratic party. But men and women journalists did not differ much with respect to educational levels, religious background, membership in journalism organizations, or employment in group-owned versus independently owned media.

BACKGROUNDS

Education

In 1971, women journalists were less likely than men to be college graduates, as Table 5.1 shows, but by 1982–1983, women were slightly more likely to hold a bachelor's degree than men and a bit less likely to have a graduate degree. By 1992, there was no significant educational gap between men and women journalists, either at the bachelor's- or graduate-degree level. In fact, just over 83% of the women journalists in 1992 held at least a bachelor's degree (or higher), compared with slightly more than 81% of men journalists. This result suggests that, for both groups, the bachelor's degree became the standard for being hired as a full-time journalist in the United States in the early 1990s.

Mary Frank Fox conducted a study that showed higher educational levels of U.S. women in general were correlated with increased participation in the paid workforce. She found 59% employed among women who had finished high school, 72% employed among women who had completed 4 years of college, and 79% employed among those with 5 or more years of college.[10] If this asso-

TABLE 5.1
Amount of Formal Education of U.S. Journalists (Percentage in Each Category)

Highest Educational Attainment	1971[a]		1982–1983[b]		1992	
	Men	Women	Men	Women	Men	Women
Some high school	2.0	1.3	0.6	—	—	0.3
High school graduate	10.6	18.4	6.2	10.1	3.6	5.4
Some college	27.4	29.5	19.1	16.3	15.0	11.0
College graduate	41.4	32.6	53.6	57.3	63.4	66.5
Some graduate training	10.2	11.6	8.3	9.2	6.3	5.9
Graduate degree	8.4	6.6	12.1	7.1	11.7	11.0

[a]From Bowman, *Distaff Journalists*, p. 132.
[b]From Weaver and Wilhoit, *The American Journalist*, p. 166.

ciation continues to hold true, higher educational levels for women journalists should mean higher levels of employment in the future.

Race

Among racial minorities in U.S. journalism, the percentage of women in 1992 was considerably higher than the 34% figure for all journalists—52.5% of Asian Americans, 53.2% of African Americans, 48.1% of Hispanics, and 42.9% of Native Americans.

Some have suggested that this trend in 1992 was due to media managers being interested in getting credit for hiring both a racial minority and a woman in the same person. However, among racial minorities—especially African Americans—women were more likely to finish college than were men and more likely to major in journalism[11]—both increasingly necessary conditions for being hired as a full-time journalist in the United States.

African-American women in the United States historically have been more likely than White women to be paid workers.[12] Giddings argued that the combination of sexism and racism forced African-American women into the paid workforce, and also increased the emphasis on education for them, especially in an economy where blue-collar men could earn as much or more as white-collar women. In such an economy, which no longer existed in the early 1990s, "sons dropped out of school to support themselves and their families, while daughters went to school to do so," Giddings wrote.[13]

Whatever the reasons for higher proportions of women among racial and ethnic minorities, it seems likely that efforts to increase minorities in journalism will also result in increases in women as well, although the reverse is not necessarily true.

Family Life

Gender of U.S. journalists in 1992 was related to their marital status and family situation, just as it was in 1982–1983. Women in 1992 were still less likely to be married (48%) than men (65%), and were much less likely to have children living with them (28%) than men (44%).

However, it should be noted that the proportion of married women in journalism increased from 43% in 1982–1983 to 48% in 1992, after a notable decline of 16 points from 1971 to 1982. The percentage of married men increased slightly from 62% in 1982–1983 to 65% in 1992, also after a decline of nearly 15 points in the previous decade. This suggests that, by 1992, more women and men journalists were managing to balance their personal and professional lives. But the difficulty of combining career and family seemed greater for women than for men, although there were some signs that this was changing in U.S. journalism.

Age

The largest increase in women journalists during the 1980s was in the youngest age category (under 25), and the only decline was in the 45–54 age bracket. But a cohort analysis suggests that it was women younger than 35 and in their mid-40s to mid-50s in 1982 who were most likely to leave journalism from the early 1980s to the early 1990s, perhaps for family reasons or because of professional frustrations, or both (see Table 1.7 in chap. 1, this volume).

The proportion of women in the youngest category in 1992 slightly exceeded that for the total U.S. labor force in 1989. This was the first time this happened in the three major studies of journalists done from 1971 to 1992. However, beginning with the next age group (25–34), the percentage of women journalists began to lag behind the percentage of women in the overall labor force. Considering all the age groups, however, the differences between the percentages of women journalists and women in the labor force declined from 1982 to 1992 in all but two categories—35- to 44-year-olds and 45- to 54-year-olds. The increase in women after the age of 55 seemed to signal a return to journalism after a career change or interruption, perhaps for family reasons.

JOBS

Work Experience

The proportion of women in U.S. journalism was analyzed by years of experience (see Fig. 1.1 in chap. 1), it steadily declined with number of years in journalism, suggesting that fewer women were hired in earlier times or that women have not stayed in journalism as long as men, or both. As noted in chapter 1, the average years of journalism experience in 1992 was 15 for men and 12 for women, and men were considerably more likely than women to have more than 15 years of journalism experience, suggesting that women generally did not stay in journalism as long as men.

This was not a matter of age alone. Table 1.7 in chapter 1 showed a higher percentage of women in the oldest (65 and up) category, whereas Fig. 1.1 showed a steady decline in the proportion of women by years of experience. As mentioned earlier, this suggests that some older women worked in journalism after other careers, or returned to journalism after interrupting careers.

News Medium

The proportion of women journalists in 1992 also varied considerably by news medium, as Table 1.6 in chapter 1 indicated—from about one fourth in the wire services and television to nearly one half in weekly newspapers and news magazines. But overall, there was not as much variation as there was in 1971, when only 5% of radio journalists were women, compared with nearly a third of those working for news magazines. The biggest increases of women during the 1980s were in news magazines and, to a lesser extent, the wire services. Despite the appearance of more female TV news announcers during the 1980s, women actually lost ground as a percentage of all journalists working in television newsrooms and held steady in daily and weekly newspapers.

Income

In our 1982–1983, study we found that the salary gap between men and women had decreased somewhat from 1970.[14] From 1981 to 1991, that gap decreased even more than in the previous decade. Overall median salaries for women in 1991 were 81% of those for men, compared with 64% in 1970, as Fig. 3.11 in chapter 3 indicated.

Figure 3.12 showed that when years of experience in journalism were considered, the gender gap in income nearly disappeared. There was a notable gender gap in median income of about $6,000 (favoring men) among journalists having 10–14 years experience. Although there is no ready explanation for that difference, it is true that women with 4 years or less experience tended to work for slightly smaller news organizations than did men. This helps explain the small salary gap of nearly $1,800 between the most recently hired men and women journalists.

When a variety of predictors of income were controlled statistically in a multiple-regression analysis (such as professional age, type of medium, size of news organization, managerial responsibilities, race, ownership of news organization, presence of a journalists union, region of country, and education level), gender predicted less than 1% of the variation in pay in 1992. There was no income gap by race of journalist, except for Native Americans, who made substantially less than others probably because they worked for very small news operations.

Table 3.12 in chapter 3 showed that the strongest predictors of U.S. journalists' income in 1992 were number of years of experience, size of news organization, type of news organization (with news magazines and wire services at the top, and weekly newspapers and radio at the bottom), and holding a managerial position. Years of experience and size of organization were especially strong predictors of income when compared with the others.

Managerial Influence

Women journalists gained managerial responsibility and influence in journalism during the 1980s. In 1992, 41% said they supervised news or editorial employees, compared with 43% of men. In addition, 18% of women journalists were owners, publishers, or upper level managers (city editor or news director and higher), compared with 22% of male journalists. Finally, 32% of women journalists were lower level managers (desk editors, assignment editors, or assistant editors), compared with 30% of men.

In terms of perceived influence on hiring and firing news employees, women newsroom managers were less likely than their male counterparts in 1992 to think they had a great deal of influence, especially in the broadcast media of radio and television. Table 5.2 shows that there were notable increases in women perceiving great influence on hiring between 1982 and 1992, but only in the print media were women managers nearly as likely as men to perceive this influence in 1992.

These figures clearly suggest that radio and TV newsrooms were more likely to be controlled by men than by women in 1992. However, this difference was not so clear in the print media of daily and weekly newspapers and news magazines, where women tended to be a higher proportion of all full-time journalists.

Taken together, the data in Tables 1.6 and 5.2 indicate that, as women became more numerous in various news media, they also gained more authority as managers. This was true especially in weekly newspapers and news magazines, where women were approaching parity with men in numbers by 1992.

Editorial Influence

Although women journalists were not as likely as men to perceive themselves having a great deal of managerial influence in 1992, they equalled and even surpassed men in the amount of editorial control they exercised, in both print and broadcast news media.

Table 5.3 shows that women journalists in broadcast media in 1992 were more likely than men to say that they almost always could select the stories they worked on, whereas in 1982–1983 men in radio and TV newsrooms were significantly more likely to claim this. There was a noticeable drop in the proportions of both men and women print journalists perceiving such great freedom during 1982–1992, however. Hence, although women in 1992 were equal to

TABLE 5.2
Male and Female Newsroom Managers' Influence on Hiring
(Percentage in Each Category)

| | 1982–1983 | | | | 1992 | | | |
| | Print | | Broadcast | | Print | | Broadcast | |
Influence	Men (n = 242)	Women (n = 111)	Men (n = 96)	Women (n = 19)	Men (n = 253)	Women (n = 128)	Men (n = 74)	Women (n = 33)
A great deal	47.1	27.0	37.5	10.5	39.9	35.2	40.5	21.2
Some	17.8	20.7	25.0	10.5	20.9	22.7	20.3	27.3
A little	12.8	16.2	12.5	26.3	18.2	16.4	25.7	27.3
None at all	22.3	36.0	25.0	52.6	20.9	25.8	13.5	24.2

TABLE 5.3
Frequencies of Being Able to Select Stories Worked on, by Gender
(Percentage in Each Category)

	1982–1983				1992			
	Print		Broadcast		Print		Broadcast	
Frequency	Men (n = 370)	Women (n = 225)	Men (n = 132)	Women (n = 67)	Men (n = 583)	Women (n = 328)	Men (n = 172)	Women (n = 63)
Almost always	60.3	60.0	67.4	44.8	47.5	46.0	44.8	54.0
More often than not	27.3	26.2	23.5	28.4	37.7	36.6	43.0	39.7
Only occasionally	11.4	12.4	8.3	22.4	14.1	16.8	11.6	6.3
Don't make proposals	1.1	1.3	0.8	4.5	0.7	0.6	0.6	0.0

TABLE 5.4
Amount of Editing Performed by Male and Female Newsroom Managers
(Percentage in Each Category)

	1982–1983				1992			
	Print		Broadcast		Print		Broadcast	
Amount	Men (n = 489)	Women (n = 264)	Men (n = 168)	Women (n = 71)	Men (n = 585)	Women (n = 329)	Men (n = 173)	Women (n = 63)
A great deal	35.8	33.0	23.2	19.8	39.1	42.6	20.8	34.9
Some	36.0	34.4	51.2	56.3	37.1	29.5	60.1	41.3
None at all	28.2	32.6	25.6	23.9	23.8	28.0	19.1	23.8

men in their ability to select stories, there was not quite as much perceived freedom to do so.

Table 5.4 indicates that women journalists were notably more likely to do a great deal of editing in 1992 than a decade earlier, especially in the broadcast news media. Women were also substantially more likely than men to do a great deal of editing in 1992, whereas men were a bit more likely to do so in 1982–1983 in radio and TV news, suggesting a significant gain in editorial influence for women during the decade.

But Table 5.5 also suggests a somewhat diminished sense of editorial autonomy, as did Table 5.3, except for women journalists in broadcast news organizations, who were more likely in 1992 than a decade earlier to say they had almost complete freedom in deciding how stories would be used. When comparing men with women, it's clear that women were more likely than men to claim almost complete freedom in deciding story use in 1992 as compared with the situation in 1982–1983, when women were less likely than men to claim this much freedom. Except for women broadcast editors, however, there were notable declines over time in those saying they had almost complete freedom

TABLE 5.5
Amount of Freedom Men and Women with Editing Duties Had in Deciding
How Stories Would Be Used (Percentage in Each Category)

	1982–1983				1992			
	Print		Broadcast		Print		Broadcast	
Amount of Freedom	Men (n = 350)	Women (n = 178)	Men (n =126)	Women (n = 56)	Men (n = 428)	Women (n = 230)	Men (n = 138)	Women (n = 48)
Almost complete	42.3	34.8	49.2	37.5	15.9	21.3	24.6	41.7
A great deal	25.7	25.8	23.0	37.5	33.9	33.0	30.4	37.5
Some	21.7	23.0	23.0	12.5	35.3	28.3	37.0	16.1
None at all	10.3	16.3	4.8	12.5	15.0	17.4	8.0	4.2

in deciding how stories would be used, raising the issue of decreasing editorial autonomy for both men and women.

Job Dimensions

Although men and women were equally likely to rate freedom as *very important* during the 1970s and 1980s, in 1992 women were slightly more likely than men to do so. Table 5.6 also shows that women consistently were more likely than men to rate helping people as *very important* from 1971 to 1992. The same was true for the editorial policies of the news organization, although here the gap between men and women was narrowing; for the first time in 1992 women were more likely to rate these policies as more important than the chance to help others.

Pay and fringe benefits also became more important aspects of work for women, with increasing numbers rating them as *very important* over time, whereas for men the figures did not change much. But compared with other aspects of journalistic work—such as editorial policies, the chance to help other people, job security, and autonomy—pay and fringe benefits were lower on the list of priorities for both men and women. Whereas men were more concerned than women about chances for advancing in 1971, and women more than men in 1982–1983, there was no significant difference between men and women on this dimension of work in 1992.

Job Satisfaction

In 1971, although women journalists in the United States received less pay and were less numerous and influential, they were more likely than men to say that they were very satisfied with their work.[15] By 1982–1983, this was no longer true—women did not express any less satisfaction than men, and both groups

TABLE 5.6
The Importance of Job Dimensions for Journalists, 1971, 1982–1983, and 1992
(Percentage Who Rated Each Dimension *Very Important*)

Dimension	1971		1982–1983		1992	
	Men	Women	Men	Women	Men	Women
Pay	28.7	15.3	24.5	18.9	22.2	19.7
Fringe benefits	25.6	23.3	25.8	25.1	33.2	37.7
A chance to get ahead in the organization	52.4	38.7	43.9	52.8	38.3	40.5
Job security	50.9	52.5	56.6	57.7	62.3	58.1
Chance to develop a specialty	43.5	48.8	41.9	50.4	38.9	41.9
Chance to help people	65.0	73.1	56.6	68.9	57.2	67.9
Editorial policies of organization	48.9	62.3	54.1	62.3	66.8	71.8
Freedom from supervision	52.4	54.8	38.1	39.3	—[a]	—[a]
Amount of autonomy	55.4	54.9	50.1	51.1	49.1	54.5

[a]Not asked in 1992.

were equally likely to want to stay in journalism—with 84% of women and 82% of men saying they would like to be working for a news organization in the next 5 years.[16] In 1992, there were again no significant differences in overall job satisfaction of men and women, with 27% of each group claiming to be very satisfied. Women were slightly less likely than men (75% vs. 79%) to say they would like to be working in the news media in 5 years.

But overall, there was a significant drop in the percentage of U.S. journalists saying they were very satisfied—from 49% in 1971 to 40% in 1982–1983 to 27% in 1992. There was also a significant increase in the percentage saying they would like to work outside the news media in 5 years—from 7% in 1971 to 11% in 1982–1983 to 22% in 1992.[17]

Some have dismissed these 1992 journalism trends as being generally true in the U.S. workforce. However, a comparison with other occupations shows that the proportion claiming to be very satisfied was considerably higher—44% in a national survey of 1,517 adult workers by the National Opinion Research Center in 1991 and 43% in a national survey of 1,008 American office workers in 1991 by Louis Harris (NORC 1991; Harris 1991).[18] These figures did not vary much during the 1980s (from 41% to 46% for Harris and from 44% to 49% for NORC).

This suggests that, in 1992, there was a special problem with declining job satisfaction in American journalism that was not common to other occupations, but it did not seem to be related to gender. A more in-depth look at this decline in chapter 3 (this volume) identified three major problems: management policies, low salaries, and inadequate opportunity for advancement.[19]

PROFESSIONAL VALUES

Role Perceptions

In 1982–1983, women and men journalists responded in mostly similar patterns in rating various news media roles. Men were less likely than women to rate avoiding stories with unverified content as *extremely important*, and women were a bit more likely than men to rate providing entertainment and relaxation as *extremely important* (see Table 5.7). But women were just as likely as men to think it was extremely important to investigate government claims and to get information to the public quickly, and were equally unlikely to rate being an adversary of government or business as *extremely important*.

These perceptions did not change much a decade later. The ratings of general media roles by men and women journalists in 1992 were quite similar, except that women were considerably less likely to consider providing entertainment and relaxation as extremely important (as compared with a decade earlier, and to a lesser extent with men) and somewhat more likely to value getting information to the public quickly.

TABLE 5.7
The Importance Journalists Assigned to Various Mass Media Roles, 1982–1983
and 1992 (Percentage Who Rated Each Dimension *Extremely Important*)

Journalistic Role	1982–1983		1992	
	Men (n = 661)	Women (n = 338)	Men (n = 760)	Women (n = 392)
Investigative government claims	64.0	68.6	68.1	64.8
Get information to public quickly	57.8	63.3	67.5	70.7
Avoid stories with unverified content	45.8	58.0	47.3	52.1
Provide analysis of complex problems	49.2	49.1	48.9	47.1
Discuss national policy	39.5	39.6	39.5	37.2
Develop intellectual/cultural interests	23.5	25.7	17.7	19.7
Provide entertainment, relaxation	18.2	23.1	15.3	11.5
Serve as an adversary of government	21.0	18.7	22.2	19.6
Serve as an adversary of business	15.1	16.0	14.7	14.0

Overall, there was little change in men's and women's news media role priorities, and very little difference in how these roles were rated by gender. These results suggest that women and men journalists in 1992 had similar and stable views of the general role priorities of the news media.

Ethical Standards

Much public debate about journalism focuses on the ethics of various reporting practices, such as using hidden cameras or microphones, paying for information, not revealing that one is a journalist, and so on. In 1982–1983, we asked about seven questionable reporting practices, and found much disagreement among journalists as to whether certain practices might be justified on occasion or would not be approved under any circumstances. As chapter 4 (this volume) indicated, the only practice that U.S. journalists overwhelmingly agreed on (95%) was that divulging confidential sources should *not* be approved under any circumstances. For the rest of the practices, the percentages ranged from 20% to 67% who thought that they might be justified on occasion.[20]

Taken together, there were not significant differences between men and women journalists in 1982–1983 regarding whether these controversial reporting practices might be justified, but older and more experienced journalists, especially those working for radio, were less likely to approve. Those journalists working for larger news organizations and making higher salaries were more likely to see these reporting practices as sometimes justifiable.

Chapter 4 indicated that, in 1992, the percentages of journalists saying that the various practices might be acceptable did not change much from 1982–1983 for five of the seven methods—getting employed to gain inside information, badgering unwilling informants to get a story, paying for information, claiming to be somebody else, and disclosing confidential sources. But there was a dramatic increase in those saying that using confidential business or government documents without authorization might be acceptable (from 55% to 82%), and in those saying that using personal documents such as letters and photographs without permission might be justified (from 28% to 48%; see Table 4.11).

In 1992, as in 1982–1983, there were almost no significant differences between men and women journalists regarding the acceptability of these controversial reporting methods (see Table 5.8). Instead, the major differences occurred by news medium and minority status. For example, in 1992, daily newspaper, news magazine, and wire service journalists were significantly more likely than others to justify the use of unauthorized documents, as were Asian-American journalists. Weekly newspaper, radio, and Native-American journalists were least likely to approve of the use of documents without permission, perhaps because they were likely to work for smaller news organizations in more cohesive communities where journalists and news sources more regularly interacted.

Another striking demonstration that gender is less important than newsroom environment and minority status in ideas about reporting ethics came from one of the three reporting practices we added in the 1992 study. Disclosing the names of rape victims was a controversial topic during much of the early 1990s, made even more salient by the William Kennedy Smith rape trial in Palm Beach, Florida, and the furor over protecting the victim's identity. Although U.S. journalists in 1992 were nearly evenly split on whether it could be considered justifiable to disclose the name of a rape victim (43% said it might), they were not split by gender, as one might expect. Exactly the same proportion of men and women journalists said it might be justifiable on occasion.[21]

TABLE 5.8
Journalists' Opinions on Reporting Practices
(Percentage Saying Each Practice May Be Justified)

Reporting Practice	Men (n = 757)	Women (n = 392)[a]
Using confidential business or government documents without authorization	81.2	82.9
Getting employed to gain inside information	61.3	66.1
Using hidden microphones or cameras	61.2	58.6
Badgering unwilling informants to get a story	49.2	48.3
Using personal letters and photographs without permission	47.7	47.3
Disclosing names of rape victims	43.1	43.2
Using re-creations of news by actors	27.1	29.3
Claiming to be somebody else	19.6	26.3
Paying for confidential information	21.9	16.5
Agreeing to protect confidentiality and not doing so	6.2	3.3

[a]Ns vary slightly by item. The largest Ns are reported here.

Native-American journalists were much less likely to agree (21%), as were news people from television (34%) and radio (28%). However, when we asked about using hidden microphones or cameras, television journalists were most likely to give a qualified approval (90%) and weekly newspaper journalists least likely (45%). Among minorities, the proportions varied from 59% for Native Americans to 72% for Asian Americans. The proportions of men (61%) and women (59%) in the overall sample did not differ significantly.

This same pattern of greater differences by news medium and race or ethnic background than by gender emerged for all the controversial reporting practices we asked about in 1992, suggesting again that newsroom environment and community/cultural setting were more powerful influences on ethical values of journalists than was gender in the early 1990s.

CONCLUSIONS

Taken together, the three major national studies of U.S. journalists conducted in 1971, 1982–1983, and 1992 suggest considerable progress for women in American journalism during 1971–1992, with a few setbacks and a few areas of little change.

Backgrounds

By the early 1990s, women journalists were clearly as educated as men at both undergraduate and graduate levels, and were more likely to be married than 10 or 20 years previous. But they were still much less likely to be married than men, and much less likely to have children living with them. This suggests that women journalists had more difficulty combining careers and families than did men.

Women were also more likely to work full time for a wide variety of news media in 1992, as compared with the past. They were also better represented in journalism overall than in other professional occupations, such as college or university teaching, dentistry, law, and medicine. But the overall representation of women in U.S. journalism in 1992 did not increase from 1982–1983 levels, although the proportion of women under the age of 25 increased notably, primarily because women have not stayed in journalism as long as men. It appears that many women have left journalism before their mid-30s and have returned in later years, resulting in fewer years of experience than men, who have stayed on the job without taking a leave.

Women actually lost ground in TV news, dropping from one third of all TV journalists in 1982–1983 to about one fourth in 1992. They held steady in daily and weekly newspapers, and made the largest gains in news magazines and wire services.

Occupational Experiences

The income gap between men and women decreased, from 64% of men's salaries overall in 1971 to 81% in 1991. When years of experience, size of news media organization, managerial responsibilities, and several other predictors were held constant, the gender gap in income virtually disappeared by the early 1990s.

Women also made significant gains in managerial responsibility, especially in the print media, and in amount of editorial control, although there seemed to be a decrease in perceived autonomy to select stories for both women and men during the previous 10–20 years. Women lagged behind men in perceived influence on hiring and firing, especially in radio and TV news. Overall, the 1992 findings suggest that radio and TV newsrooms were more likely to be controlled by men than women, but not so for the print media, where women were more numerous.

There was a notable drop in both the 1970s and 1980s in the proportion of U.S. journalists claiming to be very satisfied with their work. By the 1980s, though, there were no significant differences between men and women on perceived job satisfaction. Women were slightly less likely than men to say they would like to be working in journalism in the next 5 years. Women were equally as unlikely as men to belong to a professional journalism association (slightly more than one third claimed to), and equally likely to rate their news organization as doing a *very good* or *outstanding* job of informing the public (nearly two thirds said so).

In general, there were not many differences between men and women in job experiences or satisfaction, except in perceived influence in hiring and firing, where women were less likely to think they had a great deal of influence in the broadcast news media.

Professional Roles and Ethics

Likewise, there were few detectable differences between men and women journalists in their perceptions of which news media roles were most and least important, and in their opinions on which questionable reporting practices might be justified on occasion and which should not be approved under any circumstances. Instead, opinions on these topics were much more likely to vary by type of news organization (e.g., daily and weekly newspaper, news magazine, radio, television, and wire service) and racial and ethnic background than by gender.

This finding suggests that newsroom and community environments were stronger influences on journalists' professional values (and probably on the kind of news content they produced) than was gender, raising the question of whether news coverage is likely to change much as more women enter journalism and assume positions of increasing responsibility.

In our 1982–1983 study, we found that factors in the organizational environment—as opposed to education and demographic background measures—were most predictive of journalistic role orientation.[22] We also found that newsroom learning and family upbringing were the most often cited sources of influence on ideas about journalism ethics for both women and men.[23] The same patterns emerged in 1992, with respect to both ethical and news values: Journalistic training and newsroom learning were perceived as the most influential by the most journalists, both men and women.

These findings suggest that a larger representation of women in journalism will not automatically result in changes in news coverage of politics or other subjects unless the culture of newsrooms, the structure of news work, and the traditions of journalism change. This conclusion was supported by an additional analysis of our 1982–1983 data by Lori Bergen, who correlated the individual and organizational characteristics of journalists with samples of their best work (and also with their open-ended descriptions of their best work in our survey). She found that organizational characteristics (income, years employed at organization, amount of editing, frequency of reporting, beat assignment, perceived autonomy, type and size of media organization, type of ownership, presence of a union, and size of city) were stronger predictors of the kind of stories journalists wrote than were individual traits (age, gender, education, college major, membership in professional organizations, political leaning, and role orientation), although neither were very strong influences on news content.[24]

In analyzing the stories that journalists sent to us as examples of their best work in 1983, Bergen coded topic of the story, news values evidenced (conflict, timeliness, proximity, prominence, unusualness, and impact), sources relied on (gender, anonymous vs. named, documentary vs. person, institutional vs. private), event or issue orientation, role concepts (adversarial, interpretive, neutral disseminator), and cultural values (ethnocentrism, altruistic democracy, responsible capitalism, etc.).[25] In every aspect of the stories analyzed, the organizational characteristics were consistently stronger predictors than the individual, but the small proportions of variance predicted by both suggested that (a) there were other influences operating that were not included in this study, (b) much of the difference in news content was idiosyncratic, or (c) more subtle aspects of news coverage were not measured.

Whatever the explanations, it seems clear from this analysis and other studies, such as those by Hirsch and by Shoemaker and Reese, that most journalists, even those with great freedom, work within the constraints of specific news organizations.[26] As such, most realize that they must meet organizational, occupational, and audience expectations. In addition, the news organizations within which journalists work are influenced by external societal and cultural environments. Given these layers of influences, it was not too surprising that the individual characteristics of journalists did not correlate strongly with the kinds of news content they produced, but it would be a mistake to think that individual journalists have little freedom to select and shape news stories, or to change the nature of the news organizations for which they work.

For example, chapter 7 (this volume) reveals that, in 1992, women journalists were somewhat more likely to include female sources in their news stories than were men, who were more likely to include male news sources. There was also evidence of a shift from more traditional government and crime news to news of personalities and human interest over the decade in this set of self-selected stories, with stories written by women more likely to be concerned with social problems and protests, and less likely to emphasize getting the story quickly, than those written by men.

Changing the culture and structure of news organizations, especially large ones, is not a simple or quick matter, however. When more women attain higher levels of authority in news organizations, more changes in news coverage may be possible. But women, like men, will still be constrained by the economic realities, organizational structures, and journalistic values they worked under on their way up the journalistic ladder.

NOTES

1. Sue A. Lafky, "Women Journalists," in David H. Weaver and G. Cleveland Wilhoit, *The American Journalist*, 2nd ed. (Bloomington, IN: Indiana University Press, 1991), p. 181.
2. Victor R. Fuchs, *Women's Quest for Economic Equality* (Cambridge, MA: Harvard University Press, 1988).
3. Gilda Berger, *Women, Work and Wages* (New York: Franklin Watts, 1986); Lafky, "Women Journalists."
4. "Women in the Civilian Labor Force," *The 1993 Information Please Almanac* (Boston: Houghton Mifflin), p. 55.
5. John W. C. Johnstone, Edward J. Slawski, and William W. Bowman, *The News People* (Urbana, IL: University of Illinois Press, 1976), p. 197.
6. D. H. Weaver and G. C. Wilhoit, *The American Journalist* (Bloomington: Indiana University Press, 1991), p. 19.
7. Maurine H. Beasley and Kathyrn T. Theus, *The New Majority: A Look at What the Preponderance of Women in Journalism Means to the Schools and to the Professions* (Lanham, MD: University Press of America, 1988).
8. Paul V. Peterson, "Enrollment Surges Again, Increases 7 Per Cent to 70,601," *Journalism Educator, 33*, 4 (1979), p. 3.
9. Susan H. Russell, James S. Fairweather, and Robert M. Hendrickson, *Profiles of Faculty in Higher Education Institutions, 1988* (Washington, DC: National Center for Education Statistics, U.S. Department of Education, 1991), p. 133; Sylvia Nasar, "Women's Progress Stalled? Just Not So," *The New York Times*, October 18, 1992, p. 10.
10. Mary Frank Fox, "Women and Higher Education: Gender Differences in the Status of Students and Scholars" in Jo Freeman, ed., *Women: A Feminist Perspective*, 4th ed. (Mountain View, CA: Mayfield Publishing Company, 1988).
11. Michele Collison, "More Young Black Men Choosing Not to Go to College," *The Chronicle of Higher Education*, December 9, 1987, pp. 1, A26–A27; Paula Giddings, *When and Where I Enter: The Impact of Black Women on Race and Sex in America* (New York: W. Morrow, 1984), pp. 325–335.
12. Claudia Goldin, *Understanding the Gender Gap: An Economic History of American Women* (New York: Oxford University Press, 1990), p. 27.

13. Giddings, *When and Where I Enter*, p. 329.
14. Weaver and Wilhoit, *The American Journalist*, p. 83.
15. William W. Bowman, "Distaff Journalists: Women as a Minority Group in the News Media," Ph.D. dissertation, University of Illinois at Chicago Circle, 1974.
16. Lafky, "Women Journalists," p. 176.
17. Weaver and Wilhoit, *The American Journalist*, p. 96.
18. Louis Harris, *Steelcase Office Environment Index* (New York: Louis Harris & Associates, 1991); NORC (National Opinion Research Center), *General Social Survey* (Chicago, IL: University of Chicago, April 1991).
19. See also G. Cleveland Wilhoit and David Weaver, "U.S. Journalists at Work, 1971–1992," a paper presented to the annual meeting of the Association for Education in Journalism and Mass Communication, Atlanta, Georgia, August 1994, p. 32.
20. Weaver and Wilhoit, *The American Journalist*, pp. 127–128.
21. David Weaver and G. Cleveland Wilhoit, "The American Journalist in the 1990s," report to The Freedom Forum, Arlington, VA, November 1992, pp. 13–14.
22. Weaver and Wilhoit, *The American Journalist*, p. 117.
23. Weaver and Wilhoit, *The American Journalist*, p. 135.
24. Lori A. Bergen, "Testing the Relative Strength of Individual and Organizational Characteristics in Predicting Content of Journalists' Best Work," Ph.D. dissertation, Indiana University–Bloomington, 1991.
25. Bergen, "Testing the Relative Strength," pp. 53–65; Lori A. Bergen, "Journalists' Best Work," in David H. Weaver and G. Cleveland Wilhoit, *The American Journalist*, 2nd ed. (Bloomington: Indiana University Press, 1991), pp. 194–210.
26. Paul M. Hirsch, "Occupational, Organizational, and Institutional Models in Mass Media Research," in Paul M. Hirsch, Peter V. Miller, and F. Gerald Kline, eds., *Strategies for Communication Research* (Thousand Oaks, CA: Sage, 1977); Pamela J. Shoemaker and Stephen D. Reese, *Mediating the Message: Theories of Influences on Mass Media Content* (White Plains, NY: Longman, 1991).

Chapter 6

Minority Journalists

Perhaps no other issue in journalism (and in the larger society in general) dominated the agenda of the late 1980s and early 1990s as conspicuously as that of racial diversity and representation. Scores of speeches, papers, articles, books, and television programs criticized the mainstream news media and journalism educators for not including more members of minority groups (mainly African American, Asian American, Hispanic, and Native American) in their news organizations and classrooms and on their faculties.[1] Others criticized the news coverage of minorities and their lives in various media as sparse, unrepresentative, stereotypical, and unduly negative.[2]

This criticism of U.S. news media can be traced back at least a quarter century to the publication of the Kerner Report (the Report of the National Advisory Commission on Civil Disorders named after its chair Otto Kerner, former governor of Illinois).[3] This report recommended expanded coverage of the Negro community and of race problems by reporters familiar with urban and racial affairs, integration of Negroes and Negro activities into all aspects of coverage and content, recruitment of more Negroes into journalism and broadcasting and promotion of those qualified to positions of significant responsibility, and adoption of guidelines to ensure accurate and responsible reporting of racial news.

According to Sidmel Estes-Sumpter, past president of the National Association of Black Journalists (NABJ) and Unity '94 (an organization of the four main minority journalism associations), "The terminology is archaic, but if you substitute the words 'people of color' for the word 'Negro' or 'Negroes,' what results is a blueprint for what should have been done before the 1992 urban disturbances, but what the nation's news organizations have yet to achieve."[4]

What did the nation's mainstream, general interest news organizations achieve (or not achieve) in the hiring of minority journalists during 1971–1992? Did some news media do better than others in recruiting and retaining minority journalists? What were the educational and work backgrounds, incomes, job titles and influence, job satisfaction, professional affiliations, and views on roles and ethics of minority journalists as compared with majority White journalists? To answer these questions, we turn first to our main probability sample of all U.S. journalists for estimates of numbers of minority journalists employed in the different mainstream news media. Then we rely on the separate samples of minority journalists for answers to the other questions.

REPRESENTATION OF MINORITY JOURNALISTS IN MAINSTREAM NEWS MEDIA

During 1982–1992, numerous studies were done on how many and which kind of minority journalists worked in various news media, and how more could be recruited and retained.[5] Estimates of the percentages of minorities working in different media varied widely in these studies, as did the questions asked and the methods used. The response rates of many of these studies were quite low (27%, 31%, 38%), making generalization to larger groups highly suspect. Exceptions included the American Society of Newspaper Editors (ASNE) 1989 study, *The Changing Face of the Newsroom* (with a response rate of 89%), the ASNE annual employment surveys (with responses from 60% to 70%), and the Tan study of former Asian-American journalists (with a response of 79%).[6]

Fewer such surveys by various media industry groups, more carefully conducted and coordinated, would result in more accurate and cumulative measures of minority employment over time, including reasons for why minorities are attracted to, and leave, major news media positions. The key advantages of the 1992 survey of U.S. journalists (and the previous ones conducted in 1971 and 1982–1983) included standardized questions, similar sampling methods, and high response rates, which enabled reliable comparisons over time that were also generalizable to the larger population of U.S. journalists.

As chapter 1 (this volume) noted (Table 1.8), 3.7% of all full-time U.S. journalists working for mainstream news media in 1992 were African American. Based on our estimate of 122,015 total U.S. full-time journalists in 1992, this translates into slightly more than 4,500 African-American journalists nationwide—the largest minority group if Jewish journalists were not counted as minorities.

The next largest group was Hispanic journalists, who constituted 2.2% of the total journalistic workforce, for an estimated 2,680 nationwide. Asian-American journalists were only 1% of the total workforce, or about 1,220 in number nationwide, and Native Americans were the smallest minority group at 0.6% of the workforce, or only 732 total. Another 0.7% identified themselves as "other" minorities when asked how they would classify themselves, for a total of 854.

These figures indicate that ethnic and racial minorities in American journalism in 1992 were a small group (about 10,000 individuals), as compared with about 112,000 in the White majority. If Jewish journalists are considered an ethnic minority, then the size of the minority group increased to nearly 16,600 in 1992, compared with slightly over 105,000 in the White majority.

Trends Over Time

Although the minority group of U.S. journalists was relatively small in 1992, chapter 1 pointed out that there was improvement in the representation of racial and ethnic minorities in U.S. mainstream news media during 1982–1992—from 3.9% overall to 8.2%, if the 0.7% who identified themselves as "other" minorities is included. This percentage of 8.2 lagged far behind the 25% estimated by the U.S. Census for the total U.S. population. But when compared with the percentage of minorities who had a bachelor's degree (9.1%), the minimum requirement for most full-time journalism jobs in 1992, it is clear that U.S. journalism did not lag very far behind the *qualified* population percentage, as Stephen Hess of The Brookings Institution has pointed out.[7]

If only those full-time journalists hired during 1982–1992 are considered, Fig. 1.2 in chapter 1 showed that the overall percentage of minorities was considerably higher than 8.2% (11.9% for those with 0–4 years of experience, and 12.4% for those with 5–9 years of experience). These figures suggest that there were increased efforts, and some success, in minority hiring in U.S. journalism during the 1980s.

But Fig. 1.2 also showed that after 10 years of experience, the percentage of minority journalists dropped sharply, probably because of a combination of less emphasis on hiring minorities before the 1980s and a tendency for minorities to leave journalism. Our data show that minority journalists in 1992 had an average of 9–11 years of work experience in journalism, compared with an average of 14 years for nonminority journalists.

Differences Among Media

Chapter 1 also noted that some news media did better than others in recruiting full-time journalists of differing races and ethnic backgrounds. Figure 1.3 in chapter 1 showed that the broadcast news media of radio and television had the highest percentages in 1992, whereas weekly newspapers had the lowest. It is likely that the low percentage for weeklies reflects that, in 1992, most racial minorities in the United States lived in larger urban areas, rather than in the small towns where weeklies tend to be published. However, the same cannot be said for news magazines, which tend to be located in larger urban areas.

The higher percentages of minorities in broadcast news media were consistent with more interest in these media by minority journalism students in 1980[8] and 1987.[9] In our 1982–1983 study of U.S. journalists, we speculated that "minorities are more likely to be attracted to the faster-growing broadcast media than to the more traditional print media of newspapers, news magazines, and news services."[10]

This appears to have happened during 1982–1992, perhaps because of additional efforts by broadcast news managers to recruit minorities, or because of more interest in broadcast media by minority journalism students, or both.

Although there have been real increases in the proportions of racial minorities working in U.S. mainstream news media during the 1980s and early 1990s, chapter 1 argued that it will be difficult to retain many of the brightest and most ambitious, given the limited opportunities for advancement in a field that has not grown much during the 1980s. This prediction receives some mixed support from our data, as discussed in the section on job satisfaction later in this chapter.

BACKGROUNDS

Compared with majority White journalists in 1992, minority journalists were less likely to be male, to be of the Protestant faith (except for African Americans), to be married, to lean toward the Republican party, to have worked in journalism longer than 10 years, and to work for small news organizations (except for Native Americans). Minority journalists were more likely to be younger, to be Democrats, and to be members of a journalism association.

The "typical" African-American journalist in 1992 was a Protestant woman with a bachelor's degree from a public college, not married, a Democrat, 34 years old, working in journalism about 11 years, earning about $37,000 a year, a member of at least one professional journalism association, and employed by a large (100 journalists or more) group-owned daily newspaper.

The average Asian-American journalist in 1992 was a 33-year-old woman of Protestant or no religion with a bachelor's degree from a public college, not married, a Democrat, earning about $42,000 a year after working in journalism about 10 years, a member of at least one professional journalism association, and employed by a very large (150 journalists or more) group-owned daily newspaper.

The typical Hispanic journalist in 1992 was slightly more likely to be a male, a Catholic with a bachelor's degree from a public college, unmarried, a Democrat, 33 years old, working in journalism about 9 years, earning about $37,000 a year, a member of at least one professional journalism association, and employed by a large group-owned daily newspaper.

The average Native-American journalist in 1992 was a male of a different religion than Protestant or Catholic with a bachelor's degree from a public college, married, a Democrat or Independent, 40 years old, earning about $22,000 a year after working in journalism about 11 years, a member of at least one professional association, and employed by a very small (three journalists or less) single-owned daily newspaper or television station.

Education

Table 6.1 shows that, in 1992, minority journalists were slightly less likely than the White majority to hold a college bachelor's degree, but slightly more likely to have earned a graduate degree. Minorities were a bit less likely to have stopped

TABLE 6.1
Amount of Formal Education of U.S. Journalists (Percentage in Each Category)

Highest Educational Attainment	Minorities (n = 340)	White (n = 1,063)
Some high school	0.0	0.1
High school graduate	1.8	4.3
Some college	15.3	13.2
College graduate	59.4	64.3
Some graduate training	6.5	6.4
Graduate degree	17.1	11.4

their formal education with a high school diploma. But overall, there were not significant differences between minority and majority journalists in level of formal education.

There were some significant differences among the individual minority groups, however. Native Americans were much less likely to hold a bachelor's degree (43%) than the other groups (60%–68%). Asian Americans and African Americans were most likely to have a graduate degree (21%), and Hispanics were least likely (9%).

As a whole, minorities were a bit more likely to have majored in journalism in college (45% of those with a college degree) than the White majority (41%), but Native Americans were far less likely to have done so (30%) than African Americans and Hispanics (47% and 50%, respectively). Minorities were no more likely to have majored in radio-television than majority journalists (5% of all those with a college degree), but minorities were slightly more likely to have majored in other communication subjects (15%) than were Whites (11%). At both the undergraduate and graduate levels, minorities were significantly less likely to have majored in English and more likely to have majored in journalism or a social science other than political science.

Minorities were also more likely than majority journalists to have attended an Ivy League college at both undergraduate and graduate levels, except for Native Americans. Asian Americans were most likely to have attended an Ivy League college at both undergraduate (11%) and graduate (28%) levels combined. At the graduate level alone, Hispanics were most likely to have gone to an Ivy League school (29%). There were no significant differences in attendance at public or private schools in graduate school, but, at the undergraduate level, African Americans were most likely to have attended a private college (43%) and Native Americans were least likely (15%), with Whites in between at 30%. In general, then, minority journalists in 1992 were more likely than the majority to have attended Ivy League colleges and private graduate schools, except for Native Americans, who were least likely of all groups to have a college degree in general or to have attended more elite colleges.

Continuing Education

When asked if they felt a need for additional training in journalism or other subjects, minorities as a group were more likely to say "yes" (70%–80%) than were majority journalists (60%), with Native Americans most likely to say so at 80%. Native Americans were also most likely to say that they had taken courses, workshops, or fellowships since becoming a journalist (79%), as compared with other groups (59%–64%), suggesting that more experience with such training stimulates more interest in additional training.

Family Life

Minorities as a group were less likely to be married than were majority White journalists, perhaps because they tended to be younger and more likely to be women. Among minority groups, 38%–50% were married in 1992, compared with 60% of Whites. The least likely to be married were African-American and Hispanic journalists (38% and 39%, respectively), and the most likely were Native Americans (50%).

Native-American journalists were also the most likely to have children living with them (44%), and Asian Americans and Hispanics were least likely (20%), with African Americans (32%) and Whites (39%) in between.

Age

Whereas minority journalists in general tended to be younger than majority news people in 1992, that was not true for Native Americans, who had an average age of 40, compared with 38 for Whites. But the other three minority groups were significantly younger on average—33 for Asian Americans and Hispanics and 34 for African Americans. Younger average ages of minority journalists were not surprising, given the data in Fig. 1.2 in chapter 1, which showed the largest proportions of minorities were hired as journalists during the 1980s. But these younger average ages suggest that minorities were not as likely as majority Whites to be in positions of leadership and authority in their news organizations. The next section examines the working environment of minority journalists in 1992.

JOBS

Work Experience

Table 6.2 shows that minority journalists were more likely than majority Whites in 1992 to have 10 years or less experience in journalism, almost as likely to have 10–15 years of experience, but significantly less likely to have more than 15 years in journalism (20% vs. 37% for Whites). The average number of years of journalism experience was 14 for Whites, 10 for Asian Americans, 11 for

TABLE 6.2
Years of Experience in Journalism (Percentage in Each Category)

Experience	Minorities (n = 342)	White (n = 1,060)
1–5 years	26.9	18.7
6–10 years	33.0	22.5
11–15 years	20.2	21.8
16–20 years	12.3	17.0
21–25 years	4.1	8.7
26–30 years	2.0	4.7
31–35 years	0.6	2.4
36–40 years	0.3	2.4
More than 40 years	0.6	2.0

African Americans, 9 for Hispanics, and 11 for Native Americans. This was most likely due to less emphasis on hiring minorities into journalism before the 1980s, but it may have been due as well to minorities leaving journalism in larger proportions than Whites. When asked where they would most like to be working in 5 years, African-American and Native-American journalists were more likely to say somewhere else besides the news media (26% and 29%, respectively) than were Whites (21%). But Asian Americans and Hispanics were less likely to want to leave journalism (11% and 19%, respectively).

Income

The overall analysis of U.S. journalists' 1991 income in chapter 3 (this volume) shows that there was little impact of race, except for Native Americans, whose average salaries were lower, but who also tended to work for smaller news organizations, which typically pay less. But overall, the impact of race on income was very small after other factors, such as size of organization and years of experience, were controlled statistically, as shown in Table 3.12 in chapter 3.

Table 6.3 presents a more detailed look at income for all minority journalists combined, as compared with majority Whites. In most categories, the percentages were similar, but there were a few where minorities led Whites ($50,000–$55,000 and $55,000–$60,000), and a few where Whites were more prevalent ($15,000–$20,000 and $40,000–$45,000). At the upper levels of income, it was clear that minority journalists were equally well represented in 1991 salaries as were majority journalists, although the proportions were small for both groups.

The median incomes of the different minority groups differed substantially, but that was mainly due to the differing sizes of news organizations for which they worked. Asian Americans, who tended to work for the largest organizations (150 journalists or more), earned the highest median incomes in 1991 ($42,000), followed by African Americans and Hispanics (at $37,000), who tended to work

TABLE 6.3
Income of Journalists (Percentage in Each Category)

Income	Minorities (n = 322)	White (n = 1,032)
Less than $15,000	8.1	8.6
$15k–$20k	8.1	11.4
$20k–$25k	13.0	12.3
$25k–$30k	12.4	13.7
$30k–$35k	8.4	9.6
$35k–$40k	9.3	11.6
$40k–$45k	8.1	12.3
$45k–$50k	7.8	6.0
$50k–$55k	7.5	5.4
$55k–$60k	5.9	2.3
$60k–$65k	3.4	1.3
$65k–$70k	1.9	1.3
$70k–$75k	2.5	1.2
$75k–$85k	1.9	1.2
$85k–$100k	0.6	0.7
$100,000 & above	1.2	1.2

for large daily newspapers. Native Americans, who were likely to work for very small news organizations (with an average of only three full-time journalists), earned a median income of only $22,000 in 1992. White journalists' median income was $32,000.

Although these differences in median salaries of different racial and ethnic groups are striking, Table 3.12 in chapter 3 showed clearly that the strongest predictors of income were number of years of journalism experience, and type and size of news organization. Except for being Native American, race and ethnicity was not a significant predictor of income. Being Native American was not as strong a predictor of income as were years of experience, type of medium, size of organization, and having management responsibilities. Nevertheless, Native-American journalists did earn slightly less than others in 1991, even after these other predictors were controlled statistically.

Managerial Influence

Minority journalists were about as likely as Whites (43%) to supervise other news employees, except for African Americans, who were somewhat less likely (34%). Native Americans were most likely to say they supervised others (48%), but they were also most likely to work for very small news media and to be older on average than other groups. Hispanics (42%) and Asian Americans (41%) were somewhat less likely to be supervisors in newsrooms than were Native Americans, but were also more likely to work for much larger organizations and to be younger.

TABLE 6.4
Job Titles of U.S. Journalists (Percentage of Each Category)

Title	Asian American (n = 100)	African American (n = 77)	Hispanic (n = 78)	Native American (n = 81)	White (n = 1,043)
Owner, publisher, or upper level manager[a]	12.0	10.4	14.1	49.3	25.1
Lower level manager[b]	37.0	36.4	29.5	16.0	27.3
Writer or announcer	12.0	16.9	10.3	19.8	16.4
Reporter or staff writer	30.0	28.6	38.5	11.1	22.1
Photographer or graphics specialist	9.0	7.8	7.7	3.7	9.1

[a]Upper level managers include city editors, news directors, and higher level personnel.
[b]Lower level managers include desk editors, assignment editors, and assistant editors.

Except for Native Americans, minority journalists were less likely to be owners, publishers, or upper level managers (city editor or news director and higher) than White majority journalists, as Table 6.4 shows. Native Americans were much better represented at the top levels, but they were also inclined to work for much smaller organizations than the other groups, as noted earlier.

Minorities were generally more likely to be lower level managers than Whites, suggesting the possibility that more minorities will move into upper level positions in the years to come if they stay in journalism. It was clear that, among minorities, many were "in the pipeline" to become upper level managers. Asian Americans, African Americans, and Hispanics were somewhat more likely to be reporters or staff writers than Whites, but they were also more inclined to be younger and have fewer years of journalism experience, as well as fewer years of seniority in their present organizations (4–5 years on average, as compared with 8.5 years for Whites).

Another indicator of management level was perceived influence on hiring and firing news employees. Table 6.5 shows that minorities working in the print media (newspapers, news magazines, and wire services) were almost as likely as

TABLE 6.5
Minority and White Newsroom Managers' Perceived Influence
on Hiring (Percentage in Each Category)

Influence	Print		Broadcast	
	Minorities (n = 123)	White (n = 369)	Minorities (n = 15)	White (n = 93)
A great deal	36.6	39.3	26.7	36.6
Some	13.0	22.0	20.0	22.6
A little	26.0	17.1	26.7	25.8
None at all	24.4	21.7	26.7	15.1

TABLE 6.6
Frequencies of Being Able to Select Stories
Worked on (Percentage in Each Category)

	Print		Broadcast	
Frequency	Minorities (n = 306)	White (n = 856)	Minorities (n = 34)	White (n = 203)
Almost always	42.8	47.1	41.2	48.3
More often than not	37.3	37.7	44.1	41.4
Only occasionally	19.6	14.5	14.7	9.9
Don't make proposals	0.3	0.7	0.0	0.5

Whites to say that they had a great deal of influence on hiring, whereas those working for radio and television news departments were less likely to perceive this much authority. This pattern was also true for women, as noted in chapter 5 (this volume), suggesting that broadcast news organizations in 1992 were more likely to be controlled by White males than were print media, although minority journalists were more likely to work in the broadcast media than in print, as Fig. 1.3 in chapter 1 illustrated, whereas women were less likely to do so.

Editorial Influence

In both broadcast and print news media, minorities were slightly less likely than majority journalists to say that they almost always could select the stories they worked on. In general, however, the differences were not great, suggesting that there was little difference in the perceived freedom of journalists by race or ethnicity (see Table 6.6).

Likewise, the amount of editing done by minority and majority journalists did not differ greatly, and minorities in the broadcast media were somewhat more likely than Whites to do a great deal of editing, suggesting significant editorial influence (see Table 6.7). But Table 6.8 suggests that minorities perceived less freedom in deciding how stories would be used in the broadcast media

TABLE 6.7
Amount of Editing Performed by Minority and White
Newsroom Managers (Percentage in Each Category)

	Print		Broadcast	
Amount	Minorities (n = 305)	White (n = 859)	Minorities (n = 35)	White (n = 203)
A great deal	35.7	40.7	31.4	23.6
Some	36.1	34.5	40.0	57.6
None at all	28.2	24.8	28.6	18.7

TABLE 6.8
Amount of Freedom Those with Editing Duties Had in Deciding
How Stories Would Be Used (Percentage in Each Category)

Amount of Freedom	Print		Broadcast	
	Minorities (n = 209)	White (n = 622)	Minorities (n = 25)	White (n = 163)
Almost complete	15.8	18.5	12.0	31.9
A great deal	35.4	34.6	44.0	30.7
Some	34.4	32.0	32.0	31.3
None at all	14.4	15.0	12.0	6.1

than did Whites, compared with no difference in the print media. This finding, coupled with those in Tables 6.5 and 6.6, reinforces the conclusion that majority White journalists had more control (or at least perceived more control) in broadcast news organizations in 1992 than did women or minorities.

Job Dimensions

When asked how important a number of things were in judging jobs in journalism, the most striking differences between minority and majority journalists were in the chance to get ahead in the organization, which was rated *very important* by significantly more minorities, as Table 6.9 shows, and in the chance to influence public affairs, which again was rated *very important* by many more minorities than Whites. Minorities were also more likely to highly value the chance to develop a specialty and to help people.

In general, then, minority journalists were more likely than the White majority to rate more influence—both within and outside journalism—as *very im-*

TABLE 6.9
The Importance of Job Dimensions for Journalists
(Percentage Who Rated Each Dimension *Very Important*)

Dimension	Minorities (n = 338)	White (n = 1,049)[a]
Pay	25.1	20.1
Fringe benefits	36.8	33.8
A chance to get ahead in organization	59.5	37.2
Job security	59.3	59.5
Chance to develop a specialty	49.9	39.7
Chance to help people	76.7	60.0
Editorial policies of organization	72.1	69.8
Chance to influence public affairs	58.1	36.6
Amount of autonomy	55.0	51.4

[a]Ns vary slightly by item. The largest Ns are reported here.

portant, perhaps because of greater feelings of powerlessness or deprivation based on past discrimination. But minorities were similar to the majority in rating the chance to help people and the editorial policies of their news organizations as the most important dimensions of their jobs.

Job Satisfaction

Chapters 3 and 5 (this volume) pointed out the significant drop in the percentage of U.S. journalists claiming to be very satisfied—from 49% in 1971 to 27% in 1992—and the lack of difference between male and female journalists on this measure in 1982 and 1992. When minority journalists were compared with the majority in 1992, it was clear that Hispanics and Native Americans were as satisfied as Whites (Native Americans more so), but Asian Americans and African Americans were somewhat less likely to be very satisfied and more likely to be somewhat dissatisfied (see Table 6.10).

Reasons for job *satisfaction* did not vary significantly between minority and majority journalists. Both frequently mentioned autonomy and the challenge of writing and reporting (70% did so), the opportunity for personal and professional development (25%–30%), and pay and economics (13%–18%).

One Asian-American journalist said, "We are trying to develop a new kind of coverage in the region, and we've been given the resources and space to do this. We have the backing of management, and there is a lot of freedom to try new things."

An African-American journalist put it this way: "I have a fair amount of autonomy, I'm in a competitive market which is exciting, I work with some talented journalists, I feel I can make a difference, plus I have job security and the ability to progress."

A Hispanic journalist said, "I have a very high degree of autonomy. I run my own bureau, I have my own beat which I created, I'm writing about people in communities which normally don't get a high degree of attention, and I'm providing insight for the majority community about segments of the population

TABLE 6.10
Job Satisfaction of Journalists (Percentage in Each Group)

Level of Satisfaction	Asian American (n = 99)	African American (n = 77)	Hispanic (n = 79)	Native American (n = 82)	White (n = 1,049)
Very satisfied	21.2	19.5	27.8	32.9	27.5
Fairly satisfied	51.5	53.2	54.4	53.7	49.8
Somewhat dissatisfied	26.3	23.4	13.9	9.8	20.0
Very dissatisfied	1.0	3.9	3.8	3.7	2.8
Average level of satisfaction[a]	4.9	4.8	5.1	5.3	5.0

[a]Means based on a scale where 1 = very dissatisfied, 3 = somewhat dissatisfied, 5 = fairly satisfied, and 7 = very satisfied.

which they know nothing about. The flip side is that the minority communities are getting recognition for things other than social problems."

A Native-American journalist said, "I have a good staff that I enjoy working with, and we work well together. It has taken several years to get to this point. We don't have too much interference from the tribal government with the paper, although we do have some."

Reasons for being *dissatisfied* with the job included complaints about management (mentioned by 11%–12%), salary and economics (mentioned more frequently by minorities—10%—than by the majority—6%), and complaints about lack of opportunities to advance (mentioned by 4.1% of the minorities and 4.5% of the total sample).

As an Asian-American journalist put it, "It's very difficult as an Asian American or as a minority journalist to rise above a certain point, and when you hit the glass ceiling, which is definitely there primarily at the management level, it is incredibly frustrating whatever the editorial policy of the news."

A Hispanic journalist cited lack of advancement and the scope of the work: "I'm somewhat limited. I'd like to do a broader scope, broader stories, more long-term kinds of stories."

An African-American journalist said, "I love my job and I love what I do, but I am becoming more and more discouraged over the level of pay. I resent the inflexibility of scheduling, meaning I work on the weekends and have a great deal of difficulty getting the weekend off if I need it. I resent management not giving me the days off that I need."

A Native-American journalist mentioned the "reluctance of the more mainstream news organizations to take an interest in the Native-American community," and added, "They're only interested in stereotypical topics, and you have to take them by the hand and explain why it is important. You have to give them a history lesson too."

Commitment to Journalism

On another measure of job satisfaction—where they would like to be working in 5 years, in the news media or somewhere else—African Americans and Native Americans were most likely to say "somewhere else" (26% and 29%, respectively), and Asians were least likely to want to leave the news media (11%). Hispanics at 19% were slightly below Whites at 21%. Based on the job satisfaction scores in Table 6.10, one would expect Asian Americans and African Americans to be most likely to want to leave the news media, and Native Americans least likely. The lack of correlation between these two indicators suggests that there were different reasons for being dissatisfied with one's job and wanting to leave journalism.

Disappointment with journalism—especially superficiality of news coverage, a tendency not to look at why stories were happening, narrow-mindedness, and resistance to change—was mentioned by about 20% of the minority journalists, especially Native Americans, as compared with 15% of the total sample. A feeling that their talents were better suited to another job was expressed by 18% of the minorities, compared with only about 7% of the total sample. Excessive stress and pressure were mentioned by 12% of the minorities and 10.5% of the majority journalists. Low pay was mentioned by only 9% of the minorities, as compared with 21% of the total sample. But Native Americans were more likely to cite low pay than other minority journalists, which was not surprising given the much lower average income of this group mentioned earlier.

As one Native-American journalist remarked, "There is more money outside the news media. I'm really disillusioned with the news media in general, and that includes radio, television and newspapers, because it's a White-dominated system and doesn't want to change." Another Native-American journalist said, "I think that I'm very good at what I do, but I think my real talent lies outside of newspapers. I've gotten a little bored with daily reporting, and I want to do something a little more creative."

A Hispanic woman journalist commented that "it is very difficult for minorities to break through the 'good old boy' network and change attitudes about what needs to be covered and attitudes about women and minorities. . . . I feel that I might be better able to change attitudes by going back to journalism education in high school or at college level."

An African-American journalist said that the primary reason for wanting to leave the news media was that "the other areas allow for more creativity and are less competitive." Another mentioned that "news is very restrictive, it is stressful and it is extremely time consuming."

An Asian-American journalist leaned toward leaving the news business because "I think I could have a greater impact in terms of bringing in Asian American voices, experiences, stories, and images by working in media with a larger scope like television or film."

Among Asian Americans, those with 5 or fewer years of experience in journalism were most likely to say they wanted to leave the news media (19%); among African Americans, it was those with 6–10 years of experience (33%). Among Hispanics, it was the older journalists—those with 21 or more years of experience—who were most likely to speak of leaving journalism (40%); among Native Americans, it was those with 11–15 years in journalism who were most likely to talk about leaving (50%). It seems clear that disillusionment with the news media peaked at different stages in the careers of the different minority groups, with Hispanics and Native Americans taking the longest to become dissatisfied. Among Whites, those with 6–10 years were most likely to want to leave (28%)—the same as for African Americans.

Overall, then, there were some differences in levels of job satisfaction between minority and majority journalists. Asian-American and African-American journalists were somewhat less satisfied, but African Americans and Native Americans were somewhat more likely to want to leave journalism.

Rating of Organization

One of the strongest predictors of job satisfaction, in 1971, 1982, as well as in 1992, was how good a job a journalist thought his or her news organization was doing in informing the public. Although there was no significant difference between men and women on this measure (13% of men and 12% of women said "outstanding"), there were significant differences between the different minority groups. As would be expected from the job satisfaction scores in Table 6.10, Asian Americans (8%) and African Americans (7%) were least likely to rate their organizations *outstanding*, and Native Americans were most likely to do so (17.5%). Hispanics were nearly equal to Whites (11% vs. 13%) in their ratings of *outstanding*.

Reasons for rating their organization's performance favorably varied somewhat by racial and ethnic origin. One Native-American journalist cited "factual news, traditional stories, and racial pride through education." Another mentioned "a very diverse staff" and coverage of "a very wide range of issues," as well as skepticism of government information. A Hispanic journalist talked about being "genuinely concerned about the issues that affect our readers" and making "a real effort to have those issues reported fairly and as quickly as possible." An African-American television journalist praised the organization for doing "stories with greater depth and more perspectives so that viewers can make decisions in their own lives based on as much information as the station can give them." An Asian-American journalist mentioned "a wide range of reporting that tries to cover all segments of the community and that provides good analysis of complex issues and good coverage of cultural events."

For those who rated their news organizations more negatively, the reasons also varied. An Asian-American journalist criticized his newspaper for being "very out of touch with other communities such as people of color, the gay community and other alternative communities." An African-American journalist said, "they leave out a lot of information in a lot of stories they do. They don't always present the different sides of the story." A Hispanic journalist charged that "we shy away from controversial events, and we don't have a budget so I have a hard time covering stories." Native-American journalists were most likely to cite lack of resources for news coverage. One said, "My own goal was to provide more native coverage of their own issues and more local and regional coverage, and due to lack of resources and manpower I have not been able to meet that goal."

Thus, even though Native Americans had the highest levels of job satisfaction and were most likely to think that their news organizations were doing an outstanding job of informing the public, they were the most likely to want to leave the news media. Although Asian Americans were one of the least satisfied groups and one of the least inclined to rate their news organizations as doing an *outstanding* job, they were by far the most likely to want to stay in journalism. One possible explanation for this contradiction is average income. As noted earlier, Asian-American journalists had the highest median income ($42,000) in 1991 and Native Americans had the lowest ($22,000).

Organizational Memberships

Minority journalists as a group were significantly more likely to belong to a journalists' union (26%–46%) than White journalists (17%), probably because minorities were more likely to work for larger, urban media. Asian-American journalists were particularly likely to say they belonged to a union (46%), and they were also most likely to work for the largest news organizations.

The additional samples of minority journalists in this study were drawn from the membership lists of professional journalism associations, such as the National Association of Black Journalists (NABJ). Hence, it was not surprising that these minority journalists were more likely to belong to a professional association than were White majority journalists. But even when only those minority journalists who fell into the main national probability sample were analyzed, it was clear that Asian-American and African-American journalists were much more likely to belong to a professional association (67% and 60.5%, respectively) than were White journalists (35%), whereas Hispanic journalists were about as likely to belong as Whites (32%), and Native Americans were less likely (14%).

If belonging to a professional association is a sign of professional identity or commitment, then Asian-American and African-American journalists were more likely to have such a commitment in 1992 than were other journalists.

PROFESSIONAL VALUES

Role Perceptions

An important indicator of professional values is the priority that journalists assign to various roles of the news media. Table 6.11 indicates that the overall ranking of importance of media roles was similar for minority and majority journalists, but there were some differences in emphasis, especially among those roles that seemed to be measures of an interpretive or adversarial approach to journalism (e.g., analyzing complex problems, discussing national policy, and serving as an adversary of business or government). Minorities (most notably Asian Americans and African Americans) were somewhat more likely to consider these roles very important than were Whites. The biggest difference between the groups, however, was the much greater emphasis by minority journalists on developing intellectual and cultural interests of their publics, especially among Native-American and Hispanic journalists. This role was part of an approach to journalism that we called *populist mobilizer* in chapter 4 (this volume). We suspect that minority journalists were particularly interested in the cultural in-

TABLE 6.11
The Importance Journalists Assigned to Various Mass Media Roles
(Percentage Who Rated Each Dimension *Extremely Important*)

Journalistic Role	Minorities (n = 337)	White (n = 1,051)[a]
Investigate government claims	68.7	67.4
Get information to public quickly	63.7	68.5
Avoid stories with unverified content	46.9	48.7
Provide analysis of complex problems	55.8	48.9
Discuss national policy	43.6	38.9
Develop intellectual and cultural interests	32.8	17.8
Provide entertainment, relaxation	12.3	13.9
Serve as an adversary of government	25.7	20.9
Serve as an adversary of business	20.5	13.7
Use news of widest interest	24.0	19.2
Set the political agenda	7.7	3.9
Let ordinary people express their views	48.5	47.7

[a]Ns vary slightly by item. The largest Ns are reported here.

terests of their readers, viewers, and listeners because of a perception of dominance of other cultures by the mainstream Anglo-American culture.

Ethical Standards

As noted in chapters 4 and 5 (this volume), the ethics of reporting is one of the most controversial areas of journalism, and ethical values are usually considered an important type of professional value. Chapter 5 reported almost no significant differences between men and women journalists regarding the acceptability of various questionable reporting practices (i.e., paying for information, using confidential government or business documents without authorization, claiming to be someone else, agreeing to protect confidentiality and not doing so, badgering unwilling informants to get a story, using personal documents such as letters and photographs without permission, getting employed to gain inside information, using hidden microphones or cameras, using re-creations or dramatizations of news by actors, and disclosing the names of rape victims). When comparing minority journalists with each other and with the larger group of White journalists on these practices, we again found many similarities, but a few notable differences that probably reflected cultural backgrounds as much as individual or organizational ethical standards.

For example, Table 6.12 shows that Native-American journalists were significantly less likely than other journalists to think it might be justified to use confidential or personal documents without permission, badger unwilling informants, or disclose the names of rape victims in news stories. In contrast, Native-American and African-American journalists were more likely than others to say

TABLE 6.12
Journalists' Opinions on Controversial Reporting Methods
(Percentage of Each Category Saying May Be Justified on Occasion)

Reporting Method	Asian American (n = 98)	African American (n = 77)	Hispanic (n = 79)	Native American (n = 83)	White (n = 1,050)[a]
Using confidential business or government documents without authorization	92.9	78.9	78.5	73.5	82.3
Getting employed to gain inside information	55.1	73.7	65.4	54.2	62.9
Using hidden cameras or microphones	72.4	67.5	67.1	59.0	60.1
Badgering unwilling informants to get a story	52.6	40.3	41.6	32.5	49.9
Using personal letters and photographs without permission	59.2	52.6	48.1	42.2	47.8
Disclosing names of rape victims	46.4	39.0	38.0	20.7	43.8
Using re-creations of news by actors	25.8	40.3	31.6	33.3	26.8
Claiming to be somebody else	25.0	23.7	29.1	20.5	22.1
Paying for information	22.4	29.9	16.5	26.8	19.5
Agreeing to protect confidentiality and not doing so	3.1	5.2	5.1	12.0	5.2

[a]Ns vary slightly by item. The largest Ns reported here.

that paying people for information might be justified for an important story, and Hispanic journalists were notably less likely. Asian-American journalists were far more likely to think that using confidential government or business documents without authorization might be justified and less likely (with Native Americans) to ever approve of getting employed to gain inside information.

Some of these differences could be due to size of organization, as well as differing cultural backgrounds. Journalists of Asian heritage tended to work for the largest daily newspapers, which might help to explain their willingness to use confidential government and business documents without permission. Native Americans worked for the smallest organizations, which might have increased their reluctance to approve of badgering informants or disclosing the names of rape victims. Whatever the reasons, it seems clear that there were more differences of opinion about the acceptability of various reporting practices by race and ethnicity than by gender.

CONCLUSIONS

This chapter demonstrates that, in 1992, U.S. journalists from minority racial and ethnic backgrounds were both similar to and different from White majority journalists, and that minorities were making some slow progress in entering and climbing the management ladders in American journalism, although they were underrepresented at all levels, especially the higher ones. Because minority journalists as a whole were somewhat more likely to be lower level managers than were majority journalists, they seemed poised to move into upper level management in the years to come—if they stay in journalism and if those at the highest levels are committed to equal opportunity hiring.

But this study also demonstrates how difficult it is to generalize accurately about minority journalists. Although they were a small group (about 10,000) when compared with majority White journalists (about 112,000), there were significant differences between African Americans, Asian Americans, Hispanics, and Native Americans that should not be glossed over lightly. These differences were evident in religious affiliations, marital status, average age, median income, job titles, size and type of news medium, job satisfaction, intention to stay in journalism, rating of their news organization, and opinions on the acceptability of questionable reporting practices.

In some cases, there were differences between minorities in general and the majority White journalists. Minority journalists were less likely to be male, to be married, to identify with the Republican party, and to have worked in journalism more than 10 years. They were more likely to be Democrats, to be members of a journalism union or professional organization, to desire continuing education, to consider the opportunity for advancement and influence very important, and to favor a more interpretive or even adversarial approach to journalism.

Some of these differences posed difficult problems for minority journalists, who were eager to advance and have influence in an occupation that had not grown much since the early 1980s and may have been shrinking in the early 1990s. They also posed problems for newsroom managers, who needed to make difficult decisions about which journalists got to advance in the tight and competitive job market. Editors, too, were challenged in which journalists to assign to different stories and in their use of traditional criteria for judging the quality of news reporting.

Some of the news priorities of many minority journalists, however, seemed healthy for American journalism. Increased emphasis in 1992 on analyzing complex problems, discussing national policy, and developing the intellectual and cultural interests of the public is likely to result in higher quality journalism. Increased emphasis on adversarial reporting with respect to government and business may or may not contribute to more insightful reporting.

Like women, minority journalists were likely to find that changing the culture and structure of news organizations was not a simple or quick matter. But minorities were somewhat less susceptible to existing journalistic values than women from the majority White culture, given the greater differences in their backgrounds, experiences, and values. In other words, significant increases in minority journalists may have had greater effects on news coverage than significant increases in women journalists from the majority culture. Certainly there were greater differences in backgrounds and professional/ethical opinions between minorities and the White majority than between men and women journalists in general.

Whether increases in women and minorities in journalism will be able to counter some of the trends found in this study, such as less perceived autonomy and fewer satisfied journalists, remains to be seen. It is also not clear whether the culture of the modern corporate newsroom will be able to accommodate the diverse perspectives of minority journalists quickly enough to convince them to stay in journalism for the long term.

NOTES

1. See, for example, American Society of Newspaper Editors Minorities Committee, *Achieving Equality for Minorities in Newsroom Employment: ASNE's Goal and What It Means* (Rochester, NY: American Society of Newspaper Editors, 1986); Chuck Stone, "Journalism Schools' Students and Faculty in the Year of Kerner Plus 20," *Kerner Plus 20* (Washington, DC: National Association of Black Journalists, 1988); "Newsroom Integration Still Crawling at a Snail's Pace," *NABJ Newsletter*, April 1989; Loren F. Ghiglione, "Newspaper Recruiting Efforts Are Flagging as the Minority Share of the Population Grows," *The Bulletin of the American Society of Newspaper Editors*, 715 (July/August 1989), p. 2; Ted Pease, "Ducking the Diversity Issue: Newspapers' Real Failure Is Performance," *Newspaper Research Journal*, 11, 3 (Summer 1990), pp. 24–37; Roberto L. Moreno, "Standard 12 and the Myth of Latino Journalism Education," *Twelve* (Austin, TX: Commission on the Status of Minorities, AEJMC, July 1993), pp. 10–15; "A City Room of Many Colors," *Newsweek*, October 4, 1993, p. 82; David B. Sachsman, "Mass Communication Education: Moving Toward Diversity," *Mass Comm Review*, 20, 2&3 (1993), pp. 180–191.

2. See, for example, Carolyn Martindale, *The White Press and Black America* (Westport, CT: Greenwood Press, 1986); David Lawrence, Jr., "Where Are the Minority Comic Strip Characters?" *Minorities in the Newspaper Business*, 4, 2 (June/July 1988), p. 1; Thom Lieb, "Protest at the *Post*: Coverage of Blacks in the Washington *Post* Sunday Magazine," *Mass Comm Review*, 15, 2&3 (1988), pp. 65–66; Edward C. Pease, "Kerner Plus 20: Minority News Coverage in the Columbus *Dispatch*," *Newspaper Research Journal*, 10, 3 (Spring 1989), pp. 17–37; Carolyn Martindale, "Coverage of Black Americans in Four Major Newspapers, 1950–1989," *Newspaper Research Journal*, 11, 3 (Summer 1990), pp. 96–112; David Shaw, "Coloring the News: A Special Report," *The Quill*, 79, 4, May 1991, pp. 14–19.

3. *Report of the National Advisory Commission on Civil Disorders*, New York Times edition (New York: Dutton, 1968).

4. Sidmel Estes-Sumpter, "Responding to a Revolution," in Unity '94, *Kerner Plus 25: A Call for Action* (Oakland, CA: Unity '94, March 1993), p. 2.

5. See, for example, American Society of Newspaper Editors (ASNE) Human Resources Committee Report, *The Changing Face of the Newsroom* (Washington, DC: ASNE, May 1989); Belden Associates, "Employee Departure Patterns in the Newspaper Industry," conducted for the Task Force on Minorities in the Newspaper Business, Washington, DC, 1990; American Newspaper Publishers Association (ANPA), *Survey on Minorities and Women Employed by U.S. Daily Newspapers* (Washington, DC: ANPA, June 1990); Alexis S. Tan, "Why Asian American Journalists Leave Journalism and Why They Stay," presented at the national convention of the Asian American Journalists Association, August 1990; Center for Integration and Improvement of

Journalism, "Latinos in California's News Media: A Status Report," presented at the California Chicano News Media Association State Conference, September 1990; National Association of Hispanic Journalists (NAHJ), *Survey of Hispanics in the Newsroom, 1991* (Washington, DC: NAHJ, 1991); David Shaw, "Black, White, Read All Over?" *The Quill*, 79, 4, May 1991, pp. 20–23; Zita Arocha, "Hispanics in the News Media 1992: Still Struggling for Entry," presented at the National Association of Hispanic Journalists (NAHJ) Tenth Annual Convention, 1992; American Society of Newspaper Editors' annual employment surveys of U.S. daily newspapers, Washington, DC.

6. See footnote 5 for complete citations of these studies.

7. U.S. Bureau of the Census, *Statistical Abstract of the United States 1991* (Washington, DC: U.S. Government Printing Office, 1991), p. 386; Stephen Hess, Remarks at "The American Journalist in the 1990s," The Freedom Forum World Center, Arlington, Virginia, November 17, 1992.

8. Paul V. Peterson, *Today's Journalism Students: Who They Are and What They Want to Do* (Columbus, OH: School of Journalism, Ohio State University, 1981), p. 15.

9. Lee B. Becker and Thomas E. Engleman, "Class of 1987 Describes Salaries, Satisfaction Found in First Jobs," *Journalism Educator*, 43 (Autumn 1988), p. 6.

10. David H. Weaver and G. Cleveland Wilhoit, *The American Journalist* (Bloomington, IN: Indiana University Press, 1986, 2nd ed., 1991), p. 22.

Journalists' Best Work

Divya C. McMillin is first author of this chapter.
David Weaver revised and edited it.

Stories sent to us by journalists as examples of their "best work" covered a wide range of subjects, ranging from social problems to consumer advice. A significant change occurred, however, in the topics dealt with most frequently in 1992, compared with a decade earlier. Stories about personalities and celebrities, social problems and protests, and general human interest were more likely to be chosen by journalists in 1992 as examples of their best work than in 1982, when crime news and state or local government news were the most common topics. Crime news was notably less likely to be chosen as best work in 1992, as compared with 1982.

We asked journalists in our survey to send a sample of what they considered their "best work," on the assumption that such work might be more likely to reflect the roles and news values they considered most important than the more typical day-to-day news coverage. We were interested in the subjects covered, the roles suggested, the news values implied, and the kind of sources used in these stories.

In the 1982–1983 study, a content analysis of the best work submitted by newspaper journalists indicated that they did not limit the topics of their best stories to one or two categories, although more than one fourth of the stories dealt with crime or state and local government news. The interpretive role was most likely to be reflected in the best work, followed by the disseminator and adversarial roles. Stories that contained the news values of proximity, impact, and conflict were more likely to be considered "best work" than those containing timeliness, unusual aspects, or prominence.

HOW THE ANALYSIS WAS DONE

In this chapter, the best stories sent in 1992 are compared with those analyzed in 1982, using similar content categories.[1] The 1992 study differed from the earlier one because the sample of stories included not only those from daily and weekly newspapers, but also those from magazines, radio, television, and wire services. When direct comparisons were made between 1982 and 1992, however, only those stories submitted by newspaper journalists were included to control for possible differences between news media.

More than 14% of the 1,410 survey participants responded, sending 206 stories, compared with a 13% response (131 stories) from 1,001 U.S. journalists in 1982. In 1992, 41% of the stories were written by women, compared with 45% in 1982—slightly more than the 34% women in the surveys in both years. But we cannot assume that those who sent examples of their self-designated "best work" were a random subsample of the larger random sample of journalists in either survey. This self-selected collection of stories may not be representative of any larger group of U.S. journalists.

For the analysis, 180 stories were selected.[2] Of these, 59% were from daily newspapers, 16% from weeklies, 8% from magazines, 7% from television, 6% from wire services, and 3% from radio. For comparisons over time, only the 136 stories from daily and weekly newspaper journalists were used.

All the stories were coded by one coder. Ten percent of the stories were randomly selected and analyzed for the same content categories by a second coder.[3] (See Appendix III, this volume, for details of the coding categories.)

GENERAL STORY TOPICS

Table 7.1 shows a notable shift from news about state and local government and crime to news about personalities and celebrities, and social problems and protests during 1982–1992. Of the 19 general news categories,[4] personalities/celebrities and social problems/protests were the main topics of 35% of the "best" newspaper stories in 1992, compared with only 13% in 1982. General human interest was the main topic of 12.5% of these stories in 1992—up slightly from the 1982 figure. Crime news dropped most (nine percentage points)—from 14% of all newspaper stories in 1982 to only 5% in 1992. Aside from these differences, the percentages for the other news topics were about the same over time (see Table 7.1).

The top five news categories in the 1992 study appeared in the top five categories of the 1982 study as well, but two "hard news"[5] categories (crime and national government news) dropped and two "soft news" areas (personalities and human interest) increased, perhaps reflecting changing news values and priorities. Social problems and protests also increased significantly in newspaper journalists' best work, and this kind of news could be considered "harder" than coverage of personalities and human interest.

The stories about personalities/celebrities tended to be about people who emerged as public figures because of their courageous battles with dreaded diseases or near-fatal accidents. These people, including the occasional celebrity, were invariably from the local community. The stories from the other top five categories—social problems/protests, general human interest, state and local govern-

TABLE 7.1
Story Topics of Newspaper Journalists' Best Work

Story Topics[a]	Percent of Best Work		Ranking	
	1982 (n = 131)	1992 (n = 136)	1982	1992
Celebrities and personalities	5.0	18.0	5th-tie	1st
Social problems and protests	8.0	17.0	4th	2nd
General human interest	9.0	12.5	3rd	3rd
State and local government news	14.0	12.0	1st-tie	4th
Education and schools	5.0	7.0	5th-tie	5th
Business and finance	4.0	2.0	—	—
Crime news	14.0	5.0	1st-tie	—
Arts, leisure, and travel	5.0	5.0	5th-tie	—
Medical news	5.0	4.0	5th-tie	—
Sports	5.0	4.0	5th-tie	—
Environment and energy	3.0	3.0	—	—
Accidents and disasters	3.0	1.5	—	—
Economic news and issues	2.0	1.0	—	—
Humor	3.0	2.0	—	—
Other	0.0	1.5	—	—
National government news	4.0	1.0	—	—
International news	2.0	1.0	—	—
Science invention and space	1.0	0.0	—	—
Consumer information and advice	5.0	1.5	5th-tie	—
Religion	4.0	1.0	—	—

[a]From Judee K. Burgoon, Michael Burgoon, and Charles K. Atkin, *The World of the Working Journalist*, p. 69. These categories were specified by reporters as those most interesting to readers.

ment news, and education and schools—also dealt mostly with events and issues pertaining to the local community.

This may be a reflection of a trend in newspapers in the 1980s to emphasize features and local news.[6] However, because the stories were examples of best work, they may represent instances where the journalist tried to make a difference in the local community. To cite an example, one television reporter commented on a story on "life in the hood." This story illustrated the life of people in a project and the problems of crime, drugs, and alcohol faced every day. Commenting on why this story was thought to be best work, the journalist said: "It raises a lot of questions about how we live (and) how we treat people. It made people get involved and want to make changes. Very little is done in this situation and what little is done helps."

Another journalist describing a story about aerial spraying of herbicides on the community said the story was outstanding because: "It illustrates that small town journalism makes as big a difference in people's lives as network news, just on a smaller scale. We made a difference." In contrast to this local emphasis, there was scant representation of national government and international news.

This was undoubtedly due to the fact that not many U.S. newspapers employ Washington or foreign correspondents, and the bulk of national government and international news is provided by the wire services.

MEDIA ROLE PERCEPTIONS

In chapter 4 (this volume), the three functions most likely to be considered very important by U.S. journalists were the interpretive, disseminator, and adversarial. We tried to categorize the stories submitted by journalists as reflecting one of these general media functions. Each story was then coded for seven more specific roles.[7] For example, a strike by a workers' union received detailed coverage by a daily newspaper. The report included events leading up to the conflict, opposing viewpoints of management and employees, and background information surrounding the issue. The story was coded as an example of the general media role "interpretive," and then for its specific media role—an "analysis or interpretation of complex problems."

General Media Roles

The most dominant role, or function, found in the 1992 sample of stories was the disseminator, with almost 67% of the stories (69% of newspaper stories) falling into this category. Twenty-two percent of the stories (18% of newspaper) exhibited an interpretive function. These percentages differed from the 1982 findings, where 46% of the stories suggested an interpretive stance and 37% implied a disseminator function. Both the 1992 study and the 1982 analysis ranked the adversarial role third, with about 13% of the stories portraying this role (see Fig. 7.1).

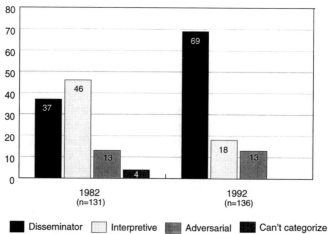

FIG. 7.1. General media roles (percentage of best work from newspaper journalists).

Overall, the best stories submitted were more likely to emphasize the disseminator role than were the journalists in the survey to rate this role as *very important* (67% vs. 51%). The stories were much less likely to suggest an interpretive role than were the journalists in the larger sample to rate this role as *very important* (22% vs. 63%). Finally, the best stories were somewhat less likely to stress the adversarial role than were those in the larger national sample to rank this role as *very important* (11% vs. 18%).

This may suggest that what these journalists said was not necessarily reflected in what they did. However, this was not a random sample of journalists' work, whereas we did have a random sample of U.S. journalists' responses to questions about roles. Also, it was difficult to classify stories as emphasizing just one general media function or role.

Specific Media Roles

Of the seven specific media roles portrayed in the stories, the top three—appeals to a wide audience, analyzes or interprets complex problems, and gets story to public quickly—were ranked similarly in both the 1982 and 1992 studies, although stories in 1982 were coded for more than one role, whereas those in 1992 were classified as emphasizing only one (see Table 7.2).

The specific role "appeals to a wide audience" was evident in 50% of the stories (51% of newspaper stories)—far more common than stories that analyzed complex problems and those that stressed getting the information to the public quickly. The adversarial role—with regard to business or government officials—was displayed in very few stories. Even fewer discussed government policy as it was being developed, and less than 2% described investigations into government claims, raising a question as to whether investigative and adversarial reporting were as common as popular images of journalism often suggested. Although the

TABLE 7.2
Specific Media Roles Emphasized in Newspaper Stories

Specific Media Roles	Percent of Best Work[a]	Ranking	
	1992 (n = 136)	1982 (n = 131)	1992 (n = 136)
Appeals to a wide audience	51.0	1st	1st
Analysis/interpretation of complex problems	14.0	2nd	3rd
Get story to public quickly	18.0	3rd	2nd
Adversary to business	8.0	7th	4th
Adversary to government	5.0	6th	5th
Discusses policy as it is developed	3.0	4th	6th
Investigates government claims	1.5	5th	7th

[a]Percentages for 1982 are not shown in this table because stories in 1982 were coded for more than one role, whereas those in 1992 were coded only for the dominant role.

rankings of this kind of reporting in 1992 did not differ much from those in 1982, the percentages were lower, especially for investigative reporting.

Journalists' Responses

Table 7.3 illustrates how a random sample of 50 journalists' open-ended comments distributed across specific media roles. Nineteen journalists said their stories were good because they analyzed and interpreted complex problems. The next most frequent response was that the stories appealed to a wide audience, followed by mentions of the timeliness of the news. The rest of the journalists said their stories were good because of their adversarial nature.

The rankings of these specific roles mentioned in the open-ended responses of 50 randomly selected journalists closely matched the rankings of these roles based on actual stories, as shown in Table 7.2. However, appealing to the widest audience dropped considerably in percentage of journalists' responses, and analyzing problems increased, again raising the question of whether what journalists said differed from what they did. But adversarial and investigative stories remained near the bottom of the list for both stories and journalists' open-ended comments (see Tables 7.2 and 7.3).

As an example considered good because it analyzed a complex problem, one reporter described a story written on high salaries received by chief executive officers, and the widening gap between executive salaries and the pay of almost all others in society. This story was considered best work because: ". . . it makes the public aware of what I perceive to be a considerable problem in the economic democracy."

Another journalist felt his story about the confrontation between pro-abortion and anti-abortion activists was an example of best work because:

> (It is a) watershed issue in our country that clearly defines where the public stands on the issue of abortion. There seems to be no middle ground. Covering the story disclosed that for me and hopefully gave readers a true picture of how divisive and important this topic is.

TABLE 7.3

Specific Media Roles in 50 Journalists' Open-Ended Descriptions of Best Work

Media Roles	Number of Responses	Rank
Analyzes and interprets complex problems	19	1
Appeals to a wide audience	14	2
Gets story to public quickly	9	3
Adversary to business	5	4
Adversary to government	2	5
Discusses policy as it is developed	—	6.5
Investigates government claims	—	6.5

Factors Influencing Media Roles

Several factors besides the journalists' personal orientations influenced the roles portrayed in their news stories. These included organizational priorities, type of beat assigned, time and resources available, nature of the news story, and type of medium. Although we could not examine the influence of organizational, economic, and time constraints on media roles stressed in the stories that were sent to us, because we could not match the individual stories with the survey data, we could check the relationships between type of news story and type of medium with story roles.

Story Orientation

Table 7.4 shows that of all the stories classified as event-oriented, most stressed the disseminator role, with the interpretive and adversarial roles trailing far behind. For stories classified as issue-oriented, almost as many emphasized the interpretive role as the disseminator. For stories that did not clearly concern issues or events (mostly features), nearly all were classified as emphasizing the disseminator role. (The substantial proportion of stories that could not be coded as either event- or issue-oriented is discussed later in this chapter.)

These findings confirm our expectations that, in our 1992 sample, issue-based stories were usually dealt with in more depth than those based on events, and were more likely to incorporate interpretation and analysis. An adversarial stance was also more likely to be conveyed in the discussion of an issue. A specific event was more likely to be reported in a breaking story, allowing primarily for quick dissemination, rather than for research and background information (see Table 7.4).

Type of Medium

Chapter 4 (this volume) discussed the role perceptions of journalists from various media. The interpretive role was emphasized slightly more than the disseminator role across all media combined, with print media journalists (particularly from wire services and news magazines) most likely to stress the importance of inter-

TABLE 7.4
The Relationship of Media Roles to Orientation of Best Stories

	Story Orientation		
Media Role	Event (%) (n = 49)	Issue (%) (n = 90)	Can't Tell (%) (n = 41)
Disseminator	84	43	98
Interpretive	8	39	2
Adversarial	8	18	—

pretation and analysis in news reporting. The disseminator function was rated *very important* by about half of all journalists combined, particularly by those working for the wire services and television. The adversarial function was rated *very important* by news magazine and daily newspaper journalists, although it trailed well behind the others, with not quite 18% of all the journalists rating it *very important*.

We were interested to see if these patterns of responses were reflected in the best stories. As Fig. 7.1 shows, contrary to the survey findings, the disseminator role was evident in many more newspaper stories than the interpretive role. But similar to the survey responses, the stories from news magazines (nearly half) were most likely to portray the interpretive role, with those from the wire services and television next (about one third). The disseminator role was most likely to be emphasized in stories from journalists at radio stations, daily newspapers, and wire services. Evidence of the adversarial role was found in a minority of stories from all the media, but the stories from news magazines and daily newspapers were most likely (13% each) to manifest this role, as was true in the survey responses.

In summary, the disseminator role emerged as the most dominant in the sample of best stories. The interpretive and adversarial roles were far more likely to be found in stories dealing with issues than events and somewhat more likely in stories from the print media. The disseminator role was much more likely to be found in stories dealing with events than issues. Except for stories from news magazines, the disseminator role was the most common in stories from all other media.

NEWS VALUES

The traditional news values of conflict, timeliness, proximity, prominence, unusualness, and impact were used as content categories in the 1982 and 1992 studies. It is possible that a single news story may contain more than one news value. For this study, however, each story was first coded for whether it had a traditional news value, and then for the most prominent news value that it exhibited.

Our 1992 findings show that about 39% of all news stories (35% of newspaper stories) were written for audience impact. This news value ranked second in the 1982 study. Most of the stories in this category dealt with such far-reaching issues as breast cancer, AIDS, and domestic abuse. The stories were tales of triumph and human endurance. For example, one story narrated the tales of four women and their battle against breast cancer, while another related the story of a courageous boy with an incurable heart disease. These stories advocated a lesson in hope, countering the time-worn belief that journalists are usually cynical or negative.

Conflict ranked second in 1992, with 20% of all best stories (24% of newspaper) containing this value. The 1982 study ranked conflict third. Timeliness placed third in the 1992 analysis, evident in 13% of the news stories. This value ranked fifth in 1982 (see Table 7.5). Proximity, which ranked first in 1982, was

TABLE 7.5
Six Traditional News Values in Newspaper Stories

News Value	Percent of Best Work[a] 1992 (n = 136)	Ranking 1982 (n = 131)	Ranking 1992 (n = 136)
Impact	35	2nd	1st
Conflict	24	3rd	2nd
Timeliness	13	5th	3rd
Proximity	10	1st	4th
Unusualness	8	4th	5th-tie
Prominence	8	6th	5th-tie

[a]Percentages for 1982 are not shown in this table because stories in 1982 were coded for more than one news value, whereas those in 1992 were coded only for the most dominant value.

evident as the major value in only 9% of the stories submitted in 1992 and was ranked fourth.[8] Also ranked fourth in both studies was unusualness. Prominence as a news value was ranked last in both the 1982 and 1992 analyses. In general, then, the traditional news values in our 1992 sample of best work were distributed in roughly the same order as in 1982–1983, with the exception of proximity (decreased) and timeliness (increased).

Journalists' Responses

A random sample of 50 journalists' reasons for why their stories were considered best work was analyzed by type of medium. Impact, or "affected many or all in the community," was the most prominent news value cited by journalists from all types of media. This value was mentioned in 25 responses. One weekly reporter described the coverage of a base closure in Texas:

> Essentially we competed with two other communities. One of the three communities was going to lose their base. I covered this for two months. It was a relief within our community that we did not lose our base and sadness for the community that did lose their base. I covered the emotions for these communities.

A radio journalist recounted: "We broke a story about a very major housing development. It showed initiative on the part of the reporter and (had) a significant impact on the community."

These comments imply that proximity was also a significant contributor to the story's newsworthiness. In fact, a recoding of the responses to determine how many dealt with local issues showed that 32 pertained to the local community. To be consistent, however, only the most prominent news value cited was coded, therefore impact was ranked first in these examples. Proximity was identified as a major contributor to the story's newsworthiness in two of the responses.

Prominence of characters in the news stories was cited as another reason for considering them best work. This value was mentioned in six responses. Timeliness, unusualness, and conflict all ranked third in the reasons for why stories were considered the best, and occurred in four responses each. One journalist said his story was thought to be "best work" because of the amount of research that went into it.

STORY ORIENTATION

Our 1992 results were consistent with the 1982 study in that more stories dealt with issues (50%) than events (27%). These results were not surprising because, in most cases, a discussion of issues allowed for greater detail, research, and flexibility of writing style. In contrast, an event may be anticipated or unanticipated; it may demand quick thinking and immediate deadlines, and may not allow for a journalist's best efforts. Thus, it seemed likely that the journalists in our survey would send samples of their best work that dealt with issues rather than events.

About 23% of the stories could not be coded as either issue- or event-oriented. These were humor columns, discussions of the arts, or descriptions of tourist attractions. A few news photographers from a TV station sent in clips of their camera work. These included a short feature on a diner waitress, a biking trip in the mountains, and parts of a travel series. Such features were light, timeless pieces. They could not be coded for story orientation because they did not deal with either an event or an issue. This proportion of 23% marked a substantial increase from the 1982 estimate of 6%. However, it tended to support the earlier finding in Table 7.2—that the largest percentage of stories was aimed at appealing to the widest audience possible.

Another reason for the increase in timeless features could be that a majority of the stories were from newspapers (59%). For many, newspapers were used to supplement the information provided on television, rather than as a primary source of information.[9] To compete with television's short news capsules and sound bites, many U.S. newspapers in 1992 seemed to be leaning toward shorter, lighter features.[10]

SOURCES

As in the 1982 study, in 1992 we were interested in the number and type of sources used in the best stories. Most of the stories in 1992 (90% of all and 87% of newspaper) used at least one source. The number of sources per story ranged from 0 to 30. Eighteen stories (17 from newspaper journalists) did not have any cited sources. These included editorials, columns, visual footage, and audio commentary for light entertainment articles. The mean number of sources per story in 1992 was 5.4—almost identical to the 1982 average of 5.3.

Seventy-eight percent of the newspaper story sources were identified. The mean number of identified sources in 1982 and 1992 was almost the same—4.6 and 4.8, respectively. Overall, 82% of the newspaper stories contained some identified sources in 1992, compared with 98% in 1982. Stories containing anonymous sources dropped from 30% in 1982 to 23% in 1992 (see Table 7.6).

Previous research has shown that institutional sources are used in news stories more often than noninstitutional sources. Herbert Gans called people affiliated with institutions "knowns." Included in this category are political, economic, social, or cultural elites. Gans found that, from 1967 to 1975, knowns appeared in news magazine and television stories about four times as often as unknowns or ordinary people, including "low level public officials."[11] Although our 1992 sample was not a random selection of general news stories, we were interested to see if the sources cited reflected Gan's observations.

Our results show that 49% of the newspaper story *sources* were institutional, whereas 45% were noninstitutional, barely supporting Gans' conclusions. Six percent were from special interest groups. In 1982, however, a notably larger proportion of the sources (70%) were institutional, and fewer were noninstitutional (26%) or from special interest groups (4%). Thus, there was a dramatic increase in the proportion of noninstitutional sources, as compared with institutional during 1982–1992.

The proportion of *stories* with institutional sources also decreased during 1982–1992 (by 22 percentage points), whereas those with noninstitutional sources

TABLE 7.6
Distribution of Sources in Newspaper Journalists' Best Stories

Sources Category	Distribution of Sources Within Category		Percent of Stories With This Type of Source	
	1982[a]	1992[b]	1982	1992
Identification of sources				
Identified	89	78	98	82
Anonymous	9	22	30	23
Type of sources				
Institutional	70	49	89	67
Noninstitutional	26	45	51	62
Special interest group	4	6	14	8
Nature of sources				
Female	15	37	41	60
Male	71	43	94	71
Document	8	20	30	32

[a]Of the 131 stories submitted in 1982, 120 were coded because 11 did not cite any sources.
[b]Of the 136 stories submitted in 1992, 119 were coded because 17 did not cite any sources.

increased by 11 points. This could have reflected the change in news emphasis from harder to softer news discussed earlier.

Of all the newspaper *sources*, 80% were people, whereas only 20% were documents. But the proportion of documentary sources increased from 8% in 1982 to 20% in 1992. Overall, however, the proportion of *stories* containing at least one documentary source remained about the same—30% in 1982 and 32% in 1992.

Of the people used as newspaper story sources in 1992, 54% were male and 46% were female, compared with 83% male and 17% female in 1982—a dramatic increase in women sources. Counting all sources including documents, the percentage of women increased from 15% in 1982 to 37% in 1992. In 1982, 41% of the *stories* contained at least one female source. In the 1992 analysis, the proportion of stories containing female sources increased by 19%, whereas those containing male sources decreased by 23%.

Thus, during 1982–1992, the proportion of noninstitutional sources and female sources increased. The greater proportion of female sources may have been because more women were present in traditionally male-dominated institutions, or because journalists, especially women, were extending their coverage to include ordinary people and nontraditional sources as the definitions of news changed. Our 1992 data show that women newspaper journalists were more likely to include female sources in their stories (an average of 1.5 female sources per story) than were men (an average of 1.1 female sources per story). Conversely, men newspaper journalists were more likely to include male sources in their stories (an average of 3.3) than were women journalists (an average of 2.4). Women's stories were more likely to be about social problems and protests (nearly one fourth) than were men's (about one tenth), and less likely (8%) to emphasize getting the story to the public quickly than were stories written by men (24%).

SUMMARY AND CONCLUSIONS

The stories in this sample covered a wide range of topics. There seemed to be more focus on features than hard news, and on local news as compared with reports across state and national borders. This suggests that journalists submitting their best work tended to choose stories they felt had an impact on the local community and made a difference to their readers, viewers, and listeners. It may also be that the stories reflected a general trend in the media (especially newspapers) to focus on community affairs and local concerns, rather than to provide a representation of news from all over the world. The higher representation of features suggests a tendency to humanize the news and highlight its emotional content, although we did not have a representative sample of U.S. journalists' reporting to analyze. This featuristic approach to the news story may be at least partly a result of television's increasing influence during 1982–1992.

Although the journalists in our 1992 survey endorsed the interpretive role over the disseminator and adversarial roles, the disseminator role emerged as the most dominant in the samples of best work submitted to us. This suggests that journalists' role perceptions may not have always corresponded with the roles manifested in their stories. An obvious reason for this difference could be that a majority of the journalists who submitted their best work may have been those who endorsed the disseminator role in the main survey. Without being able to match actual stories with survey respondents, we cannot test this hypothesis.

The changing environment of the audience and the newsroom may be another reason for this discrepancy. New technologies in the workplace and in viewers' homes, as well as increasing competition among more media, may have pushed journalists to be entertainers rather than watchdogs or interpreters. The efforts of many journalists in 1992 may have been channeled more into packaging the news so that it appealed to the widest possible audience, rather than interpreting and analyzing complex problems or investigating claims by government or businesses.

The 1992 findings for story orientation support those from 1982. More stories focused on issues than events. Most of those that could not be coded as either were columns in newspapers or video footage on travel, art, and leisure designed for audience pleasure and entertainment.

In some ways, our 1992 analysis of news sources corresponded with the findings of the 1982 study. A large majority of the sources were identified. There were more institutional than noninstitutional or special interest group sources. Males were more often news sources than females or documents. But there were some striking differences in 1992 as compared with 1982, including significantly fewer institutional and more noninstitutional sources, a notable decrease in the proportion of male sources and an increase in the proportion of female sources, and an increase in the proportion of documentary sources. This suggests that journalists, especially women, may have been stepping out of more conventional news beat systems and tapping ordinary people as sources more often. The increase in features in 1992 was consistent with the shift in news sources found in this group of stories that journalists considered their best work.

This chapter offers another glimpse into the work of U.S. journalists that goes beyond what they say in response to survey questions. But it is limited, both in scope and in analysis, and therefore is only suggestive of possible trends. A more representative sample of journalists' reporting is needed to draw firmer general conclusions about whether news coverage in the United States has changed or remained relatively stable during the 1980s.

NOTES

1. Photographs and cartoons were eliminated from the sample because they could not be adequately analyzed for a few of the content categories, such as role perception and number and type of sources.
2. Several journalists (20) sent in more than one story. In the case of unrelated stories, one was chosen randomly to be coded. For stories that reported on an ongoing issue or event (23), the major, most detailed story was selected. Also, stories sent in by editors (20) were not coded

because such stories usually included a package of news articles that was not the work of any particular journalist.

3. Overall intercoder reliability was 77%, using Holsti's simple percentage of agreement formula.

4. See Judee K. Burgoon, Michael Burgoon, and Charles K. Atkin, *The World Of the Working Journalist* (New York: Newspaper Readership Project, Newspaper Advertising Bureau, September 1982), p. 69; Lori A. Bergen, "Testing the Relative Strength of Individual and Organizational Characteristics in Predicting Content of Journalists' Best Work," unpublished doctoral dissertation, Indiana University, Bloomington, 1991. In the Burgoon et al. study, 19 news categories were defined by journalists as topics most interesting to readers. The categories were used in the 1982 study by Bergen to analyze journalists' responses and stories submitted as "best work."

5. Although *hard news* and *soft news* are difficult to define, general descriptions have been attempted. For our narrative, we used the concepts as they are defined in Gaye Tuchman, *Making News: A Study in the Construction of Reality* (New York: The Free Press, 1978), pp. 47–58. *Hard news* is defined as that which is timely and factual, and usually involving the government, accidents, disasters, and crime. *Soft news* is defined as features and human interest stories, and is not necessarily based on recent events.

6. Leo Bogart, "State of the Industry," in Philip S. Cook, Douglas Gomery, and Lawrence W. Lichty, *The Future of News* (Washington, DC: The Woodrow Wilson Center Press, 1992), pp. 85–103.

7. The specific dimensions that defined each general role were the same as those used in 1982, but not exactly the same as those used in chapter 4. We kept to the 1982 definition of the disseminator role to compare the stories more directly: *disseminator role*—get information to public quickly and concentrate on widest possible audience; *interpretive role*—provide analysis of complex problems, discuss national policy as it is developed, and investigate claims made by the government; and *adversarial role*—adversarial stance or skepticism toward government or public officials, and adversarial or skeptical stance toward business.

8. The main reason for the dramatic drop in the percentage of stories coded as stressing the news value of proximity from 1982 to 1992 was that only the most dominant value was coded for each story in 1992. Impact and proximity were closely related in numerous stories, but impact was coded over proximity in many when it emerged as the more dominant of the two.

9. Robert L. Stevenson, "The Disappearing Reader," *Newspaper Research Journal*, 15, 3 (Summer 1994), pp. 22–31.

10. Ken Auletta, "A Decade of Change: 'It's Demographics, Stupid!'" *Media Studies Journal*, 9, 1 (Winter 1995), p. 78.

11. Herbert J. Gans, *Deciding What's News: A Study of CBS Evening News, Newsweek and Time* (New York: Random House, 1980), p. 13.

Chapter 8

Conclusions

"Digitized" newsrooms were a dream of only a few visionaries in 1971, when Johnstone and colleagues carried out their landmark study. This book compares the 1971 study with those in 1982–1983 and 1992. Group ownership was common in 1971, but since then corporate mergers have touched the lives of many other journalists. By 1992, 70% worked for "chains" and 40% of all journalists were in companies traded on major stock exchanges.

Set in three different decades, these studies of journalists suggest the world around them has changed much more than they have. Part of the reason may be the way journalists have been defined in this book. In designing the 1992 survey, we did not imagine anyone asking seriously, "Is Rush Limbaugh in your study?" The answer, of course, is no. The focus was squarely on traditional journalism, or what some call the "old" news. Talk-show hosts and "tabloid" print and broadcast personnel, or the makers of the "new" news, are not included in this book.

Another reason the broad strokes of similarity seem more striking than the dots of change may be that the portrait was largely by the journalists themselves, in their own words. As media scholar Michael Schudson suggested in *The Power of News*, "This represents their own subjective experience, but at the same time it misunderstands journalism as a whole."[1] The individual accounts that form the core of our book, Schudson argued, were not as important as the "source or structure" that gave rise to them. Some important sources and structures, such as the socioeducational background of journalists and the ownership and type of media for which they worked, were included in our study. One important social structural question was: Have journalists become more removed from the general public?

ARE JOURNALISTS ELITES?

As raised most recently, the question—although not new—was in response to the late Christopher Lasch's last book, in which he saw journalists as part of America's "new professional elites" who are separated ". . . from the rest of the population by a way of life that is glamorous, gaudy, and indecently lavish." Furthermore, he saw their disdain for the larger culture as deep. In Lasch's view, "Middle Americans as they appear to the makers of educated opinion, are hopelessly dowdy, unfashionable, and provincial."[2]

Lasch, a distinguished social critic, lent a new respectability to the earlier charges during the 1992 presidential campaign by Vice President Dan Quayle that a "cultural elite" resided in "the newsrooms, sitcom studios and faculty lounges across America."[3] After hearing Quayle's characterization at the time, Mike Leonard, a columnist for the daily newspaper in Bloomington, Indiana, said he "eagerly" called home: "Hey Ma, . . . Didja hear that the vice president says I'm elite? Culturally elite? And we always thought we were lower middle class."[4]

Doubtless many journalists across the country shared Leonard's humor, pondering how a bachelor's degree from a public university and a median salary of $31,000 in 1991 could put them in the company of a cultural elite. Many must have been perplexed or amused at the success of the vice president in making Murphy Brown, the unwed mother and journalist depicted in the television show, a metaphor for much that was wrong with America and journalism.

Just how typical is Murphy Brown?

At the end of our book based on our 1982–1983 national survey of 1,001 U.S. journalists, we concluded that the skepticism of the institutional forms of professionalism among U.S. journalists was convincing evidence against the claim that they were elitists and isolated from the society at large.[5] A decade later, the findings from our 1992 survey suggest that American journalists as a whole were more representative of the larger society than remote from it. But there were a few signs that U.S. journalists were more elitist in some respects than they themselves might care to admit.

As pointed out in chapter 1 (this volume), the modal U.S. journalist in 1992 was a White Protestant male who had a bachelor's degree from a public college, was married, 36 years old, earned about $31,000 a year, had worked in journalism about 12 years, did not belong to a journalism association, and worked for a medium-size, group-owned daily newspaper. Such a profile does not suggest much elitism in American journalism.

But such a picture is also a composite of average tendencies that hides individual differences. Our findings show that there were substantial numbers of women, non-Whites, non-Protestants, single, young and old, and relatively rich and poor journalists working in this country for a wide variety of small and large news media, both group and singly owned.

For example, there can be little doubt that many of the most prestigious and influential media organizations and journalists in 1992 were located in the Northeast (especially in New York City and Washington, DC). But in 1992 U.S. journalists did not live and work in the Northeast region in disproportionately large numbers. In fact, our data show that only about 16% of all U.S. full-time mainstream journalists lived and worked in the Northeast at that time, compared with 20% of the U.S. population.

The percentage of journalists based in the Northeast declined significantly from 1971 to 1992: from more than one third in 1971 to 21% in 1982 to 16% in 1992. This was probably due to new technologies and economic constraints, which allowed for coverage of the financial and government centers of the country from almost anywhere at less cost, as well as population shifts during 1971–1992. In other regions of the country, the proportion of journalists was close to the proportion of the overall population, offering no support for the idea that journalists were disproportionately concentrated in numbers on the East Coast.

Influence, of course, is another matter. But it can be argued that the most influential people in finance and government were also located in the Northeast, and thus it was no surprise that some of the most influential journalists were there as well. This, by itself, was not evidence that journalists in 1992 were cultural elites—only that the most influential tended to cluster around the centers of financial and political power in society.

Demographics

In terms of age, U.S. journalists in 1992 were younger than some other occupations, as other studies have noted.[6] For example, college faculty were much older than journalists, with a median age of about 46. In fact, 25% of American professors were older than 55, compared with 8% of U.S. journalists who were "elders" of that age.[7] Attorneys, with a median age of 40, also tended to be older than journalists.[8]

While the median age of journalists rose from 32 in 1982 to 36 in 1992, the growth in new jobs in journalism slowed dramatically, as compared with the 1970s. This produced substantially more journalists in the 25- to 44-year-old group (74%) than in the labor force at large (54%), and relatively fewer journalists than workers in the under 24 and over 55 groups.

Thus, journalists were less likely to be very young or old than were U.S. workers as a whole. Perhaps the very young and older felt underrepresented in mainstream journalism in 1992, but we think the overall picture was one of substantial representation. The median age of all U.S. journalists (36) was virtually identical to that for the U.S. labor force as a whole.[9]

Although the overall percentage of women (34%) remained constant from 1982 to 1992, it rose to 45% among those hired between 1987–1992. In the

U.S. workforce, the percentage of women increased from just over 42% in 1981 to 45% in 1989.[10]

But compared with some other professional occupations, such as attorneys or college professors, women were better represented in journalism in the early 1990s. Only about 27% of college faculty were women in the late 1980s.[11] In law, women were 22% of the attorneys; in medicine, they were 9% of the dentists, and 18% of physicians.[12]

The number of minority journalists doubled from 1982 to 1992, at 8% in 1992, with African Americans the most numerous among minority journalists. If only those journalists hired during 1982–1992 are considered, the overall percentage of minorities (12%) suggests some success of the efforts to increase the multicultural makeup of newsrooms, especially in radio and television. Still, the figure lagged behind the 25% estimated by the 1990 U.S. Census to be minorities in the population at large.[13] In this case, universities were slightly more representative than journalism, with 11% of faculty being minorities in the late 1980s.[14]

It is clear, then, that minorities were not represented in U.S. mainstream news organizations in the same proportions as they were in the overall population in the early 1990s (nor did minorities have college degrees in the same proportion as did the White majority), but increased hiring of racial and ethnic minorities occurred during the 1980s.

Jonathan Alter of *Newsweek* wrote that "the citadels of the CE [cultural elite] that Quayle identifies—Hollywood, the press, top universities—include a disproportionate number of Jews."[15] But in terms of religious backgrounds, U.S. journalists in general did not change much from 1982 to 1992, and they reflected the overall population fairly closely. There was a drop of about five percentage points in Protestants, an increase in Catholics of three points, and an increase in "other" or "none" of about three points. Compared with the overall U.S. population, however, the proportions of journalists who claimed to be brought up as Protestants, Catholics, Jews, or "Others" were quite similar.[16]

Journalists working for news magazines and the wire services in the early 1990s were much more likely to be of the Jewish faith than the population at large (23% in news magazines and 17% in the wire services), offering some support for Alter's claim, but this was not true for the other news media.

Alter also characterized the cultural elite as "less religious and less connected to conventional standards of morality than most of the public."[17] Our survey results show that the percentage of journalists rating religion or religious beliefs as *very important* was substantially lower (38%) than the percentage in the overall U.S. population (61%). But 34% of journalists rated religion as *somewhat important*, compared with 30% of the population.[18]

Hence, there is evidence that journalists in 1992 were less likely to consider religion very important than the population in general, but most journalists said that religion was at least somewhat important to them. There were contrasts on this by medium. Journalists employed by news magazines and wire services were less likely to say their religious faith was important to them than were those working for newspapers, radio, and television.

"Real" journalists differed most from Murphy Brown on personal living arrangements. A majority (59%) were married, although male journalists were more likely to be married than were female journalists. Only 7% of journalists said they were divorced or separated. Four percent said they were cohabiting with another person. About 40% had at least one child living in the home. These percentages were close to the overall 1989 U.S. population, where 62% were married, 8% were divorced or separated, and 1.5% were cohabiting. However, journalists were slightly less likely to have a child at home (40%) than the general population (49%).

Politics

Even on political party identification, there was more diversity among journalists in 1992 than the fans of Murphy Brown—who is scripted in the situation comedy as a liberal Democrat—might have expected.[19] The Democrats were named as the party of choice by 44% of the journalists in our sample—up from about 39% in 1982. In fairness to Murphy Brown, a majority of women journalists (58%) said they were Democrats. A substantial majority of minority journalists were also Democrats.

Overall, however, there was considerable political diversity because 34% of journalists said they were Independents and Republicans numbered about 16%—both figures down a little from 1982. In addition, there was a tendency for journalists to see their organizations, a strong influence over news values, as more middle of the road politically than themselves.

When compared with the overall U.S. population, journalists were 3–10 percentage points more likely to say they were Democrats, but 10–17 points less likely to say they were Republicans, depending on which national survey was used as a measure of the overall U.S. adult population's party preference.[20] The tendencies on political party identification were not too surprising because our research was done in the middle of the 1992 election campaign. While our study was in the field (June 12–September 12), the two parties put forth sharply differing images of their positions on civil libertarian questions, which are pertinent to journalism's grounding in the ideas of the First Amendment. For example, the two party platforms were quite different on the question of a woman's right to choose an abortion—the Republicans opposed and the Democrats were in favor. On that issue, journalists diverged from the public at large.

As the now-famous episode of Murphy Brown's decision to have a child out of wedlock made clear for millions of viewers, such personal issues are so complex that framing them as survey questions often results in simplism. The question about abortion asked in Gallup's national survey—"Do you think abortions should be legal under any circumstances, legal under only certain circumstances, or illegal in all circumstances?"—by no means deals fully with the issue, but we decided to put it to our sample of journalists anyway for comparison with public opinion.

More than half (51%) of the journalists said abortion should be legal under any circumstance. Forty percent said it should be legal under certain circumstances, and 4% said all abortions should be illegal. The U.S. public at large was much less likely than U.S. journalists to think unrestricted abortion should be legal (one third) and more likely to say it should always be illegal (14%).[21]

Journalists in 1992 also diverged from the public on general political orientation. Whereas 34% of the public described their political views as conservative, only 22% of journalists did. Further, 47% of journalists considered themselves as liberal, compared with only 18% of the public.[22] The questions were not identical, but this finding, along with those from the political party and abortion questions, reinforces the idea that journalists considered themselves more liberal politically than the public, but saw their own news organizations as more centrist.

Stephen Hess found a similar tendency in 1991 for White House reporters, but slightly fewer saying they were liberal (42%) and considerably more saying conservative (33%). His finding that White House reporters were likely to think that other reporters were more liberal than they were was somewhat supported by our findings for all U.S. journalists.[23] Hess found White House reporters becoming more conservative from 1978 to 1991, whereas we found U.S. journalists in general becoming more liberal from 1982 to 1992.

Education

U.S. journalists with at least a college bachelor's degree increased from 74% in 1982 to 82% in 1992.[24] But the percentage of those with a graduate degree did not increase significantly from the 11% in 1982. In every gender and race category, a majority of journalists graduated from public, rather than private, institutions.

It is clear that a bachelor's degree has become the minimum qualification necessary for practicing journalism in all mainstream news media, and that in 1992 journalists were substantially more likely (82%) than the general population (21%) to have a college degree.[25] But compared with other professions, such as law or college teaching, where graduate degrees are the rule, journalists are far less elite in terms of formal education.

According to Hess' 1991 survey, however, about half of the White House press corps attended private universities, and many of them went to Ivy League schools, compared with only 4% of all journalism college graduates. In addition, 31% earned graduate degrees—the same as in our sample of news magazine journalists.[26] Although this may be viewed by some as a sign of elitism, or at least of upper middle-class backgrounds, we agree with Hess that journalists covering a major center of political power should be highly educated.

Income

Another stark contrast between Murphy Brown and the typical journalist in 1992 was salary. Only about 1% of American journalists earned more than $100,000 a year, and most earned considerably less. A median salary of $31,297 for journalists in 1991 placed them considerably lower in earnings than other similar occupational groups, such as internal auditors, accountants, and college professors.[27]

Media differences on salary were considerable. News magazine journalists, concentrated in the urban Northeast, earned the highest median salary of $66,071. In television, high salaries comparable to those of well-known network personnel were rare, and the typical television journalist made only $25,625.[28]

Opinions About Audience

Some critics have claimed that journalists tend to see their audiences as typically gullible and not interested in serious news. Furthermore, they see journalists as yielding much too easily to the marketing demands of the business side of media so that they accede to what some see as "the idiot culture."[29] If so, journalists don't openly admit it.

Only 14% of the journalists in our 1992 sample agreed that their audience was gullible and easily fooled—a response close to that of our 1982 study. Similarly, just 22% thought their audience was not interested in news about serious social problems such as poverty and racial discrimination. This was hardly evidence of elitist attitudes among journalists in general.

A majority (69%) did say, however, that their audience was more interested in breaking stories than in analysis. But more significant was our finding on the perception of the importance of entertainment. Fewer journalists in 1992 (14%) than a decade previous (20%)—especially among those in broadcasting—were willing to admit that entertainment was very important to news organizations.

Roles

For the most part, journalists' perceptions of the roles of the news media in 1992 were broadly similar to those of a decade previous. Although it is difficult to directly link role perceptions to the issue of elitism, a majority of journalists tended to see two responsibilities as extremely important: getting information to the public quickly and investigating government claims.

The analytical function of news media—providing analysis of complex problems—also remained about the same, with about half saying it was extremely important. Journalists for news magazines and daily newspapers were much more likely than news workers in other media to see analysis of complex problems as highly salient. Asian-American and African-American journalists were also more likely to rate this role as *extremely important*.

In the 1992 study, a new question attempted to assess journalistic initiative in setting the political agenda—a topic that received much attention during 1982–1992. Few journalists saw their role in these terms, with only 4% ranking it *extremely important* and 41% rejecting it entirely—hardly evidence of cultural elitism.

Another issue related to elitism was the extent to which journalists should attempt to give ordinary people a chance to express their views on public affairs. A little less than half the 1992 sample said this was an extremely important role, with journalists working on daily and weekly newspapers especially likely to say so. But when asked about the importance of trying to reach the widest possible audience, only one fifth—significantly fewer than in 1982—agreed that it was extremely important, perhaps because of the effect of new technologies such as cable, which have led to increasing fragmentation of the audience.

In short, the findings on journalistic roles are mixed in terms of answering the question of cultural elitism.

Ethics

The cultural elite have been described as being "less connected to conventional standards of morality than most of the public."[30] Our survey of journalists included some questions about the acceptability of questionable reporting practices that were also asked in public opinion surveys during the 1980s. A majority of journalists in 1992 said that getting employed to gain inside information may be justified on occasion. But a national survey of 1,002 adults done for the American Society of Newspaper Editors (ASNE) in 1985 found that only 32% approved of journalists not identifying themselves as reporters, as did 32% in a 1981 Gallup national survey and 38% in a 1989 Indiana statewide survey.[31] The questions were somewhat different, but it is likely there was a gap between press and public on the acceptability of undercover reporting.

Another gap with the public appeared when journalists' opinions about the use of hidden microphones or cameras were compared with the public's. Only 42% of the 1985 national sample of the public (and 46% of the 1989 Indiana sample) approved of using hidden cameras in 1985, compared with 63% of journalists in 1992 who said this practice might be justified. Again, the questions were not identical, but a gap was likely.

One practice that was approved by fewer journalists than the public was paying for information. Only 20% of the journalists in our 1992 study said this might be justified, compared with 30% of the 1985 national sample and 33% of the 1989 Indiana sample who approved. On this score, then, journalists were less permissive than the public at large.

Thus, our findings do not clearly answer the question of whether U.S. journalists in 1992 were cultural elites. On the one hand, they did not seem very elitist or removed from the general public in terms of region, age, gender, marital/family status, income, opinions of their audiences, or opinions about their roles. On the other hand, they did seem to differ from the public by being more White, less religious, more liberal politically, more highly educated and more willing to sanction questionable reporting methods, such as not identifying themselves as reporters and using hidden cameras or microphones.

Hence, they fit some of the criteria that Alter ascribed to the cultural elite: They are better educated, more liberal, and less religious. But American journalists as a whole were more representative of the larger society than remote from it, and Murphy Brown is certainly not the "typical" U.S. journalist in terms of gender, news medium, or salary.

In short, the findings on the question of cultural elitism support veteran-journalist and columnist Richard Harwood's recent essay on the topic. Harwood, a former deputy managing editor of the *Washington Post*, concluded, "The truth is that journalism as an occupational category has as many compartments as the American society, a small number of 'elitists' laboring alongside those who, like most Americans, perform relatively routine but necessary production and service functions."[32]

JOURNALISTS' WORK

It is one thing to study the characteristics and opinions of U.S. journalists, of course, and another to analyze their news coverage. Other studies of news work have made it clear that there are powerful organizational and professional constraints on what journalists cover and how they cover it, regardless of their own personal backgrounds and beliefs.[33] But our analysis of the best work sent to us by some of the journalists in our study suggests that they chose stories that had an impact on the local community and that made a difference in the lives of those in their communities. An increased use of features and noninstitutional sources from 1982 to 1992 suggested that some journalists put more emphasis on humanizing the news and highlighting social problems in 1992 as compared with a decade earlier.

Our 1992 study of journalists also provided an "inside" look at newsrooms and some significant changes in job attitudes that may have affected the quality of news. As in 1982, our 1992 data suggest that the newsroom, with all its constraints and daily hysteria of meeting deadlines, had more to do with the face of the news in America than did a statistical profile of U.S. journalists.[34] This does not detract from the value of knowing who journalists are and how they compare with the public, however, because individual backgrounds, values, and perceptions undoubtedly have some influence on how the news is covered.

These backgrounds, values, and perceptions influence news coverage within the constraints of individual news organizations, however, and our findings raise questions about whether these constraints were becoming more limiting in the early 1990s than in the decades of the 1970s and 1980s.

For example, we found a significant decline in perceived autonomy of U.S. journalists since the early 1970s, as well as diminished job satisfaction. Other comparable occupations did not experience the decline in proportions of those very satisfied with their work, and journalists who worked in smaller, privately owned news media tended to see themselves as having greater freedom and influence in the newsroom than those working in other media.

But type of corporate ownership was not a major factor in job satisfaction, nor was salary. Instead, many journalists in 1992 were less willing to suffer the dislocation and unpredictable schedules that were accepted by an earlier generation, particularly in a competitive environment in which newsrooms were expected to do more with fewer resources and where there was little hope of professional advancement in a time of stalled growth.

The perceived decline in the organizational incentives and resources to cover the news adequately—evident in the open-ended responses of the journalists in our 1992 study—has serious implications for the quality of news the public receives. Even if the constraints were more likely to be a result of a general anemia in the advertising industry than of a pervasive corporate culture that put increased emphasis on profits, the result was the same. The sense of public service that has long been an attraction for journalists does seem threatened by many of the trends reported here.

Media scholar Michael Schudson saw journalists as alternating between the goal of just trying to meet deadlines to a loftier, sometimes unreachable goal of educating audiences to be active citizens and smart observers of politics. "They try to create the world in which a classical notion of democracy would make sense," he said, and called it an "excellent guide to journalistic practice."[35] But that is not enough. In his view, journalists must go further because an informed electorate often cannot be forged, despite journalism's best effort. The journalist, then, must also act as a "stand-in," shining brightly and constantly the "searchlight of publicity" on powerful official and private interests. This may make for a kind of "schizophrenia" in journalism, he said, but in that complication lies opportunity.[36]

In many ways, the pluralism we found in the mindset of American journalists suggests they already expect of themselves the challenge Schudson presents, and that expectation became keener over the 1971–1992 period. But journalists in 1992 were likely to think their newsrooms were more successful at comprehensive and speedy coverage than at providing a real check on powerful officials and interests. The question that lurks, then, is whether the culture of the modern, corporate newsroom will sustain the democratic altruism and provide the resources for the "searchlight of publicity" to shine as brightly as before on powerful interests that often conflict with the public good. If not, there may be less real journalism—and fewer authentic journalists—in some of the major news media of this country by the end of the 1990s.

NOTES

1. Michael Schudson, *The Power of News* (Cambridge: Harvard University Press, 1995), p. 12.
2. Christopher Lasch, "The Revolt of the Elites," in *Harper's*, November 1994, p. 41—an adaption of his book, *The Revolt of the Elites and the Betrayal of Democracy* (New York: W.W. Norton, 1995).
3. Kenneth L. Woodward, "The New Class Warriors," *Newsweek*, October 5, 1992, p. 40.
4. Mike Leonard, "Elitism Seems Pretty Scarce in the H-T Newsroom," *The Herald Times*, June 11, 1992, p. C1.
5. David H. Weaver and G. Cleveland Wilhoit, *The American Journalist: A Portrait of U.S. News People and Their Work* (Bloomington, IN: Indiana University Press, 1986; 2nd ed., 1991), p. 218 of 2nd ed.
6. Ted Pease, "Who's Making the News? Changing Demographics of Newspaper Newsrooms," paper presented at the annual meeting of the Association for Education in Journalism and Mass Communication, Montreal, Canada, August 5–8, 1992.
7. Susan H. Russell, James S. Fairweather, and Robert M. Hendrickson, *Profiles of Faculty in Higher Education Institutions, 1988* (Washington, DC: Center for Education Statistics, U.S. Department of Education, 1991), p. 9.
8. Barbara A. Curran and Clara N. Carson, *Supplement to the Lawyer Statistical Report: The U.S. Legal Profession in 1988* (Chicago, IL: American Bar Association, 1988), p. 3.
9. U.S. Bureau of the Census, *Statistical Abstract of the United States: 1991*, 111th ed. (Washington, DC: U.S. Government Printing Office, 1991), p. 392.
10. *Statistical Abstract of the United States: 1991*, p. 392.
11. Russell et al., *Profiles of Faculty*, p. 133.
12. Sylvia Nasar, "Women's Progress Stalled? Just Not So," *The New York Times*, Sunday, October 18, 1992, p. 10.
13. *Statistical Abstract of the United States: 1991*, pp. 22, 56.
14. Russell et al., *Profiles of Faculty*, p. 133.
15. Jonathan Alter, "The Cultural Elite," *Newsweek*, October 5, 1992, p. 32.
16. Data for the population percentages came from a national telephone survey of 1,001 U.S. adults conducted from July 30 to August 2, 1992, by the Gallup Organization. The data were provided by The Roper Center, University of Connecticut, Storrs, CT 06268.
17. Alter, "The Cultural Elite," p. 32.
18. The population percentages came from a national telephone survey of 1,002 U.S. adults conducted from April 9 to April 12, 1992, by the Gallup Organization. Data were provided by the Political Science Data Lab, Woodburn Hall, Indiana University, Bloomington, IN 47405.
19. Richard Zoglin, "Sitcom Politics," *Time*, September 21, 1992, p. 47.
20. A Gallup Organization national telephone poll of 955 U.S. adults conducted July 17, 1992, just after the Democratic national convention, indicates the following percentages: Democrat–41%, Republican–26%, Independent–31%, reflecting the much reported convention "bounce." An earlier July 6–8, 1992, survey of 1,307 U.S. adults found 34% Democrat, 33% Republican, and 31% Independent. In both surveys, the question was, "In politics today, do you consider yourself a Republican, a Democrat, or an Independent?" Data were provided by the Political Science Data Lab, Woodburn Hall, Indiana University, Bloomington, IN 47405.
21. The data for the public came from a national telephone survey of U.S. adults conducted September 5–8, 1991. See *The Gallup Poll 1991*, p. 188.
22. The figures for the public came from a Gallup Organization national telephone survey of 1,001 U.S. adults conducted from July 31 to August 2, 1992, and provided by The Roper Center at the University of Connecticut. The question was: "How would you describe your political views—very conservative, conservative, moderate, liberal, or very liberal?" The conservative

percentage reported here is the sum of those saying *very conservative* (4.7%) and *conservative* (29.2%). The liberal percentage is the sum of those saying *very liberal* (4.5%) and *liberal* (13.7%). The question in our 1992 journalists study was, "Do you consider yourself pretty far to the left, a little to the left, in the middle of the road, a little to the right, or pretty far to the right?" As with the public, we summed the responses for the left-leaning answers (11.6% far left and 35.7% left) into *liberal* and those for the right-leaning answers (4.7% far right and 17.0% right) into *conservative*. News magazine journalists were most likely to consider themselves liberal (69.5%), and television (27.7%) and radio (29.8%) were least likely to do so. About half of the daily newspaper and wire service journalists considered themselves somewhat or very liberal.

23. Stephen Hess, "All the President's Reporters: A New Survey of the White House Press Corps," *Presidential Studies Quarterly*, 22 (Spring 1992), p. 318.
24. The 1982 figure is from D. Weaver and C. Wilhoit, *The American Journalist*, p. 48.
25. The source of the 1989 population percentage is from U.S. Bureau of the Census, *Statistical Abstract of the United States: 1991*, 111th ed. (Washington, DC: 1991), pp. 138–139.
26. Hess, "All the Presidents Reporters," pp. 311–321.
27. The mean salary for nonsupervisory management accountants in 1990 was $37,000. It was $36,800 for internal auditors. The average salary for professors at public universities in 1991–1992 was $42,352. U.S. Department of Labor Statistics, *Occupational Outlook Handbook*, May 1992, Bulletin 2400, p. 17; *The Chronicle of Higher Education*, June 10, 1992, p. A12. The mean 1991 salary for all full-time U.S. journalists was $31,500.
28. The salary estimate for television journalists was fairly close to that found by Vernon A. Stone, "News Salaries Stand Still," *Communicator*, February 1992, pp. 14–15.
29. Carl Bernstein, "The Idiot Culture," *The New Republic*, June 8, 1992, pp. 22–28.
30. Alter, "The Cultural Elite," p. 32.
31. Cecilie Gaziano and Kristin McGrath, "Measuring the Concept of Credibility," *Journalism Quarterly*, 63 (Autumn 1986), pp. 451–462; David Weaver and LeAnne Daniels, "Public Opinion on Investigative Reporting in the 1980s," *Journalism Quarterly*, 69 (Spring 1992), pp. 146–155.
32. Richard Harwood, "Are Journalists 'Elitist'?," *American Journalism Review*, June 1995, pp. 27–29.
33. See, for example, John W.C. Johnstone, Edward J. Slawski, and William W. Bowman, *The News People: A Sociological Portrait of American Journalists and Their Work* (Urbana: University of Illinois Press, 1976); Gaye Tuchman, *Making News* (New York: Free Press, 1978); Michael Schudson, *Discovering the News* (New York: Basic Books, 1978); Herbert J. Gans, *Deciding What's News* (New York: Vintage Books, 1979); Mark Fishman, *Manufacturing the News* (Austin: University of Texas Press, 1980); and David H. Weaver, *Videotex Journalism: Teletext, Viewdata, and the News* (Hillsdale, NJ: Lawrence Erlbaum Associates, 1983).
34. See Lori A. Bergen, "Journalists' Best Work," in David H. Weaver and G. Cleveland Wilhoit, *The American Journalist*, 2nd ed. (Bloomington, IN: Indiana University Press, 1991), pp. 194–210. In her 1991 dissertation from Indiana University ("Testing the Relative Strength of Individual and Organizational Characteristics in Predicting Content of Journalists' Best Work"), Bergen found that organizational characteristics (such as type, ownership, and size of news medium) were generally better predictors of the nature of news coverage than the individual traits of journalists (such as age, gender, education, political leanings, and role orientations). But neither predicted much of the variation in story topics, news values, issue versus event orientations, or what Herbert Gans termed *enduring values* in *Deciding What's News* (New York: Vintage Books, 1980).
35. Schudson, *The Power of News*, p. 223.
36. Schudson, *The Power of News*, p. 223.

Afterword:
A Calling at Risk?

Trevor R. Brown

How essential are journalists and the functions of news and truth to a fair, just, and efficient American society?

Give the people "full information of their affairs through the channel of the public papers," said Jefferson. Yes, of course. "Knowledge will forever govern ignorance. And a people who mean to be their own governors must arm themselves with the power knowledge gives," said Madison. Absolutely. David Weaver and Cleveland Wilhoit found that journalists in 1992 still defined functions and values for their profession that follow the advice of Jefferson and Madison. But how essential are journalists in an age when information is at the consumer's disposal and entertainment is the consumer's choice? Weaver and Wilhoit have sounded an alarm. They are concerned that journalists in the early 1990s were increasingly discontented because of declining support among many media owners and the public for serving a self-governing citizenry with news and truth.

One has the uneasy feeling that the world of journalism that Weaver and Wilhoit mapped has changed sufficiently since 1992 to raise the urgency they expressed from a one-alarm to at least a three-alarm.

Warren Breed, the intellectual forebear for the kind of work that Weaver and Wilhoit have been doing for 15 years, concluded in 1955 that the values shaping the newsroom culture came from the top, from the publisher or chief executive. Certainly that was so a century ago.

In 1880, for example, William Rockhill Nelson, founder and owner of the *Kansas City Evening Star*, believed that a daily newspaper was "a necessity to every intelligent person, who desires to keep posted as to the current events of the day." The *Star*, he said, would be "wholly free to labor for the interests of the people and to wage warfare upon corrupt and extravagant tax eaters of all parties." In serving these interests, said Nelson, "the reporter is the essential man on the newspaper. . . . [W]e should go to smash if we had no reporters."

When Nelson died after directing his paper for 35 years, his widow and daughter ended an editorial with this tribute: "Mr. Nelson never regarded his newspaper as a commercial proposition. To him it was always a sacred trust."

A century later, serving the people's interests with news and truth was of little apparent significance to Michael D. Eisner, chairman of the Walt Disney Company, when he acquired the *Kansas City Star* as part of the second-largest merger ever. In August 1995, Disney bought Capital Cities/ABC for $19 billion. In addition to the ABC Television Network and other properties, Capital Cities/ABC owned 21 radio stations, 8 TV stations, and several newspapers, including the *Kansas City Star*.

The deal, said Eisner, was "a once-in-a-lifetime opportunity to create an outstanding entertainment and media company." This deal, he said, "is about increasing revenues."

To finance its acquisition of Capital Cities/ABC, Disney had to borrow $10 billion and pay it off over 7 years. This process was a familiar one during the 1980s and 1990s, a decade of multimedia mergers and acquisitions. To cut costs and increase revenues, as Weaver and Wilhoit reported, some print and broadcast media reduced news staffs. Those revenues were needed, it seemed, more for debt service than public service.

The juxtaposition of the aspirations of two owners of the *Star*—Nelson's democratic idealism against Eisner's flair for gauging the entertainment tastes of the masses—may exaggerate the contrast between them across a century of social, economic, and technological change to make a point: that the requirements of lenders and stockholders in contemporary media properties have put the ability of journalists to perform their essential role in serving society at risk. In many print and broadcast newsrooms in the 1990s reduced news staffs are trying to help inform a complex, diverse domestic society that is also the surviving superpower in the world.

We had no Weaver and Wilhoit to tell us how satisfied reporters were on the *Kansas City Star* in the 1880s, when Nelson considered them essential in laboring for the interests of the people. Weaver and Wilhoit do tell us that between the early 1980s and the early 1990s, "the overall decline in job happiness was considerable." The explanation journalists offered was complex. Editorial policies and limited autonomy were factors. So were job security and salary. Weaver and Wilhoit found that the type of ownership was not a significant factor in job satisfaction. Their report suggests, however, that journalists no longer perceived owners as the source of fundamental journalistic values. These values appear to survive in newsrooms despite the indifference of many owners, although by no means all of them.

One value in particular has shown remarkable resistance. Almost 69% of the journalists surveyed in 1992 considered getting information quickly to the public extremely important—a role that rose steadily in journalists' perceptions of importance, from 56% in 1971. In contrast, from 1982 to 1992, the decade in which *infotainment* entered the dictionary and tabloidism affected print and broadcast news alike, the percentage of journalists who considered providing entertainment extremely important dropped from 20% to 14%. Here may be the sharpest division in perceptions of role and responsibility between owners and journalists, between the Eisners and the philosophical offspring of Nelson.

The pressure of the market is surely difficult to resist. The penetration in the 1980s of VCRs, cable and, toward the end of the decade, home computers, modems, and the Internet has multiplied choices in sources of information and entertainment. Advertisers have been following audience choices. Between 1984 and 1994, for example, newspapers lost 4% share of total advertiser expenditures, broadcast television lost 1.4%, while cable gained 1.3%. In their role as citizens, Americans have sought news and information; in their role as consumers and pleasure seekers, they have sought amusement and diversion. Critics have scolded journalists for blurring the distinction between news and entertainment, but public behavior has suggested that for many, perhaps most Americans, consumer/pleasure seekers, rather than citizens, have become the real us.

Given the professed values of journalists and the internal and external pressures from audience choices, advertiser spending, and owner priorities, we might expect the most experienced journalists to lose heart and leave. In 1982, Weaver and Wilhoit found that indeed the best and brightest planned to leave. In 1992, the most experienced professionals were planning to stay. However, the proportion of all journalists planning to leave rose to a 20-year high. Weaver and Wilhoit take comfort in the thousands of young people graduating annually in journalism–mass communication eager for those jobs. Anecdotal evidence suggests, however, that the discontent interns encounter in many newsrooms is turning them off journalism. The best and brightest may be staying, but the next generation of best and brightest may not be entering.

The possible loss of the most promising professionals before they even enter is alarming. As Weaver and Wilhoit reported, journalists are getting older on the average. Although the experience of mature, seasoned professionals is invaluable for the functioning of self-governance, they are communicating with audiences, particularly print audiences, that are also getting older on the average. The apparent disconnection between younger Americans and their institutions, including the press, is unlikely to be repaired if journalists lose touch with a younger audience and also lose the best of the generation of younger colleagues.

More important, and to some extent irrespective of age, journalism needs the best and brightest professionals. The Weaver–Wilhoit 1992 survey ended before the increased use of the Internet and before the accumulation of millions of bits and bytes of information in an interactive digital world. For some, this world may represent the triumph of Jefferson's view of the democratic process. We give and receive full information of a broad range of our affairs as we move into cyberspace—a universe of audio and video signals traveling at the speed of light. In that new place, perhaps we cybernauts are all journalists—all gatherers and communicators of information. But because the sheer mass of information threatens to engulf us, Madison's view defines the more important need. Yes, knowledge will forever govern ignorance. Our more urgent need is for knowledge to govern information. Weaver and Wilhoit found, however, that journalists in 1992 perceived their most and increasingly essential role to be as providers of information. Journalists considered their analytical role to be of much lesser and declining importance. The signs in 1995 are that we need journalists most as judges and analysts of what information is accurate, reliable, important and valuable.

The analytical role requires more of a journalist's education both in knowledge and in craft than does the informational role. Yet academia seems squeamish about the blend. The tonier universities in particular insist on the distinction between learning for the sake of learning and learning for the sake of earning, and they patrol the border between the liberal arts college and the professional schools. They polarize the choice for students between a liberal and a vocational education, between enlightenment and employment. News media leaders, who hire at least 70% of their entering workforce from students who have studied journalism and mass communication, often contribute to this divide. As statesmen, they extol the virtues of knowledge and a liberal education. As recruiters, they stress evidence of craft. Admiration for the bachelor's degree often seems rhetorical. The credential they revere is the clip or demo tape.

Lost in the pleasing symmetry between learning for learning and learning for earning is a uniting principle rooted in the origins of American education—learning for serving, particularly for serving as citizens of a republic. In recognition of that principle, the baccalaureate curriculum of journalism education is among the strongest on campus for its blend of liberal arts and professional craft. It seeks to create an interdisciplinary space for an education in civic thought and action. Yet as the need for knowledge to govern information—not merely to manage it—becomes even more pressing, the market pulls in the direction of volume, speed and interactivity of information set in the alluring frame of entertainment.

How essential are journalists in an interactive, wired society that informs itself if it cares to and seems to prefer that its multimedia entertain it? William Rockhill Nelson believed his newspaper should go to smash if he had no reporters. Our society could go to smash if we do not recognize our need for journalists and if we do not have enough of them—and the very best we can educate and inspire to serve us with news and truth, and to help us make sense of both.

Methods

This study was intended to be a partial replication of the 1971 national telephone survey of 1,328 U.S. journalists by John Johnstone and his colleagues[1] and the 1982–1983 national telephone survey of 1,001 U.S. journalists by ourselves.[2] Hence, we followed the definitions of *journalist* used by these earlier studies and their sampling plans closely to be able to compare our 1992 results directly with those of 1971 and 1982–1983. We also used many of the same questions used in these previous studies, but added some open-ended questions for more explanations in journalists' own words and some other questions to reflect the changes in the news media environment between 1982–1992.

Unlike the previous two studies, however, in 1992 we deliberately oversampled journalists from four key minority groups—Asian American, African American, Hispanic, and Native American—to ensure adequate numbers for comparison with each other and with White journalists. We kept these oversamples of minority journalists separate from the main probability sample when making comparisons with the earlier studies.

POPULATION

As in the earlier studies, the population of our 1992 main sample was full-time editorial or news people responsible for the information content of English-language mainstream general interest news media in the United States. In other words, this study was concerned with journalists who worked for news media targeted at general audiences, rather than special interest or ethnic groups. These mainstream news media included daily and weekly newspapers, news magazines, radio and television stations, and general news or wire services (such as the Associated Press and Reuters) based in the United States.

We included those persons who produced news, information, and opinion, rather than those who created fiction, drama, art, or other media content. We also limited our study to those news media that transmitted information more frequently than once a month, as was true in the earlier studies. Thus, no monthly (or less frequently published) periodicals were included in our main sample. Only news magazines published more than once a month were included.

DEFINITION OF A JOURNALIST

Following earlier studies, we defined *journalists* as those who had responsibility for the preparation or transmission of news stories or other information—all full-time reporters, writers, correspondents, columnists, photojournalists, news people, and editors. In broadcast organizations, only those in news and public affairs departments were included.

Our 1992 definition of journalists, as in the earlier studies, included editorial cartoonists, but not comic strip cartoonists. We did not include librarians, camera operators, or video and audio technicians because we followed the reasoning of the earlier studies that they do not have direct responsibility for news content in the various media. We did include photojournalists in this study, unlike the earlier studies, because they increasingly combine picture taking and writing, and operate independently from reporters.

SAMPLING—MAIN PROBABILITY SAMPLE

We used a three-stage sampling plan similar to that used by the 1971 and 1982–1983 studies.

1. The first step was to compile lists of daily and weekly newspapers, news magazines, news services, and radio and television stations in the United States. We used the 1991 *Editor & Publisher International Year Book* for our lists of daily and weekly newspapers and news services, *The Broadcasting Yearbook 1991* for our lists of radio and television stations, and the 1991 *Gale Directory of Publications and Broadcast Media* (Vols. 1–3) for our lists of news magazines published more than once a month. We also relied on the Summer 1991 *News Media Yellow Book of Washington and New York* for our lists of news magazines and television network personnel.

The lists of daily and weekly newspapers and radio and television stations involved no judgment on our part: We simply used what was provided in the yearbooks. But the lists of news services and news magazines did require decisions as to what constituted legitimate news services (as opposed to purely feature, picture, and comics services, which are also listed with news and press services in the *Editor & Publisher International Year Book*), and which magazines were bona fide *news* magazines (because there is no such category in the *Gale Directory*, although there is a category, "Magazines of General Circulation," with subcategories of "Business" and "General Editorial," which were helpful).

There is a "News" periodical category in the *News Media Yellow Book*, but it included only six publications, one of which was *The Economist*, a British-based publication not included here. Our final list of news magazines published more than once a month included 17 derived from both the *Gale* and the *Yellow Book* listings: *Barron's National Business and Financial Weekly, Business Week, Forbes, Fortune, Insight, The Nation, National Journal, National Review, The New Republic, Newsweek* (and *Newsweek International*), *New York, The New Yorker, People, Rolling Stone, Spotlight, Time,* and *U.S. News & World Report*.

Our final selection of general news services included The Associated Press, Reuters, and United Press International bureaus as listed in the *Editor & Publisher Year Book*. We also received helpful information from the headquarters of these wire services on numbers of full-time journalists and bureaus.

From these sources, we used systematic random sampling to compile lists of 181 daily newspapers (stratified by circulation so that we drew roughly 11% of the number of dailies in each circulation category at random), 128 weekly newspapers (every 47th one), 17 news magazines (all that we classified as such published more than monthly), 28 news service bureaus (every fifth one), 121 radio stations (every 98th one), and 99 television stations (every 15th one).

In all, our random sample of news organizations included 574 from an estimated 22,007 in the United States (or about every 38th one), as compared with 586 from an estimated 19,869 in the 1982–1983 study (or about every 34th one).

2. The second task was to obtain lists (or at least total numbers) of all full-time journalists working for the 574 news organizations in our sample. This was done in three steps. In early February 1992, we sent a letter to all editors or news directors of the 574 news organizations in our sample, explaining the study and asking for the total number of all news or editorial people working in each organization. We defined what we meant by *news people* both in print and broadcast. We also asked for the names and job titles of all full-time journalists, or at least a list of all news positions and the number of persons in each one. We audited the lists of journalists received for job titles we considered not fitting our definition of journalist.

The response to this first letter was disappointing—only about 10%—so we sent a second follow-up letter to all who had not responded in early March 1992. Again, the response was low, so after 3 weeks we began telephone calls to those who had not responded. We soon learned that most editors and news directors respond much more quickly to the telephone than to the U.S. mail. The lists began pouring in, by fax and by mail, and for small organizations by telephone.

In all, we obtained numbers of full-time journalists from 114 of the 128 weekly newspapers, 113 of the 181 dailies, 13 of 17 news magazines, 25 of 28 news service bureaus, 79 of 99 television stations, and 116 of 121 radio stations, for a total of 460 responding news organizations from the original sample of 574—a response rate of 80.1%. As in 1982, the best response was from radio stations (95.9%). Unlike 1982, the worst was from daily newspapers (62.4%). (News services had been the worst in 1982, with a response of 74.6%.) This probably reflects that in 1992 U.S. daily newspaper editors were overwhelmed with survey requests from academics like ourselves.

3. The third task was to draw a random, representative sample of individual journalists from the lists of names and positions collected in Step 2. We first used the total number of journalists working for the organizations that responded to estimate the total numbers working for news media throughout the United States. We did that by calculating the percentage of each type of news organization responding (daily newspapers, radio, television, etc.) by dividing the number responding by the total number of organizations in the population, then multiplying the total number of persons working for each type of organization by 100 divided by the percentage of such organizations in our sample.

For example, we obtained the numbers of full-time journalists working for 79 randomly selected television stations (5.37%) of the 1,472 in the United States. We divided 100% by 5.37% and got a multiplier of 18.62. Multiplying the total number of journalists from the 79 stations in our sample (955) by 18.62 yielded an estimate of 17,784 full-time television journalists in the United States. The same procedure was followed for each of the other five types of media.

Once we had estimated the total number of full-time journalists working for each type of news organization in the United States, we calculated the percentages of journalists working for each type of medium by dividing the estimated total number of journalists (122,015) by the number working for each type of medium. We then used these percentages to estimate how many journalists from each type of news medium should be included in our national probability sample of 1,500 (comparable to the 1971 sample of 1,550 and the 1982 sample of 1,250).

After going through this procedure, we found that using strict percentages of total estimated U.S. journalistic workforce would result in only 21 news magazine and 17 wire service journalists in our sample of 1,500. Because we wanted to compare journalists working for different media, we increased the news magazine sample from 21 to 135 (from 1.4% to 9.0%) and the wire service sample from 17 to 102 (from 1.1% to 6.8%). This oversampling of these journalists meant, of course, that we had to undersample other journalists. We chose to reduce the number of radio journalists from 218 to 150 and the number of television from 219 to 213, but we also added some journalists in other categories, making the main probability sample total 1,662, rather than the 1,500 we had originally planned.

A total of 1,156 interviews were completed from these 1,662, for a gross response rate of 69.5%. When the 241 who were incapacitated, ill, deceased, or no longer journalists were subtracted from the total, the *adjusted response rate*

TABLE AI.1
Actual Main Sample/Estimated Workforce

Medium	Ns	%	%	Difference (%)
Dailies	636	55.0	55.1	−0.1
Weeklies	162	14.0	13.3	+0.7
News magazines	61	5.3	1.4	+3.9
News service	58	5.0	1.1	+3.9
Television	138	11.9	14.6	−2.7
Radio	101	8.7	14.5	−5.8
Total	1,156	100.0	100.0	

for the main probability sample response rate rose to 81.3%. We ended up with percentages in each medium that were quite close to those estimated in the total workforce (see Table AI.1).

Thus, the most oversampled journalists were from news magazines and news wire services, for reasons mentioned earlier, and the most undersampled were from radio, mostly because of the very small sizes of radio news staffs, which produced small lists of radio journalists. But no group of journalists was either over- or undersampled by more than 6 percentage points, as was true in 1982, leading us to conclude that weighting by medium type was not necessary. The *sampling error* margin at the 95% level of confidence for this main probability sample of 1,156 was *plus or minus three percentage points*.

SAMPLING—MINORITY OVERSAMPLE

Unlike the 1971 and 1982–1983 studies, in 1992 we decided to include an oversample from the four major minority journalists associations to ensure enough minority journalists to compare with those from the White majority and with each other. We knew from the previous studies that we would not obtain enough minorities from the main probability sample for such a comparison because of their small proportions among all U.S. journalists. In fact, our main probability sample of 1,156 contained only 43 African Americans (3.7%), 25 Hispanics (2.2%), 12 Asian Americans (1.0%), 7 Native Americans (0.6%), and 8 who classified themselves as "some other category" (0.7%). In all, then, our main probability sample included 95 journalists (8.2%) who classified themselves as in a racial or ethnic group other than White.

To increase the number of minority journalists in our study, we drew random samples from the membership lists of the Asian American Journalists Association (AAJA), the National Association of Black Journalists (NABJ), the National Association of Hispanic Journalists (NAHJ), and the Native American Journalists Association (NAJA). We obtained the actual mailing lists from all of these organizations except the NABJ, which had a policy against releasing its membership list. In addition, the membership list for the NAHJ did not contain media organization or telephone number. For both groups, we sent letters and forms (with postage-paid return envelopes) requesting name and address of news organization, job title, full- or part-time status, business telephone (or home if preferred), and best day and time to call.

The NABJ staff were very helpful in mailing these letters and forms to every sixth professional member on their membership list from a random starting point, totaling 183 African-American journalists. We sent similar letters and forms to every sixth member of the NAHJ mailing list, totaling 173 Hispanic journalists. We also did a systematic random sample of the AAJA membership list by selecting every sixth name, totaling 160. Finally, we included all 143 members of the NAJA in our sample. We audited these lists for journalistic job titles and employment at news organizations.

From these efforts, we completed interviews with an additional 34 African-American journalists, 55 Hispanics, 88 Asian Americans, and 77 Native Americans, totaling 254 minority journalists in the oversample from 659 original names, or 38.5%. The mailings to the NABJ and NAHJ members produced only 47 and 64 replies, respectively, so the actual number of eligible respondents from the minority groups was 414, from which the 254 interviews were completed, for an *adjusted response rate of 61.3%* for the oversample of minorities. Taken together, the sampling error margin for this additional sample of minority journalists at the 95 level of confidence was plus or minus six percentage points. It was higher, of course, for the individual minority group samples.

Minorities from the oversampled groups were compared with those from the main probability sample on 15 different characteristics to check for differences between the two groups. These 15 characteristics included: age, gender, education level, public versus private college, Ivy League versus other college, journalism versus other college major, region of work, marital status, whether they had children at home, political party identification, religious upbringing, the importance of religious beliefs, level of job satisfaction, plans to stay in or leave news media, and whether their media organizations were group owned.

There were no more than four statistically significant differences for any given minority group, and these differences tended to vary by group. For example, there were no significant differences for any group by age, gender, religion, undergraduate education levels, or job satisfaction. There were some differences on region of work, with the main probability sample producing a more even spread of minority journalists throughout the country than the oversamples drawn from membership lists of the four minority journalism associations. The main samples of Asian Americans and Hispanics tended to identify more with the Republican party than the oversamples, and the main samples of Asian Americans and Hispanics were more likely to want to work outside of the news media than the oversamples. Finally, the main samples of African Americans and Native

TABLE AI.2
Frequency of Racial Groups

Group	Frequency	Percentage of Total Sample
Asian American	100	7.1
Native American	84	6.0
Hispanic	80	5.7
African American	77	5.5
Missing/other	16	1.1
White	1,053	74.7
Total	1,410	100.1 (rounding error)

Americans were more likely to work for group- or chain-owned media than the oversamples.

Despite these differences, the overall picture was certainly one of more similarity than difference between the groups. Hence, we decided to combine them in our analyses comparing minority groups with each other and with the White majority journalists in 1992. But our comparisons with the 1971 and 1982–1983 studies were based only on the main probability sample of 1,156 to preserve comparability.

Table AI.2 lists the numbers in each racial group after combining the main sample and oversample minority groups. Thus, the total number of identifiable minority journalists in this study, counting both main and oversamples, was 341.

INTERVIEWING

Telephone interviews averaging 50 minutes in length were completed with these 1,410 U.S. journalists between June 12, 1992, and September 12, 1992, by the Center for Survey Research at Indiana University's Bloomington campus. Two weeks before the interviews were conducted, letters were sent to all journalists in the sample explaining the study and urging them to cooperate. In addition, the questionnaire was pretested on a sample of journalists in the local area. Interviewers were trained for a minimum of 20 hours before actually beginning on the survey, and we met with the interviewers to explain the study and the reasoning behind the questions just before the interviewing began.

Interviewers were instructed to ask each respondent for a convenient time for the interview and to reschedule if necessary. Substitutions were allowed only if the original respondents had left journalism or could not be reached. If they had moved to another news organization, interviewers were asked to track them. Substitutions were made with another person holding the same job title in the original media organization.

NOTES

1. John W. C. Johnstone, Edward J. Slawski, and William W. Bowman, *The News People: A Sociological Portrait of American Journalists and Their Work* (Urbana, IL: University of Illinois Press, 1976).
2. David H. Weaver and G. Cleveland Wilhoit, *The American Journalist: A Portrait of U.S. News People and Their Work* (Bloomington, IN: Indiana University Press, 1986; 2nd ed., 1991).

1992 Journalists Survey Questionnaire (Final Version—June 12, 1992)

(Note: Some question numbers and parts of questions are not numbered consecutively because of deletions and rearranging of questions during pretesting and cutting of the questionnaire.)

RECORD WHETHER THIS INTERVIEW IS FROM THE NATIONAL PROBABILITY SAMPLE OR FROM ONE OF THE FOUR MINORITY GROUP MEMBERSHIP LISTS:

National probability sample 1
Asian-American journalists group 3
Hispanic journalists group 5
Native American journalists group 7
Black journalists group 8

RECORD TYPE OF NEWS ORGANIZATION:
(Ask if from a minority group and not known)

Daily newspaper 1
Weekly newspaper 3
News magazine 5
News agency (wire service) 7
TV station 9
Radio station 2

1. Thank you for agreeing to participate.

NEWN. In this survey, I will ask a number of questions about your news organization. Is there another name that you use to refer to it?

    Yes 1   (GO TO ORGN.)
    No 5

ORGN. What name do you use? (ENTER NEW NAME)

1a. First, what is your exact job title at (NAME OF ORGANIZATION)?

    JOB TITLE:_____

1b. What is your main responsibility at (NAME OF ORGANIZATION)?

2. In what year did you become a full-time employee of (NAME OF ORGANIZATION)?

    YEAR: _____   Not full-time (GO TO END)
    Don't Know (DK) 9998   Refused (RF) 9999

3. What are the titles of previous jobs you have held, if any, in journalism? (SPECIFY)

    None 99

4. How long have you worked in journalism?

    YEARS: _____   Can't estimate . . . 97 DK . . . 98 RF . . . 99

5. In looking back, why did you become a journalist? (PROBE IF NECESSARY: "Any other reasons?") (RECORD VERBATIM.)

7.A. Where would you most like to be working in five years—in the news media or somewhere else?

    In news media (go to q7b) 3
    Somewhere else (go to q7d) 1
    Don't know 9
    Refused 0

7.B. In which of the news media—newspapers, magazines, radio, television, or other news services?

    Newspapers 1
    Magazines 3

Radio 5
Television. 7
News Services 2
(VOLUNTEERED)
Other—where? (SPECIFY). 4
Don't Know 9
Refused. . . . . 0 (GO TO Q.8.A)

7.D. Where?

7.E. Why do you want to work outside the news media?

8.A. I'd like to find out how important a number of things are to you in judging jobs in your field—**not just your job**. For instance, how much difference does the pay make in how you rate a job in your field—is pay very important, fairly important, or not too important?

		VERY IMPORTANT	FAIRLY IMPORTANT	NOT TOO IMPORTANT	DK	RF
8.A.	the pay?	5	3	1	9	0
B.	fringe benefits?					
C.	the editorial policies of the organization?					
D.	job security?					
E.	the chance to develop a specialty?					
F.	the amount of autonomy you have?					
G.	the chance to get ahead in the organization?					
I.	the chance to help people?					
J.	the chance to influence public affairs?					

9. All things considered, how satisfied are you with your present job—would you say very satisfied, fairly satisfied, somewhat dissatisfied, or very dissatisfied?

Very satisfied 7
Fairly satisfied 5
Somewhat dissatisfied 3
Very dissatisfied 1
Don't know 9   (GO TO Q.12)
Refused. 0   (GO TO Q.12)

10. What are the most important reasons you say you are (very satisfied, fairly satisfied, etc.) with your present job?

12. To what extent, if at all, are you using computerized databases such as NEXIS or DIALOG in your work?

Daily .... 7 (GO TO Q.13)
Several times a week .... 5 (GO TO Q.13)
Weekly .... 3 (GO TO Q.13)
Less often than that .... 1 (GO TO Q.13)
Don't use them at all .... 8 (GO TO Q.14)
DK 9   RF 0

13. (IF DATABASES USED) For what purposes do you use these databases? (RECORD ANSWER VERBATIM)

14. Do you ever use a computer to analyze data from government agencies or other sources in your work?

Yes 3
No 1
DK 9
RF 0

16.A. How often do you get reactions or comments on your work from people who are above you in your organization—would you say regularly, occasionally, seldom or never?
(CODE IN COLUMN A BELOW.)

B. How often do you get reactions or comments on your work from people at about your level in your organization—would you say regularly, occasionally, seldom, or never?
(CODE IN COLUMN B BELOW.)

C. How often do you get reactions or comments on your work from people in other organizations who do the same kind of work you do—would you say regularly, occasionally, seldom or never?
(CODE IN COLUMN C BELOW.)

D. How often do you get reactions or comments on your work from news sources—regularly, occasionally, seldom or never?
(CODE IN COLUMN D BELOW.)

E. (How often do you get reactions or comments on your work) from readers, listeners, or viewers—regularly, occasionally, seldom or never?
(CODE IN COLUMN E BELOW.)

A. (people above)	B. (people at same level)	C. (people in other org.)	D. (news sources)	E. (readers, viewers)
Regularly	7	7	7	7
Occasionally	5	5	5	5
Seldom	3	3	3	3
Never	1	1	1	1
Not applicable	0	0	0	0
Don't know	8	8	8	8
Refused	9	9	9	9

17. Do you supervise any news or editorial employees?

   Yes (ASK Q. 18)................ 3
   No (SKIP TO Q. 20)............ 1
   DK 9   RF 0   (GO TO Q. 20)

18. About how often do you meet with individual reporters to discuss future stories—would you say several times a day, daily, several times a week, weekly, or less often than that?

   Several times a day 7
   Daily......................... 5
   Several times a week............ 3
   Weekly....................... 1
   Less often than that 0
   (VOLUNTEERED)
   Don't meet with reporters 8
   DK 98   RF 99

19. How much influence do you have in decisions on hiring and firing news or editorial employees? Would you say:

   A great deal................... 7
   Some......................... 5
   A little, or 3
   None at all................... 1
   DK 9   RF.............. 0

20. How much editing or processing of other people's work do you do? Would you say:

   A great deal................... 5
   Some......................... 3
   None at all (SKIP TO Q. 22) 1

DK 9   RF 0   (GO TO Q.22)

21. How much freedom do you usually have in deciding how the stories written by others will be used in (FILL IN MEDIUM)? Would you say:

Almost complete freedom 7
A great deal of freedom 5
Some freedom, or 3
None at all 1
DK 9   RF 0

22. How often do you do reporting? Would you say:

Regularly (ASK Q. 23) 7
Occasionally (ASK Q. 23) 5
Seldom, or 3
Never . . . . 1 (GO TO Q. 28)
DK 9   RF 0   (GO TO Q. 28)

23. Do you usually cover a specific "beat" or subject area, or do you usually cover different things?

Cover a specific "beat" . . . . 3 (GO TO Q. 23.A.)
Cover different things . . . . 1 (GO TO Q. 28)
DK 9   RF 0   (GO TO Q. 28)

23.A. (IF SPECIFIC BEAT) Which beats or areas do you usually cover?

28. Next, a question on journalistic freedom. On the whole, what do you consider to be the most significant limits on your freedom as a journalist?

24. How much editing do your stories get from others at (FILL IN ORGANI-ZATION)? Would you say:

A great deal 5
Some, or 3
None at all 1
DK 9   RF 0

25. If you have a good idea for a subject which you think is important and should be followed up, how often are you able to get the subject covered? Would you say:

Almost always 5
More often than not, or 3

Only occasionally 1
Don't make such proposals........ 9
DK .... 98 RF.................. 99

26. How much freedom do you usually have in selecting the stories you work on? Would you say:

Almost complete freedom........ 7
A great deal.................. 5
Some, or..................... 3
None at all.................. 1
DK .... 9 RF.................... 0

27. How much freedom do you usually have in deciding which aspects of a story should be emphasized? Would you say:

Almost complete freedom........ 7
A great deal.................. 5
Some, or..................... 3
None at all.................. 1
DK .... 9 RF.................... 0

30. Do you belong to a journalists' union?

Yes 3
No........................... 1
Don't know 9
Refused...................... 0

31.A. Does your news organization employ someone either full- or part-time as an ombudsman?

Yes.......................... 3
No 1
Don't know.................. 9
Refused 0

31.B. Does your news organization employ someone either full- or part-time as a writing coach?

Yes.......................... 3
No 1
Don't know.................. 9
Refused 0

32.A. Here are some statements about your (readers, viewers, listeners). Please indicate whether you strongly disagree, somewhat disagree, are neutral, somewhat agree, or strongly agree with these statements.

(Readers, viewers, listeners) are more interested in the day's breaking news than in analysis. Do you:

```
Strongly disagree . . . . . . . . . . . . . .  1
Somewhat disagree. . . . . . . . . . . .  2
Somewhat agree. . . . . . . . . . . . . .  4
Strongly agree, or. . . . . . . . . . . . .  5
Are you neutral? . . . . . . . . . . . . .  3
DK. . . . . . . . . . . . . . . . . . . . . . . . .  9
RF . . . . . . . . . . . . . . . . . . . . . . . . .  0
```

32.B. The majority of (readers, viewers, listeners) have little interest in (reading about, viewing, listening to) social problems such as racial discrimination and poverty. Do you: (Strongly disagree, etc., as in Q. 32.A.)

32.D. (Readers, viewers, listeners) are gullible and easily fooled. Do you: (Strongly disagree, etc., as in Q. 32.A.)

33. Next, some questions on influence of the media and public opinion. For each statement, I would like you to use a zero to ten rating scale to indicate the amount of influence.

First, how strong do you think the influence of the media is on the formation of public opinion? Please choose a number from zero to ten, where zero means no influence and ten means very great influence.

No Influence								Very great influence		
0	1	2	3	4	5	6	7	8	9	10

```
Don't know. . . . . . . . . . . . . . . . . . .  98
Refused . . . . . . . . . . . . . . . . . . . . . .  99
```

34. And how strong do you think the influence of the media **should** be on public opinion? Again, please choose a number from zero to ten, where zero means no influence and ten means very great influence.

No Influence								Very great influence		
0	1	2	3	4	5	6	7	8	9	10

```
Don't know. . . . . . . . . . . . . . . . . . .  98
Refused . . . . . . . . . . . . . . . . . . . . . .  99
```

37. Given an important story, which of the following, if any, do you think may be justified on occasion and which would you not approve under any circumstances?

	Justified on occasion	Would not approve	Not sure	DK	RF
37A. First, paying people for confidential information. Is it justified on occasion, or would you not approve under any circumstances?	3	1	9	8	0
B. Using confidential business or government documents without authorization. Is it (etc. as in 37.A.)					
C. Claiming to be somebody else. Is it (etc.)					
D. Agreeing to protect confidentiality and not doing so. Is it (etc.)					
E. Badgering unwilling informants to get a story. Is it (etc.)					
F. Making use of personal documents such as letters and photographs without permission. Is it (etc.)					
G. Getting employed in a firm or organization to gain inside information. Is it (etc.)					
I. Using hidden microphones or cameras. Is it (etc.)					
K. Using re-creations or dramatizations of news by actors. Is it (etc.)					
M. Disclosing the names of rape victims. Is it (etc.)					

38. Next, I'd like to ask you how important you think a number of things are that the news media do or try to do today. First,

   A. Get information to the public quickly. Is that extremely important, quite important, somewhat important, or not really important at all? (CODE IN A BELOW.)

(THEN ASK B–M: Is that extremely important, etc.?)

	Extremely Important	Quite Important	Some-what	Not Really	DK	RF
A. Get information to the public quickly.	7	5	3	1	9	0
B. Provide analysis and interpretation of complex problems.						

C. Provide entertainment and relaxation.
D. Investigate claims and statements made by the government.
E. Stay away from stories where factual content cannot be verified.
F. Concentrate on news which is of interest to the widest possible audience.
G. Discuss national policy while it is still being developed.
H. Develop intellectual and cultural interests of the public.
I. Be an adversary of public officials by being constantly skeptical of their actions.
J. Be an adversary of businesses by being constantly skeptical of their actions.
K. To set the political agenda.
L. Influence public opinion.
M. Give ordinary people a chance to express their views on public affairs.

39.A. How influential have the following been in shaping your ideas in matters of journalism ethics?

First, how influential have high school teachers been in developing your ideas about what's right and wrong in journalism? Would you say extremely influential, quite influential, somewhat influential, or not very influential in developing your ideas about what's right and wrong in journalism?

Extremely Influential	Quite Influential	Somewhat Influential	Not Very Influential	DK	RF
7	5	3	1	9	0

A. High school teachers?
B. College teachers, other than journalism teachers?
C. Journalism teachers?
D. Family upbringing?
E. Religious training?
F. Day-by-day newsroom learning?
G. A senior reporter?
H. A senior editor?
I. Publishers, owners or general managers?

40. Next, I'd like to ask about your news organization. How good a job of informing the public do you think your own news organization is doing? Would you say outstanding, very good, good, fair or poor?

Outstanding   8
Very good.   6
Good.   4
Fair   2
Poor   0
No opinion/don't know   9   (GO TO Q. 43)
Refused.   99   (GO TO Q. 43)

41. Why do you think your news organization is doing a (outstanding, very good, good, etc.) job of informing the public?_____

_____

42.A. Currently, in your day-to-day job, how influential is each of the following on your concept of what is newsworthy? Please use a scale from one to five, where **one means not at all influential** and **five means very influential**. (CIRCLE ONE NUMBER FOR EACH ITEM.)

	NOT AT ALL INFLUENTIAL		VERY INFLUENTIAL			DK	RF
42.A. Your peers on the staff?	1	2	3	4	5	9	0
B. Your supervisors?							
C. Your friends and acquaintances?							
D. Your journalistic training?							
E. Findings of readership or audience research?							
F. News sources?							
G. Priorities of network news and prestige newspapers?							
H. Local competing news media?							
I. Wire service budgets?							
J. Public opinion polls?							

43. The media are often classified politically in terms of left, right and center. On a scale from zero **which means extreme left** to one hundred **which means extreme right**, where would you place the editorial policy of your organization?

RECORD POSITION: (0–100)   DK 998   RF 999

44. And where on this scale would you place yourself, keeping in mind that zero means extreme left and one hundred means extreme right?

RECORD POSITION: (0–100)   DK 998   RF 999

45. Overall, then, does this mean that you consider yourself:

Pretty far to the left 1
A little to the left 2
In the middle of the road 3
A little to the right, or 4
Pretty far to the right 5
Don't know 9
Refused 0

49. On the issue of women's rights, where would you place yourself on a scale where zero means extreme left and one hundred means extreme right?

RECORD POSITION: (0–100)   DK 998   RF 999

50. On the issue of affirmative action for minorities, where would you place yourself on a scale where zero means extreme left and one hundred means extreme right?

RECORD POSITION: (0–100)   DK 998   RF 999

53. Do you think abortions should be legal under any circumstances, legal under only certain circumstances, or illegal in all circumstances?

Legal, any circumstances 5
Legal, certain circumstances 3
Illegal, all circumstances 1
No opinion 9
Refused 0

57.A. I'd like to talk with you about a story you think represents some of your best work. Please pick one of the best stories you've been involved in during the past year and tell me briefly what it was about.

Story given (SPECIFY) 1
No story given—(GO TO Q58.A.) 5

57.B. Why do you think that this story is particularly good?

57.C. How does this story differ, if at all, from the more routine work you do?

57.D. Could you send a copy of this story to Prof. Weaver at Indiana University?
(PROVIDE ADDRESS AGAIN IF NEEDED)

Yes 1
No 5

DK 9
RF. 0

58.A. Which professional journalism publications, if any, do you read **regularly**—that is, almost every issue?

58.C. Which professional journalism publications, if any, do you read or look at **occasionally**?

59. Which newspapers do you read regularly—that is, at least once a week? (LIST EACH PAPER—FULL NAME, CITY AND STATE OF PUBLICATION.)

60. How many days a week do you usually watch the early evening network newscasts on TV—that is CBS, NBC or ABC?

    0   1   2   3   4   5   6   7   DK—8   RF—9

61. How many days a week do you usually watch CNN news?

    0   1   2   3   4   5   6   7   DK—8   RF—9

62. How many days a week do you usually watch the MacNeil/Lehrer Newshour on public television?

    0   1   2   3   4   5   DK—8   RF—9

63. How many days a week do you usually watch local newscasts?

    0   1   2   3   4   5   6   7   DK—8   RF—9

64. How many days a week do you usually watch TV tabloid programs such as "Inside Edition," "Current Affair," and "Hard Copy"?

    0   1   2   3   4   5   6   DK—8   RF—9

64.A. How many days a week do you usually watch TV talk shows such as Oprah Winfrey or Phil Donahue?

    0   1   2   3   4   5   6   7   DK—8   RF—9

65. Please tell me the magazines you read regularly—that is, almost every issue. (LIST FULL NAMES OF ALL MAGAZINES.)

66. Now a few questions about your background and we'll be through. What is the highest grade of school or level of education you have completed?

No school or kindergarten 0
Grades 1–11... (1–11)
Completed high school (SKIP TO Q67) 12
1–3 years of college................................. (13–15)
Graduated from college (ASK Q.66A–G) 16
Some graduate work, no degree....................... 17
Master's degree (ASK Q.66A–O) 18
Doctorate, law, or medical degree 19
Vocational or technical school beyond high school 20
Don't Know... 98
Refused.. 99

(IF GRADUATED FROM COLLEGE OR MORE)

66.A. In which state or country did you do most of your undergraduate studies?
STATE/COUNTRY_____

66.B. As an undergraduate, did you attend a public or private school?
Public . . . 1   Private . . . 3   DK . . . 9   RF . . . 0

66.C. Was it an Ivy League college?
Yes 3   No 1   DK 9   RF 0

66.D. What was your undergraduate major?

Journalism.. 1
Journalism and other major (SPECIFY) 3
Other major(s)—what was it? (SPECIFY) 5
(VOLUNTEERED)
Did not have a major 7
Don't Know 8
Refused 9

66.E. What was your undergraduate minor?

Journalism.. 1
Journalism and other minor (SPECIFY) 3
Other minor(s)—what was it? (SPECIFY) 5
(VOLUNTEERED)
Did not have a minor................................. 7
Don't Know 8
Refused 9

66.F. As an undergraduate, did you take courses in journalism or in media studies?

Yes 3
No 1
Don't know 9
Refused 0

66.G. In which state or country did you do most of your graduate studies?
STATE/COUNTRY_____

66.H. Was it a public or private school?

Public 1
Private 3
Don't Know 9
Refused 0

66.I. Was it an Ivy League college?
Yes 3   No 1   DK 9   RF 0

66.J. What field were you in in graduate or professional school?
FIELD_____

(IF GRADUATE DEGREES)

66.K. Which graduate degrees do you hold? (FIRST MENTION)

MA 1   MD 5
PhD 2   Other—what? . . . . 7 (SPECIFY)
JD, law 3   Don't know 9
MBA 4   Refused 0

66.L. Which graduate degrees do you hold? (SECOND MENTION)

MA 1   MD 5
PhD 2   Other—what? . . . . 7 (SPECIFY)
JD, law 3   Don't know 9
MBA 4   Refused 0
No second mention 6

67.A. Do you feel you need additional training in journalism or other subjects?

Yes . . . . 3 (GO TO Q.67.B)
No 1
Don't Know 9
Refused 0

67.B. In what subjects?
(RECORD ANSWER VERBATIM.)

67.C. Have you had any short courses, sabbaticals, workshops or fellowships
since becoming a journalist?

Yes. 3
No. 1
Don't Know 9
Refused 0

68. Altogether, about what percentage of the people you see socially are connected in some way with journalism or the communications field?

PERCENTAGE: . . . . (0 to 100)
Can't estimate 997
Don't know 998
Refused 999

69. In what year were you born?_____

Don't know 9998
Refused 9999

70. In which one of the following groups would you place yourself?

White (Caucasian) 1
Black or African-American 3
Hispanic or Latino . . . . : . . . 5
Asian or Asian-American. 7
Native American or Indian 9
Other (SPECIFY BELOW) 8
Don't know 98
Refused. 99
OTHER:_____

71.A. In what religion, if any, were you brought up?

Protestant . . . . 1 (GO TO Q.71.B.)
Catholic 2
Jewish 3
Other . . . . 4 (GO TO Q.71.C.)
None at all. 5
Don't know 8
Refused 9

71.B. In which Protestant denomination were you brought up?

Answered (SPECIFY)_____1
DK.......................... 8
RF 9

71.C. In which religion were you brought up?

Answered (SPECIFY)_____1
DK.......................... 8
RF 9

72. How important is religion or religious beliefs to you? Would you say:

Very important................ 7
Somewhat important 5
Not very important, or.......... 3
Not at all important............ 1
Don't know................... 9
Refused 0

73. What is your marital status? Are you:

Married 7
Cohabiting 6
Divorced 5
Separated................................. 4
Widowed, or.............................. 3
Single, that is, never married 1
Refused 9

74.A. Do you have any children living with you?

Yes........................... 3 (GO TO Q.74.B.)
No 1
Don't know................... 8
Refused 9

74.B. (IF "YES") How many children are currently living with you? (SPECIFY)

Don't know................... 98
Refused 99

75.A. As of today, are you a Democrat, a Republican, or what?

Democrat................................... 1
Republican 3
(VOLUNTEERED)

Independent/no party . . . . 5 (GO TO Q.75.B.)
Other (SPECIFY BELOW). 7
Don't know 8
Refused 9

75.B.   (IF INDEPENDENT OR NO PARTY) Which of the following best describes your political leanings?

Lean toward the Republican party. 3
Lean toward the Democratic party, or. 1
Lean toward neither major party 5
(VOLUNTEERED)
Other (SPECIFY) 7
Don't know 8
Refused. 9

76.A.   Do you belong to any organizations or associations that are primarily for
people in journalism or the communications field?

Yes. . . . . 3 (GO TO Q.76.B)
No. 1
Don't know 8
Refused 9

76.B.   (IF YES) Which ones? (RECORD BELOW) Any others?

79.A.   Is your (FILL IN NEWS ORGANIZATION) owned by a public corporation whose shares are traded on an exchange?

Yes. . . . . 3 (GO TO Q.79.B.)
No. 1
Don't know 8
Refused . . . . 9 (GO TO Q.79.C.)

79.B.   (IF YES TO Q.79.A) Are the majority of the shares publicly traded?

Yes. 3
No. 1
Don't know 8
Refused 9

79.C.   Is your (FILL IN ORGANIZATION) owned by a group or chain?

Yes. 3
No. 1
Don't know 8
Refused 9

80. Is the person or company that owns your news organization located in your town or city?

    Yes 3
    No............................ 1
    Don't know 9
    Refused....................... 0

81. Finally, I'd like to ask you some financial information. I'd like to mention once again that all information you give us will be treated in strict confidence, and neither you nor your organization will ever be reported by name. Would you please tell me what your total personal income was, before taxes, from your work in the communications field during 1991? Was it:

    Less than $35,000.............. 1 (GO TO, etc.)
    Between $35,000 and $60,000, or. 3 (GO TO, etc.)
    Was it over $60,000............ 5 (GO TO, etc.)
    Don't know................... 9
    Refused .... 0 (GO TO Q.82)

82. (INTERVIEWER: RECORD RESPONDENT'S SEX. ASK ONLY IF NEC-ESSARY.)
    I'm required to ask all questions. Are you:

    Male, or 1
    Female 3
    DK/Refused 9

83. How many full-time news and editorial people are employed at your organization? (SKIP IF ALREADY KNOWN IN MAIN SAMPLE)

    NUMBER OF EDITORIAL PEOPLE:_____

    (VOLUNTEERED)
    Can't estimate 997
    Don't know 998
    Refused....................... 999

    INT Do you have any additional comments?

         Yes .... 1 (SPECIFY)
         No........................ 9

Coding Schedule for
Journalists' Best Work

I.	Item Number	000
II.	Sample	
	a. weeklies	1
	b. TV	2
	c. radio	3
	d. dailies	4
	e. wire	5
	f. news magazines	6
III.	Page Number	
	a. first/cover page	1
	b. inside page(s)	2
	c. don't know	9
IV.	General Story Categories	
	a. accidents and disasters	01
	b. state and local government news	02
	c. national government news	03
	d. crime news	04
	e. international news	05
	f. sports	06

g. personalities/celebrities   07
h. general human interest   08
i. economic news and issues   09
j. consumer information and advice   10
k. social problems/protests   11
l. business and finance   12
m. environment and energy   13
n. science, invention, and space   14
o. education and schools   15
p. religion   16
q. medical   17
r. arts, leisure, and travel   18
s. humor   19
t. other   20

V.   General Media Roles

a. disseminator   0
b. interpretive   1
c. adversarial   2

VI.   Specific Roles

a. adversarial stance or skepticism toward
    government/public official   1
b. adversarial stance or skepticism toward business   2
c. analysis or interpretation of complex problems   3
d. investigations of claims made by government   4
e. discussion of governmental policy as it's developed 5
f. timeliness (get story to public quickly)   6
g. appeal to the widest audience possible   7

VII. News Value

a. contains news value   1
b. does not contain news value   2

VIII. Specific Value

a. conflict   1
b. timeliness   2
c. proximity   3
d. prominence   4
e. unusualness   5
f. impact   6

IX.   Event/Issue Orientation

    a. event-oriented								0
    b. issue-oriented								1
    c. can't tell/don't know								2

X. Number of Sources								00

XI.   Type of Sources

    a. number identified by name								00
    b. number anonymous								00
    c. number institutional (business,								00
       government, official, or agency)
    d. number noninstitutional								00
    e. number of special interest groups								00
    f. number of female sources								00
    g. number of male sources								00
    h. number of document sources								00

Bibliography

Alter, Jonathan. (1992, October 5). The cultural elite. *Newsweek*, pp. 30–34.

Altheide, David L. (1974). *Creating reality: How TV news distorts events*. Beverly Hills, CA: Sage.

American Newspaper Publishers Association. (1990, June). *Survey on minorities and women employed by U.S. daily newspapers*. Washington, DC: Author.

American Society of Newspaper Editors. (1993, March 30). *News release*. Washington, DC: Author.

American Society of Newspaper Editors. *Annual employment surveys of U.S. daily newspapers*. Washington, DC: Author.

American Society of Newspaper Editors Human Resources Committee Report. (1989, May). *The changing face of the newsroom*. Washington, DC: Author.

American Society of Newspaper Editors Minorities Committee. (1986). *Achieving equality for minorities in newsroom employment: ASNE's goal and what it means*. Rochester, NY: Author.

APME Journalist Satisfaction Study. (1993, September). Minneapolis, MN: MORI Research Inc.

Arocha, Zita. (1992, Summer). *Hispanics in the news media 1992: Still struggling for entry*. Presented at the National Association of Hispanic Journalists tenth annual convention, Albuquerque, NM.

Associated Press. (1994, July 16). Some stations cut violent news images. *The [Bloomington, IN] Herald Times*, p. 9.

Auletta, Ken. (1993, June 28). Opening up the times. *The New Yorker*, pp. 55–71.

Auletta, Ken. (1995). A decade of change: "It's demographics, stupid!" *Media Studies Journal*, 9(1), 78.

Ayers, Brandt H. (1994, July 16). The death of civility. *The New York Times*, p. 11.

Bagdikian, Ben H. (1987). *The media monopoly*. Boston: Beacon.

Baker, Russell. (1990). *The good times*. New York: Penguin.

Baker, Russell. (1993, June 12). Terror in the sunlight. *The New York Times*, p. 15.

Bates, Stephen. (1995). *Realigning journalism with democracy: The Hutchins Commission, its time, and ours*. Washington, DC: The Annenberg Washington Program in Communications Policy Studies of Northwestern University.

Beam, Randal A. (1990, June). Journalistic professionalism as an organizational-level concept. *Journalism Monographs* (No. 121).

Beam, Randal A. (1993). The impact of group ownership variables on organizational professionalism at daily newspapers. *Journalism Quarterly*, 70, 907–918.

Beasley, Maurine H., & Theus, Kathryn T. (1988). *The new majority: A look at what the preponderance of women in journalism means to the schools and to the professions.* Lanham, MD: University Press of America.

Becker, Lee B., & Engleman, Thomas E. (1988). Class of 1987 describes salaries, satisfaction found in first jobs. *Journalism Educator, 43,* 4–10.

Becker, Lee B., & Kosicki, Gerald M. (1993a). Annual census of enrollment records fewer undergrads. *Journalism Educator, 48*(3), 55–65.

Becker, Lee B., & Kosicki, Gerald M. (1993b, August). *Summary results from the 1992 annual enrollment and graduate surveys.* Paper presented at the 1993 convention of the Association for Education in Journalism, Kansas City, MO.

Belden Associates. (1990). Employee departure patterns in the newspaper industry. Conducted for the Task Force on Minorities in the Newspaper Business, Washington, DC.

Bergen, Lori A. (1991). *Testing the relative strength of individual and organizational characteristics in predicting content of journalists' best work.* Unpublished doctoral dissertation, Indiana University, Bloomington.

Berger, Gilda. (1986). *Women, work and wages.* New York: Franklin Watts.

Bernstein, Carl. (1992, June 8). The idiot culture. *The New Republic,* pp. 22–28.

Bernstein, Carl, & Woodward, Bob. (1974). *All the president's men.* New York: Simon & Schuster.

Bogart, Leo. (1989). *Press and public: Who reads what, when, where, and why in American newspapers* (2nd ed.). Hillsdale, NJ: Lawrence Erlbaum Associates.

Bogart, Leo. (1992). State of the industry. In P. S. Cook, D. Gomery, & L. W. Lichty (Eds.), *The future of news.* Washington, DC: The Woodrow Wilson Center Press.

Borden, Sandra. (1994, May). *Does the extent to which journalists identify with outsiders affect their willingness to sacrifice the autonomy of others?* Unpublished manuscript.

Bowman, William W. (1974). *Distaff journalists: Women as a minority group in the news media.* Unpublished doctoral dissertation, University of Illinois at Chicago Circle.

Brill, Steven. (1994, December). A new code for journalists: A challenge to the press to live by the code. *The American Lawyer,* pp. 5–7, 85.

Buchanan, Brian J., Newton, Eric, & Thien, Richard. (1993). *No train, no gain: Continuing training for newspaper journalists in the 1990s.* Arlington, VA: The Freedom Forum.

Burgoon, Judee K., Burgoon, Michael, & Atkin, Charles K. (1982). *The world of the working journalist.* New York: Newspaper Advertising Bureau.

Busterna, John C. (1988). Trends in daily newspaper ownership. *Journalism Quarterly, 65,* 831–838.

Carey, James. (1969). The communications revolution and the professional communicator. *Sociological Review Monographs, 13,* 32.

Center for Integration and Improvement of Journalism. (1990, September). *Latinos in California's news media: A status report.* Paper presented at the California Chicano News Media Association State Conference.

Chang, Elizabeth. (1993, July/August). The buyout boom. *American Journalism Review,* pp. 17–21.

A city room of many colors. (1993, October 4). *Newsweek,* p. 82.

Clarke, Lee. (1989). New ideas on the division of labor. *Sociological Forum, 4,* 281–289.

Cohen, Bernard C. (1963). *The press and foreign policy.* Princeton, NJ: Princeton University Press.

Collison, Michele. (1987, December 9). More young Black men choosing not to go to college. *The Chronicle of Higher Education,* pp. 1, A26–A27.

The Commission on Freedom of the Press. (1947). *A free and responsible press.* Chicago: The University of Chicago Press.

Cranny, C. J., Smith, Patricia C., & Stone, Eugene F. (1992). *Job satisfaction: How people feel about their jobs and how it affects their performance.* New York: Lexington.

Crawford, Nelson A. (1924). *The ethics of journalism.* New York: Alfred A. Knopf.

Cronkite, Walter. (1995). A decade of change: Journalism and its public. *Media Studies Journal, 9*(1), 76–78.

Curran, Barbara A., & Carson, Clara N. (1988). *Supplement to the lawyer statistical report: The U.S. legal profession in 1988*. Chicago, IL: American Bar Association.

Demers, David P. (1994). Structural pluralism, intermedia competition, and the growth of the corporate newspaper in the United States. *Journalism Monographs* (No. 145).

Dennis, Everette E., & Merrill, John C. (1991). *Media debates: Issues in mass communication*. New York: Longman.

Denniston, Lyle. (1992, May). The high cost of burning a source. *American Journalism Review*, p. 51.

Denniston, Lyle. (1994, April). Going too far with the hidden camera. *American Journalism Review*, p. 54.

The Dow Jones Newspaper Fund. (1984). *1984 journalism career and scholarship guide*. Princeton, NJ: Author.

Editor & Publisher International Yearbook. (1995). New York: Editor & Publisher.

Engelberg, Stephen. (1995, June 25). Hostage-taking is a weapon of war whose time is now. *The New York Times*, Sec. 4, pp. 1, 3.

Estes-Sumpter, Sidmel. (1993). Responding to a revolution. In *Unity '94, Kerner Plus 25: A Call for Action* (pp. 1–2). Oakland, CA: Unity '94.

Ettema, James S., & Glasser, Theodore L. (1994). The irony in—and of—journalism: A case study in the moral language of liberal democracy. *Journal of Communication, 44*(2), 5–28.

Fink, Conrad C. (1995). *Media ethics*. Boston: Allyn & Bacon.

Fishman, Mark. (1980). *Manufacturing the news*. Austin: University of Texas Press.

Fox, Mary Frank. (1988). Women and higher education: Gender differences in the status of students and scholars. In Jo Freeman (Ed.), *Women: A feminist perspective* (4th ed., pp. 217–235). Mountain View, CA: Mayfield Publishing Company.

Frankel, Max. (1994, November 27). The shroud. *The New York Times Magazine*, p. 30.

Frankel, Max. (1995, March 19). Beyond the shroud. *The New York Times Magazine*, p. 30.

Fuchs, Victor R. (1988). *Women's quest for economic equality*. Cambridge, MA: Harvard University Press.

Gallup Organization. (1991, September). *National telephone survey of U.S. adults*. Unpublished data.

Gallup Organization. (1992, April). *National telephone survey of 1002 U.S. adults*. Unpublished data.

Gallup Organization. (1992, July 17). *National telephone poll of 955 U.S. adults*. Unpublished data.

Gans, Herbert G. (1980). *Deciding what's news: A study of CBS Evening News, NBC Nightly News, Newsweek, and Time*. New York: Vintage Books.

Gaunt, Philip. (1990). *Choosing the news: The profit factor in news selection*. New York: Greenwood.

Gaziano, Cecilie, & McGrath, Kristin. (1986). Measuring the concept of credibility. *Journalism Quarterly, 63*, 451–462.

Ghiglione, Loren F. (1989, July/August). Newspaper recruiting efforts are flagging as the minority share of the population grows. *The Bulletin of the American Society of Newspaper Editors* (No. 715).

Giddings, Paula. (1984). *When and where I enter: The impact of Black women on race and sex in America*. New York: W. Morrow.

Glaberson, William. (1993, June 11). Times Co. acquiring Boston Globe for $1.1 Billion. *The New York Times*, p. 1.

Glasser, Theodore L. (1992). Professionalism and the derision of diversity: The case of the education of journalists. *Journal of Communication, 42*(2), 131–140.

Goldin, Claudia. (1990). *Understanding the gender gap: An economic history of American women*. New York: Oxford University Press.

Gomery, Douglas. (1992). Newsworkers and newsmakers. In Philip S. Cook, Douglas Gomery, & Lawrence W. Lichty (Eds.), *The future of news* (pp. 121–126). Washington, DC: The Woodrow Wilson Center Press.

Green, Bill. (1981, April 26). The fake Pulitzer story: "How did it all happen?" *Louisville Courier-Journal*, p. D3.

Harris, Louis. (1991). *Steel case office environment index*. New York: Louis Harris & Associates.

Harwood, Richard. (1995, June). Are journalists "elitist"? *American Journalism Review*, pp. 27–29.

Hess, Stephen. (1981). *The Washington reporters*. Washington, DC: The Brookings Institution.

Hess, Stephen. (1992a). All the president's reporters: A new survey of the White House press corps. *Presidential Studies Quarterly, 22,* 311–321.

Hess, Stephen. (1992b, November 17). *The American journalist in the 1990s.* Remarks at the Freedom Forum World Center, Arlington, VA.

Hirsch, Paul M. (1977). Occupational, organizational, and institutional models in mass media research. In Paul M. Hirsch, Peter V. Miller, & F. Gerald Kline (Eds.), *Strategies for communication research* (pp. 13–42). Thousand Oaks, CA: Sage.

Hoffman, Bill. (1994, May). Nice try! *American Journalism Review*, p. 45.

International Survey Research Corporation. (1984–1992). *Employee satisfaction surveys.* Chicago, IL: Author.

Johnstone, John W. C., Slawski, Edward J., & Bowman, William W. (1976). *The news people: A sociological portrait of American journalists and their work.* Urbana: University of Illinois Press.

Journalism under fire. (1983, December 12). *Time*, pp. 76–93.

Katz, Jon. (1993, August 19). The capital gang bang: The failure of the Washington press corps. *Rolling Stone*, pp. 37–39.

Lafky, Sue A. (1991). Women journalists. In David H. Weaver & G. Cleveland Wilhoit, *The American journalist* (2nd ed., pp. 160–181). Bloomington, IN: Indiana University Press.

Lambeth, Edmund B. (1992). *Committed journalism* (2nd ed.). Bloomington: Indiana University Press.

Lasch, Christopher. (1994, November). The revolt of the elites. *Harper's*, p. 41.

Lasch, Christopher. (1995). *The revolt of the elites and the betrayal of democracy.* New York: W. W. Norton.

Lass, E. Donald. (1995, March). Pay raises in 1994 lagged those of the year before. *American Society of Newspaper Editors Bulletin*, pp. 34–35.

Lawrence, David, Jr. (1988). Where are the minority comic strip characters? *Minorities in Newspaper Business, 4*(2), 1.

Leonard, Mike. (1992, June 11). Elitism seems pretty scarce in the H-T newsroom. *The Herald Times*, p. C1.

Lichter, S. Robert, & Rothman, Stanley. (1981, October/November). Media and business elites. *Public Opinion*, pp. 4–5.

Lieb, Thom. (1988). Protest at the *Post*: Coverage of Blacks in the Washington *Post* Sunday Magazine. *Mass Comm Review, 15*(2&3), 65–66.

Lindley, William R. (1975). *Journalism and higher education: The search for academic purpose.* Stillwater, OK: Journalistic Services.

Linsky, Martin. (1983). *The adversary press.* St. Petersburg, FL: Modern Media Institute.

Margolick, David. (1995, June 12). For good or ill, the Simpson case has permeated the nation's psyche: Today marks first anniversary of the murders. *The New York Times*, p. A12.

Martindale, Carolyn. (1986). *The White press and Black America.* Westport, CT: Greenwood.

Martindale, Carolyn. (1990). Coverage of Black Americans in four major newspapers, 1950–1989. *Newspaper Research Journal, 11*(3), 96–112.

McLeod, Jack, & Hawley, Searle. (1964). Professionalization among newsmen. *Journalism Quarterly, 41,* 529–538, 577.

Menand, Louis. (1995, March 5). The trashing of professionalism. *The New York Times Magazine*, pp. 41–43.

Merritt, Davis, & Rosen, Jay. (1995, April 13). Imagining public journalism: An editor and scholar reflect on the birth of an idea. In *Roy W. Howard Public Lecture in Journalism and Mass Communication Research No. 5.* Bloomington: School of Journalism, Indiana University.

Moreno, Roberto L. (1993). Standard 12 and the myth of Latino journalism education. In *Twelve* (pp. 10–15). Austin, TX: Commission on the Status of Minorities, AEJMC.

Moyers, Bill. (1992, February 22). Old news and the new civil war. *The New York Times*, p. C1.

Nasar, Sylvia. (1992, October 18). Women's progress stalled? Just not so. *The New York Times*, p. 10.

National Association of Hispanic Journalists. (1991). *Survey of Hispanics in the newsroom, 1991.* Washington, DC: Author.

National Opinion Research Center. (1991). *General social survey.* Chicago, IL: University of Chicago Press.

Newspaper Association of America. (1993). *Facts about newspapers.* Washington, DC: Author.

Newsroom integration still crawling at a snail's pace. (1989, April). *NABJ Newsletter.*

O'Neill, Michael J. (1982, May 5). *A problem for the republic—A challenge for editors.* Address to the American Society of Newspaper Editors. Reprinted in *The Adversary Press.* St. Petersburg, FL: Modern Media Institute, 1983.

O'Reilly, Charles A., III, & Anderson, John C. (1980). Trust and the communication performance appraisal information: The effect of feedback on performance and job satisfaction. *Human Communication Research, 6,* 289–298.

Papper, Bob, & Sharma, Andrew. (1995, May). Salaries going up. *Radio Television News Directors Communicator,* pp. 14–19.

Patterson, Eugene. (1983, September 6). *The press: A few problems to solve.* Convocation address to the Indiana University School of Journalism, Bloomington, IN.

Pease, Edward C. (1989). Kerner plus 20: Minority news coverage in the Columbus Dispatch. *Newspaper Research Journal, 10*(3), 17–37.

Pease, Edward C. (1990). Ducking the diversity issue: Newspapers' real failure is performance. *Newspaper Research Journal, 11*(3), 24–37.

Pease, Edward C. (1992, August). *Who's making the news? Changing demographics of newspaper newsrooms.* Paper presented at the annual meeting of the Association for Education in Journalism and Mass Communication, Montreal, Canada.

Peterson, Paul V. (1972). Journalism growth continues at hefty 10.8 per cent rate. *Journalism Educator, 26*(4), 4, 5, 60.

Peterson, Paul V. (1979). Enrollment surges again, increases 7 per cent to 70,601. *Journalism Educator, 33*(4), 3.

Peterson, Paul V. (1981). *Today's journalism students: Who they are and what they want to do.* Columbus, OH: The Ohio State University Press.

Peterson, Paul V. (1983). J-school enrollments hit record 91,016. *Journalism Educator, 37*(4), 3–8.

Pincus, David. (1986). Communication satisfaction, job satisfaction, and job performance. *Human Communication Research, 12,* 395–419.

Prato, Lou. (1994, September). Tabloids force all to pay for news. *American Journalism Review,* p. 56.

Privacy and the need to know. (1992, October). *Presstime,* pp. 18–21.

Quindlen, Anna. (1994, July 13). Order in the court. *The New York Times,* p. A11.

Quindlen, Anna. (1994, July 16). A good fire. *The New York Times,* p. 11.

Report of the National Advisory Commission on Civil Disorders. (1968). New York: Dutton.

Reston, James. (1994). *Deadline: A memoir.* New York: Random House.

Rich, Frank. (1995, June 15). The longest year. *The New York Times,* p. A17.

Rivers, William L. (1962). The correspondents after twenty-five years. *Columbia Journalism Review, 1,* 5.

Rivers, William, Schramm, Wilbur, & Christians, Clifford. (1980). *Responsibility in mass communication* (3rd ed.). New York: Harper & Row.

Rivlin, Alice. (1992, September). Distinguished Lecturer Series, Institute for Advanced Study and the Society for Advanced Study, Indiana University, Bloomington.

Rosten, Leo. (1937). *The Washington correspondents.* New York: Harcourt, Brace.

Rothman, Stanley, & Lichter, S. Robert. (1983, Spring). Are journalists a new class? *Business Forum*, p. 15.

Russell, Susan H., Fairweather, James S., & Hendrickson, Robert M. (1991). *Profiles of faculty in higher education institutions, 1988*. Washington, DC: National Center for Education Statistics, U.S. Department of Education.

Sachsman, David B. (1993). Mass communication education: Moving toward diversity. *Mass Comm Review, 20*(2&3), 180–191.

Sander, Ernest. (1994, May). A TV tabloid vows to clean up its act. *American Journalism Review*, p. 15.

Schudson, Michael. (1978). *Discovering the news*. New York: Basic Books.

Schudson, Michael. (1995). *The power of news*. Cambridge, MA: Harvard University Press.

Sciolino, Elaine. (1995, July 10). China's prisons forged zeal of U.S. crusader. *The New York Times*, pp. A1, A4.

Seventh annual salary survey. (1992, August). *Public Relations Journal*, pp. 10–21.

Shaw, David. (1991). Coloring the news: A special report. *The Quill, 79*(4), 14–19.

Shaw, David. (1991). Black, white, read all over? *The Quill, 79*(4), 20–23.

Shepard, Alecia. (1994, January/February). Legislating ethics. *American Journalism Review*, p. 38.

Shoemaker, Pamela J., & Reese, Stephen D. (1991). *Mediating the message: Theories of influences on mass media content*. White Plains, NY: Longman.

Sigal, Leon V. (1986). Sources make the news. In Robert K. Manoff & Michael Schudson (Eds.), *Reading the news* (pp. 9–37). New York: Pantheon Books.

Smith, Shellee. (1995, May/June). Shoptalk. *Scripps Howard News*, p. 15.

Squires, James D. (1992, December). Plundering the newsroom. *Washington Journalism Review*, pp. 18–24.

Stamm, Keith, & Underwood, Doug. (1993). The relationship of job satisfaction to newsroom policy changes. *Journalism Quarterly, 70*, 528–541.

Starobin, Paul. (1995, March/April). A generation of vipers. *Columbia Journalism Review*, pp. 25–32.

Stevenson, Robert L. (1994). The disappearing reader. *Newspaper Research Journal, 15*(3), 22–31.

Stone, Chuck. (1988). Journalism schools' students and faculty in the year of Kerner Plus 20. In *Kerner Plus 20* (p. 7). Washington, DC: National Association of Black Journalists.

Stone, Vernon. (1992, February). News salaries stand still. *Communicator*, pp. 14–15.

Stone, Vernon. (1993, May). TV news work force grows, declines continue in radio. *Communicator*, p. 26.

Stone, Vernon A. (1994, February). Pay gains top cost of living. *Communicator*, pp. 68–70.

Strauss, William, & Howe, Neil. (1991). *Generations: The history of America's future, 1584 to 2069*. New York: William Morrow.

Tan, Alexis S. (1990, August). *Why Asian American journalists leave journalism and why they stay*. Presented at the national convention of the Asian American Journalists Association, New York, NY.

The Times Mirror Center for The People and The Press. (1995). *The people, the press & their leaders, 1995*. Los Angeles: Author.

Tuchman, Gaye. (1978). *Making news: A study in the construction of reality*. New York: The Free Press.

Tye, Larry. (1993, September 8). Proposed "Bill of Rights" would limit personal data. *The Boston Globe*, p. 1.

Underwood, Doug. (1988, March/April). When MBAs rule the newsroom. *Columbia Journalism Review*, pp. 23–30.

Underwood, Doug. (1993). *MBAs in the newsroom*. New York: Columbia University Press.

Underwood, Doug, & Stamm, Keith. (1992). Balancing business with journalism: Newsroom policies at 12 west coast newspapers. *Journalism Quarterly, 69*, 836–846.

U.S. Bureau of the Census. (1991). *Statistical Abstract of the United States 1991* (111th ed.). Washington, DC: U.S. Government Printing Office.

U.S. Bureau of the Census. (1992). *Statistical Abstract of the United States 1992* (112th ed.). Washington, DC: U.S. Government Printing Office.

U.S. Department of Labor Statistics. (1992). *Occupational outlook handbook* (Bulletin 2400). Washington, DC: U.S. Government Printing Office.

Weaver, David H. (1983). *Videotex journalism: Teletext, viewdata, and the news.* Hillsdale, NJ: Lawrence Erlbaum Associates.

Weaver, David, & Daniels, LeAnne. (1992). Public opinion on investigative reporting in the 1980s. *Journalism Quarterly, 69,* 146–155.

Weaver, David H., & Wilhoit, G. Cleveland. (1986). *The American journalist: A portrait of U.S. news people and their work.* Bloomington: Indiana University Press.

Weinstein, Steve, & Haithman, Diane. (1989, July 26). ABC News draws criticism of spy case re-creation. *Los Angeles Times,* Sec. 6, p. 1.

Windahl, Swen, & Rosengren, Karl Eric. (1978). Newsmen's professionalization: Some methodological problems. *Journalism Quarterly, 55,* 466–473.

Women in the civilian labor force. (1993). *The 1993 information please almanac.* Boston: Houghton Mifflin.

Woodward, Kenneth L. (1992, October 5). The new class warriors. *Newsweek,* p. 40.

Wu, Wei. (1994). *Predictions of the endorsement of the adversarial role by U.S. journalists in 1992.* Unpublished manuscript.

Zoglin, Richard. (1992, September 21). Sitcom politics. *Time,* p. 47.

About the Authors

Trevor R. Brown is Dean of the School of Journalism at Indiana University, where he has taught since 1972. He holds a BA (Honors) degree in modern history from Oxford University in England, where he was a Rhodes Scholar, an MA in communications–journalism from Stanford University, an MA in history from Oxford University, and a PhD in communications–public affairs from Stanford. He has worked as a general reporter, columnist, and sports reporter on the *Cape Times* in Cape Town, South Africa. He is a co-author (with Charlene Brown and William L. Rivers) of *The Media and the People*, and author of a section on the South African Press in William L. Rivers' *The Adversaries*.

Everette E. Dennis is Executive Director of The Freedom Forum Media Studies Center in New York and Senior Vice President of The Freedom Forum (formerly the Gannett Foundation). He is also editor-in-chief of *Media Studies Journal*, published by the Center. He holds a BA from the University of Oregon, an MA from Syracuse University, and a PhD from the University of Minnesota. He has held three post-doctoral fellowships at Harvard University and is the author, co-author, or editor of more than 20 books and numerous articles. He has taught on the journalism faculties of Kansas State, Minnesota, Northwestern, and Oregon, where he served as Dean of the School of Journalism from 1981 to 1984.

Divya C. McMillin is a doctoral student in the School of Journalism at Indiana University. She holds a BA degree in Journalism, English Literature and Psychology, and a BS degree in Mass Communication from Bangalore University in India, She obtained her MA in Mass Communication from Pittsburg State University in Kansas. She is a keen scholar of international communication and has presented papers at various conferences on the impact of globalization on national identity in India.

David H. Weaver is the Roy W. Howard Professor in Journalism and Mass Communication Research at Indiana University's School of Journalism, where he has taught since 1974. He holds a BA in journalism and sociology from Indiana University, an MA in journalism from Indiana, and a PhD in mass communication research from the University of North Carolina. He has worked as a journalist for four daily newspapers. He is author or co-author of six books, including *The American Journalist* (with G. Cleveland Wilhoit in 1986), and numerous book chapters and articles on journalists, the agenda-setting role of the media in election campaigns, foreign news coverage, and newspaper readership.

G. Cleveland Wilhoit is Professor of Journalism and Director of the Bureau of Media Research at Indiana University, where he has taught since 1967. He was Associate Director of the Institute for Advanced Study at Indiana from 1988 to 1993. He holds BA and MA degrees and a PhD in mass communication research from the University of North Carolina. He is co-author (with David Weaver) of *Newsroom Guide to Polls and Surveys* and editor of the first two volumes of the *Mass Communication Review Yearbook*. He and David Weaver have also written a Journalism Monograph on news media coverage of U.S. senators and articles on foreign news coverage. With Dan Drew, Wilhoit has conducted three national studies of American editorial writers.

Name Index

A

Acheman, Yardley, 55
Agnew, Spiro, xii
Alter, Jonathan, 234, 239, 241, 242, 279
Altheide, David L., 77, 123, 279
Anderson, John C., 123, 283
Arocha, Zita, 215, 279
Atkin, Charles K., 122, 219, 230, 280
Auletta, Ken, 122, 230, 279
Ayers, Brandt H., 122, 279

B

Bagdikian, Ben H., 122, 279
Baker, Russell, 2, 26, 51, 54, 55, 56, 99, 122, 123, 279
Barlett, Donald, 126
Bates, Stephen, 138, 174, 279
Beam, Randal, 128, 173, 279
Beasley, Maurine H., 192, 280
Becker, Lee B., 13, 27, 30, 31, 33, 40, 43, 47, 114, 215, 280
Bergen, Lori A., xviii, 191, 193, 230, 242, 280
Berger, Gilda, 192, 280
Bernstein, Carl, xix, 56, 57, 74, 77, 122, 134, 158, 175, 242, 280
Bladden, Paul, 162
Blau, Peter, 173

Bogart, Leo, 27, 28, 230, 280
Borden, Sandra, 176, 280
Bowman, Patricia, 166
Bowman, William W., xvii, 2, 5, 8, 10, 11, 14, 15, 17, 18, 20, 26, 27, 28, 34, 35, 37, 39, 44, 47, 135, 172, 173, 178, 192, 242, 247, 254, 280, 282
Breed, Warren, 243
Brill, Steven, 126, 127, 172, 280
Brown, Murphy, 232, 235, 237, 239
Brown, Trevor, xviii, 243
Bruck, Jerry, 173
Buchanan, Brian J., xviii, 47, 172, 174, 280
Buchanan, Patrick, xii
Buckley, Keith, xix
Burgoon, Judee K., 28, 123, 219, 230, 280
Burgoon, Michael, 219, 230, 280
Bush, George, xii
Busterna, John C., 122, 280

C

Carey, James, 176, 280
Carson, Clara N., 241, 281
Carter, Connie, xix
Carter, Jimmy, xii
Chang, Elizabeth, 122, 123, 280
Christians, Clifford, 175, 283
Clarke, Lee, 122, 280

K

Katz, Jon, 49, 121, 282
Keaton, Michael, 146, 156
Kennedy, John, xix
Kennedy, Ted, 166
Kerner, Otto, 195
King, Larry, x
Kline, F. Gerald, 193, 282
Knopf, Alfred A., 152
Kosicki, Gerald M., 40, 47, 280

L

Lafky, Sue A., xviii, 177, 192, 193, 282
Lambeth, Edmund B., 175, 282
Lapham, Lewis, 55
Lasch, Christopher, 232, 241, 282
Lass, E. Donald, 123, 282
Lawrence, David, Jr., 214, 282
Leonard, Mike, 232, 241, 282
Lewis, Scott, xviii
Lichter, S. Robert, 15, 16, 27, 282, 284
Lieb, Thom, 214, 282
Limbaugh, Rush, xix, 135, 231
Lindley, William R., 30, 47, 282
Linsky, Martin, 171, 176, 282
Luedke, Kurt, 153

M

Margolick, David, 172, 282
Martindale, Carolyn, 214, 282
McGrath, Kristin, 124, 242, 281
McLeod, Jack, 172, 282
Menand, Louis, 125, 127, 133, 171, 172, 173, 282
Merrill, John C., 125, 172, 281
Merritt, Davis, 125, 135, 171, 172, 173, 282
Miller, Peter V., 193, 282
Moreno, Roberto L., 214, 283
Moyers, Bill, 74, 122, 283

N

Nasar, Sylvia, 27, 192, 241, 283
Nelson, William Rockhill, 243, 244, 246
Neustadt, Richard, 49
Newton, Eric, 47, 172, 280
Nixon, Richard, 158, 159
Norton, Cathi, xix

O

O'Brien, Patricia, xv
Olick, Diana, 159
O'Neill, Michael J., 134, 173, 283
O'Reilly, Charles A., 123, 283
Overby, Charles, xviii
Overholser, Geneva, 166

P

Papper, Bob, 123, 283
Paley, William S., xiv
Parrish, Michael, xix
Patterson, Eugene, 60, 122, 283
Pavlik, John, xviii
Pease, Edward C., 172, 214, 283
Peterson, Paul V., 27, 30, 31, 47, 192, 215, 283
Pincus, David, 123, 283
Prato, Lou, 159, 175, 283
Pulitzer, Joseph, xiv, xvi, 55
Punitha, Carolyn Divya, xviii

Q, R

Quindlen, Anna, 56, 64, 77, 122, 123, 283
Quayle, Dan, 232, 234
Reagan, Ronald, xii, 56
Reese, Stephen D., 193, 284
Reston, James, 99, 123, 283
Rich, Frank, 126, 172, 283
Rivers, William L., ix, 175, 283
Rivlin, Alice, 49, 121, 283
Roch, Tim, 158
Roosevelt, Franklin D., xii
Rosen, Jay, 135, 171, 172, 173, 282
Rosengren, Karl Eric, 173, 285
Rosten, Leo, 27, 123, 283
Rothman, Stanley, 15, 16, 27, 282, 284
Russell, Susan H., 27, 123, 192, 241, 284

S

Sachsman, David B., 214, 284
Safire, William, xii
Sander, Ernest, 175, 284
Sass, Gerald, xviii
Schudson, Michael, 231, 240, 241, 242, 284
Sciolino, Elaine, 175, 284
Shaw, David, 214, 215, 284

Subject Index

A

ABC, ix, 132, 165, 244

Adversarial role; 120, 134, 137, 139, 143, 145, 170; *table*, 139
  and journalists' perception of best work, 220, 221, 224, 228; *figure*, 220

Advertising, 3, 119

African Americans (Blacks), xii, 6, 11, 14, 195–213
  in journalism, 196, 198; *tables*, 11, 203, 206, 212

Age, 6–11, 25
  distribution of journalists, 6–8; *tables*, 2, 5, 7, 8
  of journalists leaving field, 115
  of men and women journalists compared, 180, 189
  of minority and White journalists compared, 12, 200
  of print and broadcast journalists compared, 6
  of typical reporters, 1, 25, 56, 120, 233
  of women journalists compared with U.S. labor force, 10–11; *table*, 10
  relationship to income, 94, 110, 111
  relationship to job satisfaction, 108
  relationship to journalists' functions, 56, 59
  role in journalism ethics, 167

Agenda setting, 147

Altruism, 53, 127, 133, 240

American Federation of Television and Radio Artists (AFTRA), 130

American Journalism Review, 131, 159

American Society of Newspaper Editors (ASNE), xiv, 196, 238

Anonymous sources, 227

Asian American Journalists Association (AAJA), 251

Asian Americans, 6, 14, 195–223
  in journalism, 11, 196, 198; *tables*, 11, 203, 206, 212

Associated Press, 134, 156, 248

Audience (Readers), 24, 140
  as influence on newsworthiness, 150, 229
  journalists' image of, 74–77, 120, 237
  response, 174

Autonomy,
  as predictor of journalistic roles, 142, 145, 171
  degree of, 62, 118, 240; *figure*, 64; *table*, 63
  gender differences in, 184; *table*, 184
  limits on, 65–70; *figure*, 66
  predictors of, 70–72, *table*, 71
  relationship to job commitment, 115
  relationship to job satisfaction, 103–109

B

"Baby Boom Generation," 56, 58

Badgering sources, 160; *tables*, 157, 161

293